The Essential Halliday

The Essential Halliday

M.A.K. Halliday

Edited by Jonathan J. Webster

continuum

Continuum International Publishing Group

The Tower Building   80 Maiden Lane, Suite 704
11 York Road   New York
London SE1 7NX   NY 10038

British Library Cataloguing-in-Publication Data
A catalogue record for this book is available from the British Library.

ISBN: 978-0-8264-9534-1 (Hardback)
        978-0-8264-9535-8 (Paperback)

Library of Congress Cataloging-in-Publication Data
The Publisher has applied for CIP data.

Typeset by Newgen Imaging Systems Pvt Ltd, Chennai, India
Printed and bound in Great Britain by the MPG Books Group

CONTENTS

FOREWORD

I first wish to credit the idea of *The Essential Halliday* to Professor Edwin Thumboo, Emeritus Professor at the National University of Singapore, who suggested how useful it would be to identify key concepts in Systemic-Functional Linguistics, and then extract out those passages from the ten volume *Collected Works of M.A.K. Halliday*, which are most relevant to these key concepts. In other words, identify and extract out the passages which might assist those interested in gaining a better understanding of the fundamental and essential ideas of Systemic-Functional Linguistics Professor M.A.K. Halliday gave very valuable advice on identifying the key concepts to be included in *The Essential Halliday*. Together, we identified twenty such key concepts. For each one, we also identified related terms, and, with the assistance of one of my PhD students, Mr. Ian Chow, we carried out an automated search for where these concepts were referenced and discussed across the broad spectrum of topical areas covered by each of the ten volumes in *The Collected Works*. Whereas each of the ten volumes in *The Collected Works* focuses on a particular domain of application, or, in the case of volumes seven and eight, on studies related to a particular language, many of the key concepts included in *The Essential Halliday*, being as fundamental as they are to the theory, can be found to have been elaborated on in papers appearing over several volumes.

Each key concept is introduced with a brief summary, followed by selected extracts from *The Collected Works*. For the most part we have not included whole chapters, and instead carefully identified particular portions most relevant to the concept being discussed. The extracts are arranged according to their sequential occurrence in *The Collected Works*. Following the extracts, under the heading, 'Additional readings', are listed additional references to papers in *The Collected Work* which offer further insight relevant to the concept being discussed.

Intended as a resource for those wanting to gain insight into the fundamentals of Systemic-Functional Linguistics, *The Essential Halliday* should be seen as a kind of interface to the whole ten volume Collected Works, not only pointing the reader to where these concepts come up in *The Collected Works*, but also demonstrating the fundamental nature of these concepts as they relate to the various topical areas covered in each volume.

Chapter One

Act(s) of Meaning

Summary

An act of meaning is an instance of meaning formed out of an infinite meaning potential for reflecting on the world and interacting with others in it. Acts of meaning are the linguistic instances of the linguistic system of meaning potential. In Saussurean terms, acts of meaning may be considered as 'parole', and that which they instantiate, the system of meaning potential, as 'langue'. However, unlike the Saussurean distinction between langue and parole, M.A.K. Halliday sees acts of identity (parole) and meaning potential (langue) not as two distinct classes of phenomena, but instead as only a difference in the stance taken by the observer. Such that, if langue is parole seen from a distance, then parole is langue up close and in its context.

Acts of meaning are a subclass of semiotic acts that are semantic. Every act of meaning is at once a construing of experience and an enacting of interpersonal relationships; the conjunction of the experiential and the interpersonal. Acts of meaning are also acts of identity, occurring in contexts of situation.

Already at a very early age, even before the onset of adult-like linguistic structures or words, children begin to systematize acts of meaning in the course of daily life in various functional contexts. All this leading up to that "extraordinary semiotic leap" in the child's second year, when their inventory of simple signs becomes "an infinite resource for making sense of the world and interacting with the people in it."

Selected readings

On Grammar (Volume 1)

Every act of meaning has a **context of situation**, an environment within which it is performed and interpreted. For communication to take place at all, it is necessary for those who are interacting to be able to make intelligent and informed guesses about what kinds of meanings are likely to be exchanged. They do this on the basis of their interpretation of the significance – the semiotic structure – of the situation.

Let us postulate that the relevant features of a situation in which language has some place are the *field* of social process, the *tenor* of social relationships and the *mode* of discourse itself: that is, (1) what is going on, (ii) who are involved, and (iii) what part the text is playing – whether written or spoken, in what rhetorical mode and so on.

We shall then find a systematic relationship between these components of the situation and the functional components of the semantic system. It appears that, by and large, the field – the nature of the social activity – determines the ideational meanings; the tenor – the social statuses and roles of the participants in the situation – determines the interpersonal meanings; while the mode – the part assigned to the linguistic interaction in the total situation – determines the textual meanings.

I.8(1979):201

★ ★ ★

... all knowledge is like this: to "know" something is to have transformed it into meaning, and what we call "understanding" is the process of that transformation. But experience is understood in the course of, and by means of, being acted out interpersonally – and, in the same way, interpersonal relations are enacted in the course of, and by means of, being construed ideationally. The grammar flows these two modes of meaning together into a single current, such that everything we say (or write, or listen to, or read) "means" in both these functions at once. Thus every instance of semiotic practice – every *act of meaning* – involves both talking about the world and acting on those who are in it.

I.15(1996):390–1

★ ★ ★

A corpus is not simply a repository of useful examples. It is a treasury of acts of meaning which can be explored and interrogated from all illuminating angles, including in quantitative terms (cf. Hasan 1992).

I.15(1996):406

★ ★ ★

Saussure problematized the nature of the linguistic fact; but he confused the issue of instantiation by setting up langue and parole as if they had been two distinct classes of phenomena. But they are not. There is only one set of phenomena here, not two; langue (the linguistic system) differs from parole (the linguistic instance) only in the position taken up by the observer. Langue is parole seen from a distance, and hence on the way to being theorized about. I tried to make this explicit by using the term "meaning potential" to characterize the system, and referring to the instance as an 'act of meaning", both implying the concept of a 'meaning group' as the social-semiotic milieu in which semiotic practices occur, and meanings are produced and understood.

I.15(1996):412

On Language and Linguistics (Volume 3)

In using language, we are both observing the environment and intruding on it. Nearly every utterance has both an ideational meaning, relating to the processes and things of the real world, and an interpersonal meaning, relating to the roles and attitudes adopted and assigned by the speaker. The semantic system is organized around this dual focus, of reflection and of action; and because it is so organized, it also stands as a metaphor for the culture, since culture is a construct of two environments, the natural and the social. Lévi-Strauss has stressed how the two are interlocked: the natural environment is a focus both of action and of reflection, and the social system is encoded in natural as well as in behavioural symbols. This interdependence is also both expressed and symbolized in language: to speak is to be both thinker and actor at the same time, and the two together define the act of meaning – which in turn has shaped the inner structure of the semantic system.

III.3(1975):84

★ ★ ★

We cannot transform language; it is people's acts of meaning that do that. But we can observe these acts of meaning as they happen around us, and try to chart the currents and patterns of change.[21]

Note

21. As always, language also works by its example – the metaphoric processes by which language itself displays the features it is construing. Thus the patterns of change we observe amount to a form of growthism in language.

III.6(1990):171, 174

★ ★ ★

3

When human beings evolved the resource of language, it served from the beginning not only as our means of information (the ideational function) but also as our means of interaction (the interpersonal function); and the two are inseparably bonded – you cannot have one without the other. Every act of meaning is both construal and enactment at one and the same time.

III.13(2001):276

* * *

. . . by "act of meaning" I am referring to just that subclass of semiotic acts that are semantic – that is, made of specifically linguistic meanings; and this entails that all such acts are realized in the form of wordings.

III.16(1992):355

* * *

There is, so to speak, a history of meaning, and the interpretation of any act of meaning must rest on other such acts that have preceded it and created the conditions for its occurrence.

III.16(1992):358

[*Editor's note:* MAK Halliday identifies four strands or dimensions of history that make a sentence into an act of meaning: (1) the intertextual, (2) the developmental, (3) the systemic and (4) the intratextual. These are described and illustrated in III.16(1992):361–89.]

* * *

The power of language is vested in the act of meaning.

III.17(1992):375

* * *

. . . the full creative power of an act of meaning arises from the fact that language **both** construes **and** enacts. It is not only a way of thinking about the world; it is also, at one and the same time, a way of acting on the world – which means, of course, acting on the other people in it.

. . .

But this conjunction of the experiential and the interpersonal depends in turn, for its efficacy as discourse, on meaning of a third kind, the creation of texture.

III.17(1992):384

* * *

. . . an act of meaning is not the coding and transmitting of some pre-existing information or state of mind, but a critical component in a complex process of reality construction – critical in that on the one hand it is itself part of reality, and on the other hand it is a metaphor for some other part. Semiotic systems, while they are components of human experience, along with physical, biological and social ones, are also theories about that experience (including about themselves, there being no constraint on their reflexivity (Lemke 1984)). That is their metaphorical aspect; and it is the success of that metaphor, in one's semiotic acts, I think, that determines how effective one's discourse is going to be. This power of the act of meaning would not have been news to the sophists in ancient Athens, who constructed their grammatics in order to find out how language could persuade people of something even when it wasn't true. Or to the founders of modern science, who tried to design their language so that it would open up for them the gateway to new knowledge.

III.17(1992):386

The Language of Early Childhood (Volume 4)

The protolanguage is child tongue, not mother tongue. It is created by the child, in interaction with its caregivers and any other members of its small meaning group (who normally respond to it in their own adult tongue), as a primary semiotic which will eventually lead, via a transitional phase, into the "mother tongue" of childhood, adolescence and beyond. But it is still itself a primary semiotic (that is, a semiotic of primary consciousness), not a higher-order semiotic as adult languages are; that is to say, it has no lexicogrammar (no structures and no words) in it. Its elements are still simple signs, content/expression pairs. What is new is that these are no longer isolated elements; they enter into systemic contrasts, within a small number of definable functional domains. I was able to identify four such domains to start with: the instrumental, the regulatory, the interactional and the personal. I referred to these as **micro-functions**, to contrast with the more abstract functional components of the later, transitional and mother tongue, phases of children's speech.

As far as the expression is concerned, children will create their protolinguistic signifiers out of anything that is to hand, or to mouth – provided that they can perform it and that those who exchange meanings with them respond. One source I have already referred to is by borrowing from the material domain. Another source is imitation – which can also be a source of confusion for those involved, if it is an imitation of adult speech sounds, because the meaning is not (and cannot be, because the protolanguage is not yet referential) that which the others are disposed to assign to it. Other expressions seem to be just plucked out of the air, so to speak – out of the child's repertory (of sound or gesture) as it happens to be at the time.

It is when we consider the task of "representing the child", however, that with the protolanguage an entirely new issue arises. Up to this point, the child's behaviour has been pre-systemic: signs have been created instantially, and existed only at the level of performance – they could be recorded, as sounds or gestures, but not theorized in general terms. There was no general principle behind them, no systemic potential – and hence no predictability. The phase of one or two isolated signs is transitional; by the time of the protolanguage – and this is what justifies us in referring to it as a form of "language" – the meanings have become systemic. That is to say, each individual act of meaning is the instantiation of some meaning potential; the challenge now is to represent that meaning potential in such a way that the meaning of each instance can be explained by reference to it. Instances, individual acts of meaning, have to be observed within their contexts of situation; the observer's stance then has to be shifted, to allow observation from a distance, so that the child's meaningful activity can be viewed as a whole and that a comprehensive, explanatory picture can be built up.

IV.1(1998):11–2

* * *

What we are trying to do, it seems to me, is to represent the child's semiotic behaviour as a **meaning potential**, something that is functional because it is constantly changing as the child's interaction with the environment expands and develops. Once it becomes **systemic**, such that each performance of an act of meaning is an **instance** of an underlying system that is instated in the infant's brain – in other words, once it becomes a **language**, even if still "proto-", child tongue not yet mother tongue – we can represent it in the form of a network; and, while each network taken by itself is a representation of just one "moment" in the developmental progression, the sequence of several such networks presents a moving picture of the expanding consciousness of the child.

IV.1(1998):14–5

* * *

We have seen how, in the protolanguage, children first **systemized** their acts of meaning, by reference to a small number of functional contexts: obtaining goods-and-services ("instrumental"), manipulating others ("regulatory"), exchanging attention ("interactional"), manifesting their own affective states ("personal"), playing and imagining ("imaginative").

These contexts arise in the course of daily life and the meanings the child produces arise out of them; that is how the caregivers are able to interpret them, just as pet-owners identify the meanings produced by their household pets, which are evolutionarily parallel to the human protolanguage – they also are the manifestations of forms of primary consciousness. The functional orientations of the mother tongue are very different from those of the protolanguage; in fact the entire concept of linguistic "function" has to be reconstrued. In language (here as opposed to protolanguage), while it is still possible to talk informally about the "functions" of individual utterances in their contexts of situation, functionality has become **intrinsic to the system**: every instance is in fact multifunctional, because this feature is built in to the grammar – you cannot switch it off. It is impossible to activate just one "function" at a time. In our higher-order semiotic every act of meaning is at once a construing of experience and an enacting of interpersonal relationships (grammatically speaking, every clause selects both in transitivity and in mood). This is the extraordinary semiotic leap that children take in the second year of their lives, from the point where their range of meaning is an inventory of simple signs to the point where they have constructed for themselves an effectively infinite resource for making sense of the world and interacting with the people in it. Our next step in representing the child has to be that of representing **how** they make this catastrophic transition.

I remarked at the beginning that the infant brain is simultaneously directing the body both to move and to mean – to act materially and to act semiotically. The semiotic act, or "act of meaning", involves the two planes of **content** and **expression**; and each of these two planes interfaces with the material world. The interface on the expression plane is what I have called, following Thibault, the signifying body – at first the whole body, then gradually specializing out to certain parts of it (face, hands, vocal organs) and then, when the child attains the higher-order semiotic, that of language, the vocal organs take over as the dominant player (this interface is what we call "phonetics"), except in "sign", which uses mainly hands, arms and face. On the content plane, the interface is what we call "semantics"; here children are making sense of their experience of the world they find round about them (and also that they find inside themselves, the world of their own consciousness); and in the same breath, so to speak, interacting with those around them, and so enacting their own social being. As they move into this transitional phase of semiosis, leading from the primary semiotic of the protolanguage to the higher-order semiotic of the mother tongue, there is a remarkable collaboration set up by the brain between these two interfaces, something that is made possible

7

by the brain's development to the level of higher-order consciousness. The critical factors in this development, as far as the semantic interface is concerned, are two: memory, and consciousness of self.

With memory, the child is able to construe *classes* of phenomena out of repeated instances, using a re-entrant mapping to impose categories on its experience of the world. Linguistically, this means that the child is now able to construe "common" terms – generalized common nouns as opposed to individuated proper nouns; and this is the beginning of *reference*, referential meaning. (The early individuated signs of the proto-language are not yet referential; a protolinguistic mama means something like 'I want (you) mummy'.) With self-consciousness, the child is able to make a systemic distinction between two modes of meaning, the declar-ative ('this is how things are') and the imperative ('this is how I want things to be'); this distinction is something that was noticed a long time ago by observers of children's first incursions into language (e.g. Lewis 1936), and more recent evidence confirms that it is a typical strategy for the transition into the mother tongue (Halliday 1975b, see also Chapter 9; Painter 1984, 1989; Oldenburg-Torr 1987). In grammatical terms, these two steps constitute, respectively, proto-transitivity and proto-mood; taken together, they make it possible for the child to transform experi-ence into meaning – to reflect on and to act on the world and the people in it in one semiotic swoop.

But for them to be able to do this the other interface must also be involved – the body as domain of expression: now becoming specialized, as we have seen, to expression in the form of vocally originated sound. We noted that in the content there were these two motifs: construing experi-ence, by setting up categories and their interrelations to model the child's experience of the world, and enacting social processes, by getting along with others and in so doing shaping the child's own self. Let us call these two motifs the "ideational" and the "interpersonal", as used in systemic functional grammar. Now, somehow these two motifs have to be carried along simultaneously yet independently, so that all possible meanings of the one kind can be combined with all possible meanings of the other kind.

IV.1(1998):18–20

* * *

1 Functional semantics of language development

1.1 *The concept of the protolanguage*

Long before a child begins to speak in his mother tongue, he is engaging in acts of meaning.

The meanings may be expressed in various ways. The child may use either of the two modes, vocal or gestural; and, in the vocal mode, in which the expression is a complex pattern of intonation and articulation, he may either create new patterns of his own, or attempt to imitate sounds he hears in the speech of others. Most children probably use some combination of all three kinds of expression, though many show a preference for one particular kind. I made an intensive study of one child, Nigel, from birth to 3½ years (Halliday 1975b); Nigel showed a clear preference for the vocal mode, and for inventing sounds rather than imitating them, though he did use some gestures and vocal imitations as well. All three are variants of a single, more general mode of expression, that of bodily postures and movements, with which a child constructs his *protolanguage*. The essential ingredient of the protolanguage is not the form of the output but the nature of the act of meaning itself.

An *act of meaning* is a communicative act that is intentional and symbolic. A cry of hunger is a communicative act; and so, for that matter, is clamping on to the mother's breast. Both convey a message – that the child is hungry. But neither of these acts embodies the intention to communicate; they are not symbolic acts. A symbolic act is one of which the meaning and success criteria do not reside in its own performance.

The outward form of a symbolic act is sometimes iconic. If I hit you because I'm angry with you, that is not an act of meaning. If I hit you to show that I'm angry with you, that is an act of meaning, but it is one in which the expression is related to the meaning in a non-arbitrary fashion: the symbol is an iconic one. The distinction between iconic and non-iconic symbols is, needless to say, a matter of degree; the expression may be more or less iconic, and it may be both iconic and non-iconic at the same time. At nine months Nigel had a small repertory of gestures, one of which was that of grasping an object firmly, without pulling it towards him, and then letting go. The meaning was 'I want that'. This was a partially iconic gesture, but the act was clearly a symbolic one – it did not itself constitute an attempt at realizing the desire. Nigel was not acting directly on the object. The gesture was an act of meaning, addressed to the other person taking part in the situation.

Acts of meaning, in this specific sense, take place early in a child's life; much earlier than the time at which language development studies have usually been begun, and long before the child has anything that is recognizable as a "language" – if language is defined by the presence of adult-like linguistic structures or words. As far as I was aware, Nigel's earliest act that was unambiguously an act of meaning took place just before six months, when for the first time he produced a sound – a very short and rather quiet nasal squeak, on a high rising note – the meaning of which 'what's going on?'. On the other hand I was not prepared for acts of meaning at this early age, and I may have failed to notice earlier instances. Perhaps the sad tale that he told at the age of two months, after having his first injections, should be thought of as an act of meaning, given the very clear contrast between this and his usual cheerful narrative.

By the age of nine months, Nigel had a *system* of acts of meaning – a *meaning potential* – which marked the beginning of his protolanguage. At this stage the protolanguage consisted of five meanings. Three, which were expressed gesturally, were in the more active mode: 'I want that', 'I don't want that', and 'do that (again)'. The other two, which were expressed vocally, were in the more reflective mode: 'let's be together' and 'look – that's interesting'. At that time, therefore, Nigel showed a correlation between the two modes of expression, vocal and gestural, and the two modes of meaning, reflective and active: reflective meanings were expressed vocally and active ones gesturally. Within four to six weeks, however, he abandoned the gestural mode almost entirely (the exception being the demand for music, expressed by "beating time"), and settled for vocal symbols in the expression of meanings of all kinds.

1.2 Systematic and social character of acts of meaning

An act of meaning is systematic in a dual sense. First, the act itself is an act of choice, of selection within a meaning potential; and the selection is non-random, in that it is coherently related to the context of situation – the semiotic structure of whatever portion of the child's reality construct constitutes the relevant environment in the given instance.

Second, the meaning potential is also systematic. It is a resource, a network of options each one of which can be interpreted by reference to the child's total model of reality and of his own place in it. The reality, and hence the meaning potential, is constantly under construction, being added to, differentiated within, and modified.

Between the ages of 9 and 16 months, Nigel's protolanguage grew from a system of five to a system of about fifty different meanings. For example, whereas at the start he had had just one meaning of an *interactional* kind, a generalized signal of participation, exchanging attention with another person through the conversational process, he now had a resource of about fifteen. These included: (1) *greetings*, where he distinguished among the different persons that he exchanged meanings with, and between initiating and responding; (2) *sharings*, with which he distinguished between shared attention and shared regret; and (3) *responses*, to specific invitations to mean. All these were coded in the system as recognizably distinct symbolic acts.

The term "act" is, however, semantically loaded; it suggests something purely subjective. But an act of meaning is a social act, again in the same dual sense as previously discussed. First, the act itself is shared, between the actor and the attender. It is shared not merely in the sense that the one is acting and the other is attending at the same time (the one "giving" meanings and the other "receiving" them), but that both are taking part in an exchange of meanings and that there is no act of meaning in isolation from such exchange. The process is one of conversation; the act becomes meaningful only when the other (who is a "significant other" by virtue of taking part in the conversational process) joins in and so gives value to the child's symbolic intent.

Second, the act of meaning is social also in the general sense, that the meaning potential from which it derives is a social construct. The semantic system, in which the child encodes his subjective reality, must be shared between the child and the significant others if his acts of meaning are to be successful. Experience may be private, but the symbolic coding of experience is social; there can be no private symbols, in this sense. But the child is not yet approximating the others' semantic system; he is creating one of his own. To say that the creation of a semantic system is a social process means, therefore, at this stage, that the others must be approximating the child's semantic system, and this is precisely what they do. It is clear from the observations of Nigel's conversation that the others not only understood him but also actively understood him; they played the conversational game according to his rules. Here is an example at 18 months:

> Nigel set himself to eating his lunch. Some fish fell off the fork.
> "Ooh!" It was another very high-pitched squeak.
> "Ooh, you lost a bit then," said Anna. "Where did it go?"
> "Byebye." Nigel looked up at Anna, inviting her to share a memory.
> " 'yebye, byebye," he said.
> "Yes, all the trains went away, and you said 'byebye', didn't you?"
> "Byebye," said Nigel sadly, waving his hand. He finished his lunch.
> "No-more. No-more."
> "Where has it all gone?" Anna asked him.

It is obvious that Anna is, quite spontaneously, interpreting what Nigel says as relevant participation in the dialogue. At the same time, the semantic approximation is not a one-way process; it has its own natural dialectic. Anna responds with meanings of her own; and she interprets Nigel's meanings in terms of what is coded in her own semantic system – or (since she is an imaginative person) in terms of what is not necessarily coded but is at least codable. This, in fact, is the role of the others in the conversational process: to interpret and to respond with their own meanings. So the means exist whereby the child, even at the protolinguistic phase, has access to adult meanings in a context in which they can modify and feed into his own meaning potential.

1.3 Semantic continuity

A child's earliest protolanguage can perhaps best be interpreted by reference to a small set of extralinguistically defined semantic functions. At ten months Nigel's acts of meaning fell into four functionally defined categories: the *instrumental* and the *regulatory*, which are more in the active mode of meaning; and the *interactional* and the *personal*, which are more in the reflective mode. These are "extralinguistic" in the sense that they exist as modes of intent independently of being encoded into, or realized through, symbolic acts of meaning.

It seems clear that, with Nigel at least, this functional orientation of the protolanguage is the ontogenetic base of the major functional components (what I have called *metafunctions*) of the adult semantic system, the *interpersonal* or active component and the *ideational* or reflective component (Halliday 1973).

The functional organization and functional continuity are thus properties of the system. In order to represent them we express the system as a potential – as a resource, not as a set of rules. Hence in representing Nigel's protolanguage I have used an "or"-based, not an "and"-based, model of language – one in which the underlying relation is the *paradigmatic* one (system) rather than the *syntagmatic* one (structure). A system, in this technical sense, is any set of options, or range of alternatives, together with its condition of entry.

If we follow closely Nigel's development from a protolanguage (Phase I) through a transitional stage (Phase II) to the adult linguistic system (Phase III), a striking pattern of semantic continuity emerges. The "self"-oriented systems, the interactional and the personal, at first define meanings such as 'let's be together', 'here I am', 'that's pleasing', 'that's interesting'. These then evolve, through the intermediary senses of 'let's attend to this together' and 'now you say its name', to the naming of things, beginning with persons, objects and processes; and thence through observation, recall, and prediction into the narrative mode and the ideational component of the adult semantics. This seemed to be Nigel's way in to the reflective mode of meaning.

The "other"-oriented systems, the instrumental and the regulatory, at first define meanings such as 'give me that', 'do that', and 'do that again'. These then evolve, through intermediary senses such as 'you do that', 'let's do that', and 'let me do that' (command, suggestion, and request for permission), into the exchanging of things, giving, demanding, and giving on demand; and hence through the exchange of information into the dialogue mode and the interpersonal component of the adult semantics. This was Nigel's way in to the active mode of meaning.

Central to this process of the evolution of the functional modes or components of meaning is the evolution in the concept of *function* itself. Nigel's earliest system of meaning potential, the Phase 1 protolanguage, is "functional" in the sense that each element in the system, and therefore each act of meaning, realizes an intent in respect of just one of a small set of extralinguistic functions (those that we identified as instrumental, regulatory, interactional, and personal, and the one or two that are added later). Nigel's conversation is meaningful in relation to his domains of social action, those of: (1) achieving material ends; (2) controlling the behaviour of the "others"; (3) establishing and maintaining contact with them; or (4) expressing his own selfhood in the form of cognitive and affective states. These are the social contexts of his acts of meaning – parts that he can play in the symbolic interaction. If we call these the "functions" of his protolanguage, then in this context "function" is equivalent to "use."

For some months (9 months to 16 to 17 months) this system continues to expand. The meaning potential is considerably enlarged; but it remains a system of the same kind. Then, towards the middle of the second year, the system undergoes a qualitative change. Hitherto, it has been a coding system with just two levels, a level of content (the meaning) and a level of expression (the sound or gesture); the elements of the system have been individual signs, content–expression pairs. Elements like "e-e-eh": 'here I am!'; or "ùh": 'do that some more'; or "dòh": 'nice to see you, and shall we look at this picture together?', are meanings coded directly into sounds, without any intervening organization. (Needless to say, the glosses need not be taken literally as statements of meaning; they are intended as an aid to understanding. But they also serve to bring out the fact that the meanings of Nigel's protolanguage are typically not meanings that are fully coded in the adult semantic.)

Just before the middle of his second year, however (though there have been previews of what was to come), Nigel introduces a third level of

13

coding intermediate between the content and the expression, a level of formal organization consisting of words and structures. In other words, he adds a grammar – or more accurately, a lexicogrammar. The elements of the system are no longer individual signs, but configurations at three different levels: semantic, lexicogrammatical and phonological, which are related to each other by realization. The meanings are "first" realized as (encoded into) wordings and "then" realized as (recoded into) sounds. This is the way the adult language is organized.

By taking this step, Nigel made it possible for himself to combine meanings into a single complex act; and he exploited this possibility by means of a functional strategy of his own devising, by which he distinguished all acts of meaning into two broad types, the **pragmatic** and the **mathetic**. The former have a 'doing' function, and require a response from the person addressed: at first a non-verbal response, such as giving something or doing something, but later these acts increasingly call for a verbal response, such as an answer to his question. The latter require no response and serve what we may interpret as a 'learning' function. This distinction has arisen directly by generalization out of the functions of the protolanguage; but it means that Nigel can now converse in new ways, adopting and assigning roles in the conversational process (dialogue) and ranging freely over time and space beyond the confines of the here and now (narrative).

Because he has a grammar, which allows meanings to be split up and their components combined and recombined in indefinitely many ways, Nigel is able to make this distinction explicit; and he does so in an interesting way. The meaning "pragmatic" is expressed by the use of a rising tone, and the meaning "mathetic" is expressed by the use of a falling tone. In other words the functional distinction has itself now been coded, as an opposition between two **macrofunctions**; Nigel creates this pattern more or less overnight, at 19 months, and it remains his dominant semiotic strategy throughout the rest of Phase II, the transition to an adult-like language, and into Phase III. "Function" is now no longer synonymous with "use"; it has to be reinterpreted in the sense of 'mode of meaning'.

The significant others with whom Nigel exchanges meanings respond to this new language as understandingly, and as unconsciously, as they did to his protolanguage. When the tone rises, they respond with goods-and-services, or, gradually, with new meanings – that is, they offer something in exchange. When the tone falls they listen, if they are there, but they feel no need to respond; and if they do respond, it is typically not with any new meaning but with an echo of what Nigel has said, though coded in adult words and structures, or with a prompt, inviting him to continue. Nigel, in turn, makes it clear that such responses are appropriate. This is not to imply, of course, that he always gets the response he wants; but he does get it in enough instances for the system to work. It should be noted that this semantic opposition is not at all the same as the meaning of the contrast between rising and falling tone in adult English. The two are, ultimately, related, but many of Nigel's wordings come out with what is, for the adult, the "wrong" tone. For example, all his commands and "Wh"-questions rise in tone, since they require a response; while his dependent clauses (when he begins to develop them) fall, since they do not.

In this transitional phase, however, the two modes of meaning, pragmatic and mathetic, are still alternatives: an act of meaning is always either one or the other. For example, *more méat* means 'more meat' + 'do something' (pragmatic), that is, 'give me some more meat'; *chuffa stúck* means 'train stuck' + 'do something', that is, 'get it out for me'; *high wáll* means 'high place' + 'do something', that is, 'I'm going to jump – catch me!'. On the other hand, *green càr* means 'green car' + 'I'm taking note', 'I'm learning' (mathetic), that is, 'I see (or saw or will see) a green car'; likewise *loud mùsic* means 'that's loud music'; *chuffa stòp* means 'the train's stopped'. Nigel's next move, already implicit however in this scheme of things, is to combine these two modes of meaning so that every act of meaning is both one and the other. This means reinterpreting the concept of function yet again.

By the end of Phase II, near the end of his second year, Nigel's grammatical resources have developed to the extent that he can map grammatical structures one on to another the way the adult language does. For example, he can select the categories **transitive** (in the transitivity system) and **interrogative** (in the mood system) and produce the expression *did you drop the green pen* which encodes both these selections simultaneously. He still does not use this sentence in the adult sense, as a question, because his semantic system is not yet that of the adult language; but he has successfully combined in it an interpersonal meaning, represented by the interrogative structure, and an ideational meaning, represented by the transitivity structure. (The sentence, of course, contains much else besides these two selections.)

The macrofunctions have now become what we might call **metafunctions**. They are no longer just generalizations of the earlier functional categories but reinterpretations of them at another level. They have now become the functional components of the semantic system; and each has its own systems of meaning potential, having as output some specific contribution to the total lexicogrammatical coding. The adult language is structured around these two components of meaning: the ideational and the interpersonal (together with a third, the textual, which I omit from the discussion here for the sake of brevity). They represent the twin themes of reflection and action in the adult semiotic: language as a means of reflecting on reality, and language as a means of acting on reality. The really striking fact about a human infant is that these two modes of meaning are present from the start. In his earliest acts of meaning we find Nigel already engaged in an ongoing conversational process in which the exchange takes these two primary symbolic forms.

1.4 The context of an act of meaning

It is a mistake to suppose that a child's language is ever fully context-bound or that an adult's is ever fully context-free. The principle of semantic continuity and functional evolution means that: (1) an act of meaning always has a context; while (2) the way in which an act of meaning is related to its context changes in the course of development. Equally, the system as a whole (the meaning potential) has a context, and this too changes in the developmental process.

The context for the **meaning system** is the **social system**, as it exists as a semiotic construct for the child at the given time. The context for an **act of meaning** is the **situation**, which is also a semiotic construct, a recognizable configuration of features from the social system. The situation consists essentially of a **field** of social process, and a **tenor** of social relationships, together with a third element, a **mode** of symbolic action – that is, the specific part that is assigned to acts of meaning in the particular context.

Much of the speech a child hears around him is, typically, relatable to its context of situation in recognizable and systematic ways. (It is also, despite a common belief to the contrary, richly structured, grammatically well formed, and fluent.) The meanings reflect the field, tenor, and mode of the situation in which they are expressed; and they do so in a rather systematic way. Typically, ideational meanings, realized in thing-names, transitivity structures and the like, represent the "field", the nature of the social process – what is going on at the time. Interpersonal meanings, realized in moods and modalities, expressions of comment, attitude and so on, represent the "tenor", the social relationships in the situation – who-all are taking part. Textual meanings, realized as patterns of cohesion and the organization of discourse, represent the "mode", the symbolic or rhetorical channel – what part the exchange of meanings is playing in the total unfolding scene. In much adult speech, whether backyard gossip or deliberations in committee, the actual components of the situation are fictions that are construed out of the meanings that are being exchanged: persons and objects are being talked about, and even acted upon, that are not there outside of the talk. But when the child himself is part of the interactive process, the situation is typically such that its features are made manifest to him: the feelings and attitudes of the participants and the objects and actions referred to can be seen or felt or heard.

The child's own acts of meaning relate likewise to his own social constructs. At first, in Phase I, as we have seen, the relation is one in which meaning is goal-directed ('do this', 'I want that', 'let's be together'); the context **is** the goal, and the act of meaning is successful if the goal is achieved. (We should remember that right from the start there are also purely reflexive acts of meaning: 'that's pleasing', 'that's interesting'.) But this relationship changes, by the natural dialectic of development. Nigel's own ability to mean allows him to construe acts of meaning in others, in their relation to the context; but the nature of this relation in adult conversation – or rather in conversation in the Phase III system – is such that the process of understanding it changes the contextual basis of the child's own acts of meaning. Hence what happens in Phase II, when the child makes the transition to the adult system, is that meaning no longer consists in aiming a shaft at a pre-existing target; now, it also involves defining the target. Success criteria here are of two kinds, and with Nigel, as we saw, each act was clearly marked for one or the other. Either success is external (pragmatic acts – rising tone), where Nigel is, or is not, satisfied with the other's response; or it is internal (mathetic acts – falling tone), where Nigel is, or is not, satisfied with his own achievement. In neither case is success a foregone conclusion. It is obvious that, with a pragmatic utterance, such as *more méat*, Nigel may not get an acceptable response: he may get no response at all, or a response that does not accede. But it is just as often the case that, with a mathetic utterance, Nigel recognizes failures of meaning; as he did for example when, holding a toy bus in one hand and a train in the other, he was trying to encode the situation, saying *two . . . two chùffa . . . two . . . two . . .* – finally he admitted defeat and gave up. But in both cases the act of meaning here consists in more than merely specifying a function in context; it involves making explicit the context in which that function is relevant. Nigel has now taken the critical step towards freeing his conversation from the limitations of his immediate surroundings – within which, however, it was never totally confined. Not only can he ask for toast when the toast is not in front of him, he can also recall, or predict, seeing a bus when the bus is no longer, or not yet, in sight.

1.5 Functional continuity and the construction of subjective reality

The functional-semantic continuity not only enables a child to construct a language, it also enables him, at the same time that he is constructing it, to use the language in the construction of a reality.

When Nigel takes the major step of converting his protolanguage into a language, by adding a grammar, which is a new level of coding intermediate between the meanings and the sounds, this is the one major discontinuity in the development of his linguistic system. He takes it against a background of clearly recognizable continuity in the functional-semantic evolution. From his earliest acts of meaning to the complex configurations that mark his entry into the adult mode, there is an unbroken line of development in which the twin themes of action and reflection provide the central thread.

It is this same continuity that allows Nigel to construct a reality, of which the language is both a realization and a part. This is not so much because reality construction is necessarily a continuous process – whether it is or is not is likely to depend on whether or not there are discontinuities in the reality itself. Rather, it is because the continuity of meanings proclaims and symbolizes the permanence of what is "in here" and what is "out there": of the self, and of the social system that defines the self, and of the relation that subsists between the two. The act of meaning, above all others, is what creates and maintains our identity in face of the chaos of things. It is as if, having become self-conscious through learning to mean, we have to go on meaning to keep the self in suspension.

At the very outset of Phase I, around nine to ten and a half months, Nigel has developed a picture of how things are. We know this, because only with some such picture could he mean in the ways he does; we can see the structure of his thinking through our interpretation of the structure of his meaning. By ten months of age Nigel has constructed a subjective reality that we could interpret as being based on the separation of himself from the continuum of things. Given this interpretation, in order to explain the protolanguage that we find him using at that time, we would have to postulate that, at the least, he has constructed a schema of the kind shown in Figure 1. On this same basis, the schema that Nigel has developed by the end of Phase I, six months later, may be represented in Figure 2. (For the data underlying the interpretations in Figures 1 and 2, see Tables 1 and 5 in Appendix 2 of Volume 4.) Again, this schema is one which we can recover from observations of Nigel's semantic system; it is implicit in what he is able to mean at the time.

With any such representation, we are always in fact **behind** the time. These are the minimal structures that we have to recognize as the basis

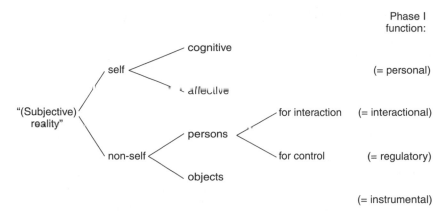

Figure 1 Nigel at 9–10½ months

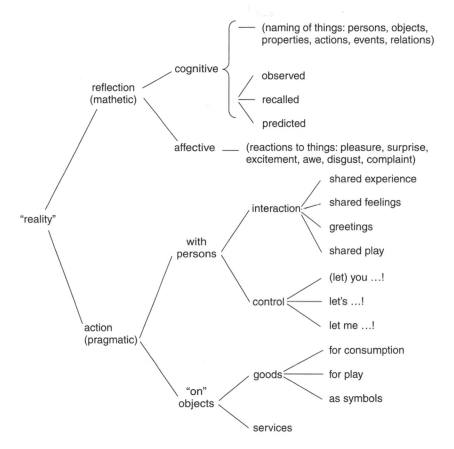

Figure 2 Nigel at 15–16½ months

of what Nigel himself can mean – what he can encode in his own speech. Since his understanding is always further developed than his powers of expression, we are seeing things long after they actually happen; as far as his model of reality is concerned, listening to Nigel speak is like observing the light rays from a distant star. And yet we have to be careful here: Nigel has got where he is not by being inducted into adult ways of thinking but by following his own route. Hence, while **his** understanding of what is meant by others (and if we continue to use the word "mean" in this rather un-English way, it is because we are talking not about what is said but about what is meant; saying is merely the outward sign and channel of meaning) shows that he knows more than he himself can mean, we cannot represent what he knows simply by describing what he must know in order to understand the meanings that are addressed to him. This is because we can only express these meanings in the terms of the adult semantic.

When Nigel moved into Phase II, the transition from protolanguage to (adult-like) language, his key functional strategy was, as we saw it, the development of an explicit opposition of pragmatic versus mathetic. It is important to stress at this point that both these modes of meaning are fundamental to the reality-constructing process. Reality, as mediated through a child's semantic system, has a twofold property, namely that it is at once both good to think and good to eat. Just as, when we observe a child using vocal or gestural signs to demand what he wants, we have to remember that he has other signs too, signs that express his pleasure in and curiosity about the surroundings, so also when we are focusing on the child's subjective reality we should not forget that it is something that is acted on as well as thought about. And this is what the pragmatic–mathetic opposition signifies. When Nigel uses a rising tone, he is acting on reality; when he uses a falling tone, he is reflecting on reality; and both action and reflection are mediated by the act of meaning. He achieves by meaning to others, and he learns by meaning to himself. It is the potential to mean – that is, by now, language – that integrates and synthesizes the two modes. Reality can be acted on and reflected on because it can be talked about; and the exchange of talk, *conversation*, is what makes it one reality not two. When Nigel enters Phase II, a word or a structure belongs to just one mode or the other; by the time he leaves Phase II, each word, and each structure, functions in both. Hence in the transition to the adult mode of meaning we can see rather clearly displayed the empirical foundations of Nigel's theory of what it is all about.

To illustrate the argument, the next section contains a number of short narratives of Nigel's interaction, starting at two and a half years and going back to the first two weeks of life.

2 Examples of conversations

(see Volume 4, Chapter 5, pp. 126–33)

3 The social construction of language, and of reality

3.1 The subjective angle: a summary

After a short preview at five months, Nigel's acts of meaning began in earnest at eight months; and by ten and a half months his conversational powers were organized into a system of meaning potential that we have referred to as a protolanguage. Unlike adult language, which is a three-level system (meaning, wording, sound), the protolanguage is a two-level system (meaning, sound), the elements of which are content–expression pairs, corresponding to the classical Saussurean notion of the "sign". These elements have meaning within a small range of semiotic functions; initially we can identify four: an instrumental, a regulatory, an interactional and a personal. These are distinct in two respects: (1) in orientation, towards persons or objects, and (2) in the type of mediation that is involved. In the instrumental function ('I want'), the child is acting on objects through the mediation of other persons; in the regulatory ('do as I say'), the child is acting directly on other persons, in the interactional ('me and you'), the child is interacting with other persons, but through the mediation of shared attention to objects; and in the personal ('here I come'), the child is becoming a self through active attention to, or rejection of, his environment.

From 8 to 17 months, that is, throughout what is referred to as Phase I, Nigel expanded his protolanguage, enlarging his conversational powers until he had a meaning potential of some 50 elements; they were still largely within the same four functions, though a fifth one had been added. This was the imaginative ('let's pretend') function, in which meaning is a mode of play. But up to this point the language had remained a two-level coding system; and, as such, it was subject to certain constraints. The "signs" of such a system are elementary particles, which can be strung together like beads but cannot be dispersed and recombined. Hence Nigel could never mean two things at once.

For this a three-level system is needed, one with an abstract level of *wording* intervening between the meanings and the sounds. This intermediate level (a lexicogrammar, in linguistic terms) is what makes it possible to name, and so to separate meaning as observation of reality from meaning as intrusion into reality. In a two-level system, such as Nigel's protolanguage, it is impossible to name something independently of acting on it. Once given a lexicogrammar, naming something and acting on it become distinct symbolic acts.

Why should Nigel want to separate these two modes of meaning? Because only in this way can conversation evolve along the lines of narrative and dialogue. Narrative and dialogue are the two cornerstones of conversation, prerequisites to the effective functioning of language in the construction of reality.

By the term **narrative** we understand the ability to make meanings context-free: to bring within the scope of conversation things that lie outside the perceptual field – processes in time past and future, states of consciousness, abstract entities, and other non-deictic aspects of subjective reality. To mean '(I see) sticks and stones' is not necessarily a narrative act; it need not imply naming, nor does it require a lexicogrammar in the system. But to mean 'I saw sticks and stones' is a narrative act, one that cannot be performed with a grammarless language; not because it requires grammatical structure (that comes later), but because it requires that the thing-name 'stick' is coded separately from any meaning such as 'I want' or 'I like'. From the moment the child has introduced this intermediate level of coding, his conversation becomes independent of the context of situation. It took Nigel about three weeks (at 17 months) to move from '(I see) sticks and stones' to 'I saw sticks and stones'; and about another three weeks after that to get to 'I will see sticks and stones' (for example, in answer to "Nigel we're going out for a walk"). The form of the utterance did not change – it was simply "stick, stone" in each case – but it now had a different significance as an act of meaning.

By the term **dialogue** we understand conversation of a particular kind, in which the interactants not only exchange meanings but also engage in dynamic role-play, each in turn both adopting a role for himself and assigning a role, or rather a role choice, to the other. Nigel made the discovery that the symbolic system he was constructing for himself as a means of **realizing** a world of meaning simultaneously **created** a world of meaning of its own, a semiotic of social roles and social acts. Since the system creates information, it can be used to exchange this information (that is, to ask and to tell) as well as to exchange goods-and-services in the way the protolanguage does. This in turn means that conversation becomes not merely a symbolic reflection of the sharing of experience but an actual alternative to it. Up to this point, when Nigel's mother suggested he should "tell Daddy what happened" it had made no sense to him. He could tell Mummy, because she had shared the experience, but how could he tell Daddy, when Daddy hadn't been there? Now he adds an **informative** function to his functional repertory – and at once becomes its prisoner for life.

Like other major forward leaps in development, this too had had its preview. It was at 15 months that Nigel took his first steps in grammar, when he came to separate the **name–choice** of the three people he conversed with from the **act–choice** of seeking versus finding. The former he expressed by articulation, the latter by intonation. In this way he was able to combine the two systems, so that each name, *ama* ('mummy'), *dada, anna*, could be used with either sense, 'where are you? I want you' (mid level + high level) or 'hullo! there you are!' (high falling + mid level). But it is in Phase II, the transition to the adult language, that this distinction between naming and acting becomes his primary semiotic strategy. Naming, as we have seen, is too narrow a concept here, if it is taken to mean merely the creation of a lexicosemantic taxonomy; we are talking about the whole ideational aspect of meaning, of which the assignment of thing-names is only a part. What Nigel did was to generalize, from his Phase I functional repertory, a simple opposition between conversation as a means of learning (a mathetic mode as we called it) and conversation as a means of doing (a pragmatic mode). So fundamental is this opposition to Nigel's construction of reality that at 19 months he took the step of encoding it systematically in prosodic form: from then on, all pragmatic acts of meaning – all utterances of a dialogic nature, demanding a response – were performed with a rising tone, and all mathetic acts – those of a narrative kind, demanding no response – were performed with a falling tone. In this way Nigel made explicit the fundamental distinction between meaning as reflection and meaning as action, a distinction that lies at the heart of the adult semantic system.

Nigel maintained this opposition intact for about six months; it was the major strategy whereby the concrete functions of his protolanguage were to evolve into the abstract functional components which are the basis of the adult semantic. At the same time, it was more than a strategy of transition; it was itself a form of the schematization of reality. By making this distinction, Nigel represented reality to himself as existing on two planes: as material to be quarried, and as terrain to be explored. Not only objects but also persons figure in this dual role; through dialogue, one person "acts on" the other, and in fact it is only through the intermediary of a person that an act of meaning can be directed onto an object, since objects are not, in principle, affected by symbolic acts.

But from the moment of its inception, Nigel's bimodal strategy, in which each act of meaning is either pragmatic or mathetic, is already breaking down. As soon as the language in which he converses has a lexicogrammar, every utterance in it is inevitably both pragmatic and mathetic at the same time. The cost of being able to mean two things at once is that it becomes impossible not to, except in very limited ways. The intonation signals what continues to be the dominant mode: response demanded (rising tone), or response not demanded (falling tone). But as Nigel moves through Phase II, the other mode becomes more and more prominent as a submotif; until by about 23 months all acts of meaning are in equal measure both pragmatic and mathetic. But in the process, these concepts have changed once again. The original functions first become macrofunctions and then metafunctions.

The pragmatic component is now, more often than not, a demand for a verbal response: giving and requesting goods-and-services has been superseded, as the favourite act of meaning, by giving and requesting information. Other elements have been added, including some that would subsequently disappear, such as the very useful distinction Nigel makes, from around 21 months, between telling listeners something he knows they already know and telling them something he knows they do not know. At this point the pragmatic function has evolved into the full interpersonal (sometimes called "socioexpressive") component in the adult semantic system; while the mathetic, meaning as a way of learning, has evolved into the ideational component. Every one of Nigel's conversational acts is now simultaneously both a reflection on and an action on reality.

But Nigel has never lost the essential links between meaning and social context that are what enabled him to make the transition from his own protolanguage to a mother tongue in the first place. Interpersonal meanings – those expressed in the grammar as mood, modality, person, key, and the like – reflect the role relationships in the communication process. Ideational meanings – expressed in transitivity, time and place, lexical taxonomies, and so on – reflect the goings-on around, the phenomenal world of processes and their participants and attendant circumstances.

This is not to say that an act of meaning typically relates directly to its immediate social context; most of them do not. We have already noted that, from the beginning of Phase II, thanks to the introduction of a lexicogrammar, Nigel's conversation has been effectively context-free, not constrained by the situation of speaking. But the meaning potential underlying his acts of meaning has its ultimate frame of reference in Nigel's experience, including, of course, his experience of his own states of consciousness; and it is a fundamental characteristic of acts of meaning that they create their own context out of this past experience. More particularly, what underlies the conversational process is not just the individual's experience of things; it is things as phenomena of intersubjective reality, as bearers of social meaning and social value. Nor is it just the face-to-face interaction of the participants in the dialogue; it is their entire function in the child's social system. Nigel has, after all, been busying himself with all this from birth. The social context of an act of meaning is far more than is made manifest in the sights and sounds around.

3.2 The intersubjective angle

A child's construction of language is at once both a part of and a means of his construction of reality; and it is natural to Western thinking to view both these processes largely from the standpoint of the individual. We tend implicitly to define the aim of the investigation as that of explaining what happens to a child in his development from infancy to maturity.

This preoccupation is embodied in and reinforced by prevailing metaphors such as "language acquisition" and "primary socialization". The former suggests that a child takes possession of a new commodity, that of language; and the latter that he is transformed into a new state, that of being social. In either case he is seen as an individual serving as the locus of external processes; and while we should not make too much of the metaphors themselves, they do perhaps reflect a tendency to think of a child as acquiring language and the rest of reality from somewhere "out there" – as if he was a pre-existing individual who, by a process of learning the rules, achieves conformity with a pre-existing scheme.

Sociolinguistic theorists of language development have attempted to place the developing child in a social context; they have removed the "nativist versus environmentalist" controversy from the agenda and offered instead some version of an "interactionist" approach. A number of investigators have suggested an interpretation in terms of the notion of communicative competence. This leads to what is essentially a socialization model of language development, according to which the child has to master, in addition to the "rules" of language, a set of socially accepted norms of language use. It is open to the objection that learning to mean cannot be reduced to a matter of learning how to behave properly in the contexts in which meanings are exchanged. A more recent interpretation is one based on the notion of the speech act, the speech act being put forward as the structural unit which a child acquires as the simultaneous representation of his conceptual, communicative, and grammatical skills (Dore 1974, 1976). But the speech act is a subjective, not an intersubjective, construct; it is supposed to take account of the fact that people talk to each other, but it represents this fact in terms of the knowledge, the belief structures, and the behaviour patterns of the individual. The consequence of this is that the theory fails to account for the dynamics of dialogue, the ongoing exchange of speech roles through which conversation becomes a reality-generating process.

I think we need to interpret language development more in terms of a conception of social or intersubjective creativity. Learning to mean is a process of creation, whereby a child constructs, in interaction with those around, a semiotic potential that gives access to the edifice of meanings that constitute social reality.

There is ample evidence that children engage in communicative interaction from birth. A newborn infant's orientation towards persons is quite distinct from his orientation towards the objects in his environment; he is aware of being addressed, and can respond. He exchanges attention with the persons who are the "others" in his social system (Bruner 1975; France 1975; Trevarthen 1974b).

In these intersubjective processes lie the foundations of the construction of reality. Reality is created through the exchange of meanings – in other words, through conversation. The exchange of attention which begins at birth already has some of the features of conversation; it has been described by Bateson (1975) as "protoconversation".

But protoconversation does not yet involve an exchange of meanings. If we adopt the distinction made previously in this chapter between an "act of meaning" and other communicative acts, then conversation proper is an exchange of acts of meaning – or, simply, an exchange of meanings; whereas protoconversation consists of communicative exchanges which do not yet take the form of acts of meaning.

Protoconversation begins at birth; conversation begins some months later. It begins, in fact, with the beginning of the protolanguage.

At this point it may be helpful to offer a tentative schematic account of the development of a child's powers of conversation (see Figure 3).

The central concept here is that of intersubjectivity (Trevarthen 1974a). The construction of reality depends on conversation – on the exchange of meanings. But the foundations are laid in the protoconversational period when the child is already engaging in intersubjective acts. A child is not born endowed with language. But he is born with the ability to recognize and respond to address; and to communicate with

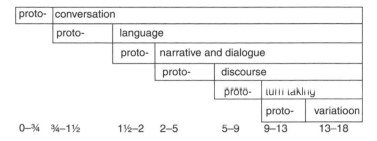

proto-	conversation					
	proto-	language				
		proto-	narrative and dialogue			
			proto-	discourse		
				proto-	turn taking	
					proto-	variatioon
0–¾	¾–1½	1½–2	2–5	5–9	9–13	13–18

Figure 3 The development of powers of conversation
0–3/4 communicative acts (protoconversation), prespeech;
3/4–1½ , acts of meaning (functional protolanguage);
1½–2, transition to language, macrofunctions mathetic/pragmatic;
2–5, narrative and dialogue, elementary lexicogrammar;
5–9, discourse, intermediate lexicogrammar;
9–13, turn taking, advanced lexicogrammar;
13(–18), variation, register and social dialect.

someone who is communicating with him. He even engages, from the age of a few weeks, in what Trevarthen calls "prespeech": the manipulation of the expressive resources that will be put to use in the protolanguage, and eventually in language itself. (It is important to distinguish between prespeech and protolanguage. Prespeech is expression only, whereas protolanguage is expression and content. There is no semantic component in prespeech. But it is significant that it typically accompanies communicative acts of this protoconversational kind.)

Patterns of intersubjective activity are thus well established by the time the child takes the crucial step of starting to mean. An act of meaning is inherently an intersubjective act, one which makes possible the exchange of meanings and hence the construction of reality. Berger and Luckmann (1966) speak in very clear terms of "the reality-generating power of conversation"; and although, as they remark, conversation usually implies language, we have stressed all along that true conversation already begins in the protolanguage. The protolanguage – if Nigel is at all typical – is not organized the way the adult language is, with a grammar and a vocabulary; but it is nevertheless a language in which conversation can and does take place.

The crucial property of conversation in Berger and Luckmann's account is that it is casual. It does not consist of explanations. Nobody instructs the child in the mysteries of things; he would not understand them if they did. Conversation consists of ongoing contextualized chatter.

Out of this a child builds an order of things and events, including his own part in them and attitudes towards them.

What makes it possible for the child to do this is the relation of an act of meaning to its context (discussed on sections 1.4 and 1.5 above). **How** he does it is a different matter. Typically, he organizes his conversation around a limited number of generalized semantic strategies, ways of meaning that are the ontogenetic analogue to, and anticipation of, the speech functions and rhetorical modes of the adult language. Here is a small example from 23 months:

> Nigel's mother and I were planning a visit to the aquarium. Nigel did not know what an aquarium was, but he heard us discussing it.
> "We're not going to see a rào ['lion']," he said to himself. "Vòpa ['fishes']. There will be some wàter."
> In other words, it was not a zoo, but it was something of the same kind, with fishes (and water for them to live in) instead of lions.

The principle of contrast – of seeing things as "same but different" – is a favourite strategy for the representation of experience at this stage. These strategies are not the same as those of an adult, nor can they be understood as unsuccessful approximations to those that an adult employs. A child uses language in different ways; not because he is trying to do what an adult does and failing, but because he is a different person engaged in a different set of tasks.

It is tempting to think of a child's construction of reality as simply his construction of a model of the outside world: of things and their properties, and how they relate and interact. This is, certainly, one important aspect of what he is doing. But it is not the whole story. The child is constructing a social semiotic, a reality in which things are because people are, and people construe them in certain ways. To say that people "construe" things means that they act on them, value them, and interpret them; and it is this construction that is shared through intersubjective acts of meaning. When the child sees things interact, typically he is seeing how people act on them; when he apprehends their significance, typically he is finding out how people value them; and when he builds them into his meaning potential, typically he is learning how people interpret them. He is not taking over a meaning potential, or a reality, that is ready-made for him "out there"; on the contrary, as the interpretation of Nigel's protolanguage makes clear, a child is **creating** meanings, not imitating those he finds around him. But this process of creation is an interactive process, in which the meanings are created in the course of being exchanged between the child and the significant others.

The exchange takes place in the context of, and in interpenetration with, the reality that is "out there"; but what is "out there" is a social construct – not a pile of sticks and stones, but a house.

As was said earlier, an act of meaning is a social act, not only in the simple sense that it is a form of interaction between people each of whom is producing meanings of his own and tracking those of others, but also in the deeper sense that the meaning potential from which these meanings derive is itself a social construct; and so is the reality beyond it. The meanings that are embodied in conversation in the protolanguage are, obviously, not very sophisticated; but they are already such that we can see them as the realization of some higher-order semiotic – of a social reality, in fact. Nigel's reality is a social reality and its construction is a social process. It is shared between Nigel and those with whom he exchanges meanings: the significant others, who are significant pre cisely for this reason, that they are the ones with whom meanings are exchanged.

One of the most remarkable features of the interaction that takes place between a child and his mother – or anyone else with whom the child regularly exchanges meanings – is the extent to which the mother (or other person) knows at each point in time what the child will and what he will not understand. This can be seen (or rather heard) not only in the way in which the mother converses with the child, but also in the way in which she tells him stories and modifies or explains for him anything she is reading aloud. (And we notice it with a shock when we come across someone we feel should have this knowledge and find they have not. One major problem for a child who is cared for in an institution is the lack of anyone who shares his language and his reality.) The phenomenon is all the more astonishing when one takes account of the fact that what the child understands is changing day by day. The mother keeps pace with this development to such an exact degree that it is not unreasonable to say that she is simultaneously building up the same language and the same reality. (I do not mean that she imitates the child's sounds. On the contrary, imitating the sounds a child makes and repeating them back to him nearly always in my experience covers up a failure to track his language adequately; it is an attempt to "con" him into thinking that one is with him in an exchange of meanings. He is never deceived, and usually rejects the attempt as insulting.) Essentially the mother is going through the processes of mental development all over again, but this time in the child's persona; under impetus from the child, the mother is creating a world of meaning along with him. It is for this reason that we call the process an *intersubjective* one.

29

If one was to attempt to characterize language development in the most general terms, it would be as the process of the intersubjective creation of meanings, and hence of a meaning potential that is a mode of the representation of reality. A child constructs, in interaction with others, a reality that has two parts to it, since it includes within itself a symbolic system – language – through which the rest is mediated. The two parts, language and non-language, are essentially continuous, each influencing and modifying the other. Hence the symbolic system through which reality is mediated is not only a part of reality, but is also, to a certain extent, a determinant of the other part. The schemata illustrated in Figures 1 and 2 represent reality as apprehended through our understanding of Nigel's protolanguage. There is a direct continuity between the infant's intersubjective experiences of mutual address, shared attention and protoconversation, on the one hand, and the social construction of reality through the natural rhetoric and natural logic of conversation on the other. In Figure 1 we know, from Nigel's ability to mean in the various modes at the outset of the protolanguage, that his subjective reality must contain certain conceptual discontinuities: at the very least, (1) reality distinguished into "out there" (non–self) and "not out there" (self); (2) non–self distinguished into persons and objects; and (3) persons distinguished into two roles, (i) for interaction and (ii) for control. The reality is an intersubjective reality, not only constructed through intersubjective acts of meaning (conversation) but also held in common with the significant others. It is a joint construction; otherwise it could not get built. The self thus lies, in Meadian fashion, at the intersection of various dimensions of social process – including, critically, processes of a symbolic or **sociosemiotic** kind.

If we then look back at our representation of Nigel's model of reality at ten months, we find in it the same preoccupation with the child as individual that was referred to at the beginning of this section. Reinterpreting in the light of what turned out to be Nigel's primary transition strategy as he moved from protolanguage to language and began to construct an adult-like semantic system, we might arrive at something more like Figure 4. This schema, suggesting an alternative interpretation of Nigel's meaning potential at ten months in terms of the ordering of persons and objects, brings out more clearly the continuity of his transition to the adult language (see Figure 2).

I have tried to outline the nature of the reality that is shared between a child and those with whom he exchanges meanings, with particular attention to the period between nine months and two years. The facts have been taken from the study of Nigel's language, and the results of

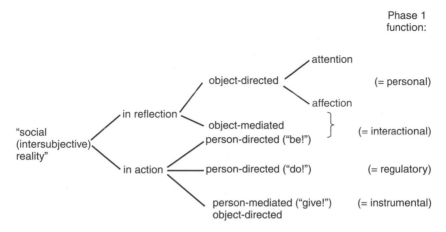

Figure 4 Nigel at nine to ten and a half months (another interpretation)

this study have been used in an interpretation of the language development process. The organizing concept is that of shared meanings. At any one moment, the child has a meaning potential, a semantic system that is shared between himself and the significant others. It has been developed by an ongoing process in which the others first track the child by participating in his acts of meaning, and then reinforce, extend and modify the child's meaning system through the effects of their own responsive acts.

IV.5(1978):113–43

★ ★ ★

At the end of the second year, when Nigel is just on the threshold of entry to the adult language, in the sense of being about to adopt the functional semantic patterns of the mother tongue, he has introduced many more delicate distinctions; but the primary distinctions he is making are now coming to approximate the speech functions of the adult language (Figure 14). It is not difficult to see how this evolves into the adult system as outlined in section 1 above, based on the exchange of meanings of the two kinds that we recognized there: goods-and-services, where language is ancillary to a (non-symbolic) process that itself is independent of language, and information, where the process is itself a symbolic one – the 'commodity' that is being exchanged **is** language, or rather is a semiotic that is realized in the form of language. It is not surprising, when seen in this light, that the concept of information, and the ability to exchange information, is relatively late in developing. By the age of nine months Nigel has a very clearly developed sense of meaning as a mediating process: by addressing another person, and exchanging symbols with that person, he can achieve a variety of intents – but the act of meaning in no way constitutes the realization of those intents. It is not until the very end of his second year that he comes to see the exchange of meanings as a goal, as a process sui generis, such that the act of meaning is itself the realization of the intent. We have seen how this awareness of exchanging information has evolved, namely through the convergence of two lines of development, starting from two of the elementary functions of the protolanguage: (1) the interactional – (a) 'let's be together'; (b) shared attention to an external object, as a form of 'togetherness'; (c) the 'naming game' ('look at this picture; now you say its name'); (d) 'what's this called?' (asking for a new name); (e) Wh-questions ('fill in the gap in this account'); and (2) the personal – (a) attention to

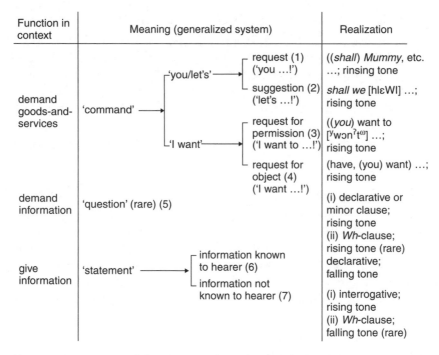

Figure 14 Incipient adult (2.0): Nigel on the threshold of the adult system of dialogue

Note: the systematic distinction between (3) and (4) is disappearing.

32

prominence ('there's a commotion?'); (b) attention to the environment ('that's interesting'); (c) observation, recall and prediction ('I see/saw/will see . . . '); (d) voicing shared experience ('I'm telling you what we both saw/heard'); (e) communicating unshared experience ('I'm telling you what I saw/heard but you didn't').

IV.10(1984):245–6

* * *

Interpersonal meanings such as protestation and reservation are just as much part of the linguistic system as are meanings of an ideational kind. The fact that interpersonal meanings often have different modes of expression from ideational ones, being prosodic or 'field'-like in their scope rather than segmental or 'particle'-like, and hence do not lend themselves so readily to representation in a constituency framework, may be one of the reasons why they have usually been treated as unsystematic. We should suggest rather that this is a reason for rejecting constituent structure as the primary organizing concept in linguistics, and for interpreting language in functional and systemic terms. In the explanation of dialogue, whether we are concerned with the most general categories or with the subtlest distinctions, and whether the focus is on the mature system of an adult or on its ontogenesis in a child, we are concerned with meanings of the interpersonal kind; it would be a mistake to adhere rigidly to theories of language which, because they reduce all linguistic organization to one type of structure, one that is typically associated with meanings of a different kind, namely ideational ones, thereby commit themselves to treating all interpersonal meanings as something secondary or tangential.

The organization of dialogue is a systematic feature of language; it is linguistically coded behaviour. It is built up by a child as part of his total semiotic potential. Neither the system nor its evolution can be satisfactorily explained in terms of a competence–performance dichotomy in which the code is so highly idealized that it cannot be used to explain what people do. Dialogue is not just a matter of "performance" (whatever that might mean). Nor, however, is it a matter of a special kind of competence ("communicative competence") that is somehow distinct from the ability to construct ideationally well-formed sentences. Taking part in dialogue is a dynamic process of selecting within a whole range of interrelated networks of interpersonal meanings. Interpersonal meanings are not 'uses of' ideational ones, or optional extras that sometimes get tacked on to them as an afterthought. The two constitute distinct but parallel components of the semantic system, and every act of meaning is the product of selections in both.

IV.10(1984):249–50

Language and Education (Volume 9)

. . . human language evolved in two primary functional contexts: construing personal ***experience***, and enacting ***interpersonal*** relations. Every human language instantiates these two metafunctions, its lexicogrammar constructing a meaning potential in which they become integrated in unitary acts of meaning (and the grammar has evolved a third component, the ***textual***, whereby such acts of meaning become discourse, a kind of virtual reality in semiotic form).

IX.15(1994):321

Additional readings

On Grammar (Volume 1) – 8(1979):206; 12(1987):348; 13(1992):354–6; 15(1996):387, 414

Linguistic Studies of Text and Discourse (Volume 2) – 2(1977):50, 52; 4(1982):145

On Language and Linguistics (Volume 3) – 4(1977):93,115; 8(1985):189; 12(1997): 249; 16(1992):355–74; 17(1992):375–89; 18(1995):415; Appendix(1994):436

The Language of Early Childhood (Volume 4) – 1(1998):6, 23; 7(1975):187; 8(1980):207; 9(1983):212–8; 10(1984):239; 11(1991):253; 13(1975):282, 303; 15(1993):327–52; 16(1999):354; Appendix 1:382-90

The Language of Science (Volume 5) – 3(1998): 51

Computational and Quantitative Studies (Volume 6) – 9(1995):198–202; 11(1995):253, 264

Language and Education (Volume 9) – 8(1978):186; 9(1986):196

Chapter Two

COMPLEMENTARITY AND COMPLEXITY IN LANGUAGE

Summary

Complementarities in grammar make it possible for our common sense grammars of daily life to accommodate multiple and possibly even contradictory perspectives on the same set of phenomena. Among examples cited by Halliday to demonstrate the need for complementarity in dealing with aspects of experience which cannot be reduced to a single construction, are tense and aspect as theories of time, and transitive and ergative as theories of agency and causality.

Complementarity also is demonstrated between the two grammatical modes of congruent common-sense grammar of daily life, on the one hand, and the metaphorical grammar of education and of the workplace, on the other hand. Common-sense discourse is characterized by a high degree of grammatical intricacy; the metaphorical or 'attic' style by a high degree of lexical density. This complementarity is also reflected in the difference between speech and writing, with the former described as dynamic and choreographic, while the latter is synoptic and crystalline. There is also a functional complementarity between writing and speech, in which either occurs in contexts different from the other.

The complementarity of lexis and grammar in the lexicogrammatical stratum is described by MAK Halliday as a metacomplementarity within the system itself, with both lexis and grammar representing different perspectives on the whole.

Selected readings

On Grammar (Volume 1)

The grammar has to impose discontinuity on the flux of experience; but the human condition – our total relationship to our environment – is complex and many-faceted, so there will be indefinitely many ways of doing this, and hence differences between one language and another, and within one language at different stages in its history: some random, some resonating with variation and change in human culture. But even within one experiential domain, at any one moment in time, the grammar has to contend with conflicting and often contradictory demands; so this same interface accommodates complementarities – in a sense analogous to that in which Niels Bohr used the term to extend Heisenberg's uncertainty principle in quantum mechanics. The grammar is unable to reduce some aspect of experience to a single construction and so introduces two distinct perspectives, two construals which are mutually contradictory and yet depend on each other to provide a theory of daily life. An example would be tense and aspect as complementary theories of time. These contradict each other: either time is a linear flow out of past through present into future, or else it isn't. Yet many languages, perhaps all, insist that it both is and is not: in very different mixtures and proportions, but each amounting to a plausible theory for coping with the everyday world. Some of these complementarities display the further property that one of the two perspectives is construed configurationally, the other iteratively (as multivariate and univariate structures), thus foregrounding respectively the synoptic and the dynamic points of view. For example, the way the grammar constructs taxonomies of things involves both locating them in configurations of properties and modifying them by means of iterative bracketing. The construction of time in English also exemplifies this point: the system of aspect is activated once at a time, while the system of tense allows for successive reentries: present, past in present, future in past in present and so on. The essence of semiotic complementarity is that it is both objective and subjective: some domain of experience is being construed both as two phenomena and as two points of view on the one phenomenon. (The complementarity of lexis and grammar in the lexicogrammatical stratum is a metacomplementarity within the system itself.)

I.14(1998):379

On Language and Linguistics (Volume 3)

5 LEVELS OF CONSCIOUSNESS IN LANGUAGE
Let me begin this section with a quotation from Prigogine and Stengers' book *Order out of Chaos* that I referred to at the outset:

[In quantum mechanics] there is an irreducible multiplicity of representation for a system, each connected with a determined [i.e. decided upon by the investigator] set of operators.

This implies a departure from the classical notion of objectivity, since in the classical view the only "objective" description is the complete description of *the system as it is*, independent of the choice of how it is observed . . .

The physicist has to choose his language, to choose the macroscopic experimental device. Bohr expressed this idea through the principle of complementarity . . .

The real lesson to be learned from the principle of complementarity, a lesson that can perhaps be transferred to other fields of knowledge, consists in emphasizing the wealth of reality, which overflows any single language, any single logical structure. Each language can express only part of reality. (p. 225)

Here Prigogine and Stengers are of course talking about "languages" in the sense of conceptual constructs; and they go on to say:

No single theoretical language articulating the variables to which a well defined value can be attributed can exhaust the physical content of a system. Various possible languages and points of view about the system may be complementary. They all deal with the same reality, but it is impossible to reduce them to one single description.

It is my contention that natural language – not as it is dressed up in the form of a scientific metalanguage, but in its common-sense, everyday, spontaneous spoken form – does in fact 'represent reality' in terms of complementarities; and that these are complementary perspectives in precisely the sense in which Bohr was using the term.[2] Only, it does so non-referentially. Just as language construes the social order without referring to the system it is constructing, so likewise language construes the natural order – through the unconscious, cryptotypic patterns in the grammar, which create their own order of reality independently of whatever it is they may be being used to describe.

I shall illustrate the complementarities inherent in this "deautomatized" sphere of the grammar in just a moment. But first we must recognise a problem. The features I am referring to in natural language are features of the "cryptogrammar"; they function way below the usual level of consciousness. And the problem is, that when we start reflecting on them, bringing them up to our conscious attention, we destroy them. The act of reflecting on language transforms it into something alien, something different from itself – something determinate and closed. There are uses for closed, determinate metalanguages; but they can represent only one point of view about a system. The language of daily life, which shapes our unconscious understanding of ourselves and our environment, is a language of complementarities, a rheomode – a dynamic open system. The question is whether we can learn to use it to think with consciously. It may be impossible. I don't mean that it is impossible to understand the cryptogrammar of a natural language, but that its reality-generating power may be incompatible with explicit logical reasoning.

I have tried out a simple strategy for exploring the more unconscious features of the grammar. I selected a text – the headlines of a news broadcast, which I had taken down verbatim from the radio; I read it aloud to a group of students, and asked them to recall it. They gave me the motifs: death, disaster, violence and the like. I pressed them further: what was actually said? This time they gave me words: a list of the lexical items used, recalled with considerable accuracy although most of them had not figured in their first responses. Let me call the motif level zero, and the lexical responses level one. I pressed them for a more specific account (still without reading the passage again), and they gave me the more exposed parts of the grammar: the word, group and phrase classes, the derivational morphology and so on. This exposed grammar we will call level two. I pressed them once more; and this time – since they were students of linguistics – they began to get to level three, the hidden grammar (the cryptotypes, in Whorf's terminology): the transitivity patterns, the grammatical metaphors and so on.

In our normal everyday concern with language we simply attend to the motifs. We are not concerned with wordings, and do not trouble even to remember them. We behave as if the metaredundancy – the realization of meanings in lexicogrammar – is simply an automatic coding. If asked to reflect on the wording, we focus on the lexical end of the spectrum: the words, or rather the lexical items – since this is the edge that is nearest the domain of conscious attention. It takes much more effort to attend to the more strictly grammatical zone, especially to its more cryototypic regions. And when we get there, we find ourselves back at the motifs again; but this time with a greatly heightened understanding, because now we can see why the text meant what it did, and we can appreciate the deeper ideological content of the discourse – the messages we had received without becoming aware of them. The process of reflecting on natural language can be modelled in terms of these four levels of consciousness:

'meaning' (semantic level) level 0: 'motifs'
'wording' (lexicogrammatical level) $\begin{cases} \text{level 1: 'words'} \\ \text{level 2: 'phenotypes'} \\ \text{level 3: 'cryptotypes'} \end{cases}$

where the spiral (cryptotypes as hidden motifs) in turn represents the dialectic of metaredundancy. Or, to put this in more familiar semiotic terms: the signified constructs the signifier (by "realization" – grammar in its automatized function), and the signifier constructs the signified (grammar, especially the cryptogrammar, in its de-automatized function). The problem of turning the cryptogrammar of a natural language into a metalanguage for reasoning with is that it has to become automatized – that is, the grammar has to be made to describe, instead of constructing reality by not describing, which is what it does best.

6 EVERYDAY LANGUAGE AS A THEORY OF THE NATURAL ORDER

I will try to enumerate some features of natural language, as embodied in our everyday informal discourse from earliest childhood, that constitute for us a theory of reality. They are features common to all languages, but in respect of which each language presents its own particular mix; I make one or two references to English, but in the main they are set out in general terms that could be applied to all.

- Clausal structures: the organization of meanings in lexicogrammatical form (as **wordings**). The gateway through which meanings are brought together and realized in ordinary grammar is the clause; and the clause nucleus is a happening (Process + Medium, in systemic terms). So natural languages represent reality as what happens, not as what exists; things are defined as contingencies of the flow.
- Projection: the general relation underlying what grammarians call "direct and indirect speech". The system of projection construes the whole of experience into two different kinds of event: semiotic events, and other events; the latter can then be transformed into semiotic events by processes of consciousness.
- Expansion: logical-semantic relationships between events. Two events provided they are of the same kind (as defined by projection) may be related to one another by one of a set of logical-semantic relations, such that the second one defines, extends, or in some way (such as time or cause) correlates with the first.

- Transitivity: the theory of processes (i). Natural languages construe experience out of different types of process; this plurality is universal, though the details of the system vary. English sets up 'outer' processes, those of the world perceived as external; 'inner' processes, those of (human-like) consciousness; and processes of attribution and representation. All are distinguished in the cryptogrammar.
- Transitivity: the theory of processes (ii). With regard to (at least) the 'outer' processes, natural languages incorporate two models: the transitive, which interprets 'mechanically', in terms of transmission, and the ergative, which interprets 'scientifically', in terms of causation. These two are complementary; the generalizations they make contradict each other, but every clause has to be interpreted as both.
- Tense and aspect: the theory of time. Similarly, natural languages embody two models of time: a theory of linear, irreversible time, out of past via present into future (tense), and a theory of simultaneity, with the opposition between being and becoming, or manifested and manifesting (aspect). Languages have very different mixtures (English strongly foregrounds linear time): but probably every language enacts both, and again the two are complementary in the defined sense.

In these and other features of their 'hidden' grammars, ordinary languages in their everyday, common-sense contexts embody highly sophisticated interpretations of the natural order, rich in complementarities and thoroughly rheomodal in ways much deeper than Bohm was able to conceive of. To be more accurate, we would say that it is these features **in a system of this dynamic open kind** that construe reality for us in this way. The system itself must be a metastable, multi-level ("metaredundant") system – that is, a human semiotic – with the further property that it is *metafunctional*: it is committed to meaning more than one thing at once, so that every instance is at once both reflection and action – both interpreting the world and also changing it.

We have been reminded of "the impossibility of recovering a fixed and stable meaning from discourse". Of course this is impossible; it would be a very impoverished theory of discourse that expected it. But it is entirely possible – as we all do – to recover from discourse a meaning of another kind, meaning that is complex and indeterminate. The reason it is hard to make this process explicit is that we can do so only by talking about grammar; and to do this we have to construct a theory of grammar: a "grammatics", let us call it. But this *grammatics* is itself a designed system, another scientific metalanguage, with terms like *subject* and *agent* and **conditional** – terms which become reified in their turn, so that we then come to think of the grammar itself (the real grammar) as feeble and crude because it doesn't match up to the categories we've invented for describing it. But of course it is the grammatics – the metalanguage – that is feeble and crude, not the grammar. To borrow Whorf's famous simile, the grammatics (grammar as metalanguage) is to the grammar (the language) as a bludgeon is to a rapier – except that a better analogy might be with the hand that wields the rapier. If the human mind can achieve this remarkable combination of incisive penetration and positive indeterminacy, then we can hardly deny these same properties to human language, since language is the very system by which they are developed, stored and powered.

7 THE NEED FOR PLURALITY OF LANGUAGE

To quote Prigogine and Stengers again: "Whatever we call reality, it is revealed to us only through active construction in which we participate" (p. 293). But, as they have already told us, "the wealth of reality . . . overflows any single language, any single logical structure. Each language can express only part of reality."

I have suggested that our natural languages do possess the qualities needed for interpreting the world very much as our modern physicists see it. But from the time when our dialogue with nature became a conscious exercise in understanding, we have come to need more than one grammar – more than one version of language as a theory of experience. Rather, we have needed a continuum of grammars, from the rheomodal pole at one end to something more fixed and constructible at the other. For our active construction of reality we had to be able to adopt either a dynamic, 'in flux' perspective or a synoptic, 'in place' perspective – or some mixture of the two, with a complementarity between them.

So our language began to stretch, beginning – as far as the West is concerned – with the explosion of process nouns in scientific Greek from 550 BC onwards (e.g. *kinesis* 'movement', from *kineo* '(I) move'), and culminating (so far!) in the kind of semantic variation found in pairs such as:

experimental emphasis becomes concentrated in testing the generalizations and consequences derived from these theories	we now start experimenting mainly in order to test whether things happen regularly as we would expect if we were explaining in the right way
1–attic	1–doric

Let me label these two styles the attic and the doric. The attic mode is not of course confined to abstract scientific discourse; 2-attic is from a television magazine:

he also credits his former big size with much of his career success	he also believes that he succeeded in his career mainly because he used to be big
2-attic	2-doric

Represented in this new, 'attic' style, the world is a world of things, rather than one of happening; of product, rather than of process; of being, rather than becoming. Whatever metaphor we use to label it with – and all these paired expressions capture some aspect of the difference – the emergence of the new attic forms of expression added a new dimension to human experience: where previously there had been one mode of interpretation, the dynamic, now there were two, the synoptic and the dynamic – or rather, two poles, with varying degrees of semantic space possible between them. There are now two ways of looking at one and the same set of phenomena.

The two are complementary, like wave and particle as complementary theories of light. Any aspect of reality can be interpreted either way; but, as with wave and particle, certain aspects will be better illuminated with the one perspective and others with the other. The doric style, that of everyday, common-sense discourse, is characterized by a high degree of grammatical intricacy – a choreographic type of complexity, as I have described it (1987): it highlights processes, and the interdependence of one process on another. The attic style, that of emergent languages of science, displays a high degree of lexical density; its complexity is crystal-line, and it highlights structures, and the interrelationships of their parts – including, in a critical further development, **conceptual** structures, the taxonomies that helped to turn knowledge into science.

There was thus a bifurcation in the metaredundancy pattern, leading to the duality of styles that Rulon Wells (1960) spoke about at the con-ference whose aftermath we are celebrating here (he referred to them as "nominal and verbal styles", but the distinction is really that of nominal and clausal). Between the doric, or clausal, style and the attic, or nominal, style is a complementarity that itself complements the various first-order complementarities that we have already seen to be present within the doric system. But this second-order complementarity is of a somewhat different kind. The two perspectives are not on equal terms. The dynamic mode is prior; it comes first.

The dynamic mode is phylogenetically prior; it evolved first, along with the human species, whereas it is only in the last few millennia that the synoptic mode has come into being. It is also ontogenetically prior; it is what we learn as children – and carry with us throughout life. Whenever we are speaking casually and unselfconsciously, in typically human dialogic contexts, we go on exploiting the dynamic mode, which as we have seen embodies the deep experience of the species in crypto-grammatic form. The synoptic mode, on the other hand, embodies the more conscious reflection on the environment that is stored in scientific knowledge; historically it is derived from the dynamic by the processes of grammatical metaphor. Of course, once in existence it can enter daily life; there is nothing very abstruse or formal about *every previous visit had left me with a feeling of discomfort* . . . Nevertheless it is a metaphoric deriva-tive; the agnate *whenever I'd visited before I'd ended up feeling uncomfortable* . . . is a prior form of semiosis. So how does the more synoptic mode, the attic style arise?

Thanks to the metaredundancy principle, it is possible to introduce variation at any one level of language without thereby disturbing the patterning at other levels of the system (that is, without catastrophic per-turbations; the consequences are seen in continued gradual changes such as I described earlier). It is even possible to replace an entire level of the system in this way; and this is what happened with the development of writing. Writing provided a new mode of expression – which could "realize" the pre-existing content patterns without disrupting them. At the same time, it provided a new interface, another kind of instantiation through which changes in the system could take place.

Writing evolved in the immediate context of the need for documen-tation and recording. But it opened the way to an alternative theory of reality.

8 THE EFFECTS OF WRITING

Conditions arise in history – essentially those of settlement – where experience has to be recorded: we need to store knowledge, and put it on file. So we invent a filing system for language, reducing it to writing. The effect of this is to anchor language to a shallower level of consciousness. For the first time, language comes to be made of constituents – sentences – instead of the dependency patterns – clause complexes – of the spoken mode. And with constituency comes a different form of the interpreta-tion of experience.

It is important not to oversimplify the argument at this point. Both language itself, and the dimensions of experience that are given form by language, are extremely complex; and instead of hoping to gain in popularity ratings by pretending all is simple we do well to admit the complexity and try to accommodate it in our thinking. Let me take just three steps at this point.

Writing brings language to consciousness; and in the same process it changes its semiotic mode from the dynamic to the synoptic: from flow to stasis, from choreographic to crystalline, from syntactic intricacy to lexical density. Note that this is **not** saying that writing imposes organization on language. On the contrary: there is every bit as much organization in spoken language as there is in written, only it is organization of a different kind. Written language is corpuscular and gains power by its density, whereas spoken language is wavelike and gains power by its intricacy. I am not, of course, talking about writing in the sense of orthography, contrasting with phonology as medium of expression; but about *written language* – the forms of discourse that arise as a result of this change of medium (by a complex historical process that is based partly on the nature of the medium itself and partly on its functions in society). Similarly in talking about spoken language I mean the forms of discourse which evolved over the long history of language in its spoken mode; the mode in which language itself evolved.

Writing puts language in chains; it freezes it, so that it becomes a **thing** to be reflected on. Hence it changes the ways that language is used for meaning with. Writing deprives language of the power to intuit, to make indefinitely many connections in different directions at once, to explore (by tolerating them) contradictions, to represent experience as fluid and indeterminate. It is therefore destructive of one fundamental human potential: to think on your toes, as we put it.

But, secondly, in destroying this potential it creates another one: that of structuring, categorizing, disciplinizing. It creates a new kind of knowledge: scientific knowledge; and a new way of learning, called education. Thus writing changed the social semiotic on two levels. Superficially, it created documentation – the filing of experience, the potential to 'look things up'. More fundamentally, it offered a new perspective on experience: the synoptic one, with its definitions, taxonomies and constructions. The world of written language is a nominalized world, with a high lexical density and packed grammatical metaphors. It is these features that enable discourse to become technical; as Martin has shown, technicality in language depends on, not writing as such, but the kind of organization of meaning that writing brings with it (Martin 1986; Wignell 1987).

Until information can be organized and packaged in this way – so that only the initiate understands it – knowledge cannot accumulate, since there is no way one discourse can start where other ones left off. When I can say

the random fluctuations in the **spin** components of one of the two particles

I am packaging the knowledge that has developed over a long series of preceding arguments and presenting it as 'to be taken for granted – now we can proceed to the next step'. If I cannot do this, but have to say every time that particles spin, that they spin in three dimensions, that a pair of particles can spin in association with one another, that each one of the pair fluctuates randomly as it is spinning, and so on, then it is clear that I will never get very far. I have to have an 'expert' grammar, the kind of grammar that is prepared to throw away experiential information, to take for granted the semantic relations by which the elements are related to one another, so that it can maximize textual information, the systematic development of the discourse as a causeway to further knowledge. That kind of grammar shuts the layman out.

It would take too long to demonstrate in detail how this written grammar works. Let me refer briefly to its two critical properties: nominalization, and grammatical metaphor. Most instances involve a combination of the two. For example,

such an exercise had the potential for intrusions by the government into the legitimate privacy of non-government schools

Apart from *had*, the clause consists of two nominal groups: *such an exercise* and *the potential for intrusions by the government into the legitimate privacy of non-government schools*. The second of these displays one of the principal devices for creating nominal structures: nominal group *nongovernment schools* embedded inside prepositional phrase *of non-government schools* embedded inside nominal group *the legitimate privacy of non-government schools* embedded inside prepositional phrase *into the legitimate privacy of non-government schools*; another prepositional phrase *by the government*; the two both embedded in the nominal group *intrusions by (a) into (b)*, itself embedded inside the nominal group *the potential for* . . . And most of these embeddings involve grammatical metaphor: *potential*, nominal expression of modality 'be able to', perhaps even a caused modality 'make + be able to'; *instrusions*, nominal expression of process 'intrude'; *privacy*, nominal expression of quality 'private'; *legitimate*, adjectival expression of attitudinally qualified projection 'as they could reasonably expect to be', and so on. (That these are marked, metaphorical realizations in contrast to unmarked, **congruent** ones is borne out in various ways: not only are the congruent forms developmentally prior – children typically learn to process grammatical metaphor only after the age of eight or nine – but also they are semantically explicit, so that the metaphorical ones can be derived from them but not the other way around. But note that the 'metaphor' is in the grammar; there is not necessarily any lexical shift.)

So to the third step. Writing and speaking, in this technical sense of written language and spoken language, are different grammars which therefore constitute different ways of knowing, such that any theory of knowledge, and of learning, must encompass both. Our understanding of the social and the natural order depends on both, and on the complementarity between the two as interpretations of experience. I sometimes ask teachers about this question: whether there are things in the curriculum they consider best learnt through talking and listening, and other things best learnt through reading and writing. They have seldom thought about this consciously; but their practice often reveals just such a complementarity – processes and process sequences, such as sets of instructions, and including logically ordered sequences of ongoing argument, are presented and explored in speech, whereas structures, definitions, taxonomies and summaries of preceding arguments are handled through writing. Thus the complementarity of speech and writing creates a complementarity in our ways of knowing and of learning; once we are both speakers and writers we have an added dimension to our experience.

Note

2. Cf. Briggs and Peat (1985: 54): "Bohr approved of the uncertainty principle itself, believing it was an aspect of a deeper idea he called "complementarity". Complementarity meant the universe can never be described in a single, clear picture but must be apprehended through overlapping, complementary and sometimes paradoxical views. Bohr found echoes of this idea in classical Chinese philosophy and the theories of modern psychology." He would have found them also in the grammar of natural languages.

III.5(1987):124–34, 137–8

★ ★ ★

One of the clear signs of extravagance in language is its fondness for complementarities – for having things both ways. Whether or not our material practices are typically discrete (we have the impression that we are always either doing this or doing that, but that in turn may be the effect of having to categorize these practices in language), in semiotic practice, at least, we are often doing – or rather meaning – two different things at once. To put this in proverbial terms: in language you can eat your cake and have it (I notice that in current usage this has become "have your cake and eat it", which is a much blander form of wording, and also makes much less sense – the parataxis is linear: you eat your cake . . . but then you still have it). I am not talking here about the discursive ambiguities of public and domestic rhetoric (although the potential for these is ultimately an aspect of the same phenomenon in language), but rather about the systemic complementarities in the way that language categorizes and "constructs reality". Kristin Davidse's theoretical work (1992, 1996) has highlighted for English one of the major complementarities that seems to pervade all languages in their systems of transitivity: that between the transitive and the ergative construal of (material and other) processes. If there are two participants involved in a process, is the one acting on the other, or is it causing the other to act? One might say: in any given instance it may be either, but the two are contradictory – the same phenomenon cannot be both. Yet the grammar wants to have it both ways: not only does the system as a whole accommodate both perspectives but many processes are construed as a tension between the two. In languages where the distinction is formally marked this dual perspective is often very clear. Another fundamental complementarity is that between aspect and tense as construals of time: is time a linear flow, out of past through present into future, or is it an emerging movement between the virtual and the actual? (This is ultimately related to the transitive/ergative nature of processes.) Again, it seems it cannot be both; yet the grammar insists that it is, in some mixture or other according to the language. (As you move across the Eurasian continent the balance tends to shift, with tense more highly systematized in languages at the western end and aspect in those at the eastern – and perhaps a more even mix in some languages in the middle, such as Russian and Hindi.) And in the construal of entities we find another complementarity, that between bounded and unbounded, or "count" and "mass".

What is characteristic of such complementarities is that they offer alternative models of experience, such that, while it would be possible to construe the entire range of the phenomena in question in just one of the two perspectives, when you bring in both the picture gains in depth. Then it turns out that certain features are better illuminated when the phenomena are viewed from one perspective, while other features show up more clearly from the other. The extravagance of modelling the same domain of experience in more than one way leads to a richer and more life-supporting account. Of course, this will always leave room for what Claude Hagège (1997) referred to as "unheeded contradictions", the leftover bits of language-building materials that continue to lie around; but the **principle** of contradictory construal is intrinsically a productive one.

III.12(1997):252–3

The Language of Early Childhood (Volume 4)

FEATURE 17

Related to the last point is the principle of ***complementarity*** in the grammar. In its ideational metafunction, a natural language is a theory of human experience. But natural language grammars do not present experience in rigid, monosystemic terms. Rather, they frame up a highly elastic space, within which the phenomena of experience can be construed from different angles of vision. I am not talking here about elaborated scientific metalanguages – these do tend to be somewhat rigidified – but about the common-sense grammars of daily life. They embody complementarities of many kinds, contradictory interpretations of some aspect of experience, each illuminating one facet of it, such that the whole is construed in terms of the tension between them. Different languages exploit this potential in different ways; these are some examples drawn from English:

- Number (countable) versus mass (uncountable) as different models of matter and substance (for example, *a stone/stones* vs. *stone*).
- Aspect (manifesting: realis/irrealis) versus tense (eventuating: past/present/future) as different models of time (for example, *doing/to do* vs. *did/does/will do*).
- Transitive (action: +/– goal) versus ergative (realization: +/– agency) as different models of material processes (for example, *they're building/what are they building?* vs. *they're breaking/what's breaking them?*).
- Active versus middle as different models of mental processes (for example, *it didn't strike me* vs. *I didn't notice it*).

In construing these complementarities children come to see their own experience in depth. Note how Nigel (just 7;0) is playing with transitivity in the following.

> "I wish I lived in a caravan with a horse to drive like a pedlar man." Roger thinks it's a horse to **ride**. He thinks you can't drive horses. But horses can drive caravans. He thinks you can't drive horses – well you can't,

48

really; but horses can drive caravans – you know, pull them: you can call that driving, can't you? Roger thinks it's a horse to ride; but pedlars don't ride horses – they ride in the caravans, and the horse drives the caravan.

Nigel is interpreting *with a horse to drive* in the original verse both ergatively 'a horse for me to drive' and transitively 'a horse to drive it'. The grammar of daily life is rich in multiple perspectives of this kind.
...

FEATURE 21

This leads to the final heading, which is that of ***synoptic/dynamic complementarity***. All learning – whether learning **language**, learning **through** language, or learning **about** language – involves learning to understand things in more than one way. In a written culture, in which education is part of life, children learn to construe their experience in two complementary modes: the dynamic mode of the everyday commonsense grammar and the synoptic mode of the elaborated written grammar. Any particular **instance**, of any kind of phenomenon, may be interpreted as some product of the two – once the adolescent has transcended the semiotic barrier between them. Modern scientists have become increasingly dissatisfied with their own predominantly "written", objectified models and often talk of trying to restore the balance, the better to accommodate the dynamic, fluid, and indeterminate aspects of reality (cf. Lemke 1990: especially Chapter 7). They do not know how to do this (I have commented elsewhere on Bohm's 1980 search for the "rheomode"; cf. Halliday and Martin 1993: Chapter 6). One suggestion we might make, as linguists, is that they should go back and replenish their meaning potential at the fountain of everyday speech.

Teachers often have a powerful intuitive understanding that their pupils need to learn multimodally, using a wide variety of linguistic registers: both those of the written language, which locate them in the metaphorical world of things, and those of the spoken language, which relate what they are learning to the everyday world of doing and happening. The one foregrounds structure and stasis, the other foregrounds function and flow. The kind of complementarity that we have already seen in the grammar (cf. feature 17) exists also between these two grammatical modes, the congruent common-sense grammar of daily life and the metaphorical grammar of education and of the workplace. This dynamic/synoptic complementarity adds a final critical dimension to the adolescent learner's semantic space.

IV.15(1993):345, 349–50

The Language of Science (Volume 5)

Written technical discourse, in particular, is characterised by rather simple clause and sentence structures: each sentence typically one clause, that clause consisting of just one or two nominal groups (one of them perhaps 'governed' by a preposition), propped up by a verbal group, usually a relational process and most typically the verb *be*. The nominal groups, on the other hand, may be enormously long and complex – since all the lexical material is compressed into these one or two groups. I have referred to these two complementary types of complexity as "lexical density" and "grammatical intricacy" (Halliday 1987): density measured as the number of lexical words per clause, intricacy as the length and depth of the tactic structures whereby clauses come together to make up a clause complex.

V.2(1998):33

Computational and Quantitative Studies (Volume 6)

Diachronically, frequency patterns as revealed in corpus studies provide explanations for historical change, in that when interpreted as probabilities they show how each instance both maintains and perturbs the system. "System" and "instance" are of course not different things; they form yet another complementarity. There is only one phenomenon here, not two; what we call language (the system) and what we call text (the instance) are two observers of that phenomenon, observing it from different distances. (I have used the analogy of "climate" and "weather".) To the "instance" observer, the **system** is the potential, with its set of probabilities attached; each instance is by itself unpredictable, but the system appears constant through time. To the "system" observer, each **instance** redefines the system, however infinitesimally, maintaining its present state or shifting its probabilities in one direction or the other (as each moment's weather at every point on the globe redefines the global climate). It is the system which has a history – that is, it is the system observer who perceives depth in time; but the transformation of instance into system can be observed only through the technology of the corpus, which allows us to accumulate instances and monitor the diachronic variation in their patterns of frequency.

VI.4(1991):66–7

* * *

Many years ago I started measuring lexical density, which I defined as the number of lexical items (content words) per ranking (nonembedded) clause.

I found a significant difference between speech and writing: in my written language samples the mean value was around six lexical words per clause, while in the samples of spoken language it was around two. There was of course a great deal of variation among different registers, and Jean Ure (1971) showed that the values for a range of text types were located along a continuum. She, however, counted lexical words as a proportion of total running words, which gives a somewhat different result, because spoken language is more clausal (more and shorter clauses) whereas written language is more nominal (clauses longer and fewer). Michael Stubbs (1996), using a computerized corpus, followed Jean Ure's model, reasonably enough since mine makes it necessary to identify clauses, and hence requires a sophisticated parsing program. But the clause based comparison is more meaningful in relation to the contrast between spoken and written discourse.

What turned out to be no less interesting was what I called "grammatical intricacy", quantified as the number of ranking clauses in the clause complex. A clause complex is any sequence of structurally related ranking clauses; it is the spoken language analogue of (and of course the underlying origin of) what we recognize in written language as a sentence. In spontaneous spoken language the clause complex often became extraordinarily long and intricate. If we analyse one of these in terms of its hypotactic and paratactic nexuses, we get a sense of its complexity. Now, it is very seldom that we find anything like these in writing. In speech, they tend to appear in the longer monologic turns that occur within a dialogue. (That is, they are triggered dialogically, but constructed by a single speaker, rather than across turns.) Since dialogue also usually has a lot of very short turns, of just one clause, which is often a minor clause which doesn't enter into complex structures in any case, there is no sense in calculating a mean value for this kind of intricacy. What one can say is, that the more intricate a given clause complex is, the more likely it is that it happened in speech rather than in writing.

VI.8(2002):168–9

★ ★ ★

The key question is: what is it that enables a grammar – the grammar of a natural language – to do these wonderful things? Let me try to identify some of the salient properties of grammars that seem to be crucial in this respect. (1) They are **comprehensive**: they can 'mean' anything we want. (2) They are **extravagant**: they always pack extra power. (3) They are **telescopic**: they carry their history with them. (4) They are **non–autonomous**: they interact with their environment. (5) They are **variable**: they change

51

under differing conditions. (6) They are ***indeterminate***: they work with approximations and tendencies. I shall discuss briefly each of these properties in turn. (For theory and method of discourse analysis in systemic functional terms see Martin 1992.)

...

(2) Extravagant. The grammar offers multiple perspectives – different angles, or ways of looking at things. It often displays ***complementarities***: different construals of experience (like tense and aspect as theories of time, or transitive and ergative as theories of agency and causality) which contradict each other, yet where the contradiction opens up new meanings in unpredictable ways. It has an unending reserve of ***metaphor***, both ideational and interpersonal, constantly "de-coupling" itself from the semantics and re-coupling in other alignments, again in this way extending the overall meaning potential. Brief examples from English: (i) complementarity: conscious processes are grammaticized both as 'subject acting mentally, with object as scope' e.g. *I notice it, I believe it* and as 'object acting materially, with subject as goal' e.g. *it strikes me, it convinces me*; (ii) metaphor: event as 'process' [verb], e.g. *an electron moves in an orbit* is regrammaticized with event as 'entity' [noun], e.g. *the orbital motion of an electron.*

Implications for grammatics. In principle there is no unique grammatical representation for a piece of text. But the different representations are systemically related; e.g. (i) by ***agnation*** (systematic proportionality within the grammar; thus *I notice it* : *it strikes me* :: *I believe it* : *it convinces me*), (ii) by ***semantic junction*** ("re-entrant" analysis from the semantics, showing e.g. that *motion* is both process and entity).

VI.10(1995):222–4

Language and Education (Volume 9)

Writing does not simply duplicate the functions of speech. It did not originate, or develop, as a new way of doing old things. Writing has always been a way of using language to do something different from what is done by talking. This is what children expect, when they learn to read and write; as Hammond (1990) pointed out, in explaining why a class of children who had just been talking about a recent experience in very complex terms regressed to more or less infantile language when asked to write about it, it made no sense to them to go over the same task again in writing. They expect what we can call a "functional complementarity" between speech and writing.

Historically, as already implied, writing evolved with settlement; and if we think about it historically, we can construct the metaphor linking writing with its contexts in other social processes. Under certain conditions, people settle down: they take to producing their food, rather than gathering it wherever it grows or hunting it wherever it roams. Instead of moving continuously through space-time, these people locate themselves in a defined space, marked out into smaller spaces with boundaries in between. (We can notice how this unity of people and place becomes lexicalized, in terms such as *village, homestead, quarter.*)

These people create surplus value: they produce and exchange durable objects – goods and property. The language that accompanies these practices is similarly transformed: it becomes durable, spatially defined, and marked with boundaries – it settles down. This is writing. In the process it also becomes an object, capable of being owned and exchanged like other objects (written text and books).

The meanings construed by this language-as-object are themselves typically 'objects' (inventories, bills of lading, etc.) rather than processes. Meanings as things split off from meanings as events; the nominal group replaces the clause as the primary meaning-producing, or **semogenic**, agent in the grammar. This is written language. The nominal group then functions to construe other phenomena into objects (nominalization), thus 'objectifying' more complex forms of social organization (noun as institution) and their ideological formations (noun as abstraction).

Production processes are technologized; objects are created by transformation out of events (e.g., heating). The nominalizing power of the grammar transforms events into objects, and their participants into properties of those objects (grammatical metaphor). These transformed 'objects' become the technical concepts of mathematics and science.

All experience can now be objectified, as the written language construes the world synoptically – in its own image (writing is language synoptically construed). Writing is itself technologized (printing). The flux of the commonsense environment, reduced to order, is experimented with and theorized. Writing and speech are maximally differentiated; written knowledge is a form of commodity (education), spoken knowledge is denied even to exist.

What I am trying to show, in this highly idealized account (of processes that are in fact messy, sporadic and evolving, not tidy, continuous and designed), is that our material practices and our linguistic practices – not forgetting the material interfaces of the linguistic practices – collectively and interactively constitute the human condition. They therefore also change it. In our present era, when information is replacing goods and services as the primary form of productive activity, it seems certain that the split between speech and writing will become severely dysfunctional. But it is still with us, and throughout this long period of history writing has had contexts different from those of speech. In some ways these are complementary; in other ways they are contradictory and conflicting.

Malinowski gave us the concepts of 'context of situation' and 'context of culture'; we can interpret the context of situation as the environment of the text and the context of culture as the environment of the linguistic system. The various types of social process can be described in linguistic terms as contexts of language use. The principle of functional complementarity means that we can talk of the contexts of written discourse.

IX.6(1996):116–7

Additional readings

On Grammar (Volume 1) – 9(1981):229; Editor's Introduction:290; 12(1987): 328–32, 335, 341–3, 351; 14(1998):374, 382; 15(1996):400, 404, 410, 412

Linguistic Studies of Text and Discourse (Volume 2) – 2(1977):61; 5(1987):150, 164; 7(1992):204; 8(1994): 242, 244

On Language and Linguistics (Volume 3) – 5(1987):137; 6(1990):159; 12(1997): 260, 265; 18(1995):421–2, 427

The Language of Early Childhood (Volume 4) – 16(1999):369

The Language of Science (Volume 5) – 6(1989):168–9,172; 7(1997):195–6

Computational and Quantitative Studies (Volume 6) – 3(1991):43–4; 4(1991):66; 5(1992):78, 87; 9(1995):209; 10(1995):214

Studies in English Language (Volume 7) – 5(1970):174, 181; 12(1998):334

Language and Education (Volume 9) – 4(1979):73–4, 77; 6(1996):104, 109, 123, 125–6; 15(1994):310; 18(1990):363; 19(1994):377–9

Language and Society (Volume 10) – 3(1974):93–4, 113

Chapter Three

Context of Culture and of Situation

Summary

Context of culture, on the one hand, defines the potential, or range of possibilities available in language as a system. Context of situation, on the other hand, specified with respect to field, tenor and mode, plays a significant role in determining the actual choices among these possibilities.

The nature of the activity – *field* – is a determinant in the selection of options from experiential systems, including choices related to transitivity structure, or process, participant, circumstance. Role relationships – *tenor* – have a hand in determining the selection of interpersonal options, such as those from the systems of mood and modality. The symbolic organization of the text – *mode* – is involved in the selection of options in *textual* systems, which relate to the overall texture of the text, including choices involving cohesion, and thematic and information structures.

Selected readings

Linguistic Studies of Text and Discourse (Volume 2)

4 Text and situation

4.1 The situation as a determining environment
We have taken as our starting point the observation that meanings are created by the social system and are exchanged by the members in the form of text. The meanings so created are not, of course, isolates; they are integrated systems of meaning potential. It is in this sense that we can say that the meanings **are** the social system: the social system is itself interpretable as a semiotic system.

Persistence and change in the social system are both reflected in text and brought about by means of text. Text is the primary channel of the transmission of culture; and it is this aspect – text as the semantic process of social dynamics – that more than anything else has shaped the semantic system. Language has evolved as the primary mode of meaning in a social environment. It provides the means of acting on and reflecting on the environment, to be sure – but in a broader context, in which acting and reflecting on the environment are in turn the means of **creating** the environment and transmitting it from one generation to the next. That this is so is because the environment is a social construct. If things enter into it, they do so as bearers of social values.

Let us follow this line of reasoning through. The linguistic system has evolved in social contexts, as (one form of) the expression of the social semiotic. We see this clearly in the organization of the semantic system, where the ideational component has evolved as the mode of reflection on the environment and the interpersonal component as the mode of action on the environment. The system is a meaning potential, which is actualized in the form of text; a text is an instance of social meaning in a particular context of situation. We shall therefore expect to find the situation embodied or enshrined in the text not piecemeal, but in a way which reflects the systematic relation between the semantic structure and the social environment. In other words, the "situation" will appear, as envisaged by Hymes (1971), as constitutive of the text; provided, that is, we can characterize it so as to take cognizance of the ecological properties of language, the features which relate it to its environment in the social system.

A text is, as we have stressed, an indeterminate concept. It may be very long, or very short; and it may have no very clear boundaries. Many things about language can be learnt only from the study of very long texts. But there is much to be found out also from little texts; not only texts in the conventional forms of lyric poetry, proverbs and the like, but also brief transactions, casual encounters, and all kinds of verbal micro-operations. And among these there is a special value to the linguist in children's texts, since these tend to display their environmental links more directly and with less metaphorical mediation. (For a description of a short piece of child language, showing its relationship to the context of situation which engendered it, see Halliday (1975a)). We find all the time in the speech of young children examples of the way in which they themselves expect text to be related to its environment: their own step-by-step building up of layers of metaphorical meaning affords a clear and impressive illustration of this point.

The question to be resolved is, how do we get from the situation to the text? What features of the environment, in any specific instance, called for these particular options in the linguistic system? It may be objected that this is asking the old question, why did he say (or write) what he did; and that is something we can never know. Let us make it clear, therefore, that we are not asking any questions that require to be answered in terms of individual psychology. We are asking: what is the potential of the system that is likely to be at risk, the semantic configurations that are typically associated with a specific situation type? This can always be expressed in personal terms, if it seems preferable to do so; but in that case the question will be: what meanings will the hearer, or reader, expect to be offered in this particular class of social contexts? The meanings that constitute any given text do not present themselves to the hearer out of the blue; he has a very good idea of what is coming. The final topic that will be discussed here is that of text and situation. In what sense can the concept of "situation" be interpreted in a significant way as the environment of the text?

4.2 Semiotic structure of the situation: field, tenor and mode

It was suggested in the first section that the options that make up the semantic system are essentially of three or four kinds – four if we separate the experiential from the logical, as the grammar very clearly does.

We shall be able to show something of how the text is related to the situation if we can specify what aspects of the context of situation "rule" each of these kinds of semantic option. In other words, for each component of meaning, what are the situational factors by which it is activated?

The question then becomes one of characterizing the context of situation in appropriate terms, in terms which will reveal the systematic relationship between language and the environment. This involves some form of theoretical construction that relates the situation simultaneously to the text, to the linguistic system, and to the social system. For this purpose we interpret the situation as a semiotic structure; it is an instance, or instantiation, of the meanings that make up the social system.

Actually it is a class of instances, since what we characterize will be a situation **type** rather than a particular situation considered as unique.

The situation consists of:

(1) the social action: that which is "going on", and has recognizable meaning in the social system; typically a complex of acts in some ordered configuration, and in which the text is playing some part; and including "subject-matter" as one special aspect,

(2) the role structure: the cluster of socially meaningful participant relationships; both permanent attributes of the participants and role relationships that are specific to the situation; including the

speech roles, those that come into being through the exchange of verbal meanings,

(3) the symbolic organization: the particular status that is assigned to the text within the situation; its function in relation to the social action and the role structure; including the channel or medium, and the rhetorical mode.

We shall refer to these by the terms "field", "tenor" and "mode". The environment, or social context, of language is structured as a *field* of significant social action, a *tenor* of role relationships, and a *mode* of symbolic organization. Taken together these constitute the situation, or "context of situation", of a text.

We can then go on to establish a general principle governing the way in which these environmental features are projected on to the text.

Each of the components of the situation tends to determine the selection of options in a corresponding component of the semantics. In the typical instance, the field determines the selection of experiential meanings, the tenor determines the selection of interpersonal meanings, and the mode determines the selection of textual meanings.

Semiotic structure of situation	associated with	Functional component of semantics
field (type of social action)	" "	experiential
tenor (role relationships)	" "	interpersonal
mode (symbolic organization)	" "	textual

The selection of options in *experiential* systems – that is, in transitivity, in the classes of things (objects, persons, events, etc.), in quality, quantity, time, place and so on – tends to be determined by the nature of the activity: what socially recognized action the participants are engaged in, in which the exchange of verbal meanings has a part. This includes everything from, at one end, types of action defined without reference to language, in which language has an entirely subordinate role, various forms of collaborative work and play such as unskilled manipulation of objects or simple physical games; through intermediate types in which language has some necessary but still ancillary function, operations requiring some verbal instruction and report, games with components of scoring, bidding, planning, and the like; to types of interaction defined solely in linguistic terms, like gossip, seminars, religious discourse and most of what is recognized under the heading of literature. At the latter end of the continuum the concept of "subject-matter" intervenes; what we understand as subject-matter can be interpreted as one element in the structure of the "field" in those contexts where the social action is inherently of a symbolic, verbal nature. In a game of football, the social action is the game itself, and any instructions or other verbal interaction among the players are **part of** this social action. In a discussion about a game of football, the social action is the discussion, and the verbal interaction among the participants is **the whole of** this social action. Here the game constitutes a second order of "field", one that is brought into being by that of the first-order, the discussion, owing to its special nature as a type of social action that is itself defined by language. It is to this second-order field of discourse that we give the name of "subject-matter".

The selection of *interpersonal* options, those in the systems of mood, modality, person, key, intensity, evaluation and comment and the like, tends to be determined by the role relationships in the situation. Again there is a distinction to be drawn between a first and a second order of such role relationships. Social roles of the first order are defined without reference to language, though they may be (and typically are) realized through language as one form of role-projecting behaviour; all social roles in the usual sense of the term are of this order. Second-order social roles are those which are defined by the linguistic system: these are the roles that come into being only in and through language, the discourse roles of questioner, informer, responder, doubter, contradicter and the like. (Other types of symbolic action, warning, threatening, greeting and so on, which may be realized either verbally or nonverbally, or both, define roles which are some way intermediate between the two.) These discourse roles determine the selection of options in the mood system. There are systematic patterns of relationship between the first-order and the second-order roles. An interesting example of this emerged from recent studies of classroom discourse, which showed that in the teacher-pupil relationship the role of teacher is typically combined with that of questioner and the role of pupil with that of respondent, and not the other way round (cf. *Five to Nine* (1972), Sinclair et al. (1972)) – despite our concept of education, it is not the learner who asks the questions.

The selection of options in the *textual* systems, such as those of theme, information and voice, and also the selection of cohesive patterns, those of reference, substitution and ellipsis, and conjunction, tend to be determined by the symbolic forms taken by the interaction, in particular the place that is assigned to the text in the total situation. This includes the distinction of medium, written or spoken, and the complex subvarieties derived from these (written to be read aloud, and so on); we have already noted ways in which the organization of text-forming resources is dependent on the medium of the text. But it extends to much more than

59

this, to the particular semiotic function or range of functions that the text is serving in the environment in question. The rhetorical concepts of expository, didactic, persuasive, descriptive and the like are examples of such semiotic functions. All the categories under this third heading are second-order categories, in that they are defined by reference to language and depend for their existence on the prior phenomenon of text. It is in this sense that the textual component in the semantic system was said to have an "enabling" function *vis-à-vis* the other two: it is only through the encoding of semiotic interaction **as text** that the ideational and interpersonal components of meaning can become operational in an environment.

The concept of genre discussed in Section 3 (II.2(1977):44)) is an aspect of what we are calling the "mode". The various genres of discourse, including literary genres, are the specific semiotic functions of text that have social value in the culture. A genre may have implications for other components of meaning: there are often associations between a particular genre and particular semantic features of an ideational or interpersonal kind, for example between the genre of prayer and certain selections in the mood system. Hence labels for generic categories are often functionally complex: a concept such as "ballad" implies not only a certain text structure with typical patterns of cohesion but also a certain range of content expressed through highly favoured options in transitivity and other experiential systems – the types of process and classes of person and object that are expected to figure in association with the situational role of a ballad text. The "fable" is a category of a similar kind.

The patterns of determination that we find between the context of situation and the text are a general characteristic of the whole complex that is formed by a text and its environment. We shall not expect to be able to show that the options embodied in one or another particular sentence are determined by the field, tenor and mode of the situation. The principle is that each of these elements in the semiotic structure of the situation activates the corresponding component in the semantic system, creating in the process a semantic configuration, a grouping of favoured and foregrounded options from the total meaning potential, that is typically associated with the situation type in question. This semantic configuration is what we understand by the ***register***: it defines the variety ("diatypic variety" in the sense of Gregory (1967)) that the particular text is an instance of. The concept of "register" is the necessary mediating concept that enables us to establish the continuity between a text and its sociosemiotic environment.

II.2(1977):52–8

The Language of Early Childhood (Volume 4)

4 STRUCTURE OF THE SOCIAL CONTEXT

From a sociological point of view a text is meaningful not so much because we do not know what the speaker is going to say, as in a mathematical model of communication, as because we do know. Given certain facts, we can predict a good deal of what is coming with a significantly high probability of being right. This is not, of course, to deny the creative aspect of language and of text. The speaker can always prove us wrong; and in any case, his behaviour is nonetheless creative even if our predictions are fulfilled to the letter.

What are these 'certain facts'? They are the general properties of the situation, in the abstract sense in which the term is being used here. Essentially what we need to know is the semiotic structure of the situation.

A number of linguists, notably Firth, Pike and Hymes, have suggested interesting ways of characterizing the context of situation. Hymes' list of categories could be summarized as follows: form and content of the message, setting, participants, ends (intent and effect), key, medium, genre and interactional norms. The problem is, however, to know what kind of status and validity to accord to a conceptual framework such as this one. Are these to be thought of as descriptive categories providing a framework for the interpretation of text in particular situation instances, as conceived of by Malinowski? Or are they predictive concepts providing a means for the determination of text in generalized situation types?

Either of these would be of interest; but in the present context, in which we are trying to see how a child constructs the social system out of text instances, and are therefore concerned to relate text, situation and linguistic system, it is the second of these perspectives which we need to adopt. We are thinking not in terms of this or that situation but of a situation type, a generalized social context in which text is created; and of the situational factors not merely as descriptive but as constitutive of the text. The semiotic properties of the situation specify the register, the semantic configurations that characterize text associated with that type of situation – the meaning potential that the speaker will typically draw on.

So if we set up a conceptual framework for the representation of situation types, we do so in order that the categories we use will serve to predict features of the text. But this is not enough. Such categories are two-faced; they not only related "downwards" to the text but also "upwards" to some higher order of abstraction – in this case, two such higher orders, the social and the linguistic. In other words the concepts that we use in describing a situation type, or social context, whatever concepts they are, have to be interpretable both in terms of the culture and in terms of the linguistic system.

The second of these requirements is particularly strong, since it is not immediately obvious how situational factors like the setting, the statuses and roles of the participants, and the like, can relate to linguistic categories. But it is this requirement which may lead us to select one from among the number of existing and possible schemes; and we shall return to one proposed by Halliday, McIntosh and Strevens (1964), which was a three-fold analysis in terms of the concepts of *field, tenor* and **mode**. It was not entirely clear at the time why such a scheme should be preferred, except that intuitively it seemed simpler than most others. But it can now be seen to offer a means of making an essential link between the linguistic system and the text.

A framework of this general kind has been discussed subsequently by a number of writers on the subject; for example, Spencer and Gregory in *Linguistics and Style* (1964). Doughty, Pearce and Thornton in *Exploring Language* (1971), Halliday in *Language and Social Man*, and Ure and Ellis in 'Register in descriptive linguistics and descriptive sociology' (1972). We can relate the general concepts of field, tenor and mode to the categories set out by Hymes in 'Models of interaction of language and social setting' as these were summarized above. A situation type, or social context, as we understand it, is characterized by a particular semiotic structure, a complex of features which sets it apart from other situation types. This structure can then be interpreted on three dimensions: in terms of the ongoing activity (field), the role relationships involved (tenor), and the symbolic or rhetorical channel (mode). The first of these, the field, corresponds roughly to Hymes' "setting" and "ends"; it is the field of action, including symbolic action, in which the text has its meaning. It therefore includes what we usually call "subject-matter", which is not an independent feature but is a function of the type of activity. The second, the tenor, which corresponds in general terms to Hymes' "participants" and "key", refers to the role relationships that are embodied in the situation, which determine levels of formality and speech styles but also very much else besides. The third heading, that of mode, is roughly Hymes' "instrumentalities" and "genre"; this refers to the symbolic channel or wavelength selected, which is really the semiotic function or functions assigned to language in the situation. Hence this includes the distinction between speech and writing as a special case.

Field, tenor and mode are not kinds of language use; still less are they varieties of language. Nor are they, however, simply generalized components of the speech situation. They are, rather, the environmental determinants of text. Given an adequate specification of the situation in terms of field, tenor and mode, we ought to be able to make certain predictions about the linguistic properties of the text that is associated with it; that is, about the register, the configurations of semantic options that typically feature in this environment, and hence also about the grammar and vocabulary, which are the realizations of the semantic options. The participants in the situation themselves make just such predictions. It is one of the features of the social system, as a semiotic system, that the members can and do make significant predictions about the meanings that are being exchanged, predictions which depend on their interpretation of the semiotics of the situation type in which they find themselves. This is an important aspect of the potential of the system, and it is this that we are trying to characterize.

The possibility of making such predictions appears to arise because the categories of field, tenor and mode, which we are using to describe the semiotics of the situation, are in their turn associated in a systematic way with the functional components of the semantic system. This is not, of course, a coincidence. The semantic system evolved, we assume, operationally, as a form of symbolic interaction in social contexts; so there is every reason that it should reflect the structure of such contexts in its own internal organization.

We referred above to the tripartite functional composition of the adult semantic system, with its components of ideational, interpersonal and textual. It was mentioned that this scheme was not something that is arrived at from the outside; this organization is clearly present in the lexicogrammatical system – as seen, for example, in the threefold structuring of the clause in English in terms of transitivity (ideational), mood (interpersonal) and theme (textual). Now it appears that each of these different components of meaning is typically activated by a corresponding component in the semiotic structure of the situation. Thus, the *field* is associated with the **ideational** component, the **tenor** with the **interpersonal** component, and the **mode** with the **textual** component.

Let us see how this works, using another example from Nigel's interaction with his mother, this time at age 1;11.

Text – Nigel at age 1;11:
MOTHER [in bathroom, Nigel sitting on chair]: Now you wait there till I get your facecloth. Keep sitting there. [But Nigel is already standing up on the chair.]

NIGEL [in exact imitation of mother's intonation pattern, not in a
correcting intonation]: Keep standing thére. Put the mug
on the flóor.

MOTHER: Put the mug on the floor? What do you want?

NIGEL: Daddy tòothbrush.

MOTHER: Oh you want Daddy's toothbrush do you?

NIGEL: Yés . . . you (= 'I') want to put the fròg in the múg.

MOTHER: I think the frog is too big for the mug.

NIGEL: Yes you can put dùck in the múg . . . make búbble . . .
make búbble.

MOTHER: Tomorrow. Nearly all the water's run out.

NIGEL: You want Mummy red tóothbrush . . . yes you can have
Mummy old red tóothbrush.

Situational features:

Field: Personal toilet, assisted (mother washing child); concurrently
(child) exploring (i) container principle (that is, putting things
in things) and (ii) ownership and acquisition of property (that
is, getting things that belong to other people).

Tenor: Mother and small child interaction; mother determining
course of action; child pursuing own interests, seeking permission; mother granting permission and sharing child's interests,
but keeping her own course in view.

Mode: Spoken dialogue; pragmatic speech ('language-in-action') the
mother's guiding, the child's furthering (accompanying or
immediately preceding) the actions to which it is appropriate;
co-operative, without conflict of goals.

Determination of linguistic features by situational features:

- Field determines:
  - transitivity patterns – the types of process, for example, relational
    clauses, possessive (*get, have*) and circumstantial:locative (*put*);
  - material process clauses, spatial:posture (*sit, stand*);
  - the minor processes, for example, circumstantial:locative (*in*);
  - perhaps the tenses (simple present);
  - the content aspect of the vocabulary, for example, naming of
    objects.

All these belong to the ***ideational*** component of the semantic system.

- Tenor determines: patterns of mood, for example, [mother] imperative (*you wait, keep sitting*);
  - of modality, for example, [child] permission (*want to, can*);

- non-finite forms such as *make bubble* meaning 'I want to be allowed to . . .');
- of person, for example, [mother] "second person" (*you*), [child] "first person" (*you* = 'I'), and of key, represented by the system of intonation (pitch contour, for example, child's systematic opposition of rising tone, demanding a response, versus falling tone, not demanding a response).

All these belong to the ***interpersonal*** component of the semantic system.

- Mode determines: forms of cohesion, for example, question-and-answer with the associated type of ellipsis (*What do you want? – Daddy toothbrush*);
  - the patterns of voice and theme, for example, active voice with child as subject/theme;
  - the forms of deixis, for example, exophoric (situation-referring) *the* (*the mug*, etc.);
  - the lexical continuity, for example, repetition of mug, toothbrush, put in.

All these belong to the ***textual*** component of the semantic system.

IV.13(1975):290–4

Language and Education (Volume 9)

1.1 CONTEXT OF SITUATION

Originally, the context meant the accompanying text, the wording that came before and after whatever was under attention. In the nineteenth century it was extended to things other than language, both concrete and abstract: *the context of the building, the moral context of the day*; but if you were talking about language, then it still referred to the surrounding words, and it was only in modern linguistics that it came to refer to the non-verbal environment in which language was used. When that had happened, it was Catford, I think, who suggested that we now needed another term to refer explicitly to the verbal environment; and he proposed the term "co-text". But how did *context* come to be extended in this way?

Here is Malinowski writing in 1923, about what at that time was referred to as a "primitive" (that is, unwritten) language. He writes "In a primitive language the meaning of any single word is to a very high degree dependent on its context. . . . [An expression such as] *we paddle in place* demands the context of the whole utterance, . . . [and] this latter again, becomes only intelligible when it is placed within its *context of situation*, if I may be allowed to coin an expression which indicates on the one hand that the conception of context has to be broadened and on the other hand that the situation in which words are uttered can never be passed over as irrelevant to the linguistic expression" (Malinowski 1923: 306). (In passing, we might note that on the very next page he also wrote "The conception of meaning as *contained* in an utterance is false and futile".) Ten years or so later, Malinowski had changed his view that this was a special feature of "primitive" languages; writing in 1935 he said all languages were alike in that "the real understanding of words is always ultimately derived from active experience of those aspects of reality to which the words belong" (Malinowski 1935:58; cf. Hasan 1985c). By this time Malinowski is extending the notion of context still further: over and beyond the context of situation lies "what we might call [the] context of culture", so that "the definition of a word consists partly of placing it within its cultural context" (ibid.: 18). What this means is that language considered as a **system** – its lexical items and grammatical categories – is to be related to its context of **culture**; while **instances** of language in use – specific texts and their component parts – are to be related to their context of **situation**. Both these contexts are of course outside of language itself.

Although Malinowski was the first to use the expression **context of situation**, the concept of 'situation', in the sense of the events and actions that are going on around when people speak, had been invoked before in linguistics, in a very different domain of inquiry, namely dialectology. Linguistic field studies were not only of culturally exotic, unwritten languages such as those studied by anthropologists; they were also carried out with rural dialects, and the Swiss dialectologist Wegener had developed a "situation theory" to account for the "special" features of informal, spoken language – that is, features that **appeared** special at a time when the only form of text that was recognized in linguistics was a written text, preferably written in a language long since dead (i.e., no longer spoken at all) (Firth 1957b). What led linguists to take account of the situation was when they turned their attention to speech. Here, they had to recognize factors like reference to persons, objects and events within the speaker's attention (technically, **exophoric deixis**), as well as other, more oblique forms of dependence on and interaction with environment. What Malinowski was saying was that because of these things, in spoken language the "situation" functioned by analogy as a kind of context. The situation was like the text by which a piece of spoken discourse was surrounded.

Malinowski was an anthropologist, who became a linguist in the service of his ethnographic pursuits. His younger colleague J.R. Firth, who was a linguist, saw the possibility of integrating this notion, of the "situation" as a kind of context, into a general theory of language. Firth was also interested in spoken language; but not as something quaint or exotic like rural dialects and aboriginal languages. On the contrary, Firth was concerned with the **typical** – what he referred to as "typical texts in their contexts of situation" (Firth 1957a: 224), by which people enacted their day-to-day interpersonal relationships and constructed a social identity for themselves and the people around them. A text was an object of theoretical study in its own right; and what Firth did was to map the notion of "context of situation" into a general theory of levels of language. All linguistic analysis, Firth said, was a study of meaning, and meaning could be defined operationally as "function in context"; so to study meaning you took each of the traditional divisions of linguistic theory – phonetic, phonological, lexical, morphological, syntactic – and treated it as a kind of context. You could then include the *situation* as just another linguistic level. But the context of situation did have a special place in the overall framework, since it was here that the text as a **whole** could be "contextualized". (And if it was a written text it could be tracked through time, as it came to be "recontextualized" with changes in the contexts in which it was read and the cultural background and assumptions of those who read it.)

1.2 CONTEXT OF CULTURE

What about the "context of culture"? Firth made very little use of this idea. Although, to use Robins' words (Robins 1963:17), Firth considered that a language was "embedded in the life and culture of its speakers", he was actually very skeptical about general notions such as 'the language' and 'the culture', because he didn't see either a language or a culture as any kind of homogeneous and harmonious whole. The notion of culture as a context for a language – for language considered as a system – was more fully articulated in the work of their contemporaries Sapir and Whorf. Sapir did not use the **expression** *context of culture*; but he did interpret a language as expressing the mental life of its speakers, and from this starting point he and Whorf developed their powerful view of the interplay between language and culture, the so-called "Sapir–Whorf hypothesis". In this view, since language evolved as part – moreover the most unconscious part – of every human culture, it functioned as the primary means whereby the deepest perception of the members, their joint construction of shared experience into social reality, were constantly reaffirmed and transmitted. Thus in this sense the culture provided the context within which words and, more generally, grammatical systems were interpreted. (Many of Whorf's example involved what he called "cryptotypes": systems of meaning that were hidden rather deep beneath the surface construction of the grammar and could only be revealed by a penetrating and thorough grammatical analysis) (Whorf 1956b).

These two founding traditions of the study of language in context, the British, with Malinowski and Firth, on the one hand, and the American, with Sapir and Whorf, on the other, are in an important way complementary to each other. The former stress the *situation* as the context for language as *text*; and they see language as a form of action, as the enactment of social relationships and social processes. The latter stress the *culture* as the context for language as *system*; and they see language as a form of reflection, as the construal of experience into a theory or model of reality. From these two sources, taken together, we have been able to derive the foundations of a functional semantics: a theory of meaning that is relevant to applied linguistic concerns.

IX.13(1991):271–3

Language and Society (Volume 10)

While we still lack a detailed description of the registers of a language on the basis of their formal properties, it is nevertheless useful to refer to this type of language variety from the point of view of institutional linguistics. There is enough evidence for us to be able to recognize the major situation types to which formally distinct registers correspond; others can be predicted and defined from outside language. A number of different lines of demarcation have been suggested for this purpose. It seems most useful to introduce a classification along three dimensions, each representing an aspect of the situation in which language operates and the part played by language in them. Registers, in this view, may be distinguished according to *field of discourse, mode of discourse* and *style of discourse*.

"Field of discourse" refers to what is going on: to the area of operation of the language activity. Under this heading, registers are classified according to the nature of the whole event of which the language activity forms a part. In the type of situation in which the language activity accounts for practically the whole of the relevant activity, such as an essay, a discussion or an academic seminar, the field of discourse is the subject-matter. On this dimension of classification, we can recognize registers such as politics and personal relations, and technical registers like biology and mathematics.

There are on the other hand situations in which the language activity rarely plays more than a minor part: here the field of discourse refers to the whole event. In this sense there is, for example, a register of domestic chores: 'hoovering the carpets' may involve language activity which, though marginal, is contributory to the total event. At the same time the language activity in a situation may be unrelated to the other activities. It may even delay rather than advance them, if two people discuss politics while doing the washing up. Here the language activity does not form part of the washing up event, and the field of discourse is that of politics.

Registers classified according to field of discourse thus include both the technical and the non-technical: shopping and games-playing as well as medicine and linguistics. Neither is confined to one type of situation. It may be that the more technical registers lend themselves especially to language activity of the discussion type, where there are few, if any, related non-language events; and the non-technical registers to functional or operational language activity, in which we can observe language in use as a means of achievement. But in the last resort there is no field of activity which cannot be discussed; and equally there is none in which language cannot play some part in getting things done. Perhaps our most purely operational language activity is "phatic communion", the language of the establishment and maintenance of social relations. This includes utterances like **how do you do!** and **see you!**, and is certainly non-technical, except perhaps in British English where it overlaps with the register of meteorology. But the language activity of the patient consulting the doctor in the surgery, or of research scientists in the performance of a laboratory experiment, however technical it may be, is very clearly functioning as a means of operation and control.

This leads to "mode of discourse", since this refers to the medium or mode of the language activity, and it is this that determines, or rather correlates with, the role played by the language activity in the situation. The primary distinction on this dimension is that into spoken and written language, the two having, by and large, different situational roles. In this connection, reading aloud is a special case of written rather than of spoken language.

The extent of formal differentiation between spoken and written language has varied very greatly among different language communities and at different periods. It reached its widest when, as in medieval Europe, the normal written medium of a community was a classical language which was unintelligible unless learnt by instruction. Latin, Classical Arabic, Sanskrit and Classical Chinese have all been used in this way. By comparison, spoken and written varieties of most modern languages are extremely close. The two varieties of French probably differ more than those of English; even popular fiction in French uses the simple past (preterite) tense in narrative. But spoken and written English are by no means formally identical. They differ both in grammar and in lexis, as anyone by recording and transcribing conversation can find out.

Within these primary modes, and cutting across them to a certain extent, we can recognize further registers such as the language of newspapers, of advertising, of conversation and of sports commentary. Like other dimensions of classification in linguistics, both descriptive and institutional, the classification of modes of discourse is variable in delicacy. We may first identify 'the language of literature' as a single register; but at the next step we would separate the various genres, such as prose fiction and light verse, as distinct registers within it. What is first recognized as the register of journalism is then subclassified into reportage, editorial comment, feature writing and so on.

Some modes of discourse are such that the language activity tends to be self-sufficient, in the sense that it accounts for most or all of the activity relevant to the situation. This is particularly true of the various forms of the written mode, but applies also to radio talks, academic discussions and sermons. In literature particularly the language activity is as it were self-sufficient. On the other hand, in the various spoken modes, and in some of the written, the utterances often integrate with other non-language activity into a single event. Clear instances of this are instructions and sets of commands. The grammatical and lexical distinction between the various modes of discourse can often be related to the variable situational role assigned to language by the medium.

Third and last of the dimensions of register classification is "style of discourse", which refers to the relations among the participants. To the extent that these affect and determine features of the language, they suggest a primary distinction into colloquial and polite ("formal", which is sometimes used for the latter, is here avoided because of its technical sense in description). This dimension is unlikely ever to yield clearly defined, discrete registers. It is best treated as a cline, and various more delicate cuts have been suggested, with categories such as 'casual', 'intimate' and 'deferential'. But until we know more about how the formal properties of language vary with style, such categories are arbitrary and provisional.

The participant relations that determine the style of discourse range through varying degrees of permanence. Most temporary are those which are a feature of the immediate situation, as when the participants are at a party or have met on the train. At the opposite extreme are relations such as that between parents and children. Various socially defined relations, as between teacher and pupil or labour and management, lie somewhere intermediately. Some such registers may show more specific formal properties than others: it is probably easier to identify on linguistic evidence a situation in which one participant is serving the others in a shop than one involving lecturer and students in a university classroom.

Which participant relations are linguistically relevant, and how far these are distinctively reflected in the grammar and lexis, depends on the language concerned. Japanese, for example, tends to vary along this dimension very much more than English or Chinese. There is even some formal difference in Japanese between the speech of men and the speech of women, nor is this merely a difference in the probabilities of occurrence. In most languages, some lexical items tend to be used more by one sex than the other; but in Japanese there are grammatical features which are restricted to the speech of one sex only.

It is as the product of these three dimensions of classification that we can best define and identify register. The criteria are not absolute or independent; they are all variable in delicacy, and the more delicate the classification the more the three overlap. The formal properties of any given language event will be those associated with the intersection of the appropriate field, mode and style. A lecture on biology in a technical college, for example, will be in the scientific field, lecturing mode and polite style; more delicately, in the biological field, academic lecturing mode and teacher to student style.

The same lecturer, five minutes later in the staff common room, may switch to the field of cinema, conversational mode, in the style of a man among colleagues. As each situation is replaced by another, so the speaker readily shifts from one register to the next. The linguistic differences may be slight; but they may be considerable, if the **use** of language in the new situation differs sharply from that in the old. We cannot list the total range of uses. Institutional categories, unlike descriptive ones, do not resolve into closed systems of discrete terms. Every speaker has at his disposal a continuous scale of patterns and items, from which he selects for each situation type the appropriate stock of available harmonies in the appropriate key. He speaks, in other words, in many registers.

X.1(1964):19–22

* * *

It was Malinowski from whom Firth derived his notions of 'context of culture' and 'context of situation' (Malinowski 1923); and Malinowski's ideas about what we might call cultural and situational semantics provide an interesting starting point for the study of language and social man, since they encourage us to look at language as a form of behaviour potential. In this definition, both the 'behaviour' and the 'potential' need to be emphasized. Language, from this point of view, is a range of possibilities, an open-ended set of options in behaviour that are available to the individual in his existence as social man. The context of culture is the environment for the total set of these options, while the context of situation is the environment of any particular selection that is made from within them.

Malinowski's two types of context thus embody the distinction between the potential and the actual. The context of culture defines the potential, the range of possibilities that are open. The actual choice among these possibilities takes place within a given context of situation.

Firth, with his interest in the actual, in the text and its relation to its surroundings, developed the notion of 'context of situation' into a valuable tool for linguistic enquiry. Firth's interest, however, was not in the accidental but in the typical: not in this or that piece of discourse that happened to get recorded in the fieldworker's notebook but in repetitive patterns which could be interpreted as significant and systematizable patterns of social behaviour. Thus, what is actual is not synonymous with what is unique, or the chance product of random observations. But the significance of what is typical – in fact, the concept 'typical' itself – depends on factors which lie outside language, in the social structure. It is not the typicalness of the words and structures which concerns us, but the typicalness of the context of situation, and of the function of the words and structures within it.

Malinowski (1935) tells an interesting story of an occasion when he asked his Trobriand Island informant some questions about the Trobrianders' gardening practices. He noted down the answers, and was surprised a few days later to hear the same informant repeating what he had said word for word in conversation with his young daughter. In talking to Malinowski, the informant has as it were borrowed the text from a typical context of situation. The second occasion, the discussion with the little girl, was then an instance of this context of situation, in which the socialization of the child into the most significant aspect of the material culture – the gardening practices – was a familiar process, with familiar patterns of language behaviour associated with it.

There is not, of course, any conflict between an emphasis on the repetitive character of language behaviour and an insistence on the creativity of the language system. Considered as behaviour potential, the language system itself is open-ended, since the question whether two instances are the same or not is not determined by the system; it is determined by the underlying social theory. But in any case, as Ruqaiya Hasan (1971) has pointed out, creativeness does not consist in producing new sentences. The newness of a sentence is a quite unimportant – and unascertainable – property, and 'creativity' in language lies in the speaker's ability to create new meanings: to realize the potentiality of language for the indefinite extension of its resources to new contexts of situation. It is only in this light that we can understand the otherwise unintelligible observation made by Katz and Fodor (1963), that "almost every sentence uttered is uttered for the first time" (p. 171). Our most 'creative' acts may be precisely among those that are realized through highly repetitive forms of behaviour.

Firth did not concern himself with Malinowski's 'context of culture', since he preferred to study generalized patterns of actual behaviour, rather than attempting to characterize the potential as such. This was simply the result of his insistence on the need for accurate observations – a much-needed emphasis in the context of earlier linguistic studies – and in no way implied that the study of language could be reduced to the study of instances, which in fact he explicitly denied (1968). More to the point, Firth built his linguistic theory around the original and fundamental concept of the 'system', as used by him in a technical sense; and this is precisely a means of describing the potential, and of relating the actual to it.

A 'system', as the concept was developed by Firth, can be interpreted as the set of options that is specified for a given environment. The meaning of it is 'under the conditions stated, there are the following possibilities'. By making use of this notion, we can describe language in the form of a behaviour potential. In this way the analysis of language comes within the range of a social theory, provided the underlying concepts of such a theory are such that they can be shown to be realized in social context and patterns of behaviour.

X.2(1971):44–6

* * *

(a) **Field**. The kind of language we use varies, as we should expect, according to what we are doing. In different contexts, we tend to select different words and different grammatical patterns – simply because we are expressing different kinds of meaning. All we need add to this, in order to clarify the notion of register, is that the 'meanings' that are involved are a part of what we are doing; or rather, they are part of the expression of what we are doing. In other words, one aspect of the field of discourse is simply the subject matter; we talk **about** different things, and therefore use different words for doing so. If this was all there was to it, and the field of discourse was **only** a question of subject matter, it would hardly need saying; but, in fact, 'what we are talking about' has to be seen as a special case of a more general concept, that of 'what we are doing', or 'what is going on, within which the language is playing a part.' It is this broader concept that is referred to as the "field of discourse". If, for example, the field of discourse is football, then no matter whether we are playing it or discussing it around a table we are likely to use certain linguistic forms which reflect the football context. But the two are essentially different kinds of activity and this is also reflected in the language. This difference, between the language of playing football and the language of discussing football, is also a reflection of the "mode of discourse"; see below.

The "field", therefore, refers to what the participants in the context of situation are actually engaged in doing, like 'buying-selling a newspaper' in our example above. This is a more general concept than that of subject matter, and a more useful one in the present context since we may not actually be **talking about** either buying and selling or newspapers. We may be talking about the weather; but that does not mean that the field of discourse is meteorology – talking about the weather is part of the strategy of buying and selling.

(b) *Mode*. Secondly, the language we use differs according to the channel or wavelength we have selected. Sometimes we find ourselves, especially those of us who teach, in a didactic mode, at other times the mode may be fanciful, or commercial, or imperative: we may choose to behave as teacher, or poet, or advertiser, or commanding officer. Essentially, this is a question of what function language is being made to serve in the context of situation; this is what underlies the selection of the particular rhetorical channel.

This is what we call the "mode of discourse"; and fundamental to it is the distinction between speaking and writing. This distinction partly cuts across the rhetorical modes, but it also significantly determines them: although certain modes can be realized through either medium, they tend to take quite different forms according to whether spoken or written – written advertising, for example, does not say the same things as sales talk. This is because the two media represent, essentially, different **functions** of language, and therefore embody selections of different kinds. The question underlying the concept of the mode of discourse is, what function is language being used for, what is its specific role in the goings-on to which it is contributing? To persuade? To soothe? to sell? to control? to explain? or just to oil the works, as in what Malinowski called "phatic communion", exemplified above by the talk about the weather, which merely helps the situation along? Here the distinction between the language of **playing** a game, such as bridge or football, and the language of **discussing** a game becomes clear. In the former situation, the language is functioning as a part of the game, as a pragmatic expression of play behaviour; whereas in the latter, it is part of a very different kind of activity, and may be informative, didactic, argumentative, or any one of a number of rhetorical modes of discourse.

(c) *Tenor.* Thirdly, the language we use varies according to the level of formality, of technicality, and so on. What is the variable underlying this type of distinction? Essentially, it is role relationships in the situation in question: who the participants in the communication group are, and in what relationship they stand to each other.

This is what, following Spencer and Gregory, we called the "tenor of discourse". Examples of role relationships, that would be reflected in the language used, are teacher/pupil, parent/child, child/child in peer group, doctor/patient, customer/salesman, casual acquaintances on a train, and so on. It is the role relationships, including the indirect relationship between a writer and his audience, that determine such things as the level of technicality and degree of formality. Contexts of situation, or settings, such as public lecture, playground at playtime, church service, cocktail party, and so on can be regarded as institutionalized role relationships and hence as stabilized patterns of "tenor of discourse".

It will be seen from the foregoing that the categories of *field of discourse, mode of discourse* and *tenor of discourse* are not themselves kinds or varieties of language. They are the backdrop, the features of the context of situation which determine the kind of language used. In other words, they determine what is often referred to as the register: that is, the types of meaning that are selected, and their expression in grammar and vocabulary. And they determine the register collectively, not piecemeal. There is not a great deal that one can predict about the language that will be used if one knows **only** the field of discourse or **only** the mode or the tenor. But if we know all three, we can predict quite a lot; and, of course, the more detailed the information we have, the more linguistic features of the text we shall be able to predict.

It is possible, nevertheless, to make some broad generalization about each of these three variables separately, in terms of its probable linguistic consequences.

The field of discourse, since it largely determines the "content" of what is being said, is likely to have the major influence on the selection of vocabulary, and also on the selection of those grammatical patterns which express our experience of the world that is around us and inside us: the types of process, the classes of object, qualities and quantities, abstract relations, and so on.

The mode of discourse, since it specifies the "channel" of communication, influences the speaker's selection of mood (what kind of statements he makes, such as forceful, hesitant, gnomic, qualified or reassertive; whether he asks questions and so on) and of modality (the judgement of probabilities); and also, in the distinction between speech and writing, it affects the whole pattern of grammatical and lexical organization, the **density** of the lexical content.

In general, written language is more highly 'lexicalized' than spoken language; it has a more complex vocabulary. This does not necessarily mean that written language uses words that are more unusual, though this may be true too; but it means that it has a greater lexical **density**, packing more content words into each phrase or clause or sentence. To express this in another way, written language contains more lexical information per unit of grammar. By the same token, written language also tends to be simpler than spoken language in its grammatical organization; speech, especially informal speech such as casual conservation, displays complexities of sentence structure that would be intolerable (because they would be unintelligible) in writing. Naturally, there is considerable variety within both the written and the spoken modes: there are forms of writing that are more like speech, and forms of spoken language that are very close to the written ('he talks like a book'). But this kind of variation also largely depends on the rhetorical channel or genre, as it is still a function of the mode of discourse. Jean Ure remarks, for example, that the lexical density is determined by the extent to which the language is what she calls "language-in-action".

Both the choice of vocabulary, which is largely a matter of the field of discourse, and its distribution in grammatical structures, which is mainly dependent on the mode, are also affected by factors of the third type, the tenor of the discourse: the types of social relationship, both temporary and permanent, that obtain between a speaker and his hearers, or between a writer and his readers (and such a relationship is presumed to exist even if a writer is writing for an unknown public – this is often a big factor in his success), tend to influence the level of formality and technicality at which the speaker or writer is operating, and hence lead him to prefer certain words over others and to pitch his discourse at a certain point on the Joosian style scale[7]. Equally, however, it is the tenor of discourse that primarily determines which dialectal or other speech variant the speaker is going to select for the occasion: whether he is going to put on his verbal Sunday best and talk proper, or wear the linguistic garb that is suited to the works, the family or the club.

So there is some tendency for the field of discourse to determine the content of what is said, and for the mode and tenor to determine the manner or style of it, with the mode selecting the particular genre to be used and the tenor determining the social dialect. But this is, at best, only a crude approximation. In the first place the distinction between style (or "form", or "manner") and content is largely illusory; we cannot really separate what is said from how it is said, and this is just as true of everyday language as it is of myth and poetry. In the second place, the factors of field, mode and tenor operate as a whole, not in isolation from each other; the linguistic reflection of any one of them depends on its combination with the other two. There is not a great deal that one can say about the language of football, taken as a rubric just by itself (field of discourse), or the language of public lectures (mode), or the language of teacher and pupil (tenor), although these are certainly meaningful concepts, as is proved by the fact that if we hear a recording or read a passage out of context we can usually identify it in precisely such terms as these. But such identification is often made by means of linguistic clues which are themselves rather trivial, like the lecturer's voice quality or the urgent 'sir!' of the schoolboy; whereas in order to predict the interesting and important features of the language that is used we need to characterize the situation in terms of all three variables in interaction with each other. Suppose, on the other hand, that the setting is described in some such terms as these:

Field: Instruction: the instruction of a novice
       – in a board game [e.g. Monopoly] with equipment present
       – for the purpose of enabling him to participate
Mode: Spoken: unrehearsed
       Didactic and explanatory, with undertone of non-seriousness
       – with feedback: question–and–answer, correction of error
Tenor: Equal and intimate: three young adult males, acquainted
       – but with hierarchy in the situation [two experts, one novice]
       – leading to superior-inferior role relationship

Here we can predict quite a lot about the language that will be used, in respect of the meanings and the significant grammatical and lexical features through which they are expressed. If the entries under field, mode and tenor are filled out carefully and thoughtfully, it is surprising how many features of the language turn out to be relatable to the context of the situation. This is not to claim that we know what the participants are going to say; it merely shows that we can make sensible and informed guesses about certain aspects of what they might say, with a reasonable probability of being right. There is always, in language, the freedom to act untypically; but that in itself confirms rather than denies the reality of the concept of what is typical.

There is an experiment well known to students of linguistics in which the subject listens to a recording that is 'noisy' in the technical sense (badly distorted or jammed), so much so that he cannot understand anything of what is being said. He is then given a simple clue as to the register; and next time he listens he understands practically the whole text. We always listen and read with expectations, and the notion of register is really a theory about these expectations, providing a way of making them explicit.

To gain some impression of 'language in the life of the individual', it is hardly necessary, or possible, to keep detailed records of who says what, who to, when and why. But it is not too difficult to take note of information about register, with entries for field, mode and tenor in the language diary. This can give valuable insights into what language means to the individual. It will also effectively demolish any suspicion that there are individuals whose language is impoverished or deficient, since it goes straight to language as behaviour potential, to the semantic system that lies behind the wordings and the 'soundings' which are so often ridiculed or dismissed from serious attention.

Points to look for:

(a) What does the language profile of an individual's daily life look like? What roles has he adopted, that have been expressed through language?
    What forms of interaction have these involved (e.g. the role of 'eldest daughter' implies interaction with parent(s) on the one hand and with younger brother(s) or sister(s) on the other; that of 'teacher' suggests interaction with pupils and also, perhaps, with headmaster)?
In what language events (types of linguistic situation) has he participated?
Has he made use of different variants (dialect switching), and if so, with what kind of linguistic variation and under what circumstances?

(b) What is the pattern of register variation?
Can we specify the relevant background features for particular instances
    of language use?
    field of discourse: the nature of the activity, and subject matter
    mode of discourse: the channel, and the part played by language in the
    total event
    tenor of discourse: the role relationships among the participants
Where are the properties of the field, mode and tenor revealed in the
    language spoken or written? How far could the eavesdropper fill in
    the situational background; and conversely, what features of the lan-
    guage could have been predicted from the structural information?
(c) How much more difficult would it have been for the individual to
    survive **without** language?

5 LANGUAGE AND THE CONTEXT OF SITUATION

Like all the headings in our list, this is closely related to the others; in
particular, it overlaps with the previous one, that of language in the life
of the individual. But there is a difference of perspective: here we are
focusing attention on the generalized contexts of language use and the
function of language within these contexts, rather than on the linguistic
profile of an individual speaker. The question that is raised is not so much
what language means to an individual in his daily life as what the typical
social contexts are in which he participates as an articulate being.

As in the last section, there is no difficulty in understanding the
general principle: it is obvious that we use language in contexts of
situation, and that these can be described in various ways. The problem
here has always been how best to describe the various kinds of setting,
and especially how to bring out what is significant and distinguish it
from all the irrelevant particularities that are associated with specific
instances.

This already arises in the treatment of register, as a problem of what
Ellis calls "delicacy of focus". Suppose, to take a trivial example, that the
field of discourse is shopping: do we characterize this as simply 'transaction', or as 'buying' (as distinct from, say, borrowing), or as 'buying in
a shop' (as distinct from in the market), or as 'buying in a chemist's shop'
(as distinct from a grocer's), or as 'buying a toothbrush' (as distinct from
a cake of soap)? And since the criterion is bound to be our assessment,
in some form or other, of whether it matters or not, we may as well ask
whether we are likely to take any interest in a situation of this kind in
the first place.

One way of deciding whether a particular type of situation is of interest or not is to consider, in terms of the second of the headings above, whether it is of any significance for the socialization of a child. For example, it is a good working hypothesis to assume that any type of situation in which a parent is controlling the child's behaviour is potentially important for linguistic and social development; and this suggests not only that these situations are of interest to us but also that a certain amount of information needs to be given about them, specifically information about what aspect of the child's behaviour it is that is being regulated: whether, for example, attention is being focused on his personal relationships ('don't talk to Granny like that!') or on his behaviour towards objects ('don't tear it').

Generally speaking the concept of social man provides the grounds for assessing the importance of a given class of context. The fact that a particular type of language use is relevant to the socialization of the child is one guarantee of significance; but it is not the only one – there are other ways in which it may be of importance in the culture. We might for example think of a linguistic setting such as 'teacher-parent consultation', subdivided into individual contact, parents' association meeting, exchange of letters, and so on; this may be assumed to be of some significance in an educational context, and therefore the forms of linguistic interaction between teacher and parent might well be worth looking into. Even more interesting are the forms of linguistic interaction between teacher and pupil in the classroom, and in other school settings. There have now been a number of useful studies of classroom language, and these all depend on some notion of the relevant contexts of situation.

Another quite different reason for thinking about 'language and situation' is the fact that the pupil, in the course of his education, is expected to become sensitive to the use of language in different situation types, and to be able to vary his own linguistic behaviour in response to them. The move, in schools, away from a total preoccupation with formal composition towards an awareness of the many different types of language use involved a fairly drastic redefinition of the educationally relevant contexts of situation – a redefinition which was not without its dangers and difficulties, as subsequent debate revealed, but which was very necessary nevertheless. Both *Breakthrough to Literacy and Language in Use* demand an enlightened and imaginative view of language and situation; because of this, they are an excellent source of insight into questions of relevance. As we have stressed all along, there is no difference between knowing language and knowing how to use it; success in the mother tongue is success in developing a linguistic potential for all the types of context that are engendered by the culture. From this point of view, if we think that a pupil when he leaves school should be able to use language adequately in this or that particular range of contexts, then those contexts are important even if they do not seem to provide any great scope for linguistic virtuosity or the exercise of the creative imagination. And there is some value to be gained from an occasional glance at those types of language use which are not normally regarded as the responsibility of the school. An example is the language of technical instructions: if one looks carefully (and sympathetically) at the leaflets issued by the manufacturers of appliances, not to the general public but to those responsible for the installation and maintenance of these appliances, one can get a very clear picture of how language is related to the context of situation in which it is functioning – or rather that in which it is **intended** to function: one should always remember that a leaflet of this kind is as out of context in the classroom as would be the gas boiler itself, or whatever other object it is designed to accompany.

These are very clearly questions of register, and we almost inevitably use concepts relating to field, mode or tenor of discourse when we talk about language in relation to the situation. Formulations like "the language of the classroom"', "the language of technical instructions", are all characterizations of this kind, sometimes relating to just one of the three dimensions, often combining features of more than one. It is, in fact, very revealing to analyse some of the formulations that are commonly used, and taken for granted as meaningful descriptions of types of language use, in order to see what information they provide which might enable us to make predictions about the text; and we can do this by relating them to field, mode and tenor. Anthropologists often use terms like "pragmatic speech", "ritual language" or Malinowski's "phatic communion"; the question is what we can gather from these about the field of activity, the part played by language within it, and the participant roles and role relationships involved.

Some of the terms that typically figure in discussions of language in the context of English teaching are worth considering from this point of view, terms such as "creative writing", "imaginative language", "jargon", "ordinary language". These are rarely as objective and precise as they are made to seem. Jargon, for instance, often means no more than technical terms which the speaker personally dislikes, perhaps because he is not sure how to use them. If we try to interpret these labels in terms of field, mode and tenor, we find that it is not easy to see what they really imply about the kind of language used. It is not that they are not meaningful; but there is no consensus as to **what** they mean, so we have very little clue as to what would be generally regarded as a specimen of such language. What is creative in one type of situation (or in one person's opinion) would not be so in another.

The term "situation" is sometimes misleading, since it conjures up the idea of 'props', the specific concrete surroundings of a particular speech event such as might appear in a photograph of the scene. But this image is much too particular; what is significant is the situation **type**, the configuration of environmental factors that typically fashions our ways of speaking and writing.

Points to look for:

(a) What are examples of socially significant situation types, considered from an educational point of view?

How accurately and specifically do we define them? What is the 'delicacy of focus', e.g. school – classroom – English class – "creative writing" session?

In what ways are such situation types significant for the pupils' success in school (as distinct from those that are critical for the child's 'socialization' in general, as in 2 above)? What do we expect to learn from an imaginative enquiry into the use of language in these contexts?

(b) What are the generalized functions of language within these situation types?

What do we mean when we talk of "creative", "transactional", "practical", "expressive" (etc.) language? How far is an interpretation of language in these terms dependent on our awareness of the situation?

Can we relate the use of language to the interaction of social roles within these situation types? (The notion that the type of language used – expressive, creative, etc. – is solely governed by the free choice or whim of the individual is very much oversimplified, and leads to some highly artificial and unrealistic classroom exercises.)

Are there 'pure' types of language use, or do real situations always generate some kind of mixed type? (This is a vast topic in its own right. Probably most use of language is neither rigidly pure nor hopelessly mixed, but involves a dominant register and one or two subsidiary motives. *Language in Use* provides opportunities for exploring this notion further.)

Note

7. Martin Joos recognizes five points: intimate, casual, consultative, formal and fro-
zen; see his book *The Five Clocks*, and also the discussion in Chapters 10 and 11
of *Exploring Language* ('Accent and dialect' and 'Diversity in written English', by
John Pearce). It is worth remarking, perhaps, that the term "formality" (or "level
of formality") is the source of some confusion in discussions of language, because
it is used in two difference senses. On the one hand it refers to the use of forms
of the language – words, or grammatical structures – that are conventionally
associated with certain modes: with impersonal letters or memoranda, various
types of interview and the like. On the other hand it is used to refer to the
degree of respect that is shown linguistically to the person who is being addressed:
languages differ rather widely as regards how (and also as regards how much)
they incorporate the expression of respect, but there are ways of addressing parents and elders, social and occupational superiors, and so on, that are recognized
as the marks of the social relationship involved. Although there is some overlap
between these two senses of 'formality', they are in principle rather distinct and
have very different manifestations in language.

X.3(1974):110–20, 130

Additional readings

On Grammar (Volume 1) – 1(1957):29, 35; 8(1979):201, 211, 217; 9(1981):221,
225–31, 243, 246; 10(1985):263, 283–5; 11(1984):311; 13(1992):357, 359;
15(1996):405
Linguistic Studies of Text and Discourse (Volume 2) – 2(1977):38, 44, 51–64;
5(1987):150–2; 8(1994):229–34, 243–4, 251, 254
On Language and Linguistics (Volume 3) – 2(1966):65; 3(1975): 79; 4(1977):101;
5(1987):121; 6(1990):154–6; 8(1985):185, 195–7; 9(1992):210; 12(1997):260;
13(2001):273, 279; 14(1973):298–9; 16(1992):358, 362; 17(1992):382;
18(1995): 420; Appendix(1994):437
The Language of Early Childhood (Volume 4) – 2(1975):56; 3(1976): 81, 87;
4(1974): 95, 101, 111; 5(1978):121, 134; 8(1980):204, 207; 10(1984):249;
13(1975):286–95, 302–4; 15(1993):344; 16(1999):369
The Language of Science (Volume 5) – 1(1995):18; 3(1998):93; 5(1988): 140
Computational and Quantitative Studies (Volume 6) – 1(1956):9; 3(1991):60;
4(1991):71; 8(2002):177; Editor's Introduction:193; 9(1995):207–8; 10(1995):
217, 225, 238; 11(1995):249, 256, 260, 266
Studies in English Language (Volume 7) – 5(1970):199; 12(1998)
Studies in Chinese Language (Volume 8) – 1(1959):10, 13, 16, 20, 64; 3(1956):238;
7(1984):327; 9(2001):355–7

Chapter Four

FUNCTION IN LANGUAGE

Summary

Function in language deals with how people use language and how language varies according to its use. The study of function in language offers insight into the way language is learnt, and why language is as it is. The functional origin of language is most evident in the language of young children. Among the functions which language serves in the life of the child are the following: (1) instrumental, (2) regulatory, (3) interactional, (4) personal, (5) heuristic, and (6) imaginative. These functions or uses of language are to be distinguished from the macro- or meta-functions, including ideational, interpersonal and textual, which constitute major components of meaning in the adult language system.

Selected readings

On Language and Linguistics (Volume 3)

1 FUNCTION AND USE

What do we understand by a "functional approach" to the study of language? Investigations into "the functions of language" have often figured prominently in linguistic research; there are several possible reasons for wanting to gain some insight into how language is used. Among other things, it would be helpful to be able to establish some general principles relating to the use of language; and this is perhaps the most usual interpretation of the concept of a functional approach.

But another question, no less significant, is that of the relation between the functions of language and language itself. If language has evolved in the service of certain functions that may in the broadest sense be called "social" functions, has this left its mark? Has the character of language been shaped and determined by what we use it for? There are a number of reasons for suggesting that it has; and if this is true, then it may be an important factor in any discussion of language and society.

There is one aspect of the relation between language and its use which immediately springs to mind, but which is not the one we are concerned with here. The social functions of language clearly determine the pattern of language varieties, in the sense of what have been called "diatypic" **varieties**, or *registers*; the register range, or linguistic repertoire, of a community or of an individual is derived from the range of uses that language is put to in that particular culture or subculture. There will probably be no bureaucratic mode of discourse in a society without a bureaucracy. The concept "range of uses" has to be understood carefully and with common sense: there might well, for example, be a register of military diction in a hypothetical society that does not make war – because it observes and records the exploits of others that do. Its uses of language do not include fighting, but they do include historiography and news reporting. This is not a departure from the principle, merely an indication that it must be thoughtfully applied.[1]

But diatypic variation in language, the existence of different fields and modes and tenors of discourse, is part of the resources of the linguistic system; and the system has to be able to accommodate it. If we are able to vary our level of formality in talking or writing, or to switch freely between one type of context and another, using language now to plan some organized activity, now to deliver a public lecture, now to keep the children in order, this is because the nature of language is such that it has all these functions built in to its total capacity. So even if we start from a consideration of how language varies – how we make different selections in meaning, and therefore in grammar and vocabulary, according to the context of use – we are led into the more fundamental question of the relation between the functions of language and the nature of the linguistic system.

Hence, the interpretation of our original question which concerns us here is this: is the social functioning of language reflected in linguistic structure – that is, in the internal organization of language as a system? It is not unreasonable to expect that it will be. It was said to be, in fact, by Malinowski, who wrote in 1923 that "language in its structure mirrors the real categories derived from the practical attitudes of the child . . .".[2] In Malinowski's view all uses of language, throughout all stages of cultural evolution, had left their imprint on linguistic structure, although "if our theory is right, the fundamental outlines of grammar are due mainly to the most primitive uses of language".

It was in the language of young children that Malinowski saw most clearly the functional origins of the language system. His formulation was, actually, "the practical attitudes of the child, and of primitive or natural man"; but he later modified this view, realizing that linguistic research had demonstrated that there was no such thing as a "primitive language" – all adult speech represented the same highly sophisticated level of linguistic evolution. Similarly all uses of language, however abstract, and however complex the social structure with which they were associated, were to be explained in terms of certain very elementary functions. It may be true that the developing language system of the child in some sense traverses, or at least provides an analogy for, the stages through which language itself has evolved; but there are no living specimens of its ancestral types, so that any evidence can only come from within, from studying the language system and how it is learnt by a child.

Malinowski's ideas were rather ahead of his time, and they were not yet backed up by adequate investigations of language development. Not that there was no important work available in this field at the time Malinowski was writing; there was, although the first great expansion of interest came shortly afterwards. But most of the work – and this remained true until very recently, right throughout the second wave of expansion, the psycholinguistic movement of the 1960s – was concerned primarily with the mechanism of language rather than with its meaning and function. On the one hand, the interest lay in the acquisition of sounds – in the control of the means of articulation and, later on, in the mastery of the sound system, the phonology, of the language in question. On the other hand, attention was focused on the acquisition of linguistic forms – the vocabulary and the grammar of the mother tongue. The earlier studies along these lines were mainly concerned with the learning of words and word-grammar – the size of the child's vocabulary month by month, and the relative frequency of the different parts of speech – backed up by investigations of his control of sentence syntax in the written medium.[3] More recently the emphasis has tended to shift towards the acquisition of linguistic structures, seen in terms of a particular psycholinguistic view (the so-called "nativist" view) of the language-learning faculty.

These represent different models of, or orientations towards, the language-learning process. They are not, however, either singly or collectively, adequate or particularly relevant to our present perspective. For this purpose, language acquisition – or rather language development, to revert to the earlier term; "acquisition" is a rather misleading metaphor, suggesting that language is some sort of property to be owned – needs to be seen as the mastery of linguistic functions. Learning one's mother tongue is learning the uses of language, and the meanings, or rather the meaning potential, associated with them. The structures, the words and the sounds are the realization of this meaning potential. Learning language is learning how to mean.

If language development is regarded as the development of a meaning potential it becomes possible to consider the Malinowskian thesis seriously, since we can begin by looking at the relation between the child's linguistic structures and the uses he is putting language to. Let us do so in a moment. First, however, we should raise the question of what we mean by putting language to this or that use, what the notion of language as serving certain functions really implies. What are "social functions of language", in the life of *homo grammaticus*, the talking ape?

One way of leading into this question is to consider certain very specialized uses of language. The languages of games furnish many such instances; for example, the bidding system of contract bridge. The language of bidding may be thought of as a system of meaning potential, a range of options that are open to the player as performer (speaker) and as receiver (addressee). The potential is shared; it is neutral as between speaker and hearer, but it presupposes speaker, hearer, and situation. It is a linguistic system: there is a set of options, and this provides an environment for each option in terms of the others – the system includes not merely the option of saying *four hearts* but also the specification of when it is appropriate. The ability to say *four hearts* in the right place, which is an instance, albeit a trivial one, of what Hymes explains as "communicative competence", is sometimes thought of as if it was something quite separate from the ability to say *four hearts* at all; but this is an artificial distinction: there are merely different contexts, and the meaning of four hearts within the context of the bidding stage of a game of contract bridge is different from its meaning elsewhere. (We are not concerned, of course, with whether four hearts is 'a good bid' in the circumstances or not, since this cannot be expressed in terms of the system. We are concerned, however, with the fact that four hearts is meaningful in the game following *three no trumps* or *four diamonds* but not following *four spades*.) We are likely to find ourselves entangled in this problem, of trying to force a distinction between meaning and function, if we insist on characterizing language subjectively as the ability, or competence, of the speaker, instead of objectively as a potential, a set of alternatives. Hence my preference for the concept of "meaning potential", which is what the speaker/hearer **can** (what he can mean, if you like), not what he knows. The two are, to an extent, different ways of looking at the same thing;

but the former, "interorganism" perspective has different implications from the latter, "intraorganism" one.

There are many "restricted languages" of this kind, in games, systems of greetings, musical scores, weather reports, recipes and numerous other such generalized contexts. The simplest instance is one in which the text consists of only one message unit, or a string of message units linked by 'and'; a well-known example is the set of a hundred or so cabled messages that one was permitted to send home at one time while on active service, a typical expression being *61 and 92*, decoded perhaps as 'happy birthday and please send DDT'. Here the meaning potential is simply the list of possible messages, as a set of options, together with the option of choosing more than once, perhaps with some specified maximum length.

The daily life of the individual talking ape does not revolve around options like these, although much of his speech does take place in fairly restricted contexts where the options are limited and the meaning potential is, in fact, rather closely specifiable. Buying and selling in a shop, going to the doctor, and many of the routines of the working day all represent situation types in which the language is by no means restricted as a whole, the transactional meanings are not closed, but nevertheless there are certain definable patterns, certain options which typically come into play. Of course one can indulge in small talk with the doctor, just as one can chatter idly while bidding at bridge; these non-transactional instances of language use (or, better, "extracontextual", since "transactional" is too narrow – the talk about the weather which accompanies certain social activities is not strictly transactional, but it is clearly functional within the context) do not at all disturb the point. To say this is no more than to point out that the fact that a teacher can behave with his students otherwise than in his contextual role as a teacher does not contradict the existence of a teacher–student relationship in the social structure. Conversation on the telephone does not constitute a social context, but the entry and the closure both do: there are prescribed ways of beginning and ending the conversation.[4] All these examples relate to delimitable contexts, to social functions of language; they illustrate what we use language for, and what we expect to achieve by means of language that we should not achieve without it. It is instructive here to think of various more or less everyday tasks and ask oneself how much more complicated they would be to carry out if we had to do so without the aid of language.[5]

We could try to write a list of "uses of language" that we would expect to be typical of an educated adult member of society. But such a list could be indefinitely prolonged, and would not by itself tell us very much. When we talk of "social functions of language", we mean those contexts which are significant in that we are able to specify some of the meaning potential that is characteristically, and explainably, associated with them. And we shall be particularly interested if we find that in doing so we can throw light on certain features in the internal organization of language.

2 AN EXAMPLE FROM CHILD LANGUAGE

With this in mind, let us now go on to consider the language of the child, and in particular the relation between the child's linguistic structures and the uses to which he puts his language. The language system of the very young child is, effectively, a set of restricted language varieties; and it is characteristic of young children's language that its internal form reflects rather directly the function that it is being used to serve. What the child does with language tends to determine its structure. This relatively close match between structure and function can be brought out by a functional analysis of the system, in terms of its meaning potential. We can see from this how the structures that the child has mastered are direct reflections of the functions that language serves for him.

Figures 1 to 3 give an actual example of the language system of a small child. They are taken from the description of Nigel's language at age nineteen months; and each represents one functional component of the system – or rather, each represents just a part of one such component, to keep the illustration down to a reasonable size. The total system is made up of five or six functional components of this kind.[6] Figure 1 shows the system Nigel has developed for the instrumental function of language. This refers to the use of language for the purpose of satisfying material needs: it is the "I want" function, including of course "I don't want". Here the child has developed a meaning potential in which he can request either goods or services, the latter in the form either of physical assistance or of having something made available to him. We show some examples of these requests. In addition his demand may be in response to a question *do you want . . .?*, in which case the answer may be positive or negative; or it may be initiated by himself, in which case it is always positive. Furthermore, under one set of conditions, namely where the demand is initiated by himself and it is a demand for a specific item of food, there is a further option in the meaning potential since he has learnt that he can demand not only a first instalment but also a supplementary one, *more*. (This does not correspond to the adult interpretation;

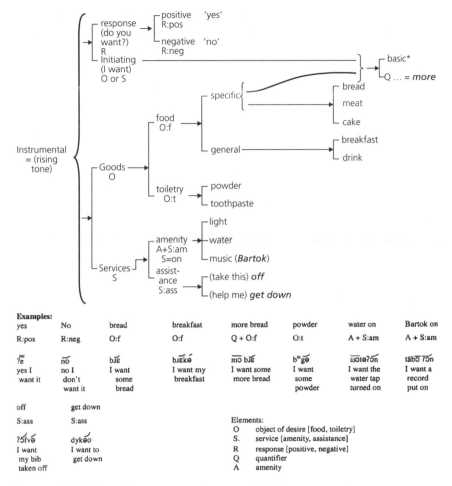

Figure 1 Nigel at nineteen months: part of the instrumental component

he may ask for more bread when he has not yet had any bread but has had something else. Note that he has not yet learnt the meaning 'no more'.) With toiletry, and with general demands for food, this option does not arise. In the system of "basic" versus "supplementary", therefore, the term "basic" is the unmarked one (indicated by the asterisk), where "unmarked" is defined as that which must be selected if the conditions permitting a choice are not satisfied.

Each option in the meaning potential is expressed, or "realized", by some structure-forming element. In the instrumental component there are just five of these: the response element, the object of desire, the service desired, the amenity, and the quantifier. The selection which the child makes of a particular configuration of options within his meaning potential is organized as a structure; but it is a structure in which the elements are very clearly related to the type of function which the language is being made to serve for him. For example, there is obviously a connection between the "instrumental" function of language and the presence, in the structures derived from it, of an element having the structural function "object of desire". What is significant is not, of course, the label we put on it, but the fact that we are led to identify a particular category, to which a label such as this then turns out to be appropriate.

The analysis that we have offered is a functional one in the two distinct but related senses in which the term "functional" is used in linguistics. It is an account of the functions of language; and at the same time the structures are expressed in terms of functional elements (and not of classes, such as noun and verb). It could be thought of as a kind of "case grammar", although the structural parts are strictly speaking "elements of structure" (as in system-structure theory) rather than "cases"; they are specific to the context (i.e. to the particular function of language, in this instance), and they account for the entire structure, whereas cases are contextually undifferentiated and also restricted to elements that are syntactically dependent on a verb.

We have assumed for purposes of illustration a relatively early stage of language learning; at this stage Nigel has only one- and two-element structures. But it does not matter much which stage was chosen; the emphasis is here on the form of the language system. This consists of a meaning potential, represented as a network of options, which are derived from a particular social function and are realized, in their turn, by structures whose elements relate directly to the meanings that are being expressed. These elements seem to be more appropriately described in terms such as "object of desire", which clearly derives from the 'I want' function of language, than in any "purely" grammatical terms, whether these are drawn from the grammar of the adult language (like "subject") or introduced especially to account for the linguistic structures of the child (like "pivot"). I shall suggest, however, that in principle the same is true of the elements of structure of the adult language: that these also have their origin in the social functions of language, though in a way that is less direct and therefore less immediately apparent. Even such a "purely grammatical" function as "subject" is derivable from language in use; in fact, the notion that there are "purely grammatical" elements of structure is really self-contradictory.

The same principle is noticeable in the other two functions which we are illustrating here, again in a simplified form. One of these is the "regulatory" function of language (Figure 2).

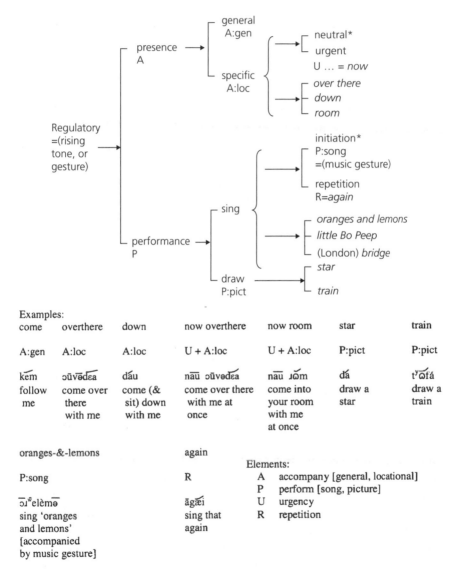

Examples:

come	overthere	down	now overthere	now room	star	train
A:gen	A:loc	A:loc	U + A:loc	U + A:loc	P:pict	P:pict
kém	ɔūvɛdɛa	dáu	nāū ɔūvɛdɛa	nāū jóm	dá	t'ɑ́fá
follow	come over	come (&	come over there	come into	draw a	draw a
me	there	sit) down	with me at	your room	star	train
	with me	with me	once	with me		
				at once		

oranges-&-lemons	again
P:song	R
ɔɪʷelèmə	ágǽi
sing 'oranges	sing that
and lemons'	again
[accompanied	
by music gesture]	

Elements:

A	accompany [general, locational]
P	perform [song, picture]
U	urgency
R	repetition

Figure 2 Nigel at nineteen months: part of the regulatory component

This is the use of language to control the behaviour of others, to manipulate the persons in the environment – the 'do as I tell you' function. Here we find a basic distinction into a demand for the other person's company and a demand for a specific action on his or her part. The demand for company many be a general request to 'come with me', or refer to a particular location 'over there', 'down here', 'in the (other) room'; and it may be marked for urgency. The performance requested may be drawing a picture or singing a song; if it is a song, it may be new (for the occasion) or a repeat performance. It is interesting to note that there is no negative in the regulatory function at this stage; the meaning 'prohibition' is not among the options in the child's potential.

The third example is of the 'interactional' function (Figure 3). This is the child's use of language as a means of personal interaction with those around him – the 'me and you' function of language. Here the child is either interacting with someone who is present ("greeting") or seeking to interact with someone who is absent ("calling"). That someone may either be generalized, with *hullo* used (i) in narrow tone accompanied by a smile, to commune with an intimate or greet a stranger, or (ii) in wide tone, loud, to summon company; or it may be personalized, in which case it is either a statement of the need for interaction, . . . *come!*, or a search, *where . . .?* And there is here a further choice in meaning, realized by intonation. All utterances in the instrumental and regulatory functions end on a high rising tone, unless this is replaced by a gesture, as in the demand for music; this is the tone which is used when the child requires a response of any kind. In the interactional function there are two types of utterance, those requiring a response and those not; the former have the final rise, the latter end on a falling tone (as do utterances in the other functions which we have not illustrated here).

It would be wrong to draw too sharp a line between the different functions in the child's linguistic system. There is a clear connection between the instrumental and the regulatory functions, in that both represent types of demand to be met by some action on the part of the addressee; and between the regulatory and the interactional, in that both involve the assumption of an interpersonal relationship. Nevertheless, the functions we have suggested are distinguishable from one another; and this is important, because it is through the gradual extension of his meaning potential into new functions that the child's linguistic horizons become enlarged. In the instrumental function, it does not matter who provides the bread or turns the tap on; the intention is satisfied by the provision of the object or service in question. In the regulatory function on the other hand the request involves a specific person; it is he and no

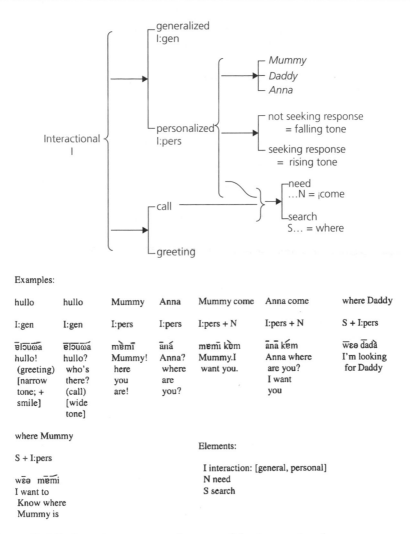

Figure 3 Nigel at nineteen months: part of the interactional component

one else who must respond, by his behaviour. The interactional also involves a specific person; but he is not being required to do anything, merely to be there and in touch. There are, to be sure, borderline cases, and there are overlaps in the realization (e.g. *come* is sometimes regulatory, sometimes interactional in meaning); but such indeterminacy will be found in any system of this kind.

These extracts from the account of Nigel's developing linguistic system will serve to illustrate the types of structure that are encountered in the language of the very young child, and how they relate directly to the options that he has in his meaning potential. The networks show what the child can do, in the sense of what he can mean; the structural interpretations show the mechanism by which he does it – how the meanings are expressed, through configurations of elementary functions.

3 FROM FUNCTIONS TO MACROFUNCTIONS

In another paper (1969) I have suggested what seem to me to be the basic functions that language comes to fulfil in the early life of the child, listing the instrumental, the regulatory, the interactional, the personal, the heuristic, the imaginative and the representational. (The last was badly named; it would have been better called "informative", since it referred specifically to the use of language for transmitting information.) These are the generalized social functions of language in the context of the young child's life. When the child has learnt to use language to some extent in any of these functions, however limited the grammatical and lexical resources he can bring to bear, then he has built up a meaning potential for that function and has mastered at least a minimal structural requirement – it may be a "configuration" of only one element – for purposes of expressing it.

The social functions which language is serving in the life of the child determine both the options which he creates for himself and their realizations in structure. We see this clearly in the language of young children, once we begin to think of language development as the development of the social functions of language and of a meaning potential associated with them. However, although this connection between the functions of language and the linguistic system is clearest in the case of the language of very young children, it is essentially, I think, a feature of language as a whole. The internal organization of natural language can best be explained in the light of the social functions which language has evolved to serve. Language is as it is because of what it has to do. Only, the relation between language function and language structure will appear less directly, and in more complex ways, in the fully developed adult system than in children's language.

To say this is in effect to claim, with Malinowski, that ontogeny does in some respect provide a model for phylogeny. We cannot examine the origins of language. But if we can relate the form of the adult language system to its social functions, and at the same time show that the language of the child, in its various stages, is explainable in terms of the uses that he has mastered up to the particular stage, then we have at least opened up the possibility of interesting discussion about the nature and social origins of language.

It is characteristic, it seems, of the utterances of the very young child that they are functionally simple; each utterance serves just one function. If an utterance is instrumental in function, seeking the satisfaction of some material desire, then it is just instrumental and nothing else. This represents a very early stage of language development. It is shown in our illustrations by the fact that each utterance is totally specified by just one network: to derive *more bread!* we need only the instrumental system network, which fully describes its structure.

The adult language bears the marks of its humble origins in systems like these. But it differs in fundamental ways; and perhaps the most fundamental – because this is what makes it necessary to develop a level of linguistic form (grammar and vocabulary) intermediate between meanings and sounds – is the fact that utterances in the adult language are functionally complex. Every adult linguistic act, with a few broadly specifiable exceptions, is serving more that one function at once.

One very familiar type of phenomenon which illustrates this fact is that of denotation and connotation in word meanings. For example, after the FA Cup Final match between Leeds and Chelsea a friend of mine who is a Londoner greeted me with I *see Chelsea trounced Leeds again,* using the word *trounce* which means 'defeat' plus 'I am pleased'. But the functional utterance goes much further than is signalled by the word-meaning of *trounce.* The speaker was conveying a piece of information, which he suspected I already possessed, together with the further information (which I did not possess) that he also possessed it; he was referring it to our shared experience; expressing his triumph over me (I am a Leeds supporter and he knows it); and relating back to some previous exchanges between us. There is no simple functional category from which we can derive this utterance, corresponding to categories such as regulatory or instrumental in the linguistic system of the young child.

The problem for a socio-linguistic theory is: what is there in the adult language which corresponds to the functional components, the systems of meaning potential, that make up the early stages in the child's language development? Or, since that is a rather slanted way of asking the question, what is the relation of the fully developed language system to the social functions of the adult language? And can we explain something of the form that languages take by examining this relation?

In one sense, the variety of social functions of language is, obviously, much greater in the adult. The adult does more different things than the child; and in a great many of his activities, he uses language. He has a very broad diatypic spectrum. Yet there is another sense in which the adult's range of functional variation may be poorer, and we can best appreciate this if we take the child as our point of departure. Among the child's uses of language there appears, after a time, the use of language to convey new information: to communicate a content that is (regarded by the speaker as) unknown to the addressee. I had referred to this in a general way as the "representational" function; but it would be better (as I suggested above) if one were to use a more specific term, such as "informative", since this makes it easier to interpret subsequent developments. In the course of maturation this function is increasingly emphasized, until eventually it comes to dominate, if not the adult's use of language, at least his conception of the use of language. The adult tends to be sceptical if it is suggested to him that language has other uses than that of conveying information; and he will usually think next of the use of language to **mis**inform – which is simply a variant of the informative function. Yet for the young child the informative is a rather minor function, relatively late to emerge. Many problems of communication between adult and child, for example in the infant school, arise from the adults' failure to grasp this fact. This can be seen in some adult renderings of children's rhymes and songs, which are often very dramatic, with an intonation and rhythm appropriate to the content; whereas for the child the language is not primarily content – it is language in its imaginative function, and needs to be expressed as pattern, patterns of meaning and structure and vocabulary and sound. Similarly, failures have been reported when actors have recorded foreign language courses; their renderings focus attention only on the use of language to convey information, and it seems that when learning a foreign language, as when learning the mother tongue, it is necessary to take other uses of language into account, especially in the beginning stages.

What happens in the course of maturation is a process that we might from one point of view call "functional reduction", whereby the original functional range of the child's language – a set of fairly discrete functional components each with its own meaning potential – is gradually replaced by a more highly coded and more abstract, but also simpler, functional system. There is an immense functional diversity in the adult's use of language; immense, that is, if we simply ask "in what kinds of activity does language play a part for him?" But this diversity of usage is reduced in the internal organization of the adult language system – in the grammar, in other words – to a very small set of functional components. Let us call these for the moment *macrofunctions* to distinguish them from the functions of the child's emergent language system, the instrumental, the regulatory and so on. These "macro-functions" are the highly abstract linguistic reflexes of the multiplicity of social uses of language.

The innumerable social purposes for which adults use language are not represented directly, one by one in the form of functional components in the language system, as are those of the child. With the very young child, "function" equals "use"; and there is no grammar, no intermediate level of internal organization in the language, only a content and an expression. With the adult, there are indefinitely many uses, but only three or four functions, or "macro-functions" as we are calling them; and these macrofunctions appear at a new level in the linguistic system – they take the form of *grammar*. The grammatical system has as it were a functional input and a structural output; it provides the mechanism for different functions to be combined in one utterance in the way the adult requires. But these macro-functions, although they are only indirectly related to specific uses of language, are still recognizable as abstract representations of the basic functions which language is made to serve.

4 IDEATIONAL, INTERPERSONAL AND TEXTUAL

One of these macro-functions is what is sometimes called the representational one. But just as earlier, in talking of the use of language to convey information, I preferred the more specific term "informative", so here I shall also prefer another term – but this time a different one, because this is a very distinct concept. Here we are referring to the linguistic expression of ideational content; let us call this macro-function of the adult language system the *ideational* function. For the child, the use of language to inform is just one instance of language use, one function among many. But with the adult, the ideational element in language is present in all its uses; no matter what he is doing with language he will find himself exploiting its ideational resources, its potential for expressing a content in terms of the speaker's experience and that of the speech community. There are exceptions, types of utterance like *how do you do?* and *no wonder!* which have no ideational content in them; but otherwise there is some ideational component involved, however small, in all the specific uses of language in which the adult typically engages.

This no doubt is why the adult tends to think of language primarily in terms of its capacity to inform. But where is the origin of this ideational element to be sought within the linguistic repertoire of the very young child? Not, I think, in the informative function, which seems to be in some sense secondary, derived from others that have already appeared. It is to be sought rather in the combination of the personal and the heuristic, in that phase of linguistic development which becomes crucial at a particular time, probably (as in Nigel's case) shortly after the emergence of the more directly pragmatic functions which we illustrated in Figures 1 to 3. At the age from which these examples were taken, nineteen months, Nigel had already begun to use language also in the personal, the heuristic and the imaginative functions; it was noticeable that language was becoming, for him, a means of organizing and storing his experience. Here we saw the beginnings of a grammar – that is, a level of lexico-grammatical organization, or linguistic "form"; and of utterances having more than one function. The words and structures learnt in these new functions were soon turned also to pragmatic use, as in some of the examples quoted of the instrumental and regulatory functions. But it appears that much of the initial impetus to the learning of the formal patterns (as distinct from the spontaneous modes of expression characteristic of the first few months of speech) was the need to impose order on the environment and to define his own person in relation to and in distinction from it. Hence – to illustrate just from vocabulary – we find the word *bus*, though it is **recognized** as the name of a toy bus as well as of full-sized specimens, being used at first exclusively to comment on the sight or sound of buses in the street and only later as a demand for the toy; and the one or two exceptions to this, e.g. *bird* which was at first used **only** in the instrumental sense of 'I want my toy bird', tend to drop out of the system altogether and are relearnt in a personal–heuristic context later.

It seems therefore that the personal-heuristic function is a major impetus to the enlarging of the ideational element in the child's linguistic system. We should not however exaggerate its role *vis-à-vis* that of the earlier pragmatic functions; the period fifteen to twenty-one months was in Nigel's case characterized by a rapid development of grammatical and lexical resources which were (as a whole) exploited in all the functional contexts that he had mastered so far. The one function that had not yet emerged was the informative; even when pressed – as he frequently was – to 'tell Mummy where you went' or 'tell Daddy what you saw', he was incapable of doing so, although in many instances he had previously used the required sentences quite appropriately in a different function. It was clear that he had not internalized the fact that language could be used to tell people things they did not know, to communicate experience that had **not** been shared. But this was no barrier to the development of an ideational component in his linguistic system. The ideational element, as it evolves, becomes crucial to the use of language in all the functions that the child has learnt to control; and this gives the clue to its status as a macro-function. Whatever specific use one is making of language, one will sooner or later find it necessary to refer explicitly to the categories of one's experience of the world. All, or nearly all, utterances come to have an ideational component in them. But, at the same time, they all have something else besides.

When we talk of the ideational function of the adult language, therefore, we are using "function" in a more generalized sense (as indicated by our term "macro-function") than when we refer to the specific functions that make up the language of the young child. Functions such as "instrumental" and "regulatory" are really the same thing as "uses of language". The ideational function, on the other hand, is a major component of meaning in the language system that is basic to more or less all uses of language. It is still a **meaning potential**, although the potential is very vast and complex; for example, the whole of the transitivity system in language – the interpretation and expression in language of the different types of process of the external world, including material, mental and abstract processes of every kind – is part of the ideational component of the grammar. And the structures that express these ideational meanings are still recognizably derived from the meanings themselves; their elements are in this respect not essentially different from those such as "object of desire" that we saw in Figures 1–3. They represent the categories of our interpretation of experience. So for example a clause such as *Sir Christopher Wren built this gazebo* may be analysed as a configuration of the functions "agent" *Sir Christopher Wren*, "process: material: creation" *built*, "goal: effected" *this gazebo*, where "agent", "process", "goal" and their subcategories reflect our understanding of phenomena that come within our experience. Hence this function of language, which is that of encoding our experience in the form of an ideational content, not only specifies the available options in meaning but also determines the nature of their structural realizations. The notions of agent, process and the like make sense only if we assume an ideational function in the adult language, just as "object of desire" and "service" make sense only if we assume an instrumental function in the emergent language of the child. But this analysis is not imposed from outside in order to satisfy some theory of linguistic functions; an analysis in something like these terms is necessary (whatever form it finally takes for the language in question) if we are to explain the structure of clauses. The clause is a structural unit, and it is the one by which we express a particular range of ideational meanings, our experience of processes – the processes of the external world, both concrete and abstract, and the processes of our own consciousness, see-

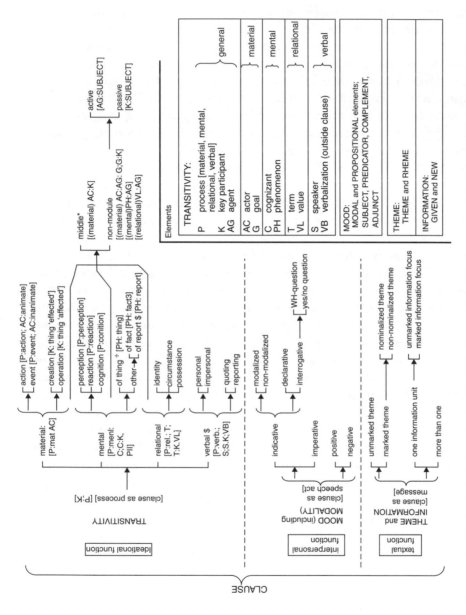

Figure 4 Summary of principal options in the English clause (simplified; structural indices for transitivity only)

ing, liking, thinking, talking and so on. Transitivity is simply the grammar of the clause in its ideational aspect.

Figure 4 sets out the principal options in the transitivity system of English, showing how these are realized in the form of structures. It can be seen that the structure-forming elements – agent, process, phenomenon etc. – are all related to the general function of expressing processes. The labels that we give to them describe their specific roles in the encoding of these meanings, but the elements themselves are identified syntactically. Thus, in the English clause there is a distinct element of structure which expresses the cause of a process when that process is brought about by something other than the entity that is primarily affected by it (e.g. *the storm* in *the storm shook the house*); we can reasonably label this the "agent", but whether we do so or not it is present in the grammar as an element deriving from the ideational function of language.

The clause, however, is not confined to the expression of transitivity; it has other functions besides. There are non-ideational elements in the adult language system, even though the adult speaker is often reluctant to recognize them. Again, however, they are grouped together as a single macro-function in the grammar, covering a whole range of particular uses of language. This is the macro-function that we shall refer to as the *interpersonal*; it embodies all use of language to express social and personal relations, including all forms of the speaker's intrusion into the speech situation and the speech act. The young child also uses language interpersonally, as we have seen, interacting with other people, controlling their behaviour, and also expressing his own personality and his own attitudes and feelings; but these uses are specific and differentiated. Later on they become generalized in a single functional component of the grammatical system, at this more abstract level. In the clause, the interpersonal element is represented by mood and modality – the selection by the speaker of a particular role in the speech situation, and his determination of the choice of roles for the addressee (mood), and the expression of his judgments and predictions (modality).

We are not suggesting that one cannot distinguish, in the adult language, specific uses of language of a socio-personal kind; on the contrary, we can recognize an unlimited number. We use language to approve and disapprove; to express belief, opinion, doubt; to include in the social group, or exclude from it; to ask and answer; to express personal feelings; to achieve intimacy; to greet, chat up, take leave of; in all these and many other ways. But in the structure of the adult language there is an integrated "interpersonal" component, which provides the meaning potential for this element as it is present in all uses of language, just as the "ideational" component provides the resources for the representation of experience that is also an essential element whatever the specific type of language use.

These two macro-functions, the ideational and the interpersonal, together determine a large part of the meaning potential that is incorporated in the grammar of every language. This can be seen very clearly in the grammar of the clause, which has its ideational aspect, transitivity, and its interpersonal aspect, mood (including modality).

There is also a third macro-function, the *textual*, which fills the requirement that language should be operationally relevant – that it should have a texture, in real contexts of situation, that distinguishes a living message from a mere entry in a grammar or a dictionary. This third component provides the remaining strands of meaning potential to be woven into the fabric of linguistic structure.

We shall not attempt to illustrate in detail the interpersonal and the textual functions. Included in Figure 4 are a few of the principal options which make up these components in the English clause; their structural realizations are not shown, but the same principle holds, whereby the structural mechanism reflects the generalized meanings that are being expressed. The intention here is simply to bring out the fact that a linguistic structure – of which the clause is the best example – serves as a means for the integrated expression of all the functionally distinct components of meaning in language. Some simple clauses are analysed along these lines in Figure 5.

What we know as "grammar" is the linguistic device for hooking up together the selections in meaning which are derived from the various functions of language, and realizing them in a unified structural form. Whereas with the child, in the first beginnings of the system, the functions remain unintegrated, being in effect functional varieties of speech act, with one utterance having just one function, the linguistic units of the adult language serve all (macro-) functions at once. A clause in English is the simultaneous realization of ideational, interpersonal and textual meanings. But these components are not put together in discrete fashion such that we can point to one segment of the clause as expressing one type of meaning and another segment as expressing another. The choice of a word may express one type of meaning, its morphology another, and its position in sequence another; and any element is likely to have more than one structural role, like a chord in a polyphonic structure which participates simultaneously in a number of melodic lines. This last point is illustrated by the analyses in Figure 5.

	this gazebo	was built	by Sir Christopher Wren
IDEATIONAL material (action/ creation/(non-middle:passive))	G:K; effected	P:material/ action	AC:AG; animate
INTERPERSONAL declarative/non modalized	Modal	Propositional	
	Subject	Predicator	Adjunct
TEXTUAL unmarked theme one information unit: unmarked	Theme	Rheme	
	Given	New	

	I	had	a cat ...
IDEATIONAL relational: (possession/middle)	T:K	P:rel-ational	VL
INTERPERSONAL declarative/non-modalized	=did have		
	Modal	Propositional	
	Subject	Predicator	Complement
TEXTUAL unmarked theme one information unit: unmarked	Theme	Rheme	
	Given	New	

	... the cat	pleased	me
ID.mental:(reaction/ fact/(non-middle active)	PH:AG; thing	P:mental: reaction	C:K.
INT.declarative/ non-modalized	Modal	=did | please	Propositional
	Subject	Predicator	Complement
TEXT.unmarked theme one information unit: unmarked	Theme	Rheme	
	Given	New	

	such a tale	you would	never believe
ID.mental:(cognition/ report/middle)	PH: report	C:K | P: mental: cognition	
INT.declarative/ modalized negative	Propo-.	Modal	-sitional
	Complement	Subject	Predicator
TEXT.marked theme: non-nominalized two information units	Theme	Rheme	
	New	Given	New

Figure 5 Analysis of clauses, showing simultaneous structures

a SYSTEM

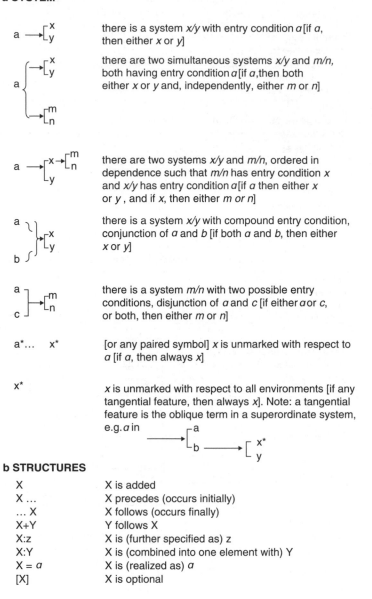

there is a system *x/y* with entry condition *a* [if *a*, then either *x* or *y*]

there are two simultaneous systems *x/y* and *m/n*, both having entry condition *a* [if *a*, then both either *x* or *y* and, independently, either *m* or *n*]

there are two systems *x/y* and *m/n*, ordered in dependence such that *m/n* has entry condition *x* and *x/y* has entry condition *a* [if *a* then either *x* or *y*, and if *x*, then either *m* or *n*]

there is a system *x/y* with compound entry condition, conjunction of *a* and *b* [if both *a* and *b*, then either *x* or *y*]

there is a system *m/n* with two possible entry conditions, disjunction of *a* and *c* [if either *a* or *c*, or both, then either *m* or *n*]

a*... x* [or any paired symbol] *x* is unmarked with respect to *a* [if *a*, then always *x*]

x* *x* is unmarked with respect to all environments [if any tangential feature, then always *x*]. Note: a tangential feature is the oblique term in a superordinate system, e.g. *a* in

b STRUCTURES

X	X is added
X ...	X precedes (occurs initially)
... X	X follows (occurs finally)
X+Y	Y follows X
X:z	X is (further specified as) z
X:Y	X is (combined into one element with) Y
X = *a*	X is (realized as) *a*
[X]	X is optional

Figure 6 Summary of notational conventions

We hope to have made it clear in what sense it is being said that the concept of the social function of language is central to the interpretation of language as a system. The internal organization of language is not accidental; it embodies the functions that language has evolved to serve in the life of social man. This essentially was Malinowski's claim; and, as Malinowski suggested, we can see it most clearly in the linguistic system of the young child. There, the utterance has in principle just one structure; each element in it has therefore just one structural function, and that function is related to the meaning potential – to the set of options available to the child in that particular social function.

In the developed linguistic system of the adult, the functional origins are still discernible. Here, however, each utterance has a number of structures simultaneously – we have used the analogy of polyphony. Each element is a complex of roles, and enters into more than one structure (indeed the concept "element of structure" is a purely abstract concept; it is merely a role set, which is then realized by some item in the language). The structure of the adult language still represents the functional meaning potential; but because of the variety of social uses of language, a "grammar" has emerged whereby the options are organized into a few large sets in which the speaker selects simultaneously whatever the specific use he is making of language. These sets of options, which are recognizable empirically in the grammar, correspond to the few highly generalized realms of meaning that are essential to the social functioning of language – and hence are intrinsic to language as a system. Because language serves a generalized "ideational" function, we are able to use it for all the specific purposes and types of context which involve the communication of experience. Because it serves a generalized "interpersonal" function, we are able to use it for all the specific forms of personal expression and social interaction. And a prerequisite to its effective operation under both these headings is what we have referred to as the "textual" function, whereby language becomes text, is related to itself and to its contexts of use. Without the textual component of meaning, we should be unable to make any use of language at all.

If we want to pursue this line of interpretation further, we shall have to go outside language to some theory of social meanings. From the point of view of a linguist the most important work in this field is that of Bernstein, whose theories of cultural transmission and social change are unique in this respect, that language is built into them as an essential element in social processes. Although Bernstein is primarily investigating social and not linguistic phenomena, his ideas shed very considerable light on language; in particular, in relation to the concept of language as meaning potential, he has been able to define certain contexts which are crucial to the socialization of the child and to identify the significant orientations in the behaviour of participants within these contexts. The behavioural options of the participants are, typically, realized through language; and with a functional interpretation of the semantic system we can begin to appreciate how it is that, in the course of expressing meanings that are specific to particular contexts of situation, language at the same time serves to transmit the essential patterns of orientation in the total context of the culture.

This provides the backdrop to a functional view of language. In front of our eyes, as it were, are the "uses of language"; we are interested in how people use language and in how language varies according to its use. Behind this lies a concern with the nature of language of itself; once we interpret the notion "uses of language" in sufficiently abstract terms we find that it gives us an insight into the way language is learnt and, through that, into the internal organization of language, why language is as it is. Behind this again is a still deeper focus, on society and the transmission of culture; for when we interpret language in these terms we may cast some light on how language, in the most everyday situations, so effectively transmits the social structure, the values, the systems of knowledge, all the deepest and most pervasive patterns of the culture. With a functional perspective on language, we can begin to appreciate how this is done.

Notes

This chapter was based on a preliminary interpretation of some of my early records of child language development. I had begun working on linguistic ontogeny in the context of our "Breakthrough to Literacy" project, while at the same time continuing with the systemic functional analysis of the grammar of (adult) English. The account given here was considerably modified in the course of more detailed, corpus-based study on both these fronts; among other things, the development of linguistic functionality was reinterpreted in terms of three stages: micro-functions (in protolanguage), macro-functions (in the transition to mother tongue), meta-functions (in the mother tongue). My essays on child language development are collected in Volume 4. Volumes 1 and 3 are concerned with systemic functional theory; specific chapters on the grammar of English will appear in a later volume.

1. For diatypic variety in language, see Gregory 1967; Ellis 1966.
2. Bronislaw Malinowski, 'The problem of meaning in primitive languages', Supplement 1 to Ogden and Richards 1923.
3. See for example Watts 1944.

4. Emanuel A. Schegloff, 'Sequencing in conversational openings', in Gumperz and Hymes 1972.

5. This was in fact a task assigned to the mothers in relation to the socialization of children in a study by Bernstein and Henderson, 'Social class differences in the relevance of language to socialization': they were asked to say how much more difficult it would be for parents who could not speak to do certain things with young children, such as disciplining them or helping them to make things. It should be borne in mind that in the present discussion we are using 'language' always to refer to the meaning potential; we assume some means of expression, but not any linguistic forms in particular.

6. The analyses given in Figures 1 to 3 represent a provisional interpretation of the material. A full account of Nigel's language development from nine to twenty-four months is presented in Volume 4 of the Collected Work, *The Language of Early Childhood*.

III.14(1973):298–322

The Language of Early Childhood (Volume 4)

The question then is: what are the functions that we recognize as determining the child's semiotic system at this stage, and how do we arrive at them? Here we have, as always, to keep a sense of proportion, and to try and face both ways, shunting between sensible observation on the one hand and imaginative but at the same time goal-directed theory on the other. On the one hand, we can see ourselves, as any parent can see, what the child is doing when he is uttering speech sounds, and what contributions these speech sounds are making to his total activity. We have some reasonably clear impression of function in a context; and we can characterize this very adequately in quite general terms in relation to the context of a situation. In other words, proceeding solely from observation, and using just the amount of common sense the researcher ought to possess if he did not suspend it while on duty, we could reach generalizations such as "this child says *nananana* whenever he wants to get something handed to him". And we could reach this on a purely inductive basis, or as nearly inductive as one ever gets: the educated adult cannot really proceed without imposing some kind of theory as he goes along.

On the other hand, while we could draw some interesting conclusions in this way, there would be a very severe limitation on how far we could go. If we want to understand the nature of the developmental process, and in particular to make the bridge between the language that the child creates for himself at the very first stage and the adult language that he comes out with at the end, then we have to relate the generalizations that we make about these uses of language to some hypothesis about the overall functions of language in the life of social man.

Clearly we will not be able to do this from a purely empirical standpoint, since by the time a child is, say, two and a half, we will no longer be able to give any kind of significant general account of his uses of language. By this time, like the adult, he already uses language for so many different purposes that if we try to list them, we shall simply get an endless catalogue; or rather, we shall get a whole series of catalogues with no reason for preferring one over another. We have to find some other more theoretical basis for matching the observations about language use with some theoretical construct of a functional nature. And there are two possible sources for this type of a theory of language functions, one from within language itself and one from outside it.

3 SOURCES OF FUNCTIONAL CONCEPTS

Let us look at each of these briefly in turn. If we consider first the linguistic system itself, we find that the adult language displays certain features which can only be interpreted in functional terms. These are found, naturally, in the area of meaning: the semantic system of the adult language is very clearly functional in its composition. It reflects the fact that language has evolved in the service of certain particular human needs. But what is really significant is that this functional principle is carried over and built into the grammar, so that the internal organization of the grammatical system is also functional in character. If we consider language as a meaning potential, an open-ended and theoretically infinite range of options in meaning, then we find that these options are grouped into a very small number of sets such that each set of options is subject to strong internal constraints but very weak external constraints. In other words, when the speaker makes selections in the system (which are essentially selections in meaning), a choice that he makes in one set of options has a great deal of effect on the other choices that he makes within the same set, but practically no effect on the choices he makes among the options in the other sets. These sets of options constitute the functional components of the semantic system.

Broadly speaking we can characterize these functional components as follows. First, there are the ***ideational*** options, those relating to the content of what is said. With this component, the speaker expresses his experience of the phenomena of the external world, and of the internal world of his own consciousness. This is what we might call the ***observer*** function of language, language as a means of talking about the real world.

It also includes a subcomponent concerned with the expression of logical relations which are first perceived and interpreted by the child as relations between things.

Second, there is the *interpersonal* component of the semantic system, reflecting the function of language as a means whereby the speaker participates in the speech situation. This we may call the *intruder* function of language. Through the options in this component, the speaker adopts a role, or a set of roles, *vis-à-vis* the participants in the speech situation, and also assigns roles to the other participants, while accepting (or rejecting) those that are assigned to him; he expresses his own judgements, his own attitudes, his own personality, and in so doing exerts certain effects on the hearers. These have been known as the "expressive–conative" functions of language. The options that the speaker takes up in this area of meaning, while they are strongly interrelated among one another, are in large measure independent of the options which he takes up of an ideational kind, those under the first heading.

And then, finally, there is a third semantic function which is in a sense an enabling function, one without which the other two could not be put into effect; this we shall refer to as the *textual* function, the function that language has of creating text. It is through the options in this component that the speaker is enabled to make what he says operational in the context, as distinct from being merely citational, like lists of words in a dictionary, or sentences in a grammar book. The textual function we can regard as being that which breathes life into language; in another metaphor, it provides texture, and without texture there is no text.

We can take account of this functional organization of the semantic system of the adult language in helping us to determine what are likely to be the developmental functions from which the child starts. Somehow, the child moves from the one to the other, from his own system to that of the adult; and our hypothesis must be such as at least to show that it would have been possible for him to make the transition. Ideally, of course, we would like it to be rather stronger, in the sense that it should show some clear motivation why the child should move into the adult language as the means of extending the functional potential that he already has. All this is looking at the question from inside language.

Outside language, we turn to some kind of social theory that accommodates language as an essential element, and in particular one that embodies some notion of functional contexts of language use that are likely to be critical for the child. Here we turn, obviously, to the work of

Basil Bernstein (1971), whose theory of social structure and social change embodies a concept of cultural transmission in which he has been able to identify a number of what he calls "critical socializing contexts", types of situation involving the use of language which play a key part in the transmission of culture to the child. Bernstein has identified a certain number of such contexts in what amounts to a sociological theory of linguistic functions. At one point he enumerates four such contexts, which he refers to as the regulative, the instructional, the imaginative or innovative, and the interpersonal. The fact that in Bernstein's work language is the central factor in cultural transmission makes it likely that contexts which Bernstein recognizes as critical for cultural transmission will also be critical in the language learning process.

4 PHASE I FUNCTIONS

We can now put together the various strands that make up a pattern in thinking about language in functional terms: in the first place, observations relating to the use of language by a very small child and, in the second place, theoretical considerations about linguistic function, which break down in turn into those which are essentially linguistic in nature, functional theories of language and of the semantic system, and those which are essentially extralinguistic in nature, sociological theories embodying a concept of cultural transmission and processes of socialization.

Taking these factors into account, I suggest a set of functions which would serve for the interpretation of the language of a very young child; that is, as an initial hypothesis for some kind of functional or sociolinguistic approach to early language development. The particular set of functions which I suggest is as follows: (1) instrumental, (2) regulatory, (3) interactional, (4) personal, (5) heuristic, and (6) imaginative. Let me comment briefly on each of these in turn.

1. The **instrumental** function is the function that language serves of satisfying the child's material needs, of enabling him to obtain the goods and services that he wants. It is the 'I want' function of language; and it is likely to include a general expression of desire, some element meaning simply 'I want that object there' (present in the context), as well as perhaps other expressions relating to specific desires, responses to questions 'do you want ...?' and so on.

2. The **regulatory** function is related to this, but it is also distinct. It is the function of language as controlling the behaviour of others, something which the child recognizes very easily because language

is used on him in this way: language is used to control his own behaviour and he soon learns that he can turn the tables and use it to control others. The regulatory is the 'do as I tell you' function of language. The difference between this and the instrumental is that in the instrumental the focus is on the goods or services required and it does not matter who provides them, whereas regulatory utterances are directed towards a particular individual, and it is the behaviour of that individual that is to be influenced. Typically therefore this function includes meanings such as, again, a generalized request 'do that', meaning 'do what you have just been doing' (in the context), 'do that again'; as well as various specific demands, particularly in the form of suggestions 'let's do ...' such as 'let's go for a walk', 'let's play this game', 'let's sing a song' and so forth.

3. The **interactional** function is what we might gloss as the 'me and you' function of language. This is language used by the child to interact with those around him, particularly his mother and others that are important to him, and it includes meanings such as the generalized greetings 'hello', 'pleased to see you', and also responses to calls 'yes?' as well as more specific forms. For example, the first names of particular individuals that the child learns are typically used with a purely interactional function; and there may be other specific meanings of an interactional kind involving the focusing of attention on particular objects in the environment, some favourite objects of the child which are used as channels for interacting with those around him.[4]

4. Fourth, there is the **personal** function. This is language used to express the child's own uniqueness; to express his awareness of himself, in contradistinction to his environment, and then to mould that self – ultimately, language used in the development of the personality. This includes, thus, expressions of personal feelings, of participation and withdrawal, of interest, pleasure, disgust, and so forth, and extends later on to more specific intrusion of the child as a personality into the speech situation. We might call this the 'here I come' function of language.

5. Fifth, once the boundary between the child himself and his environment is beginning to be recognized, then the child can turn towards the exploration of the environment; this is the **heuristic** function of language, the 'tell me why' function, that which later on develops into the whole range of questioning forms that the young child uses. At this very early stage, in its most elementary

113

form, the heuristic use of language is the demand for a name, which is the child's way of categorizing the objects of the physical world; but it soon expands into a variety of more specific meanings.

6. Finally we have the *imaginative* function, which is the function of language whereby the child creates an environment of his own. As well as moving into, taking over, and exploring the universe which he finds around him, the child also uses language for creating a universe of his own, a world initially of pure sound, but which gradually turns into one of story and make-believe and 'let's pretend', and ultimately into the realm of poetry and imaginative writing. This we may call the 'let's pretend' function of language.

Later on there is in fact a seventh to be added to the list; but the initial hypothesis was that this seventh function, although it is the one which is undoubtedly dominant in the adult's use of language, and even more so in the adult's image of what language is, is one which does not emerge in the child until considerably after the others. This is the one that we can call the *informative* function of language, the 'I've got something to tell you' function. Now, the idea that language can be used as a means of communicating information to someone who does not already possess that information is a very sophisticated one which depends on the internalization of a whole complex set of linguistic concepts that the young child does not possess. It is the only purely intrinsic function of language, the only use of language in a function that is definable solely by reference to language. And it is one which is not at all present in the phase of language development which we are considering here. In Nigel's case, for example, it did not begin to appear until a much later stage, at about 22 months. It is useful, however, to note it at this point particularly because it tends to predominate in adult thinking about language. This, in fact, is one of the reasons why the adult finds it so difficult to interpret the image of language that the very young child has internalized. The young child has a very clear notion of the functions of his own linguistic system. He knows very well what he can do with it. But what he can do with it is not at all the same thing as what the adult does (still less what the adult thinks he does) with his linguistic system.

These, then, are the initial functions with respect to which we identify the content of what the child is learning to say, the meanings that are present in this very early linguistic system. All those utterances which we identify as language can be interpreted in the light of some such set of functions as these. Within each one of these functions, we shall recognize a range of alternatives, a range of options in meaning, that the child has mastered at this particular stage; this is the set of possibilities that is open and accessible to him in this particular function of language.

It is this notion of a range of alternatives, a set of options, that I think provides the real foundation of a functional approach to early language development. Somewhat surprisingly, perhaps, the distinction between what is and what is not part of the system seems very easy to draw at this stage; at least I found it so. It was very rare that there was any doubt as to whether a particular sound was or was not functional in the defined terms, and so was or was not an expression in the language.

This is part of the value of the functional approach: it provides a criterion for identifying what is language and what is not. It should be noted that this criterion excludes all instances which are interpreted as linguistic practice. When the child is practising speech sounds, or later on words, phrases, structures, or whatever they are, this is not regarded as language in use; it is not an instance of meaning. This is merely tantamount to saying that the learning of a particular system cannot be categorized in terms of the use of that system, and therefore in the present study those utterances which were purely directed towards the learning of the system were omitted from consideration. It happened that Nigel was a child who did very little practice of this kind; some children apparently do a great deal more.

IV.3(1976):68–74

Additional readings

On Grammar (Volume 1) – 8(1979):217
On Language and Linguistics (Volume 3) – 15(1972):324, 350
The Language of Early Childhood (Volume 4) – 2(1975):47, 51–6; 3(1976): 81–7; 4(1974): 94; 7(1975): 179, 192; 9(1983):222; 12(1969): 270–80
Language and Education (Volume 9) – 2(1971): 41–2; 3(1977):50–3, 56–7
Language and Society (Volume 10) – 3(1974):88–92, 120–2

Chapter Five

GRAMMATICAL METAPHOR

Summary

Grammatical metaphor involves the junction of category meanings, not simply word meanings. Examples of grammatical metaphor include length, which is 'a junction of (the quality) "long" and the category meaning of a noun, which is "entity" or "thing" ', and motion, which is 'a junction of the (the process) "move" and the category meaning, again of a noun'. With grammatical metaphor, the scientist can make the world stand still, or turn it into one consisting only of things, or even create new, virtual realities.

All human adults and all human languages possess this ability to shift from the clausal to the nominal construal of experience, but this inherent potential in the grammar, which enables us to de-couple the lexicogrammatical/semantic interface and to re-couple it with a different ordering, is most characteristic of scientific discourse and the need to construct technical taxonomies and sequential argument.

Selected readings

On Language and Linguistics (Volume 3)

The principle of congruence depends on the association among the three dimensions of rank, metafunction and stratification. It is important because of the potential for departing from it, which is a way of adding to the overall meaning potential.

Departing from the congruent is what we refer to as ***metaphor***. Metaphor is an inherent property of higher-order semiotic systems, and a powerful meaning-making resource.

Let us set up a familiar example of a realizational chain as we find it operating in English. Come back once again to the child's observation man clean car. Semantically, in its experiential mode, this is a *figure*; more specifically, it is a figure of "doing" with a process 'clean', a doer 'man' and a done-to 'car'. This construes one particular instance in the child's experience in such a way as to relate it to a large variety of other instances. Grammatically, the figure is realized by a clause; we can describe it as a selection expression having a number of systemic features including material, effective, doing, dispositive, . . . ; this particular combination of features is realized by the structural configuration Actor · Process · Goal; the Process is realized in the syntagm as a verbal group; the two partici- pants, Actor and Goal, by nominal groups; and the relationship among them by their arrangement in this particular linear sequence. The groups, in turn, have their own distinct sets of features, also with their chains of realization which could be followed through in analogous ways.

Each link in this realizational chain exemplifies the way the grammar is first developed by children learning English as their mother tongue. The child who produced this particular utterance, at twenty-one months of age, was heading rapidly along the path of transition from protolan- guage to post-infancy, adult-like language. By the same token, this is also the pattern in which the language itself first evolved. It is this primary pattern of realization that is being referred to as "congruent". Congruent relations are those that are evolutionarily and developmentally prior, both in the construal of experience (as illustrated here) and in the enacting of interpersonal relationships.

This pattern is a powerful resource with which children make sense of their experience, theorizing it in terms of categories and their relations. The grammar sets up proportionalities which create multiple analogies – numerous and varied dimensions along which different phenomena can be construed as being alike. But its semogenic power is vastly increased when any of these links can be severed and a different chain of realiza- tion can be constructed. In time the child will learn wordings such a *give the car a good clean, a well-cleaned car, the cleaning of the car, car-cleaning materi- als, a carclean* (or at least *a carwash*), and so on.

All these depart in some way from the congruent pattern; they are all to a certain degree metaphorical. The process of metaphor is one of **reconstruing** the patterns of realization in a language – particularly at the interface between the grammar and the semantics. A meaning that was originally construed by one kind of wording comes instead to be construed by another. So, for example, processes are congruently con- strued as verbs; in a carwash, however, a process is realized instead in the form of a noun. But nouns congruently construe entities, not processes;

so something that started off as a 'doing', namely wash, is being recon-strued as if it was a 'thing'.

In calling this "metaphor" I am not indulging in any fancy neologism. I am simply extending the scope of the term from the lexis into the grammar, so that what is being "shifted" is not a specific word – a lexical item – but a word **class**; and I am looking at it from the perspective opposite to that which is traditionally adopted in the discussion of meta-phor: instead of saying "this wording has been shifted to express a differ-ent meaning" (i.e. same expression, different content), I am saying "this meaning has been expressed by a different wording" (same content, dif-ferent expression). We can represent this as in Figures 4 and 5.

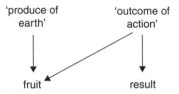

Figure 4 Lexical metaphor

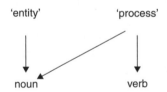

Figure 5 Grammatical metaphor

The point is, however, that it is no longer the same meaning. If a pro-cess (congruently realized by a verb) is reconstrued in the grammar as a noun (which congruently realizes an entity), the result is a semantic hybrid, which combines the features of 'process' and of 'thing'. In an iso-lated instance, such as *taking the car in for a wash*, this is of no great significance. But when large areas of human experience are reconstrued wholesale, through a wide range of different metaphoric processes in the grammar, as has happened in the evolution of the languages of science, the result is dramatic. It is no exaggeration to say that grammatical metaphor is at the foundation of all scientific thought. You cannot con-struct a theory – that is, a designed theory, as distinct from the evolved, commonsense theory incorporated in the grammar of everyday discourse – without exploiting the power of the grammar to create new, "virtual" phenomena by using metaphoric strategies of this kind.

III.Introduction(2003):20–2

* * *

In metaphor in its traditional sense, one **word** moves into the domain of another; looked at from the other end, a lexico-semantic construct that is typically realized by one word is instead realized by another, which typically realizes something else: e.g. *sowed suspicion*, where 'provided grounds for', more typically realized as *caused*, is realized instead by sowed, which typically realizes 'scattered for cultivation'. This kind of metaphor is lexical. In grammatical metaphor, on the other hand, a grammatical-semantic construct that is typically realized by (a member of) one **class** is instead realized by (a member of) another class, which typically realizes something else: e.g. *planetary motion*, where 'process: do, etc', more typically realized as a verb (e.g. *move*), is realized instead by a noun, a class which typically realizes 'participating entity'. As long as we say *planets move* we are still in the realm of the first grammar, the primary semiotic construal of experience, in which the phenomenon is construed as happening (grammatically, a clause), with a process/verb *move* and a participating entity/noun *planets*. When this is reworded as a nominal group *planetary motion*, it takes on the grammar that is characteristic of classes of **things**. And just as in lexical metaphor there is a semantic **junction**, such that *sowed* (in *sowed suspicion*) carries over features of its typical sense as scattering seeds (and the metaphor is readily extended to *seeds of suspicion*), so also there is semantic junction in grammatical metaphor, such that the noun *motion* carries over features of the typical sense of a noun as the name of a participating entity. There now exists a thing called *motion*, and *planetary motion* is one kind, a sub-class of this thing. The sense of 'change location', as in *move*, has become objectified (in Whorf's sense; i.e. 'made into an object'; not 'made objective').

Grammar has always had this potential for "cross-coupling". But it came well to the fore in the classical languages of the iron age, such as Chinese, Sanskrit and Greek, where it became the resource for creating abstract, technical objects: in Greek, on the model of *praxis, poiēsis* 'doing, making' and *pragma, poiēma* 'thing done, thing made', hundreds of verbs were nominalized as technical terms, and these nouns, together with their associated nominal group constructions, formed the core of a new, typically written, mode of discourse. Such "junctional" meanings provide the cornerstones of a **theory**, which is a designed semantic subsystem for reorganizing experience in a technological environment. But then in the "modern" period, with the emergence of experimental science, another major semiotic shift took place, further exploiting the stratal potential of language. In Newton's *Opticks*, for example, we regularly find patterns such as (pp. 156–7): *For in all whites produced by Nature, there uses to be a mixture of all sorts of Rays, and by consequence a composition of all Colours*, where *mixture* and *composition* are not functioning as technical terms; they are instantial nominalizations in which kinds of 'doing' have been construed as temporary 'things' to meet the requirements of the argument – as we find if we track them back in the text: this is preceded by *I could never yet by mixing only two primary Colours produce a perfect white. Whether it may be compounded of a mixture of three . . . I do not know*, where both 'mixing' and 'compounding' start off as verbs. We do not find this kind of discoursal grammatical metaphor in Chaucer's technical writings. But the theorizing discourse of physical science involved sustained reasoning from observation and experiment, and this was achieved by extending the metaphoric potential still further. A typical sequence from modern scientific writing would be the following (*New Scientist* no. 1916, 21 March 1994, p. 37): . . . *rapid changes in the rate of evolution are caused by external events*. Let us look at the textual environment in which this clause occurs.

The previous paragraph contained the clause *life does not evolve gradually but intermittently*; followed by various pieces of observational evidence (e.g. *from the study of fossil records*) and ending with *found . . . that extinctions occur in waves*. The writers now turn all this into a 'thing', *rapid changes in the rate of evolution*, so that they can then take the next step of postulating what brings this phenomenon about (. . . *are caused by* . . .). It happens to be someone else's postulate, but that does not affect the grammatical structure of the argument; the same pattern recurs later in the sentence when they give an example: (*evolutionary biologists have sought*) *an explanation of the demise of the dinosaurs in a meteorite impact*. We now have not only *change, evolution, extinction* but also *demise, impact* construed metaphorically as nouns. This is what enables the argument to proceed; it would be difficult to construct the logical-semantic progression and flow of information from one thesis to another if each had to be construed clausally every time. Thus each step gets "packaged" so that it can become a participant in a further process; and this "process" is itself the outcome of another grammatical metaphor whereby the logical-semantic relation '*x* happens, so *y* happens' is reconstrued in the form of a verb, *caused* – which may then be further metaphorized into a noun *cause* (*is the cause of*; cf. *sought an explanation of* above).

Thus the metaphoric reconstruction of the grammar is adapted to the evolution of forms of discourse embodying technical taxonomies and sequential argument (of which the present sentence is a typical example); it is useful for building theories. By the same token, it brings about a secondary semanticization, a semiotic reconstrual of human experience in which the flux (the "primitive ooze" as Firth used to call it, punning on Greek *protousia*) is not only analysed and "parsed out", as in the clausal grammar of our mother tongues, but made stable, bounded and determinate by the nominalizing grammar of systematic knowledge. Where the grammar of daily life presents the world as a mix of things and going-on, of order and disorder, stability and flux, the elaborated grammar of science reconstrues it as a world of things: it holds the world still, symbolically, while it is observed and measured – and also experimented with and theorized about. If this was the only grammar we had, of course, there would be nothing metaphorical about it; it would be the unmarked mode of categorizing experience. But it is not. **In all three dimensions of semohistory** – the evolution of the language system, the development of each child's meaning potential and the individuated unfolding of the text – **there is the same ordering**: the mixed, more compromising clausal grammar comes first, and the other is built up as an elaboration upon it.[21]

Ontogenetically, the metaphorical grammar comes fairly late: children can master the abstract (meanings without a perceptual correlate) at around age four to five (so this is when we put them into school); but they cannot cope with the metaphorical, in this sense of the semiotic reconstrual of experience, until puberty, the threshold of the adult condition. There seems to be a developmental semiotic progression along the following lines:

classifying:	specific to general	from age 1–2 (into mother tongue)
technicalizing:	concrete to abstract	from age 4–5 (into primary school)
theorizing:	congruent to metaphorical	from age 9–13 (into secondary school)

This is obviously highly schematic; but it draws attention to what I think is an important point. By the time the secondary grammar is developed, the everyday grammar has been in place for some time; it is already deeply installed as a theory of experience. Hence it does not get **replaced** by the metaphorical model; rather, the two co-exist and interpenetrate, and (in most cases at least!) the individual continues to move freely between more and less elaborated modes of discourse. There is no insulation between the two. But there is **conflict** – they cannot both be "true"; and so a complementarity is set up, such that experience has to be modeled from both standpoints in order to get a rounded picture of "reality", one which will enable us to go on interacting in increasingly complex ways with our environment. But the **principle** of semiotic complementarity is nothing new; it is there from the start in the grammar of the mother tongue, where many systems already embody competing and contradictory interpretations of experience: e.g. transitive and ergative as modelings of process, tense and aspect as modellings of time, count and mass as modelings of substance and so on.[22] The coexistence of competing representations is in fact built in to the semiotic mode of activity; that is how it is able to remain in cohort with activities in the material mode.

So it happens that when we come to construct our scientific models, the daily grammar's view of things is very much in the picture, even if typically below the level of conscious attention. This is perhaps especially true when we try to model **ourselves**, as we do when we come to elaborate the concept of "mind". Matthiessen has shown how the object of study of "cognitive science" is constructed out of the grammar of daily life: from the transitivity system of our Standard Average European languages, and in particular from the grammar of mental and symbolic processes (the "grammar of m semiosis", as he puts it). It is quite natural that fundamental domains of human experience, even when theorized at the highest scientific level, should still be grounded in the inherited wisdom of the species, the categorization that lies at the heart of its grammar. But Matthiessen's contention is that this particular development has been one-sided: on the one hand privileging the "mental" over the "symbolic" in the grammar's construal of consciousness, and on the other hand, more broadly, privileging the experiential aspect of the grammar over the interpersonal. We might get a richer, more rounded conception, one less tuned to computational and information-processing notions, if we complemented the folk grammar of 'thinking' with that of 'meaning' (saying, symbolizing); and still more – though much harder to achieve – if we complemented the wisdom deriving from the folk construal of experience with that which could be derived from the enactment of interpersonal relationships (harder because the latter is non-referential: it is "meaning-as-doing" rather than "meaning-as-knowing"). In other words, we can use our grammatics – our metatheory of grammar as theory – as a tool for thinking with, deconstruing the everyday grammar of experience to reveal the assumptions that lie beneath some of our fundamental organizing concepts.[23]

The metaphoric power of grammar is inherent in the stratal organization of language, which enables us to de-couple the lexicogrammatical/ semantic interface and to re-couple it with a different ordering. All human adults can do this; and all human languages, however variable their primary construction of reality, have the same potential for reconstruing in another form. With current advances in biology and physics – not to mention changes in the social order, leading to less elitist and more democratic formations of knowledge – probably in the next period of history we will again be engaging in such a reconstrual. But perhaps the next one will be more of a synthesis, a new semantic arising out of the contradictions between the primary and secondary construals that some of us are living with today.

Notes

21. This metaphoric shift from the clausal to the nominal construal of experience seems to be a characteristic of scientific discourse in every language; for a brief discussion of scientific Chinese in this respect see chapter 7 of Halliday and Martin (1993). We do not know, of course, how much this is the effect of linguistic "borrowing", through translation and other processes of contact. It should be clearly stated that every natural language has the same potential for being extended metaphorically in this way (and also of course in other ways; language is itself an inherently metaphoric process, in its relationship to processes of the material world); the most plausible view would be that the particular form of grammatical metaphor that evolved in English and other "standard" languages of Europe selects for the same (or analogous) patterns from the total potential of other languages as they extend into the registers of science – especially, perhaps, because of the eco-social pressures which require this to happen very fast.

22. On transitive and ergative, see Davidse (1991, 1992); on tense and aspect, see e.g. Dahl (1985); on count and mass, Whorf (1956/1964, esp. pp. 140ff.). Cf. also chapter 6 of Halliday and Martin (1993); Halliday (1967/68).

23. See discussion in Matthiessen (1993a); also Matthiessen (1991) on the "grammar of semiosis".

III.18(1995):419–23, 431

The Language of Early Childhood (Volume 4)

FEATURE 20

But there is yet another reconstruction still to come: that in terms of **grammatical metaphor**. Children know very well, as already remarked, that animals bite and sting. They also know why. Nigel himself said this, quite unprompted, at age 3;5:

> Cats have no else to stop you from tossing them – cats have no other way to stop children from hitting them; so they bite.

Notice how he said it first of all in his own lexicogrammar and then translated it into adult speech. But he could not have expressed it in the way that it is presented in the book. For one thing, children would say *by biting and stinging*, using a verb instead of a noun to name these actions. In the classroom text, meanings that would typically be expressed by verbs, because they are construed as actions, have been represented instead by nouns: *with bites and stings*. The experience has been reconstrued, in metaphorical terms, but with the metaphor being in the grammar, instead of in the vocabulary like metaphor in its traditional sense (Halliday and Martin 1993).

A written text is itself a static object (or has been until the advent of computers): it is language to be processed synoptically. Hence it projects a synoptic perspective onto reality: it tells us to view experience like a text, so to speak. In this way writing changed the analogy between language and other domains of experience; it foregrounded the synoptic aspect, reality as object, rather than the dynamic aspect, reality as process, as the spoken language does. This synoptic perspective is then built into the grammar of the written language, in the form of grammatical metaphor: processes and properties are construed as nouns, instead of as verbs and adjectives. Where the spoken language says *whenever an engine fails, because they can move very fast, . . . happens if people smoke more,* the written language writes *in times of engine failure, rely on their great speed, . . . is caused by increased smoking.*

Pairs of this kind are not synonymous. Each of the two wordings is representing the same phenomenon, but because the prototypical meaning of a noun is a thing, when you construe a process or property as a noun you objectify it: endow it with a kind of "thinginess". It is this particular feature which is at the centre of grammatical metaphor; while numerous other, concomitant changes take place, they combine to form a syndrome around such nominalizations. If there was no natural relationship between the semantics and the grammar, the difference between the two kinds of wording would be purely formal and ritualized; but there **is** such a natural relationship, and so the metaphor brings about a reconstrual of experience, in which reality comes to consist of things rather than doing and happening.

Children apparently do not normally come to grips with grammatical metaphor until they are approaching the age of puberty, say round about the age of nine. We thus have to postulate a three-step model of human semiotic development:

(protolanguage →) generalization → abstractness → metaphor

with a three- to five-year gap between the three post-infancy steps. As grammatical generalization is the key for entering into language, and to systematic common-sense knowledge, and grammatical abstractness is the key for entering into literacy, and to primary educational knowledge, so grammatical metaphor is the key for entering into the next level, that of secondary education, and of knowledge that is discipline-based and technical. As Martin (1990) has shown, specialized technical discourse cannot be created without deploying grammatical metaphor. Such discourse evolved as the language of technology and science, and was moulded by the demands of the physical sciences into its modern form; but today it invades almost every register of adult English that is typically written rather than spoken, especially the institutionalized registers of government, industry, finance, commerce, and the like. We are so familiar with wordings like *prolonged exposure will result in rapid deterioration of the item* (from a care label), *he also credits his former big size with much of his career success* (from a television magazine), that we forget how far these are from the language of daily life – or how far the language of daily life has had to evolve for these to become a part of it.

IV.15(1993):348–9

The Language of Science (Volume 5)

In order to illustrate the metaphoric processes that actually take place, let us look in greater detail at one further example:

Recognition of the tremendous heat resistance of bacterial spores was essential to the development of adequate procedures for sterilisation.

We might try unpacking this as:

Until <people> recognised that bacterial spores could resist <even> being made tremendously hot they could not develop adequate procedures (?) by which <objects> could be made sterile.

125

We could of course offer numerous alternative versions; but these will not change the metaphoric quality of the original. Let me enumerate some of the salient features.

(1) There are various instances of nominalization: processes, and qualities, (re)construed as nouns; e.g. *recognition, resistance, development, sterilisation, heat*. But these are not all of the same kind, nor are they all present for the same reasons.

(a) Some are early technical terms from classical times, e.g. *heat*: Greek θερμον, θερμοτης, derived from θερω 'heat up', meaning 'quality of being hot' or 'measurement of how hot'. This is originally created as a **semantic junction**: a quality construed as a thing – that is, by a class of word (noun) that congruently construes things: so it is in origin a complex element having the features of both. It is taken over, already as a technical term, into Latin *calor* and thence into modern European languages such as English. Since it has become a thing, it can be measured (cf. the expression *quantity of heat*, as used for example by John Dalton in the early nineteenth century); it can be a participant, in different participant roles within the clause; and it can be expanded to form taxonomies using the resources of the nominal group: *latent heat, radiant heat* and so on.

In other words, *heat* has become a technical element in a scientific theory; and in the process, the original metaphor has died. It is now a "dead metaphor". And once it is dead, it can no longer be unpacked. The semogenic process that begins with transcategorising an adjective *hot* into a noun *heat*, whereby a new type of complex phenomenon is brought into being (one that is both 'quality' and 'thing'), is now complete; the semantic feature of 'quality' has been transformed, and there has emerged a virtual thing, a thing that exists on a higher, more abstract level, functioning as part of an ordered chain of explanation. (Hence, just as the **relation** of grammatical metaphor is analogous to that of metaphor in its canonical, lexical sense, so also the **process** whereby a metaphor comes into being, lives, and dies, is also analogous. The only difference is that whereas in classical metaphor one **word** takes over from another, in grammatical metaphor one **grammatical class** takes over from another.)

(b) A similar process has taken place with the term *resistance*, except that here the congruent form is a verb, semantically a process; so the semantic junction that takes place is that of **process** construed as thing. This term also has become technicalized – the metaphor is dead: and it appears in a variety of theoretical contexts from electricity to immunology each with its own specialized taxonomic environment.

(c) Such taxonomies are typically construed in English as Classifier + Thing structures in the nominal group; and here we find these two metaphorical terms combining to form just this structure: *heat resistance*. And once again a semantic junction has taken place. The congruent meaning of this Classifier + Thing structure is 'a kind of', 'a class of'; so *heat resistance* becomes a kind of resistance, analogous (say) to resistance to various kinds of disease or disease bearing agents (e.g. *phylloxera resistance*, resistance to attack by a particular species of louse); *heat resistance* has thus become a complex technical term on its own. We may note that *heat resistance* is not equivalent to *resists being made hot* – heat-resistant bacteria are not bacteria which resist being heated; they are bacteria which survive even when they **are** heated. This grammatical metaphor is also dead; 'heat resistance' is a complex virtual thing, and the metaphor can no longer be unpacked.

(2) Common to all these instances of grammatical metaphor is the fact that they have become **systemic**. We may contrast, in this respect, the word *recognition*. *Recognition was essential* is agnate to *people had to recognize*; here the metaphor is not systemic – it is, and remains, **instantial**. The context for it is purely discursive: the need to organise the information as 'recognise . . . only then could develop', with 'recognise' construed as the Theme, and hence nominalized. This grammatical metaphor is not dead, and can readily be unpacked.

Except in special cases of designed systematic taxonomies, like those of chemistry, and some in medicine, all grammatical metaphors begin as instantial, created in response to the needs of the unfolding discourse. Some of them – the majority, in fact – remain this way, being recreated on each occasion. There is no thing as 'recognition' in the sense in which the word is being used here (there is, of course, in diplomacy, where *recognition* **has** become technicalized). Others become systemic: that is, they become systemic options within the meaning potential of a given register. This is a normal semogenic process within languages as a whole; what creates technical terminology is the combination of two processes: **from instantial to systemic and from congruent to metaphorical**.

(3) It would be wrong, however, to equate grammatical metaphor with nominalization. Nominalization is predominant, in the sense that most metaphoric shift is shift into a nominal group. But not all of it is. This is not the sole driving force, even in technical discourse: one that is perhaps equally critical in this context is the experientializing of logical-semantic relationships: that is, reconstruing 'so' as *cause*, 'then' as *follow* and so on. In this sentence there is a sequence of two processes, 'recognizing' and 'making sterile', with a relator 'only then' (or, in English, 'not until') between them. The congruent construal of this relationship is as a nexus of two clauses joined by a conjunction. We can set up the principle of

congruence between semantic and grammatical categories in the following way:

Congruence in rank		Congruence in status (elements)	
semantic	*grammatical*	*semantic*	*grammatical*
sequence	clause nexus	thing (entity)	noun (/nominal group)
figure	clause	quality	adjective (in nominal group)
element	group/phrase	process	verb (/verbal group)
		circumstance (1)	adverb (/adverbial group)
		circumstance (2)	prepositional phrase
		minor process	preposition
		relator	conjunction

The grammatical metaphor thus shifts both the rank and the class status:
the sequence, from being a clause nexus, becomes a single clause; and
the relator, from being a conjunction, becomes typically a verb – in this
instance, there is a further shift whereby the relator is nominalized to
become an adjective *essential*. And here again there is a semantic junction: a verb such as *cause, follow, result in* is **both** process **and** relator. It
may then become further metaphorised into a noun, such as *cause* or
consequence; this in turn may become technicalised, the metaphor dies,
and the instances can no longer be unpacked.

These are some of the grammatical metaphors contained in that particular sentence. I have discussed them, rather sketchily, case by case, with
just passing reference to the general principles involved. A summary of
the types of grammatical metaphor I have come across in analysing typical passages of technical discourse in English is given in Figure 2.3 (for a
fuller account see Halliday and Matthiessen 1999).

The interesting question that arises is: is there a single principle that
we can observe to lie behind these various shifts – a 'general drift' in the
direction taken by all the varied types of grammatical metaphor? I think
there is; it seems that we can discern a pattern as set out in Figure 2.4,
where the arrows numbered 1–10 show the various metaphoric movements that are found to be taking place. The general drift is, in fact, a
drift towards the concrete, whereby each element is reconstrued in the
guise of one that lies further towards the pole of stability and persistence
through time. Thus, entities are more stable than qualities, and qualities
than processes; while logical semantic relators like 'and', 'or', 'but', 'then',
'so', are the least stable – and hence the most complex – of all.

Key to figure:	semantic element	grammatical class
	grammatical function	example

1. quality ⇒ entity	adjective ⇒ noun
Epithet = Thing	unstable = instability

2. process ⇒ entity	verb ⇒ noun
(i) Event → Thing	transform ⇒ transformation
(ii) Auxiliary = Thing	
(tense)	will/going to = prospect
(phase)	try to = attempt
(modality)	can/could = possibility, potential

3. circumstances ⇒ entity	preposition ⇒ noun
Minor Process = Thing	with = accompaniment; to = destination

4. relator = entity	conjunction ⇒ noun
Conjunctive = Thing	so = cause/proof; if = condition

5. process ⇒ quality	verb ⇒ adjective
(i) Event ⇒ Epithet	[poverty] is increasing = increasing [poverty]
(ii) Auxiliary =	
(tense)	was/used to = previous
(phase)	begin to = initial
(modality)	must/will [always] = constant

6. circumstance ⇒ quality	adverb/prepositional phrase ⇒ adjective*
(i) Manner = Epithet	[decided] hastily = hasty [decision]
(ii) Other = Epithet	[argued] for a long time = lengthy [argument]
(iii) Other = Classifier	[cracked] on the surface ⇒ surface [cracks]

7. relator ⇒ quality	conjunction ⇒ adjective
Conjunctive = Epithet	then = subsequent; so = resulting

8. circumstance ⇒ process	*be / go* + preposition ⇒ verb
Minor Process = Process	be about = concern; be instead of = replace

Figure 2.3 Typology of grammatical metaphors

9. relator ⇒ process	conjunction ⇒ verb
Conjunctive = Event	then = follow; so = cause; and = complement
10. relator = circumstance	conjunction ⇒ preposition/-al group
Conjunctive = Minor Process	when = in times of/in ... times
	if = under conditions of/under ... conditions
11. [zero] ⇒ entity	| = the phenomenon of ...
12. [zero] ⇒ process	| = ... occurs/ensues
13. entity ⇒ [expansion]	noun ⇒ [various] (in env. 1, 2 above)
Head = Modifier	the government [decided] = the government's [decision], [a/the decision] of/by the government, [a] government(al) [decision] the government [couldn't decide/was indecisive] = the government's [indecision], [the indecision] of the government, government(al) [indecision]

* or noun; cf. mammal [cells]/mammalian [cells]

Figure 2.3 Cont'd

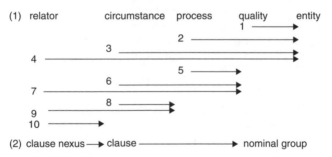

(1) relator   circumstance process   quality   entity

(2) clause nexus → clause → nominal group

Figure 2.4 The 'general drift' of grammatical metaphor: (1) status, (2) rank

V.2(1998):37–43

Studies in Chinese Language (Volume 8)

The phenomenon I would like to talk about has no general name; so let me give it one, and call it grammatical metaphor. It is related to metaphor in the normal sense – in fact it is metaphor in the normal sense; but whereas metaphor as we usually understand it is a lexical phenomenon, illustrated by such familiar transferences as *flow* in *flow of ideas*, *source* in *the source of the trouble, current* in *currents of opinion, tide* in *stem the tide of inflation, ooze* in *he oozes geniality* and so on, the kind of metaphor I am referring to is grammatical rather than lexical, although in any particular expression we often find both of these coming together.

Let me exemplify from English. Suppose we read in a report of a mountaineering expedition:

The fifth day saw them at the summit.

There are various things to note about this clause. First, is that at one level it ought to be wrong, ungrammatical, because it contains a verb of mental process *see*, in active voice, with an unconscious entity as subject, *the fifth day*. Days cannot see. Second, a competent speaker of English knows that this is metaphorical, and can compare it with its nonmetaphorical agnate *on the fifth day they arrived at the summit*. A machine translation programme, say from English to Chinese, could demetaphorize it in either of two ways: (i) by replacing it in English with the non-metaphoric form, and then translating it 第五天他們達到了山頂 *Dìwǔ tiān tāmen dádàole shāndǐng*, or (ii) by translating it as it stands 第五天看見他們在山頂上 *Dìwǔ tiān kànjiàn tāmen zài shāndǐngshàng*, and then rewriting it in acceptable Chinese. There are advantages and disadvantages in either approach; which of the two works better will tend to depend on the socio-semantico-grammatical **distance** between the two languages (the closer they are, the more likely the second solution is to pay off).

Examples of this kind are reasonably clear; their metaphoric nature is obvious, because of internal contradictions (here between *day* and *see*). The only question is, why is the metaphoric form used? No doubt this is partly for rhetorical embellishment: such locutions carry a certain value in certain types of context. But there are other more systematic semantic and communicative reasons why this metaphoric form is used: it enables *the fifth day* to function as the unmarked Theme of the clause – that is, in initial position as Subject, and thus gets the message structured the way the writer wants it. If we put *on the fifth day* first, as in the non-metaphoric form, it is still thematic, but it is **marked** Theme, because it is not the Subject, and hence carries foregrounding that the writer may not want. In other words, the motivation lies in what the Prague school called the "functional sentence perspective".

But many instances of grammatical metaphor fall into one or other of two kinds which are rather less tractable, whether to the language student or to the programmer:

(1) learned metaphors, typical of written language, especially rather weighty written language – scientific, bureaucratic, etc. – to which

we *can* find non-metaphoric equivalents, even though it is sometimes not very easy; and

(2) everyday metaphors, belonging to the system of the language
(automatized, or "dead" in rhetorical terms), which have taken
over the field and become a natural mode of expression.

There is no sharp line between the two, but they may need different
treatment in relation to particular tasks. For both these classes of metaphor we can usually find some explanation by relating them to general
features of the system of the language, although the explanation may
involve a fairly long and complex chain of reasoning.

I would like to consider mainly the everyday kind of metaphors, but
let me look briefly at the learned ones first. These are expressions like

braking distance increases more rapidly at high speeds

(to date) this latter proposition has not been pursued into practice

advances in technology are speeding up the writing of business programmes

sex differences in cognitive style have been observed in a wide variety of
groups

the analysis of the processes of social structural change requires a historical
perspective

In order to demetaphorize examples like these we have to sort out which
are the *processes* (actions, events, mental processes, relations), which are
the *participants* in the processes, and which are the *circumstantial*
elements associated with them. So the last one might be 'interpreted'
(reworded) as *if we want to analyse how the structure of society changes we must
study it over a long period of time.* Learned metaphors of this kind tend to
occur in all learned languages. Presumably we could render this into
Chinese as something like 社會結構變遷程序的分析需要歷史上的觀點
Shèhuì jiégòu biànqiān chéngxù de fēnxī xūyào lìshǐshangde guāndiǎn. I do not
know whether such patterns evolve independently in different languages,
or whether they are borrowed, spreading out by processes of language
contact from Western European languages (especially English). But they
appear to be generally associated with these registers, and to be felt as
reasonably natural (otherwise people would not need to protest about
them, which they do from time to time). Hence to learn the Chinese
equivalent is not a major problem for the student; one just takes over the
metaphor. The non-metaphoric form would also go readily into Chinese:

我們如果想要分析社會的結構怎麼樣來變化，就必須長期的研究

In other words, not only are both forms possible in both languages, but there is the same kind of relationship between them. Note that the metaphoric form would not have been possible in the English of Swift or the Chinese of Cao Xueqin; at least I think not.

Not all instances are quite so easy to handle as this one. Consider

braking distance increases more rapidly at high speeds

I find this difficult to translate into English, let alone into Chinese. You can say *the faster you're going the longer it takes to stop*, but that is not the whole story; what it means is *the faster you're going the more the time it takes to stop gets longer*. This is one interesting example of a concept, namely 'rate of acceleration', which is simply not coded in the ordinary non-metaphoric grammar of English. I do not know how to translate that into Chinese of any kind; but I suspect that in Chinese too it would be easier to represent it metaphorically – that is, it would be easier to translate it horizontally, at the same metaphoric level, than diagonally into some non-metaphoric form. Incidentally, it is difficult to find any systematic studies of concepts of this kind, concepts for which the language lacks a coded, non-metaphorical mode of expression.

These things tell us very little about the nature of the socio-semantic distance between English and Chinese. They show that both languages are used for learned purposes, which we know already; and they suggest that when a language develops for such functions it will always develop along the same lines, although it will never be possible to prove this. We can never know what would have happened to the Chinese language if the processes of technological and economic change that were starting in the Song dynasty had not been arrested and deflected instead of leading on, as happened in England five hundred years later, to an industrial revolution. But it is not improbable that the changes that take place reflect the vast range of new functions that languages are called upon to serve, the increased demands on their overall semantic resources, a process that we are seeing again today as our languages are further extended to cope with moving into the high technology age.

Let me pass on, however, to look at the category of everyday metaphors. There are two kinds of these: the interpersonal, having to do with the mood, modality and key of the clause, and the ideational, having to do with transitivity, the clause in its representational function. An example of an interpersonal metaphor in English is found in the expression

I don't think he's coming

In fact there are two metaphors here. First, a non-metaphoric form would be something like *probably* or *in my opinion he isn't coming*. Now, by one of these metaphors the modality *probably* has been represented as the primary clause *I think*. We can tell that this is a metaphor because the tagged form is

I think he's coming, isn't he?

not *I think he's coming don't I?* which would be the appropriate form if the clause was really a clause about my thoughts. Second, in addition to the modal metaphor there is a polarity metaphor whereby the negative has gone into the primary clause; so, *I don't think he's coming*, instead of *I think he isn't coming*. Compare *it isn't likely he's coming* instead of *it's likely he isn't coming*. Note that both of these metaphorical clauses are on the face of it absurd: you cannot have non-thoughts and negative probabilities. If we compare the Chinese pattern, Chinese accepts the first of these metaphors: 我想他會來 *Wǒ xiǎng tā huì lái* as semantically related to 他大概會來 *Tā dàgài huì lái*. Note here again that if I say 我想他會來 and you answer 對 *Duì* then the question at issue is 他來不來 *Tā lái bùlái* and not 我想不想 *Wǒ xiǎng bùxiǎng*. But Chinese does not accept the second; you cannot normally say 我不想他會來 *Wǒ bù xiǎng tā huì lái*, as far as I am aware.

Another type of interpersonal metaphor is the familiar type studied in speech act theory, in which one speech function is represented metaphorically as another; for example, *I wouldn't do that if I was you, do that again and I'll clobber you*, both usually regarded as embellished forms of 'don't do that (again)!' Chinese, like (presumably) all languages, has plenty of this kind; for example 你不如不再繼續這樣做才好，你再次這樣 做就 會挨打 *Nǐ bùrú bù zài jìxù zhèyàng zuò cái hǎo, nǐ zàicì zhèyàng zuò jiù húi ái dǎ*. It is not their existence that causes a problem to the learner, but the specific principles on which those in the second language are constructed. The student of Chinese who asks for directions and gets the familiar answer 恐怕你一個人一定找不到 *Kǒngpà nǐ yīge rén yīdìng zhǎobúdào* 'I'm afraid you wouldn't be able to find it on your own' has to guess whether this means 'don't go there', or 'I'll come with you' or 'I don't know the way; ask someone else!' But many of the examples cited in speech act theory are conventional mannerisms that do not have any general validity as grammatical principles. Many ideational metaphors, on the other hand, are built into the grammar of every language. One common type in English is that exemplified by

he has black hair
I have a sore arm

These the student learns very early on do not go into Chinese, where the process must be represented congruently as an attributive clause, such as 他(的) 頭髮黑, 我胳臂疼 *Tā (de) tóu fa hēi, wǒ gēbei téng*, not metaphorically as a possessive clause, such as 他有黑頭髮, 我有一個疼胳臂。 *Ta yǒu hēi tóufa, wǒ yǒu yīgo téng gēbei* These have arisen in English so that the pronoun can function as the unmarked Subject Theme; in other words, the clause is about me or him, not about hairs or arms. In Chinese this message structure is achieved without the aid of this grammatical device, since there is no need to use the pronoun as a possessive.

A second type common in English is that of *she gave a smile, he had a bath, I made a mistake, they did a dance*, where the process is represented not as a verb, which would be its congruent form as in *she smiled, he bathed, I erred, they danced*, but as a noun. The noun functions as what in traditional grammar was labelled a "cognate object", with the verb being one of the semantically "empty" words *do, have, give, make, take*.

Again it is not difficult to find the motivation for this structure; the process is nominalized in order that it can be quantified and/or qualified, as in *she gave a welcoming smile, he had a relaxing hot bath, I made two serious mistakes, they did this well-known Rumanian folk dance* and so on. This has its parallel in the Chinese constructions like 洗澡, 犯錯誤, perhaps also 跳舞 (cf. 跳了那個很有名的羅馬尼亞的民舞) *xǐzǎo, fàncuòwù, (tiàole nèige hěn yǒumíngde Luómǎníyàde mínwǔ)* although not all the same set of processes exist in both languages. In Chinese the process tends to be specified twice: 跳了一個舞 *Tiàole yīge wǔ* not 做了一個舞 *Zuòle yīge wǔ.* We might say 他給了一個微笑 *Tā gěile yīge wēixiào*, but certainly not 他有了一個澡 *Tā yǒule yīge zǎo.* The pattern is more like English *play a game*, where *play* and *game* are both names of playing.

Both these types are metaphorical in origin, although now they are fully coded in the system of the language. They have become the unmarked forms. The reason in each case is a textual one: to get the message organized in the way that is appropriate at that point in the discourse. Let us look at one other type in English, a type not obviously recognizable as metaphorical although in fact it is, where the same motivation emerges very clearly. For example:

> they called the meeting off
> they left the best part out

where the process is represented as verb plus discontinuous adverb: *call + off* ('cancel'), *leave + out* ('omit'). Before we look for an equivalent in Chinese, let us explain this construction in English. Why is it so highly favoured, especially in the spoken language? The answer is to be sought in this discourse structure, and it is entirely systematic. Suppose we have the following piece of dialogue:

What are you doing here? I thought you were in Canberra.
They cancelled the meeting. / They called off the meeting.

There is nothing to choose between the two forms of the response. But suppose the initiating turn had been:

What are you doing here? I thought you were at a meeting.

If I want to give a non-metaphoric response, using the verb *cancel*, I have to say:

They *cancelled* the meeting.

Note that the focus of information, signalled by tonic prominence, is now on *cancel*, because *meeting* has already been mentioned, and therefore is treated as Given. But in English the unmarked place for the tonic prominence is at the end; the result, therefore, is a form that is **marked**, and marked information focus is typically contrastive ('they cancelled the meeting; they didn't just postpone it'), whereas this is not the meaning that is intended. What is required is a form with the focus unmarked, in other words with 'cancel' coming at the end. There are two ways of achieving this. One is to use the passive, *the meeting was cancelled*, and the fact that the passive solves this problem is the main reason why it is used as frequently as it is in spoken English. But the passive is marked in another dimension – it is the marked term in the voice system; so another strategy has evolved, that of splitting the verb into two parts. Instead of *cancel* we use *call off*; and this allows the *off* to come at the end, where it can carry the tonic in its unmarked place:

They called the meeting *off*.

(This is why, if the object is a pronoun, it almost always comes **before** the adverb, since a pronoun is by definition 'given'.) Hence the strong preference for phrasal verbs, which represent the process metaphorically, rather than single word verbs in spoken English. In written English, of course, there is no such pressure, so phrasal verbs are felt as rather colloquial.

Chinese is like English in two respects that are relevant here: (1) it is a Subject–Verb–Object (SVO) language, (2) the information focus typically comes at the end. But Chinese has no phrasal verbs. In Chinese, the problem is solved by another metaphor, the 把 metaphor. As in English, this also involves pretending to split the process into two; but in Chinese you first 'grasp' the object, and then do something to it:

他們把會議取消了　　*Tāmen bǎ huìyì qǔxiāole*

Note that there is a proportionally here between Chinese and English, as shown in the following pairs:

我扔掉了我的破衣服	is to	我把我的破衣服扔掉了
Wǒ rēngdiàole wǒde pò yīfu		*Wǒ bǎ wǒde pò yīfu rēngdiàole*
	as	

I {discarded / threw away} my old clothes　is to　I threw my old clothes away

Like the English, moreover, the Chinese construction is also subject to a phonological restriction: the verb in a 把 clause must contain at least two syllables, to carry the weight of the information. If the lexical verb does not consist of two syllables, the second syllable must be made up by the aspectual marker. Likewise in English, a phrasal verb must have at least two syllables: *eat + up*, *put + out*, etc.

What lies behind the similarity in these two constructions is the fact that Chinese and English share a common concern with getting the message right. Specifically, each language is concerned to make it clear what the speaker is on about, which it does by identifying a ***thematic*** element – signalled by position at the beginning of the clause; and each language is concerned to make it clear what the speaker wants the learner to attend to, which it does by identifying a ***focal*** element – signalled by tonic prominence, but with favourite (unmarked) position at the end. In English, this feature is part of a very general pattern which pervades the grammar in numerous ways; superficially very disparate but all part of a highly coherent (but at the same time highly unstable) design. I am sure that in Chinese there is an equally coherent pattern, probably also in process of continuous change. Chinese, of course, is very far from having the same semantic system as that of English; but in this particular respect, the organization of the clause as a message in the context of the discourse, there are striking instances of similarity.

These features of grammatical metaphor, therefore, provide some interesting clues to the general fashions of meaning in a language, its overall semantic styles. Those of the everyday kind – and there are certainly many other features of Chinese that belong in this category – have become part of the linguistic system, for one reason or another. The reason is usually, it seems, something to do with the structure of discourse, the way the individual messages are represented in clause structure to give the language its natural texture. Such metaphors are learnt by children very early, as part of the foundation of the linguistic system. Those of a more learned kind, which children do not learn till much later – typically not until early adolescence – and tend to find rather difficult at first, also relate to the overall texture of the language, but in a different way and only in certain registers. These seem to represent tendencies common to the elaborated discourse of science and technology, government and bureaucracy, in all languages. Both types require a great deal of further study, not only to help in the more effective teaching of languages but also as a contribution to our general understanding of grammar, discourse structure and semantic styles.

VIII.7(1984):325–33

Additional readings

On Grammar (Volume 1) – 9(1981); 10(1985):282; Editor's Introduction:290; 12(1987):346–8; 13(1992):358–60; 15(1996): 397, 401

Linguistic Studies of Text and Discourse (Volume 2) – 2(1977); 5(1987):160,164; Editor's Introduction:195–6; 7(1992):219–23, 226; 8(1994): 242

On Language and Linguistics (Volume 3) – 5(1987):130–4; 6(1990); 8(1985):192; 10(1993):231; 12(1997); 13(2001): 282, 284–5; 16(1992): 366; 17(1992): 384, 388; 18(1995):415, 431

The Language of Early Childhood (Volume 4) – 15(1993):339–40, 347–9; 16(1999):367–9

The Language of Science (Volume 5) – 1(1995): 7–23; 2(1998): 32–7, 39; 3(1998): 49–101; 4(1999): 102–134; Editor's Introduction:137–9; 5(1988): 143, 147–52, 156–7; 6(1989): 162, 171–9; 7(1997):190–7; 8(1993):214–6, 220–5

Computational and Quantitative Studies (Volume 6) – 3(1991); 4(1991); 5(1992):86; 9(1995); 10(1995); 11(1995):265

Studies in Chinese Language (Volume 8) – Editor's Introduction:323; 8(1993):339–44

Language and Education (Volume 9) – 4(1979); 5(1988):91; 6(1996):105–10, 117, 123, 126–8; 14(1986): 301–3; 15(1994):323; 18(1990); 19(1994):379, 381

Language and Society (Volume 10) – 8(1994):239, 243–4; 10(1976):278

Chapter Six

GRAMMATICS

Summary

Linguistics is language about language – or as Halliday quotes Firth, "language turned back on itself." Parallel to linguistics as the study of language is grammatics as the study of grammar. A grammar is a theory of experience of everyday life. It is that abstract stratum of coding between meaning and expression; it is a resource for making meaning. Grammatics, on the other hand, is a theory of grammar; it is a theory for explaining how the grammar constructs a theory of experience. Grammatics is theorizing about a theory; it is a theory of a second order, a part of a more general theory of meaning. Grammatics, i.e. metagrammar, enables one to reflect consciously on how the grammar enables one to unconsciously construe experience.

Selected readings

On Grammar (Volume 1)

But when it comes to metalinguistic matters, linguistics presents a special case. It is not just another science. It is 'language turned back on itself', to use Firth's (very British) expression; or, in Weinreich's (very American) formulation, 'language as its own metalanguage'. As a consequence, where other sciences need two terms, we need three: one for the phenomenon, and two for the metaphenomenon, one grammatical and the other semantic. To return to the example of number: we need to be able to say that the grammatical category of 'plural' typically expresses (realizes) the semantic category of, say, 'manifold', which typically expresses (redounds with) more than one of a thing.

But notice what has happened. The grammatical category of 'plural' was set up in the first place to account for a morphological phenomenon:

suppose this had been in English, then the *–s* / *–z* / *–iz* of *cats, dogs* and *horses*. At this point, therefore, we ought to have come round in a circle: *–s* / *–z* / *–iz* means *–s* / *–z* / *–iz*. But instead we have tried to escape from the circle by finding a gloss for *–s* / *–z* / *–iz* – that is, an exact synonym for it, in natural language wording; and that is an extremely difficult thing to do. We might try glossing it as more than one, or several, or many; but the trouble is we don't actually say *I like more than one cat*, or *I like many cat* – we say *I like cats*. The meaning of the *–s* on *cats* is impossible to gloss in natural language, except by means of itself. The category is, quite simply, ineffable.

2 DIFFICULTIES WITH THE SUBJECT

Why should this be so? One hypothesis might be that natural languages are not good things for glossing with; in that connection, Reddy remarked, 'As a metalanguage, English, at least, is its own worst enemy.' We can certainly point to some deplorable habits that English has, both in its vocabulary and in its grammar. For example, we frequently use the same lexical item to stand both for the study of a particular phenomenon and for the phenomenon itself, as when we talk of someone's *psychological make-up* instead of their *psychic make-up*. It can be disastrous for students of linguistics (not to mention the general public) that *grammar* is both the name of a stratum in language and the name for the study of that stratum; and likewise with *phonology* and *semantics*. Not even the conduit metaphor excuses a ragged polysemy such as these.

Even worse are some of English's grammatical pathologies. For our metalinguistic **vocabulary**, we usually draw on some parallel semiotic as already illustrated, bringing in new words so as to be freed from the accumulated associations of the old ones. (The freedom is often short-lived, since the new term may soon be borrowed into the daily language, like the *psychological* above.) But for the grammar of our metalanguages we are usually content to stick with the everyday forms of English; and this can lead to serious misconstructions – such as the following, perpetrated by myself, when I wrote some time ago:

the Theme of an English clause is the element that is put in first position.

Now I meant this as Value ^ Token, with *is* meaning 'is represented by'. But all such clauses in English, if they have the verb *be*, are ambiguous; and this one was frequently misread as Token ^ Value, with *is* taken to mean 'represents'. In other words, a clause that was intended to say how the Theme in English is to be recognized was taken as a statement of how it is to be defined – one of the most fundamental confusions in linguistics.

It would all have been avoided if the verb *be* had had a passive; I should, therefore, have created the appropriate metagrammar and written:

> The Theme of an English clause is been by the element that is put in first position.

So there are problems in using natural language as a metalanguage, for whatever purpose: its logical and ideational systems were not designed for the task. Some combinations of features may be realized in ways that are ambiguous, others may carry a baggage of unwanted corollaries, and so on (this does sometimes lead to the creation of minor neologisms in the grammar, like the prepositional phrases that appear in the language of mathematics (I mean mathematical English) such as *the inequations over O, symmetry about a certain point for various angles of rotation*). And using natural language as a metalanguage for natural language itself is likely to inflate the problems still further, since whatever shortcomings it has are compounded by the factor of self-reference – the metalanguage being a form of the same semiotic system that it is also being used to describe.

The problem of self-reference is a familiar one; nevertheless it is not the central issue. The real problem lies in the nature of language as object, and particularly the nature of lexicogrammar. It is not so much that language is not good for glossing with. The problem is rather that language is not good for being glossed.

I.11(1984):296–8

★ ★ ★

Let me first say what I mean by "grammar" in the title of the paper. I mean the lexicogrammatical stratum of a natural language as traditionally understood, comprising its syntax and vocabulary, together with any morphology the language may display: Lamb's "lexical system", in his current (1992: Chapter 5) 'three-level architecture' – in commonsense terms, the resources of **wording** in which the meanings of a language are construed. And here I have in mind particularly the evolved, spontaneous grammar that construes the discourse of daily life. This is not to exclude from the picture the elaborated grammars of scientific and other metalanguages; but these can only be understood as what they are: an outgrowth, supported by design, of the original grammar that is learnt at mother's knee and on father's shoulders.

Now English is not very efficient at creating technical nomenclature, since it tends to confuse the study of a phenomenon with the phenomenon itself. So while the term "grammar" is commonly used in the way in which I have defined it, to mean the wording system, the central processing unit of a natural language, it is also used indiscriminately to mean the **study** of that system: grammar$_2$ meaning 'the study of grammar$_1$'. Since the study of language is called "linguistics", I have been calling the study of grammar "grammatics" in order to make the distinction clearer. A grammatics is thus a theory for explaining grammar.

But is not a grammar itself also a theory? Clearly it is. A grammar is a resource for meaning, the critical functioning semiotic by means of which we pursue our everyday life. It therefore embodies a **theory** of everyday life; otherwise it could not function in this way. A grammar is a theory of human experience: or rather, let us say, it **includes** a theory of experience, because it is also something else besides. Like any other theory, a grammar is something to think with. It is through grammar that we make sense out of our experience, both of the world we live in (what we experience as taking place "out there") and of the world that lives in us (what we experience as taking place "in here", inside our own consciousness), construing a "reality" such that the one can be reconciled against the other (Matthiessen 1991; Halliday and Matthiessen 1999).

During the past twenty years leading neurobiologists, such as Harry Jerison and John Allman, have been investigating the way the brain evolved; and they explain its evolution as the evolution of the organism's resource for constructing reality. Changes in the ecological environment require changes in the representation of experience (Edelman 1992; Lemke 1993). One critical step was the evolution of the cerebral cortex, which transformed the mammalian map of the external environment. The second was the evolution of language, which added a new dimension to reality, that of introspective consciousness; this latter step is associated with the development of the prefrontal zone of the cortex, allowing a major reorganization of neural circuitry (Dunbar 1992). Linguists can show that the corresponding unique feature of human language, distinguishing it from semiotic systems of other genera and species, is that it has a grammar, an abstract stratum of coding in between the meaning and the expression. Grammar is what brings about the distinctively human construction of reality; and by the same token, grammar makes it possible for us to reflect on this construction.

As a teacher I have often said to my students that they should learn to 'think grammatically'. By this I mean that they should use the unique power of the human brain to reflect on the way their experience is construed in their grammar: use grammatics to think about what grammar thinks about the world. I suggest they might do this with problems of any kind, such as relationships with family and friends, or whether to go for the job that pays more or for the one they would more enjoy. Let me give a small example of what I mean by thinking grammatically. You're feeling a bit down. What's the matter, someone asks. 'I have a headache.' So how does the grammar construe your unfortunate condition? Of course, **you** construed it, using your grammatical potential; but you did so quite unconsciously, in the way that it has been done countless other times by countless other people, so it is reasonable to talk about the condition being construed 'by the grammar'.

In *I have a headache* the grammar construes a kind of thing, called an *ache*; it then uses a part of the body to classify this thing, setting up a taxonomy of aches including *stomachache, backache* and various others. (Not all the parts of the body are allowed to *ache*, however; you cannot have a *footache* or a *thighache*.) The grammar then sets up a configuration of possession between the ache and some conscious being, in this case the speaker *I*. The speaker becomes the owner of one specimen of that complex class of things. It is not a prototypical form of possession; the possessor does not want the thing possessed but cannot get rid of it – cannot give it away, or put it back where it came from. Why then does the grammar not favour *my head aches*; or *my head's aching?* – in which the aching is a process, a state of being, rather than a thing, and the entity involved in that state of being is my head rather than me. The grammar has no trouble in constructing the clause *my head aches*; yet it is not the most usual way in which the experience is worded. Why is *I have a headache* preferred instead?

In English, as in many other languages (though not all), there is a particular meaning associated with being the first element in the clause. What is put first is being instated by the speaker as the theme of the coming message; it is the setting for the information that follows (Fries 1995). This pattern of the clause, a structure of "Theme + Rheme", was apparently identified by the earliest rhetorical grammarians of ancient Greece, the sophists, who seem to have recognized in the thematic organization of the clause a potent resource for constructing legal and political discourse. In modern times it was first investigated in detail by Mathesius, the founder of the Prague school; it is a particularly prominent feature of English, appearing not only in the clause but also as a "fractal" pattern in both smaller and larger structures – inside word groups, both nominal and verbal, on the one hand and extending over a nexus of clauses on the other. The following example, taken from natural conversation, shows thematic predication of a whole clause complex (from Svartvik and Quirk 1980: 304):

. . . in my last year at college I said to myself: "You want to do applied chemistry, right? What industries are now just being born which will blossom in the next quarter of a century, which is going to be my working lifetime?" And I said "Plastics, sure as the nose on your face. I'm going to get into this." . . .

I'm dazzled, you know . . . It's being able to see your working life will span a period in which so–&-so is the topmost industry which I find so dazzling.

Now if I say *my head aches*, the first element in that clause is *my head*: I have constructed a message in which *my head* is enunciated as Theme. My head is instated as what I want to elaborate on. But it isn't; I'm the one that's suffering, so the Theme of the clause should more appropriately be 'me'. How does the grammar accommodate this alternative? Most naturally, by making 'me' the Subject, since there is a strong association of these two functions in English. The 'ache' becomes a thing separated from myself, something that I possess, with my head identified as its location: *I have an ache in my head*. Better still, if my head is used as a classifier, the ache and its location become a single complex thing; and this now occupies the culminative position in the clause: *I have a headache*. The flow of information here is very different from that of *my head's aching*.

If this was just a feature of the grammar of localized aches and pains, it might remain a curiosity, a special effect rather than a principle. But this pattern has evolved in English as the prototypical form for construing bodily qualities and states; rather than *her hair is long, his throat is sore*, we tend to say *she has long hair, he has a sore throat*, putting the person rather than the body part into the thematic role.[1] And in certain other languages where initial position is thematic we also regularly find the person, rather than the body part, lodged at the beginning of the clause. The overall patterns are of course different: in particular, there may be no strong bond between Theme and Subject, and this makes it clear that the relevant function is that of Theme. We can give examples from Chinese, Russian and French. In Chinese it is possible to say *wǒdi tóu tèng* 'my head aches', where as in the English *wǒdi tóu* 'my head' is a single element in the clause and so functions as the Theme. The preferred form, however, is *wǒ tóu tèng* 'me the headaches', where the 'head' is detached from the personal pronoun; *wǒ* 'me' and *tóu* 'head' are now independent elements in the clause and only the first one, *wǒ*, is thematic. Again, this is the typical pattern for all such expressions in Chinese: *tā tóufǎ cháng* 'her the hair (is) long', *tā hóulóng tòng* 'him the throat (is) sore' and so on. In Russian, likewise, one can say *moja golova bolit* 'my head aches'; but this also is not the preferred form. Russian however displays a different pattern: *u menja golova bolit* 'at me the head aches', where again it is the 'me' that has thematic status. In French instead of *ma tête me fait mal* 'my head is hurting me' one can use possession as in English: *j'ai mal à la tête* 'I have an ache at the head'. French also has a further device, of detaching the Theme altogether from the structure of the clause, and announcing it as a key signature at the beginning: *moi j'ai mal à la tête* 'me I've got an ache at the head'. Neither Chinese *wǒ* nor Russian *u menja* nor French *moi* is Subject; what they have in common is the status of Theme.

At this point we might think once more of the sufferer and say to him or her: pity you've got a headache. But try de-construing this, in the grammar, and then re-construing it – rewording it – as *my head aches;* or better still *my head's aching*, which makes it an external rather than an internal phenomenon. This is rather less self-centered: it is no longer a fact about me, and my inner self, but an external fact about my head. This won't make the headache go; but it does put it in its place. It has now become a problem of my head, which is just one part of my physical make-up. One might offer this as a form of logotherapy, a kind of grammatical acupuncture. But here I just want it to serve as an instance of "thinking grammatically".

Thus the grammar enables us, unconsciously, to interpret experience; and the metagrammar, or grammatics, enables us to reflect consciously on how it does so. The grammatics, of course, is part of a more general theory of meaning: of language as a semiotic system, and of other semiotic systems brought into relation with language. Without such a general theory, the excursion into other languages is no more than a piece of tourism; it assumes significance only when we can show how this small corner of experience is construed in relation to the meaning potential of each language as a whole.

I.14(1998):369–73

* * *

1 THE PROBLEM

Most of us are familiar with the feeling that there must be something odd about linguistics. We recognize this as a problem in the interpersonal sphere because as linguists, probably more than other professionals, we are always being required to explain and justify our existence. This suggests, however, that others see it as a problem in the ideational sphere.

The problem seems to arise from something like the following. All systematic knowledge takes the form of 'language about' some phenomenon; but whereas the natural sciences are language about nature, and the social sciences are language about society, linguistics is language about language – "language turned back on itself", in Firth's often quoted formulation. So, leaving aside the moral indignation some people seem to feel, as if linguistics was a form of intellectual incest, there is a real problem involved in drawing the boundary: where does language end and linguistics begin? How does one keep apart the object language from the metalanguage – the phenomenon itself from the theoretical study of that phenomenon?

The discursive evidence rather suggests that we don't, at least not very consistently. For example, the adjective *linguistic* means both 'of language', as in *linguistic variation*, and 'of linguistics' as in *linguistic association* (we never know, in fact, whether to call our professional bodies *linguistic associations* or *linguistics associations*). But a situation analogous to this occurs in many disciplines: objects in nature have *physical properties*, physicists have *physical laboratories*; there are *astronomical societies* and *astronomical forces* (not to mention *astronomical proportions*). It is easy to see where this kind of slippage takes place: astronomers observe stars, and an expression such as *astronomical observations* could equally well be glossed as 'observations of stars', or as 'observations made during the course of doing astronomy'. Likewise *linguistic theory* is 'theory of language', but it is just as plausibly 'theory in the field of linguistics'.

To a certain extent this is a pathological peculiarity of the English language, because in English the ambiguity appears even in the nouns: whereas *sociology* is the study of society, *psychology* – originally the study of the psyche – has since slipped across to mean not only the study but also that which is studied, and we talk about *criminal psychology* (which means the psyche characteristic of criminals, though it "ought to mean" theories of the psyche developed by scholarly criminals). So now *psychology* is the study of psychology; and an expression such as *Australian psychology* is unambiguously ambiguous. Such confusion is not normally found for example in Chinese, where typically a clear distinction is made between a phenomenon and its scientific study; thus *shehui : shehuixue :: xinli : xinlixue* (society : sociology :: psyche : psychology) and so on. But one can see other evidence for the special difficulties associated with linguistics. For example, it is a feature of linguistics departments that, in their actual practice, what they teach is often not so much the study of language as the study of linguistics. (And one of the few fields where the terminological distinction is not consistently maintained in Chinese is that of grammar, where *yufa* often does duty also for *yufaxue*.) There do seem to be special category problems arising where language is turned back on itself.

2 GRAMMAR AND GRAMMATICS

In fact the ambiguity that I myself first became aware of, as a teacher of linguistics (and before that, as a teacher of languages), was that embodied in the term *grammar*. Here the slippage is in the opposite direction to that of *psychology*: *grammar*, the name of the phenomenon (as in *the grammar of English*), slides over to become the name of the study of the phenomenon (as in *a grammar of English*). This was already confusion enough; it was made worse by the popular use of the term to mean rules of linguistic etiquette (for example *bad grammar*). As a way of getting round part of the problem I started using the term *grammatics*. This was based on the simple proportion grammatics : grammar :: linguistics : language. I assumed it was unproblematic: the study of language is called *linguistics*; grammar is part of language; so, within that general domain, the study of grammar may be called *grammatics*.

But this proportion is not quite as simple as it seems. The relationship of linguistics to language is unproblematic as long as we leave language undefined; and we can do this – as linguists, we can take language for granted, as sociologists take society for granted, treating it as a primitive term. Grammar, on the other hand, needs defining. Although the word is used in a non-technical sense, as in the *bad grammar* example, one cannot take this usage over to define a domain of systematic study: in so far as it has any objective correlate at all, this would refer to an inventory of certain marginal features of a language defined by the fact that they carry a certain sort of social value for its speakers. We can study ethnographically the patterns of this evaluation, and their place in the social process; but that is a distinct phenomenal domain. Grammatics, in fact, has no domain until it defines one for itself (or until one is defined for it within general linguistics – exactly at what point the term *grammatics* takes over from *linguistics* is immaterial). And it is this that makes the boundary hard to draw. Since both the grammar and the grammatics are made of language, then if, in addition, each has to be used to define the other, it is not surprising if they get confused.

Now you may say, as indeed I said to myself when first trying to think this through: it doesn't matter. It does no harm if we just talk about *grammar* without any clear distinction between the thing and the study of the thing. They are in any case much alike: if you turn language back on itself, it is bound to mimic itself in certain respects. But this comforting dismissal of the problem was belied by my own experience. If I had become aware of the polysemy in the word *grammar* it was because it got in the way of clear thinking – my own, and that of the students I was trying to teach. (It does not help, incidentally, to take refuge in the term *syntax*, where precisely the same polysemy occurs.) There was confusion in certain concepts, such as "universals of grammar" and "rule of grammar", and in the status and scope of grammatical categories of various kinds. But also, I suspect, a problem that has been so vexing in recent years — that of relating the system to the text (so often discourse is analysed as if there were no general principles of meaning behind it) — is ultimately part of the same overall unclarity.

I.15(1996):384–6

★ ★ ★

20 A FINAL NOTE ON GRAMMATICS

As I said at the beginning, when I first used the term "grammatics" I was concerned simply to escape from the ambiguity where "grammar" meant both the phenomenon itself — a particular stratum in language — and the study of that phenomenon; I was simply setting up a proportion such that grammatics is to grammar as linguistics is to language. But over the years since then I have found it useful to have "grammatics" available as a term for a specific view of grammatical theory, whereby it is not just a theory about grammar but also a way of using grammar to think with. In other words, in grammatics, we are certainly modelling natural language; but we are trying to do so in such a way as to throw light on other things besides. It is using grammar as a kind of logic. There is mathematical logic and there is grammatical logic, and both are semiotic systems; but they are complementary, and in some contexts we may need the evolved logic of grammar rather than, or as well as, the designed logic of mathematics.

This reflects the fact that, as I see it, grammatics develops in the context of its application to different tasks. As Matthiessen (1991b) has pointed out, this, in general, is the way that systemic theory has moved forward. Recently, a new sphere of application has been suggested. As mentioned above [I.15(1996):399–401], Sugeno has introduced the concept of "intelligent (fuzzy) computing": this is computing based on natural language (Sugeno 1995). He has also called it "computing with words", although as I have commented elsewhere (Halliday 1995) this is really "computing with meanings". Sugeno's idea is that for computers to advance to the point where they really become intelligent they have to function the way human beings do — namely, through natural (human) language. This view (and it is more than a gleam in the eye: Sugeno has taken significant steps towards putting it into practice) derives ultimately from Zadeh's "fuzzy logic"; it depends on reasoning and on inferencing with fuzzy sets and fuzzy matching processes. But to use natural language requires a grammatics: that is, a way of modeling natural language that makes sense in this particular context. Systemic theory has been used extensively in computational linguistics; and the Penman nigel grammar, and Fawcett's communal grammar, are among the most comprehensive grammars yet to appear in computational form (Matthiessen 1991; Matthiessen and Bateman 1992; Fawcett and Tucker 1990; Fawcett, Tucker and Lin 1993). But, more importantly perhaps, systemic grammatics is not uncomfortable with fuzziness. That is, no doubt, one of the main criticisms that has been made of it; but it is an essential property that a grammatics must have if it is to have any value for intelligent computing. This is an exciting new field of application; if it prospers, then any grammarian privileged to interact with Sugeno's enterprise will learn a lot about human language, as we always do from applications to real-life challenging tasks.

I.15(1996):416–7

On Language and Linguistics (Volume 3)

And yet – no language, and no variety of a language, is ineluctably tied to any one subculture, or to any one ideology or any one construction of reality. There is no semiotic construal that cannot be deconstrued. And here the most significant fact is that, whenever we deconstruct a text or critically analyse a discourse or unpack a latent ideology, we are not only using **grammatics** (that is, a **theory** of grammar) with which to do so; we are also using **grammar**. All theories, and this includes theories of language, are made out of meanings; and meanings are construed in the grammar. The fact that our grammar enables us to deconstrue the (nonneutral) grammars of commonsense or uncommonsense modes of discourse is the proof that, in the last resort, this grammar is neutral. But it takes work – grammatical energy – to keep it that way. So we, who are grammarians, cannot afford to be neutral.

III.13(2001):286

★ ★ ★

Some time ago I started using the term "grammatics" to refer distinctively to grammar as a theoretical pursuit: grammatics as the study of grammar, parallel to linguistics as the study of language – but more especially applying the term to grammatical theory used as a source of explanation. Like all theories, a theory of grammatics is a semiotic system; but with the special characteristic that the phenomena it is designed

149

to explain are themselves also semiotic systems – languages. Traditionally, linguists have usually tried to model their theories on theories that were designed to explain systems of other kinds; but in semiotics (which is not a discipline, but a thematic organization of knowledge like mathematics) all phenomena are being investigated and interpreted as systems of meaning, and this makes it possible to use grammatics as a way of explaining them. The most immediately accessible are other, non-linguistic, semiotics such as forms of art: not just literature, which can naturally be apprehended through the grammar (by means of a grammatics) because it is made of language (cf. Butt 1984, 1988; Gregory 1985; Threadgold 1988), but also performance (dance and drama), music, and forms of visual art. Michael O'Toole (1989, 1995) uses grammatics for his investigations of painting, architecture and sculpture; Steiner (1988) and van Leeuwen (1988) for music; and Paul Thibault (1991a), starting from narrative theory, exploits grammatics as a resource for integrating the text into a broader framework of "social semiotics as praxis".

But it is now being suggested that some **physical** systems might be better understood if they could be modelled "as if" they were semiotic ones. This motif began to appear some time ago in the writings of postquantum physicists, perhaps in conjunction with their renewed interest in the language of their own science; and as far as I call tell it seems to have an interpretation on two different levels: (1) that some physical systems **incorporate** semiotic ones (e.g. Prigogine and Stengers' example of the communication among molecules that is necessary for them to operate as a "chemical clock" – and compare, in biology, communication among the eggs in a clutch getting ready to be hatched); and (2) that some physical systems **are** semiotic (e.g. Bohm's interpretation of the speed of light as the maximum speed of propagation of a signal) (Prigogine and Stengers 1982: 147–8; Bohm 1980: 123). In either case, the critical event is an act of meaning. A physical system is no longer "just" a physical system. But, by the same token, a grammatics is no longer just a theory of grammar.

III.17(1992):385

Language and Education (Volume 9)

Deepening and extending the "grammatics". Perhaps the most significant domain for the operation of the dynamic/synoptic complementarity is in the grammar itself. As we use language to construe the domains of our experience, the features that are more accessible, more specific, and more volatile are construed in words (as vocabulary), and the more hidden, more general and more lasting features are construed as grammar. This means that the grammar of a natural language is a general theory of experience. For example, the grammatical system of transitivity (types of process, their participants and circumstantial relations) constitutes a theory about events in the real world – including of course the world inside our heads, and the world of language. So when we construct a theory about grammar, in order to understand how the grammar constructs a theory about experience (or rather, how speakers do this, using grammar as their strategic resource), our theory is already a theory of a second order – a theory about a theory. I have called this higher order theory of grammar "grammatics".

IX.18(1990):363

Additional readings

On Grammar (Volume 1) – 13(1992):365–6
On Language and Linguistics (Volume 3) – 5(1987):128;9(1992):211;10(1993):222; 12(1997):264–5; 13(2001):274–6; 16(1992):362, 373; 18(1995):410
The Language of Science (Volume 5) – 5(1988):158
Computational and Quantitative Studies (Volume 6) – 8(2002):158; 10(1995):213–238
Language and Education (Volume 9) – 5(1988):92; 6(1996):111

Chapter Seven

INDETERMINACY IN LANGUAGE

Summary

Indeterminacy in language occurs (i) where distinctions in meaning are more continuous discrete; (ii) where meanings become fused to the extent that one cannot select between them; and (iii) where some domain of experience may be construed in contradictory or competing ways.

From a systemic-functional perspective, indeterminacy is both necessary and positive, enabling language to achieve its richness. Indeterminacy, therefore, must be accounted for in the grammar.

Selected readings

On Grammar (Volume 1)

10 INDETERMINACY IN GRAMMAR

It seems obvious that grammars are indeterminate (or "fuzzy", to borrow the term from its origins in Zadeh's "fuzzy logic"), if only because of the effort that goes into tidying them up. Formal logic and even mathematics can be seen as the result of tidying up the indeterminacies of natural language grammars.

The typology of indeterminacy is itself somewhat indeterminate. For the present discussion I will identify three types: (a) clines, (b) blends, and (c) complementarities, with (d) probability as a fourth, though rather different case.

Clines are distinctions in meaning which take the form of continuous variables instead of discrete terms. The prototype examples in grammar are those distinctions which are construed prosodically, typically by intonation (tone contour): for example, in English, "force", from strong to mild, realized as a continuum from wide to narrow pitch movement – if the tone is falling, then from wide fall (high to low) to narrow fall (midlow to low). But one can include in this category those distinctions where, although the realizations are discrete (i.e. different wordings are involved), the categories themselves are shaded, like a colour spectrum: for example, colours themselves; types of motorized vehicles (*car, bus, van, lorry, truck, limousine* . . . etc.); types of process (as illustrated on the cover of the revised edition of my *Introduction to Functional Grammar* 1994). In this sense, since in the grammar's categorization of experience fuzziness is the norm, almost any scalar set will form a cline: cf. *humps, mounds, hillocks, hills* and *mountains*; or *must, ought, should, will, would, can, could, may, might*.

Blends are forms of wording which ought to be ambiguous but are not. Ambiguity in the strict sense, as in lexical or structural puns, is not a form of indeterminacy as considered here, because it does not involve indeterminacy of categorization. Blends also construe two (or more) different meanings; but the meanings are fused – it is not a matter of selecting one or the other. A favourite area for blends, apparently in many languages, is modality; in English, oblique modal finites like construing and enacting *should* provide typical examples, for example *the brake should be on*, meaning both 'ought to be' and 'probably is'. There is then the further indeterminacy between an ambiguity and a blend, because a wording which is clearly ambiguous in one context may be blended when it occurs in another. A metaphor is the limiting case of a blend.

Complementarities are found in those regions of (typically experiential) semantic space where some domain of experience is construed in two mutually contradictory ways. An obvious example in English is in the grammar of mental processes, where there is a regular complementarity between the "like" type (*I like it*; cf. *notice, enjoy, believe, fear, admire, forget, resent* . . .) and the "please" type (*it pleases me*; cf. *strike, delight, convince, frighten, impress, escape, annoy* . . .). The feature of complementarities is that two conflicting proportionalities are set up, the implication being that this is a complex domain of experience which can be construed in different ways: here, in a process of consciousness the conscious being is on the one hand 'doing', with some phenomenon defining the scope of the deed, and on the other hand 'being done to' with the phenomenon functioning as the doer. All languages (presumably) embody complementarities; but not always in the same regions of semantic space (note for example the striking complementarity of tense and aspect in Russian). One favourite domain is causation and agency, often manifested in the complementarity of transitive and ergative construals.

Strictly speaking probability is not a "fuzzy" concept; but probability in grammar adds indeterminacy to the definition of a category. Consider the network of the English verbal group in Figure 2 [I.15(1996):394].

As an exercise in grammatics this network is incomplete, in that there are distinctions made by the grammar that the network fails to show: in that sense, as already suggested, no network ever can be complete. But it is incomplete also in another sense: it does not show probabilities. If you are generating from that network, you are as likely to come up with *won't be taken* as with *took*; whereas in real life positive is significantly more likely than negative, active than passive, and past than future. Similarly a typical dictionary does not tell you that *go* is more likely than *walk* and *walk* is more likely than *stroll*, though you might guess it from the relative length of the entries. A grammar is an inherently probabilistic system, in which an important part of the meaning of any feature is its probability relative to other features with which it is mutually defining. Furthermore the critical factor in register variation is probabilistic: the extent to which local probabilities depart from the global patterns of the language as a whole; for example a register of weather forecasting (and no doubt other kinds of forecasting as well), where future becomes more probable than past; or one in which negative and passive suddenly come to the fore, like that of bureaucratic regulations (Halliday 1991a & b). Probabilities are significant both in ideational and in interpersonal meanings, as well as in the textual component; they provide a fundamental resource for the constitutive potential of the grammar.

11 SOME MATCHING FEATURES

In the last few sections I have picked out certain features of natural language grammars which a theory of grammar – a "grammatics" – is designed to account for. The purpose of doing this was to provide a context for asking the questions: how does the grammatics face up to this kind of requirement? Given that every theory is, in some sense, a lexicogrammatical metaphor for what it is theorizing, is there anything different about a theory where what it is theorizing is also a lexicogrammar?

There is (as far as I can see) no way of formally testing a grammar in its role as a theory of human experience: there are no extrinsic criteria for measuring its excellence of fit. We can of course seek to evaluate the grammar by asking how well it works; and whatever language we choose it clearly does – grammars have made it possible for humanity to survive and prosper. They have transmitted the wisdom of accumulated experience from one generation to the next, and enabled us to interact in highly complex ways with our environment. (At the same time, it seems to me, grammars can have quite pernicious side-effects, now that we have suddenly crossed the barrier from being dominated by that environment to being in control of it, and therefore also responsible for it; cf. Halliday 1993). I suspect that the same holds true for the grammatics as a theory of grammar: we can evaluate such a theory, by seeing how far it helps in solving problems where language is centrally involved (problems in education, in health, in information management and so on); but we cannot test it for being right or wrong. (This point was made by Hjelmslev many years ago, as the general distinction between a theory and a hypothesis.) By the same token a grammatics can also have its negative effects, if it becomes reductionist or pathologically one-sided.

The special quality of a theory of grammar, I think, is the nature of the metaphoric relationship that it sets up with its object of enquiry. If we consider just those features of language brought into the discussion construing and enacting above – the size (and growth) of the grammar, its trinocular perspective, and its fuzz – how does the grammatics handle these various parameters? To put this in very general terms: how do we construe the grammatics so as to be able to manage the complexity of language?

It seems to me that there are certain matching properties. The grammatics copes with the immense size of the grammar, and its propensity for growing bigger, by orienting itself along the paradigmatic axis, and by building into this orientation a variable delicacy; this ensures that the grammar will be viewed comprehensively, and that however closely we focus on any one typological or topological domain this will always be contextualized in terms of the meaning potential of the grammar as a whole. It copes with the trinocular vision of the grammar by also adopting a trinocular perspective, based on the strata organization of the grammar itself. And it copes with the indeterminacy of the grammar by also being indeterminate, so that the categories of the theory of grammar are like the categories that the grammar itself construes.

Theories in other fields, concerned with non-semiotic systems, begin by generalizing and abstracting; but they then take off, as it were, to become semiotic constructs in their own right, related only very indirectly and obliquely to observations from experience. The prototype of such a theory is a mathematical model; and one can theorize grammatics in this way, construing it as a formal system. But a grammatics does not need to be self-contained in this same manner. It is, as theory, a semiotic construct; but this does not create any disjunction between it and what it is theorizing – it remains permeable at all points on its surface. The grammatics thus retains a mimetic character: it explains the grammar by mimicking its crucial properties. One could say that it is based on grammatical logic rather than on mathematical logic. In some respects this will appear as a weakness: it will lack the rigour of a mathematical theory.

But in other respects it can be a source of strength. It is likely to be more relevant to understanding other semiotic systems: not only verbal art, but also other, non-verbal art forms, as demonstrated by O'Toole's masterly interpretation of painting, architecture and sculpture in terms of systemic grammatics, referred to already (O'Toole 1994). And the new field of "intelligent computing", associated with the work of Sugeno, and explicitly defined by him as "computing with (natural) language", requires a theory that celebrates indeterminacy (it is a development of fuzzy computing) and that allows full play to the interface between wording and meaning.

I.15(1996):399–402

* * *

16 INDETERMINACY IN GRAMMATICS

That the grammatics should accommodate indeterminacy does not need explaining: indeterminacy is an inherent and necessary feature of a grammar, and hence something to be accounted for and indeed celebrated in the grammatics, not idealized out of the picture – just as the grammar's construal of experience recognizes indeterminacy as an inherent and necessary feature of the human condition.

But construing indeterminacy is not just a matter of leaving things as they are. Construing after all is a form of complexity management; and just as, in a material practice such as looking after a wilderness, once you have perturbed the complex equilibrium of its ecosystem you have to intervene and actively manage it, so in semiotic practice, when you transform something into meaning (i.e. perturb it semiotically) you also have to manage the complexity. We can note how the grammar manages the complexity of human experience. In the first instance, it imposes artificial determinacy, in the form of discontinuities: thus, a growing plant has to be construed either as *tree* or as *bush* or as *shrub* (or . . .); the line of arbitrariness precludes us from creating intermediate categories like *shrush*. Likewise, one thing must be *in* or *on* another; you are either *walking* or *running*, and so on. At the same time, however, each of these categories construes a fuzzy set, whose boundaries are indeterminate: *on* and *run* and *tree* are all fuzzy sets in this sense. Furthermore, the grammar explicitly construes indeterminacy as a semantic domain, with expressions like *half in and half on, in between a bush and a tree, almost running* and the like. The specific types of indeterminacy discussed in Section 10 above, involving complex relationships between categories, are thus only special cases, foregrounding something which is a property of the grammar as a whole.

Now consider the grammatics from this same point of view. The categories used for construing the grammar – things like *noun* and *subject* and *aspect* and *hypotaxis* and *phrase* – are also like everyday terms: they impose discontinuity. Either something is a *noun* or it is a *verb* (or . . .); we cannot decide to construe it as a *nerb*. But, in turn, each one of these itself denotes a fuzzy set. And, thirdly, the same resources exist, if in a somewhat fancier form, for making the indeterminacy explicit: *verbal noun, pseudo-passive, underlying subject*, and so on.

What then about the specific construction of indeterminacy in the overall edifice constructed by such categories? Here we see rather clearly the grammatics as complexity management. On the one hand, it has specific strategies for defuzzifying – for imposing discontinuity on the relations between one category and another; for example, for digitalizing the grammar's clines (to return to the example of "force", cited in section 10 [I.15(1996):399–401], it can establish criteria for recognizing a small, discrete set of contrasting degrees of force). A system network is a case in point: qualitative relationships both within and between systems may be ironed out, so that (i) the system is construed simply as *a* or *b* (or . . .), without probabilities, and (ii) one system is either dependent on or independent of another, with no degrees of partial association. But, at the same time, the grammatics exploits the various types of indeterminacy as resources for managing the complexity. I have already suggested that the concept of lexicogrammmar (itself a cline from "most grammatical" to "most lexical") embodies a complementarity in which lexis and grammar compete as theoretical models of the whole. There are many blends of different types of structure, for example the English nominal group construed both as multivariate (configurational) and as univariate (iterative) but without ambiguity between them. And the two most fundamental relationships in the grammatics, realization and instantiation, are both examples of indeterminacy.

I have said that a grammar is a theory of human experience. But that does not mean, on the other hand, that it is not also part of that experience; it is. We will not be surprised, therefore, if we find that its own complexity comes to be managed in ways that are analogous to the ways in which it itself manages the complexity of the rest. In the last resort, we are only seeing how the grammar construes itself.

I.15(1996):409–10

On Language and Linguistics (Volume 3)

We are familiar enough with indeterminacies in the realization patterns of language: the puns (lexical and structural ambiguities) when we have to decide between two meanings, opting for either one or the other. Children start to play with these ambiguities from their earliest encounters with the mother tongue. But the more significant types of indeterminacy – significant because they create new meanings – are those which do not resolve by enforcing choice: the overlaps, the borderline cases, and the blends. Overlapping categories are things like behavioural processes in English, which have some of the features of material processes and some of the features of mentals. A borderline case is something that can be interpreted in either of two ways, with different consequences for agnation; e.g., in English, participant$_1$ + *get* + participant$_2$ + *to* + process (*we got it to stick*), either as simple causative, like *we made it stick* (cf. agentive *we stuck it*), or as causative modulation, like *we forced it to stick* (cf. two processes: *we forced it, so it stuck*). Blends arise when, in some paradigmatic or syntagmatic environment, features which would otherwise be kept apart tend to lose their clear-cut distinction and become neutralized. With English modal verbs, for example, whereas in their non-oblique forms such as *can* and *may* the meanings of probability, usuality, obligation and readiness are typically rather distinct, in the oblique forms such as *could* and *might* these become somewhat blurred: he can be tough means either 'is sometimes tough' or 'is capable of being tough [if he needs to be]' (one or the other); but in *he could be tough* there seems to be a blending of the two, and the listener does not find it necessary to choose.

Indeterminacy is bound to arise in language because the grammar is constantly juggling with conflicting categorizations, accommodating them so as to construe a multidimensional meaning space, highly elastic and receptive to new meanings. In doing so, the grammar adopts a kind of trinocular vision, giving it a threefold perspective on the categories and their configurations. In the first place they are viewed as it were from above – the phenomena are construed according to their significance in some higher order construct; and in the second place they are viewed from below, the phenomena being construed by reference to how they appear and become manifest. But there is also the third angle of vision, that from round about: all phenomena are construed as being agnate to other phenomena – no categories are set up in terms of themselves alone. The indeterminacy comes from reconciling the three perspectives of this trinocular vision: since all yield different pictures, the result will always be compromise. All grammatical description is the product of compromise.

III.12(1997):254–5

★ ★ ★

Our theory is indeterminate, I think, again in two different ways. First, it celebrates the indeterminacy in language itself, instead of sweeping it under the carpet and then treading on it to force it into shape. What this means is that it becomes possible to operate with descriptive categories that are themselves fluid and unstable – that constitute fuzzy sets like the categories of language itself. Describing a language demands the same kind of trinocular vision that language has, and in a very specific sense that is defined by stratification: in setting up grammatical systems, for example, we are necessarily approaching them from above (semantic perspective: what meanings they realize), from below (morphological and phonological perspective: how they are realized) and also from roundabout (lexicogrammatical perspective: what are their patterns of agnation). This means that the categories themselves are inescapably the product of **compromise**, since the different perspectives locate the boundaries **between** categories at different places.

Secondly, the general theoretical framework offers ways of modelling indeterminacy. The most important of these, perhaps, is the notion of probability. Probability has been accorded rather little place in linguistics; but that is because mainstream linguistics is largely preoccupied with syntagmatic considerations, whereas probability is inherently a paradigmatic concept – it relates to system, not to structure. In a systemic grammar, probability has a central place: firstly as a feature of any given system, so that a system a/b is characterized not just as "either a or b" but as either "a or b **with a certain probability attached**"; secondly as a feature of the relationship (association) between systems, so that two systems a/b and x/y are not simply "either freely associated (simultaneous) or not at all" but "partially associated, such that $a + x$, $b + y$ are the favoured combinations" (cf. Halliday 1996). Another concept that allows for indeterminacy is stratification, and in particular the representation of the content plane. There is no doubt that the content plane requires to be modelled bistratally, with a distinction being drawn between lexicogrammar and semantics (without this separation there would be no possibility of metaphor). But the boundary between the two strata is not determinate, and it will be shifted "up" and "down" according to circumstances: in particular, the nature of the task and the state of knowledge about the language concerned (cf. Fawcett 1992; Hasan 1996, ch. 5).

III.12(1997):266–7

Computational and Quantitative Studies (Volume 6)

Let me try to summarize what I have been saying about the nature of **complexity** in language. The picture I have been trying to suggest to you, in this brief sketch, is one of **networks** of **grammatical systems** which together **construe** a **multidimensional semantic space**. Each such system, taken by itself, is just a choice among a small set of options, like 'positive or negative?', 'past, present or future?', 'possible, probable or certain?' and so on. What is important is how these systems relate to one another; and that is where the complexity arises. They are not fully independent; but nor do they form any kind of strict taxonomy. There are various degrees and kinds of partial association among them, and this makes the network extremely complex. But, by the same token, there is plenty of "play" (flexibility) in it, so that the system as a whole becomes manageable. It can be learnt, step by step, by children; it can be varied to suit the situation; and it can be modified as the discourse proceeds.

In other words, there is a great deal of indeterminacy, both in the systems themselves and in their relationship one to another. The overall picture is notably fuzzy. We do not normally use the term "fuzzy" – we refer to this property as "indeterminate"; and we try to model language in such a way as to capture the indeterminacy (a "fuzzy grammatics", as in the title of my pre-Conference written paper).

As Matthiessen has pointed out in his paper for Professor Ralescu's workshop (n.d.), when we talk about indeterminacy in language we are not referring to the explicit **formulation** of fuzziness in the lexico-grammar. All languages have ways of **referring to** different kinds of inexactness; for example, degrees of assignment to a property, like *rather, fairly, slightly*; expressions of uncertainty, like *perhaps, apparently, surely*; degrees of generality, like *on the whole, for the most part*; but these are quite marginal, in relation to language as a whole.

When we say that language is indeterminate, or fuzzy, we are talking about the whole set of categories that the lexicogrammar construes – the basic meanings of words and of grammatical features. Both ideationally, in construing our experience, and interpersonally, in enacting our social relationships, language is inherently fuzzy. It is always needing to **compromise**. This is because human experience, and human relationships, are much too complex and many-sided to be captured in categories that are well-formed, bounded and stable. Any system of rigid definitions and clear-cut boundaries would impose far too much constraint. The only determinate language is a dead one (as my teacher Professor Firth used to say, rigour in a linguistic context could only mean *rigor mortis*). Thus the indeterminacy is not an incidental feature, something added on to the grammar as a kind of optional extra; still less is it a pathological condition to be ignored or done away with. On the contrary: indeterminacy is an essential property on which the effective functioning of language depends.

IV

It has been recognized by neurobiologists for some time that the mammalian brain evolved in the context of the increasingly complex relationship of the organism to its environment. This explanation, however, focuses exclusively on the *experiential*. For the human brain, at least – that is, for the evolution of higher-order consciousness – we need to add the *interpersonal* component of the picture: the brain has evolved also in the context of the increasingly complex relationship of organisms one to another. This then coincides closely with our functional interpretation of language. Language evolves in the course of managing these two complementary types of complexity.

To take the experiential aspect first. Ellis (1993) has pointed out that there are no "natural classes": all classes – the categories of human experience – have to be **construed** in language, by what I have called the transformation of experience into meaning. The grammar does not proceed by **recognizing** things that **are alike**. It proceeds by **treating as alike** things that are in fact **different**. Another way of looking at this is to say that things may be alike **in indefinitely many ways**; the grammar **picks out** just a few of these as **parameters** for its categorization. Then, rather than saying that there are no natural classes, we might say that there are far too many, and that transforming experience into meaning involves selecting the ones to be construed. Either way, it is obvious that this construal cannot be achieved by means of a single, flat, compartmentalized categorical schema. The construal of experience has to be multifaceted, multidimensional and fluid. Things have to be seen from many angles, be related along many vectors, and have boundaries that are indeterminate and may shift in the course of time. Hence the lexicogrammar of every HAL is based on the principle of **compromise**.

Turning to the interpersonal aspect of meaning, we find exactly the same is true. Social relationships in human cultures cannot be enacted in terms of simple 'yes' or 'no', 'this' or 'that' options. Negotiation and assignment of speech roles, forms of address and personal reference, maintenance of power and distance, and the like, all need to be modulated, cushioned, hedged around, coded and disguised in various ways. The management of interpersonal relationships, in other words, is also dependent on lexicogrammatical compromise, although the forms that this compromise takes will be different in the two metafunctions.

161

It is possible to enumerate some general forms of grammatical compromise, as follows:

1. Clines (gradations, continuities): categories as a continuous scale rather than as discrete classes.
2. Overlaps ("borderline cases"): categories lying across the border of two or more others, having some of the features of each.
3. Blends: categories arising from the mixing of the features of two or more others.
4. Neutralizations: categories whose difference disappears in certain environments.
5. Metaphors: categories created by metaphoric transfer ("reconstrual").
6. Complementarities: categories construed as multiple perspectives, competing and often contradictory.

Such "compromises" occur in all languages, but in different places and different mixes. I give a few brief examples from the grammar of English in the table at the end of this chapter [See VI.9(1995):211].

The above are what we might call "categorization strategies", used by the grammar in construing our experience of processes (actions and events, and the participants and other elements involved), and in enacting our everyday *speech functions*, the small-scale semiotic roles of telling, asking, ordering and the like. Over and above the construction of particular categories, however, the grammar takes the further step of construing the relationship of one such category to another. An example would be the conditional relation, as in *Hold on to it, or it'll fall! . . . if it falls, it'll break.* There is a special component in the grammar which construes iterative relationships of this kind, which we refer to as the *logical* metafunction. (Note that this is "logical" in the grammatical sense, the logic of natural language, not the derived sense of formal or mathematical logic. Formal logic is often cited as a criterion for evaluating natural language; but formal logic is itself an idealization of natural language in the first place.) In effect, this logical component adds a further dimension of complexity into the meaning potential; this is a **dynamic** complexity, whereby "one thing leads on to another".

We sometimes tend to think of this feature in the grammar – relating phenomena to each other by time, cause, condition and so on – as a special property of the designed discourses of science and technology, or at least of the discourse of educational as distinct from commonsense knowledge. But it is not. Hasan's (1992) study of "Rationality in everyday talk", together with other studies based on her extensive corpus of natural interaction between mothers and their three-year-old children, shows how the semantic relations of cause and condition are well established in the discourse of children before they become literate or go into school. And among adults, the grammar reaches its highest level of *intricacy* (in constructing *clause complexes*, grammatically structured sequences of clauses) in informal casual conversation, where there is a rapid process of ongoing "recontextualization" – the logical significance of each clause is updated in the light of what has been said before, or in the light of changes in the context of situation. We find this happening both in monologue and in dialogue, as speakers build semantic sequences in their own discourse or in interplay with other people.

I want to make it clear that all these features which make language seem disorderly and unmanageable (the indeterminacy of the categories, or the unpredictable dynamic of the discourse) are truly features of language **as a system**. They are essential properties of knowing, understanding, reasoning and planning – of the human ability to "mean". There is no distinction to be made between "system" and its "use": no Cartesian dichotomy to be made between an idealized "competence" and a hopelessly messy "performance". The task for *grammatics*, therefore, is to account for the disorder and the complexity, not as accidental and aberrant, but as systemic and necessary to the effective functioning of language.

VI.9(1995):204–7

★ ★ ★

(6) Indeterminate. A language is not an inventory of well-formed structures. On the contrary; it is a highly indeterminate, open-ended resource for making and exchanging meaning. It is indeterminate in many ways (not the least being the indeterminacy among the different types of indeterminacy).

Most obvious (but perhaps least significant) are *ambiguities*, where a distinction in meaning is obscured by identity of form. Some of these, such as puns, are random and unpredictable; others arise out of conflicts and neutralizations in the system of the grammar (e.g., in English, *her training was highly effective*: was she the trainer, or the trainee?). Less obvious, but more problematic, are indeterminacies within the meaning itself: (a) *clines*, categories which shade one into another without clear boundaries; (b) *overlaps*, categories which display some features from each of two (or more) others; (c) *blends*, categories which combine two (or more) features that are normally contrastive. Examples from English: (a) grammatical systems realized by intonation, such as *key*, ranging from "strong" [high falling tone] to "mild" [low falling tone]; (b) in the system of

process type, there are "behavioural" processes like *sleep, chatter, laugh* which have some features of "material" and some features of "mental" processes; (c) modals, which are ambiguous in the "direct/immediate" form (e.g. *can*), become blended in "oblique + remote" (e.g. *could have*): *she can be happy* = **either** 'she is sometimes happy' **or** 'she is capable of being happy', **but not both**; whereas in *she could have been happy* the distinction seems to disappear.

Implications for grammatics. In formal linguistics indeterminacy was often seen as a pathological feature of language, something that needed to be excised by surgical idealization. In fact it is a positive characteristic, without which language would not be able to achieve its richness or its variety; so it needs to be given status in a theory. Of the types mentioned above, ambiguity is unproblematic, since it is simply the juxtaposition of two descriptions (the issue then being which, if either, is to be preferred). Perhaps the most problematic are blends, where we have to find the general conditions under which the ambiguity which "ought" to be present is somehow dissipated or neutralized. The overall challenge is to achieve significant generalizations about such indeterminacies without imposing on them an artificial exactitude. For a discussion of other, more general types of indeterminacy, see Halliday and Matthiessen 2000.

VI.10(1995):226–7

Additional readings

Linguistic Studies of Text and Discourse (Volume 2) – 2(1977):33, 51; 3(1971):93; 4(1982):139–40, 145–6
On Language and Linguistics (Volume 3) – 9(1992):201; 18(1995):427
The Language of Science (Volume 5) – 7(1997):183
Computational and Quantitative Studies (Volume 6) – 9(1995):207, 211; 10(1995):226–30
Language and Society (Volume 10) – 5(1975):193, 200

Chapter Eight

INTONATION

Summary

Intonation, which expresses both textual and interpersonal meanings, may be analysed as a complex of three phonological systems, or (more accurately) systemic variables: tonality, tonicity and tone; these in turn being interdependent with a fourth, that of rhythm.

Intonation and rhythm, especially the pitch contour of speech, figure prominently in the information system, foregrounding the new information (New) from that which is otherwise recoverable from the discourse and its context of situation (Given).

Choice of tone also plays a significant role in realizing interpersonal meanings associated with mood and modality. Already in the transition from protolanguage to language, children have been observed to use tone (rising vs. falling) to systematically distinguish between the functions of doing/telling ("pragmatic") and learning/asking ("mathetic").

Selected readings

The Language of Early Childhood (Volume 4)

From the start language is the main instrument we have for interpreting and organizing our experience. Not everything we perceive is "processed" by language, but most of it is; language is far and away the most significant instrument for building up our model of the universe and of our own place in it.

What is the origin of this process in a young child's developing language system? Our understanding of this is still very tentative and incomplete; but it appears that, as a child begins the transition from protolanguage to language – from child tongue to mother tongue – he comes to make a rather systematic distinction between two basic functions of language, which I have referred to as the "pragmatic" and the "mathetic", the doing function and the learning function. I have described this in earlier chapters, showing how my own child made the distinction explicit by his intonation pattern, expressing pragmatic by a rising tone and mathetic by a falling tone. The striking thing about this was that not only did he introduce into his own speech, more or less overnight at the age of 19 months, a fundamental semantic distinction which has nothing corresponding to it in the mother tongue, but also that his mother and those around him understood straight away what this opposition meant. Not consciously, of course; they were not aware of what was happening, and nor was I until I got to that point in my analysis. But they responded immediately to the different meanings he was expressing. This is how it happened.

When Nigel was using language for pragmatic purposes, in the sense of 'I want', for example "more meat!", "butter on!" (put some butter on my toast), "train stuck!" (get it out for me), he used a rising intonation. The meaning of this intonation pattern was 'somebody *do* something!'; and the significant observation was that somebody always did. Not that they immediately jumped up to do whatever he asked or give him whatever he wanted; the answer would often be "You can't have any more", or "I'm busy; try and get it out yourself". But they responded – thereby unconsciously acknowledging the fact that the meaning had been a request for action, and making it clear to the child that they recognized it as such.

When he was using language in a "mathetic" function, saying things like "green light" (there's a green light there), "Mummy book" (that's Mummy's book) or "two buses", the intonation was falling. And I noticed that on these occasions nobody felt it necessary to say or do anything. Sometimes they acknowledged, saying things like "yes, that's a green light", or they corrected him, "no, that's blue, not green"; but often they said nothing at all. And whereas if he got no response to a pragmatic utterance Nigel was clearly dissatisfied, and went on saying it until he did, if he got no response to a mathetic utterance, he was not in the least concerned: he didn't really expect one. The meaning was: this is how things are; you can confirm (or deny) it if you like, but I'm really sorting things out just for myself. Nigel maintained this distinction between language as a means of doing and language as a means of learning consistently for about six months, until the time came when the grammar of speech functions of the adult language was well established in his own system; then he abandoned it.

Nobody was setting out to teach him anything. Nigel's learning, his construction of reality, was taking place through these little micro-encounters in which he decided what he wanted to talk about. Usually – always, at first – the experience he was representing in words was one that was being or had been shared with someone else; and that person might correct him if they thought he'd got things wrong. But the knowledge he was storing up was common-sense everyday knowledge which the others could not have imparted to him consciously because they were not aware of having it themselves.

IV.14(1980):317–9

The Language of Science (Volume 5)

At the same time as construing instances of human experience the grammar also has to construe itself, by creating a flow of discourse. This is often referred to as "information flow"; but this term – as always! – privileges the ideational meaning, whereas the discursive flow is interpersonal as well as ideational. It is as if the grammar was creating a parallel current of semiosis that interpenetrates with and provides a channel for the mapping of ideational and interpersonal meanings. The metafunctional component of the grammar that engenders this flow of discourse is the *textual* (cf. Martin 1992, especially Chapter 6; Matthiessen 1992, 1995).

Many features contribute to the discursive flow; those that primarily concern us here are those that form part of, or are systemically associated with, the grammar of the clause – because it is there that the explicit mapping of textual and ideational meanings takes place. The two systems involved, in English, are those of theme and information. The *theme* system is a system of the clause, where it sets up a structural pattern that we can interpret as a configuration of the functions Theme and Rheme. The *information* system has its own distinct structural domain, the *information unit*, where it sets up a configuration of the functions Given and New. The management of these two systems is one of the factors that contributes most to the overall effectiveness of a text (Martin 1992, Chapter 6; Hasan and Fries 1995).

(1) The theme system maps the elements of the clause into a pattern of movement from a point of departure, the Theme, to a message, the Rheme. The point of departure may be a consolidation of various elements; the part that is relevant here is its experiential

module, defined grammatically as that part which has some function in the transitivity of the clause (semantically, some participant, circumstance or process). This thematic structure, in English, is realized lineally – the Theme comes first; furthermore there is a strong bond between the (textual) system of theme and the (interpersonal) system of mood, such that, if the clause is declarative, then other things being equal the same element will function both as Subject and as Theme – which means that it will be a nominal of some kind, since only a nominal element can function as Subject. So *those Convex glasses*, in the clause *for those Convex glasses supply the defect of Plumpness in the Eye*, is a typical "unmarked" Theme of this kind.

(2) The information system maps the discourse into a pattern of movement between what is already around, the Given, and what is news, the New. The "Given" is what is being presented in the discourse as recoverable, to be taken as read; while the 'New' is what is being foregrounded for attention. This system is not directly represented in written English because it is realized by patterns of intonation and rhythm, especially the pitch contour of speech; it constructs its own domain, in the form of a ***tone group***, and hence is independent of the grammatical clause – which means that the movement of 'information' (in this technical sense) can vary freely with the thematic movement. However, the two systems are associated: other things being equal, one information unit will be mapped onto one clause – and, within the information unit, the Given will precede the New, so that, in the "unmarked" case, the Theme of a clause is located within the Given portion, and the New, that which is under focus of attention, within the Rheme. What this means is that, typically, a speaker takes as point of departure something that is (or can be presented as being) already familiar to the listener, and puts under focus of attention something that forms part of (and is typically at the culmination of) the message.

It is this pattern of association between the information system and the thematic system which guides the readers – and the writers – of written text. Unless there is some clear indication to the contrary, the default condition will be assumed. (Such counterindication might be lexical – repetition, or synonymic echo, marking a later portion as Given; or grammatical – the predication of the Theme, as in *it was the drummer who stole the show*, marking *the drummer* as New.) The two systems together give a rhythm to the discourse, at this micro level, creating a regular pattern whereby in the unmarked case each clause moves from one peak of prominence to another – but the two prominences are of different kinds. The initial prominence, that of Theme, is the speaker/writer's angle on the message: this is the point from which I am taking off. The culminative prominence, that of New, is still of course assigned by the speaker/writer; but it carries a signal to the listener/reader: this is what you are to attend to. Of course, this underlying discursive rhythm gets modulated all the time by the other meaning-making currents that are flowing along in the grammar, as well as being perturbed by the larger-scale fluctuations – moves in dialogue, shifts of register and the like. But it provides the basic semiotic pulse, not unlike the chest pulse that gets modulated by the sound-making antics of the organs of articulation.

V.3(1998).69–71

Studies in English Language (Volume 7)

In VII.8(1963) I suggested a possible form of phonological statement for English intonation, such as might be found suitable for the purpose of describing the grammar of the spoken language. The description was based on the analysis of recorded texts of natural conversation in educated British English, supplemented by observations of speech events in daily life and by an examination of my own usage as a speaker of the language. Intonation was analysed as a complex of three phonological systems, or (more accurately) systemic variables: tonality, tonicity and tone; these in turn being interdependent with a fourth, that of rhythm. This required the setting up of three phonological units in hierarchical relation: tone group, foot and syllable; and the recognition, within the tone group, of tonic and pretonic elements of structure. Rhythm was concerned with the operation of syllables in foot structure; tonality and tonicity with the operation of feet in tone group structure. Tone was the selection by the tone group from a set of systems characterized by contrastive pitch movement and interrelated in delicacy.

The phonological categories were then provisionally ordered on the basis of meaningful grammatical contrasts, the attempt being to suggest how the phonological resources of the language are distributed into a number of sets of contrastive terms, each such set representing one grammatical selection. The aim of the present paper is to take the next step: to establish the sets of contrasts as grammatical systems, referable to and in mutual definition with other grammatical systems set up for the total description of the language. In other words, while the previous paper was so to speak looking from the phonological end, the question being 'what are the phonological resources of intonation that expound grammatical meaning?', in the present paper I am attempting to look at the same patterns from the grammatical end, asking 'what are the grammatical systems that are expounded by intonation?' The overall grammatical description on which the statements made here depend, and of which indeed they form a part, is still in course of preparation; no claim is made that the description is "complete", in the sense of being exhaustive in delicacy: although some features are, it is believed, being described for the fi rst time, the attempt is rather to use a particular model to shed additional light on facts already known.

It may be helpful here to summarize in tabular form the phonological categories that are referred to (Figure 9.1); and to list the notational conventions used in the examples (Figure 9.2).

Tone, primary and secondary, is shown by Arabic figures, alone or with diacritics (see Figure 9.1), placed immediately after the tone group boundary marker.

The convention adopted in the presentation of the systems is as follows:

(serial number) SYSTEM: term – exponent // example //; term – exponent // example //.

In some instances explanatory material is added in parenthesis; since this is intended primarily as an aid to the identification of the items concerned it has been formulated in reference to the specific examples, rather than in the more lengthy form that would be necessitated by a general explanation.

Of the systems expounded by intonation in English, the majority are referable to one particular grammatical unit, the clause. The remainder are of two kinds: those referable to one of the two adjacent units, the sentence or the group; and those whose terms represent precisely a choice among different relations between the clause and an adjacent unit, such as the choice between a sentence having two elements of structure (and thus consisting of two clauses) and one having only one.

In a general description of English grammar it seems preferable to consider systems expounded by intonation as in no way different from other grammatical systems; their place in the description is determined by the total picture, so that those referable to the sentence will be described in relation to other systems of the sentence, and so on. Here, however,

Tonality
 Distribution of utterance into tone groups (location of tone
group boundaries).
Tonicity
 Distribution of tone group into tonic and pretonic (location of
tonic foot).
Tone (primary; pitch movement on tonic)
   1 fall
   2 rise; sharp fall-rise
   3 low rise
   4 fall-rise
   5 rise-fall
   13 fall plus low rise
   53 rise-fall plus low rise
Tone (secondary)

Pretonic		*Tonic*	
1 1 even (level, falling, rising)		1 +	high fall
−1 uneven (low "spiky")	×	1	mid fall
...1 suspended ("listing")		1 −	low fall
2 2 high (level, falling, rising)		2	rise
−2 low (level, rising)	×	2	sharp fall-rise
3 3 mid (level)			
−3 low (level)			
4		4 high fall-rise	
		4 low fall-rise	
5		5 high rise-fall	
		5 low rise-fall	

Figure 9.1

//	tone group boundary (always also foot boundary)
/	foot boundary
bold	tonic syllable
^	silent ictus

Figure 9.2

where the intention is to summarize the grammatical values of intonation,
it is simpler to relate all systems in the first place to the clause; those which
are not directly referable to the clause can be shown to be derivable, by
generalization across grammatical units, from those that are. An analogy

may be found with other systems such as polarity and tense–aspect, which are also referable to more than one grammatical unit.

It is thus convenient to take as the starting point the syntagmatic equivalence of clause and tone group, in the sense that the unmarked value of the phonological unit "tone group" will be that it is exponent of the grammatical unit "clause". The condition of coextensiveness of one tone group with one clause is referred to as "neutral tonality". This does not imply that neutral tonality, in a grammatical system where it contrasts as exponent with "marked tonality", always necessarily expounds an unmarked term; there are indeed systems in which a grammatically unmarked term is expounded by marked tonality. Neutral tonality is a postulate which simplifies the descriptive statement: it means in effect the isolation of one variable, which can then be separately examined. In the same way, as will appear later, another variable can be isolated, that of "tonicity" or location of the tonic, and a "neutral tonicity" postulated. Again, neutral tonicity does not necessarily imply a grammatically unmarked term; it is simply a name for the condition that the tonic begins on the final lexical item in the tone group.

It is impossible to **define** the clause in abstraction from a total grammatical description; the clause is that unit which enters into sentence structure and whose own structure is stated in terms of (classes of) the group. But for recognition purposes a clause is any item whose parts enter into a clause-type structural relation: this means any item in which can be identified any two or more of the elements Subject, Predicator, Complement, Adjunct and "Absolute" nominal, and with certain restrictions only one such element. The Predicator may be either a finite or a non-finite verbal group; moreover not every clause contains a Predicator.

No attempt has been made here to present the full grammatical framework within which the intonation-expounded systems operate; this would require nothing less than the comprehensive description of the grammar of the language. But grammatical notes have been added where these might help to show the range of operation of the systems concerned. The sequence in which the systems are presented is determined by the desire for clarity; the general pattern is: first, systems expounded by tonality; second, those expounded by tonicity; third, those expounded by tone.

(1) INFORMATION: (i) one information unit – tonality neutral // I saw John yesterday //; (ii) two information units – tonality marked (two tone groups) // I saw John // yesterday //.

If, however, the clause has a marked theme (Complement or lexical Adjunct preceding the Subject), "two information units" represents the grammatically unmarked term:

(1.1) // John // I saw yesterday //, // in those circumstances //
I would agree //, // John I saw yesterday //, // in those
circumstances I would agree //.

This system also operates in compound sentences (those consisting of more than one clause). Here its operation depends on sentence structure: on whether the elements are related (a) in dependence (non-transitive depth-ordering), specifically (i) as in *I came because he told me*, (ii) as in *he said he was coming* or (iii) as in *John, who arrived late, missed the speeches*; or (b) in co-ordination (transitive depth-ordering), specifically (i) by linking, as in *I asked him and he told me*, or (ii) by apposition, as in *that's another thing; I don't know yet*.

In (a)(i), the system operates as in clause structure:

(1.2) // I came because he told me // (= 'that's why I came'; *I came* is "given"), // I'm leaving now to catch the train //; // I came // because he told me //, // I'm leaving now // to catch the train //.

Note that the potentiality of operation of this system is a structural criterion. If *he came to hear about it* is one clause with two Predicators in phase, it is one tone group; if it is two clauses in dependence relation, it is subject to system (1.2). In *he left me to get on with the job*, the difference lying in the presence of what if the item is one clause is a Complement-Subject, here *me*, the situation is more complex: if it is one clause, it is subject to system (1), and if it is two clauses it is subject to (1.2). The distinction is that here the **unmarked** term is neutral tonality in each case: // he left me to get on with the job // if one clause, // he left me // to get on with the job // if two.

If the independent clause is negative, the same system operates:

(1.3) // I didn't come because he told me // (I *didn't come* is "given"); // I didn't come // because he told me //.

Here the term "one information unit" carries a sub-system:

(2) NEGATION TYPE: (i) simple negative – tone 1 //1^
I / didn't / come because he / **told** me // (= 'it was because he told me that I didn't come'; (ii) transferred negative – tone 4 // 4 ^I / didn't / come because he / **told** me // (= 'it

wasn't because he told me that I came'). (The optional variant //.../ come be/cause he /...// is possible in each case, but more likely in simple negative.)

This system operates with the items *because, so* (*that*); alternatively it could be regarded as operating with all items but neutralized with the others, as in *I won't come if you don't want me*; the latter, however, is probably better regarded as an instance of (15) with marked tonality.

The selection of transferred negative is possible only where the independent clause precedes. With the sequence dependent-independent, system (1) again operates but with "two information units" as the unmarked term as in (1.1):

> (1.4) // if you want me // I'll come //; // if you want me I'll come //. Note that the latter is subject to (8) below: either // ∧ if you / want me I'll **come** // (*if you want me* "given": = 'I know you do want me'), or // ∧ if you / **want** me I'll / come// (*I'll come* "given": = 'you know I may come; this is what determines it').

The first term, "two information units", also carries a sub-system, which may be taken together with (3.1), following (15), below:

> (3) DEPENDENCE CONTRAST: (i) dependent clause unmarked – tone 4 // 4 ∧ if you /**want** me I'll // 1 **come** // (= 'I don't know whether you do or not'); (ii) dependent clause confirmatory – tone 3 // 3 ∧ if you / **want** me I'll // 1 **come** // (= 'I think you do'); dependent clause contrastive – tone 4 // 4 ∧ if you / **want** me I'll // 1 **come** // (= 'I think you don't').

Sentences of type (a)(ii) are subject to system (1) as in (1.2); and, with sequence dependent-independent, as in (1.4). With the latter sequence, the possibilities vary according to the items in the independent clause (contrast here for example *say* with *know*, and *I know* with *you know*); and with the term "one information unit" neutral tonicity is rare: // ∧ he was / coming he / **said** // is infrequent, although possible in concord with tone **4** by non-systemic selection of a term in (15).

With type (a)(iii) tonality is the defining criterion of the structure in question, so that here a different system must be recognized:

> (4) SENTENCE STRUCTURE: (i) compound – WH- clause is separate tone group // John // who arrived late // missed the speeches //, // we never saw John // who arrived late// ("non-defining relative clause"); (ii) simple – WH- clause is

not separate tone group // we never saw those who arrived late//("defining relative clause").

Tonality is thus neutral in each case: if the sentence consists of two clauses, with the WH- clause dependent, there are two tone groups (three if the WH- clause is included); if the sentence consists of one clause, with the WH- clause not dependent but rankshifted, there is one tone group. The compound structure resembles appositional structures (see (6) below) in being subject to tone concord: the dependent clause takes the tone of the preceding clause, for example // 4 John // 4 ˄ who ar/rived / **late** // I missed the / **speeches** //.

Within (a)(iii) there is a distinct sub-type exemplified by // John arrived late // which was a pity //. These are not subject to system (4), since there is no corresponding simple term. Moreover they are not subject to tone concord: the dependent clause selects freely for tone.

The reasons why (a)(iii) is not regarded as an appositional structure are: first, the structure resembles other types of dependence in being non-transitive, whereas apposition is transitive ("transitive" being used here in its meaning in logic); second, WH- clauses are bound whereas appositional items are free (i.e. capable of operating as a simple structure of the rank above); third, WH- clauses such as that in *John arrived late, which was a pity* would in any case not be appositional since they are not subject to tone concord, which is a defining criterion of apposition. There is, however, as intonation shows, some resemblance between appositional structures and this type of dependence.

Sentences of structure (b)(i), co-ordinate linked, select in system (1) as in (1.2) above. The term "two information units" carries a sub-system related to (3) but with a different term unmarked:

(5) CONTRAST: (i) unlinked clause unmarked – tone 3 // 3 ˄ I **asked** him and he //1 **told** me // ; (ii) unlinked clause contrastive – tone 4 // 4 ˄ I /**asked** him and he // 1 **told** me //.

Here, of course, the degree of marking depends on other features; a linked clause with *and* and polarity constant is more likely to correlate with tone 3 in the unlinked clause, one with *but* and polarity reversed with tone 4: // 4 ˄ I / **asked** him but he //1 didn't / **tell** me //. One could treat this as a separate system, but the two would be joined by a continuum. The point is that here, as regularly with intonation choices, there is a probabilistic correlation but the choice remains: this is the significance in such cases of regarding one term as grammatically unmarked. The linked clause in this structure selects freely for tone.

Neutral tonality operates as an exponent of structure where ambiguity would otherwise arise (cf. under (1.2) above) between a compound sentence of two linked clauses and a single clause with two linked groups; this can be regarded as the operation of system (4):

> (4.1) SENTENECE STRUCTURE: (i) compound – two tone groups // he washed // and brushed his hair //; (ii) simple – one tone group // he washed and brushed his hair //

(with tonality neutral in each case), where *he fell and hurt his foot*, being unambiguous, selects normally from system (1); and likewise between two linked groups and a single group with linked words, for example, at head in nominal group structure: // white paper // or cardboard // as against // white paper or cardboard //. (The reason why the first example determines **sentence** structure while the second does not determine **clause** structure is that two co-ordinate clauses expound two elements of sentence structure, this being a primary dimension of sentence structure, whereas two co-ordinate groups together expound one element of clause structure.)

In sentences of structure (b)(ii), co-ordinate appositional, tonality with tone concord provides the defining criterion. This is in fact the defining criterion of apposition at all ranks:

> (6) SENTENCE STRUCTURE: (i) compound sentence, appositional – two tone groups with tone concord //1 that's a/**noth**er thing I //1 don't / **know** yet //; (ii) two sentences – two tone groups without tone concord // 1 that's a/**nother** thing I // 4 don't / **know** yet //; (iii) simple sentence (with rankshifted clause as Qualifier in nominal group) //1 that's a/nother thing I / don't / **know** yet //.

Compare at other ranks, where the non-appositional terms have various values:

> (6.1) //1 ∧ he / **died** a //1 happy / **man** //, intransitive clause with discontinuous subject (two groups in apposition); //1 ∧ he / died a / happy / **man** // and // 4 ∧ he / **died** a //1 happy / **man** //, transitive clause with intensive Complement. (This explains why *he seemed a happy man* can only occur as the two latter, and not as two tone groups in concord; apposition is here impossible.)
>
> (6.2) //1 ∧ I'll / ask my / **broth**er the //1 **heart** specialist //, two groups in apposition (= 'my brother already identified', perhaps 'my only brother') ; //1 ∧ I'll / ask my / brother the

/ **heart** specialist //, one group with rankshifted Qualifier
defining *brother* : apposition in contrast with qualification.

(6.3) //1 ˄ I'll / come to/**morr**ow //1 after the / **meet**ing //, two
adverbial groups in apposition (= "the meeting is today");
//1 ˄ I'll /come to/morrow / after the / meeting //, two
Adjuncts in recursive relation (= 'the meeting is tomorrow'):
apposition in contrast with "narrowing".

So far we have been considering the choice between one tone group
and two tone groups. Within "one tone group", there is a further choice
between a simple tone group, with tone 1 2 3 4 or 5, and a compound
tone group, with tone 13 or 53. This could be regarded as an intermediate term in three-term system, representing one and a half information
units; system (1) could then be rewritten as follows:

(1*) (i) One information unit – one simple tone group // ˄ I / saw
/ John / **yesterday** //; (ii) one and a half information units
– one compound tone group // ˄ I / saw / **John** / **yes**terday
//; (iii) two information units – two simple tone groups // ˄ I
/ saw / **John** // **yes**terday //.

But the value of this "intermediate term" varies with different structures,
so that it is best regarded as a term in a separate subsystem of "one information unit" which can be represented as follows (and compare (19)):

(7) INFORMATION SUB-SYSTEM: (i) major information point
– simple
tone group // ˄ I / saw John / **yes**terday // or // ˄ I / saw /
John / yesterday // (see (8)); major plus minor information
point – compound tone group // ˄ I / saw / **John** /
yesterday //.

Which of these two terms is unmarked depends on the structure of the
clause. There is a high correlation between minor information point and
clause-final Adjunct; so that in a clause with final Adjunct "major plus
minor" can be regarded as the unmarked term: // ˄ I / saw / **John** /
yesterday //, // ˄ I / saw / **John** on the / **train** //. In all other clauses
"major" is the unmarked term: // ˄ I / saw / **John** //. As usual, however,
the system represents an independent choice and the correlation is one
of probability only.

Parallel to (1.1)–(1.4) can be recognized subsystems (7.1)–(7.4). In
(7.2), "major plus minor" is the unmarked term, with independent clause
as major and dependent clause as minor information point: // ˄ I'll /
come if you / **want** me //. In (7.1) and (7.4), however, "major" is the

unmarked term: it is unlikely, though not impossible, for // **John** I saw / **yes**terday // and // ˄ if you / **want** me I'll / **come** // to be structured as major plus minor information point. This system does not allow for minor preceding major; something like this can be achieved only by more delicate contrasts within the pretonic. In (7.3), "major plus minor" is unmarked provided that system (2) does not apply (is "neutralized"); where it does, "major plus minor" is marked and, in fact, extremely unlikely except in transferred negative with marked tonicity (tonic on negative word): // ˄ I / **did**n't / come because he / **told** me //.

The information sub-system will serve here as a bridge between tonality and tonicity. Tonicity refers to the location of the tonic within the tone group; here, as with tonality, it is useful to recognize one condition as "tonicity neutral", namely the occurrence of the tonic on the final lexical item within the tone group. If neutral tonality is taken as the starting point, then this is equivalent to the fi nal lexical item in the clause. This then contrasts with marked tonicity as follows:

(8) INFORMATION FOCUS: (i) information point unmarked – tonicity
neutral // ˄ I / saw / John on / **Tues**day //, // ˄ I /saw /
John / there //, // ˄ I / saw / **John** //, // ˄ I / **saw** him //,
// John's de/**part**ed //, // **John** / has done // ; (ii) information
point marked – tonicity marked // ˄ I / saw / **John**
on / Tuesday // etc.

The range of possible places where a marked information point can fall in any tone group is determined by the rhythm: only a strong syllable can be tonic. It is important to note that variation in rhythm represents a different choice from that represented by variation in tonicity; the two are interconnected, but either may vary while the other remains constant. The grammatical meaning of rhythm requires a separate study; as an instance of it might be cited the contrast between // ˄ the / question / which he / **asked** is // surely ir/**rel**evant // (= 'the question "which did he ask?" ') and // ˄ the / question which he / **asked** is // surely ir/**rel**evant // (= 'the question that he asked'). Here, although only tonicity is being considered, this must be taken to subsume those variations in rhythm which are determined by tonicity, that is, where the contrast is between a weak syllable and a strong syllable **that is also tonic**, for example // ˄ I / **saw** him // as against // ˄ I / saw / **him** //.

Within "information point marked" it is useful to recognize a sub-system:

(9) MARKED INFORMATION FOCUS: (i) information point final (non-
lexical) – tonic "post-neutral" // ˄ I / saw / **him** //; (ii)

information point non-final (lexical or non-lexical) – tonic "pre-neutral" // **I** / saw him //, // **John's** de/parted //.

The marked information point is either contrastive, or new by reference to another item as given: // ∧ I / saw / **him** // either = 'not her' or in answer to *who did you see?* The difference, especially with non final marked information point, is often expounded by tone: see system (15) below. (The man in the London underground who was worried because he had no dog had read the well-known notice as //1 **dogs** must be / carried //, with *dogs* marked as new.) With certain high frequency collocations the marking is reversed; these are found especially in intransitive clause structure, with inanimate nouns as subject: // ∧ my / **head** aches //, // ∧ the / **door's** / locked //. This may also happen if the final lexical item is itself of very high frequency, at the grammatical end of lexis as it were: // ∧ the / **doc**tor's / coming //. In such cases neutral tonicity expounds a marked information point.

In transitive clause structure tonicity distinguishes extensive from intensive clauses, since an intensive complement always carries the tonic as unmarked information point even when fully grammatical (hence the obligatory use of *–self* items for personal pronouns as intensive Complement): intensive // ∧ he / seemed him/**self** // contrasts with extensive // ∧ he / **hurt** him/self //, // ∧ he / **hurt** him //. Again of course these can be reversed to give a marked information point, as in // ∧ he / **seemed** him/self // (but, rhythmically, not *// ∧ he / **seemed** himself //, though // ∧ he / **hur**t himself // is regular), // ∧ he / hurt him/**self** //. It is perhaps useful to recognize a distinct system here:

(10) EXTENSION IN TRANSITIVE CLAUSE: (i) grammatical Complement extensive – tonicity neutral // ∧ he / felt him/**self** // (= 'to see if he was bruised'); (ii) grammatical Complement intensive – tonicity marked // ∧ he / felt him/**self** //.

In a clause with final *–self* item the same distinction in tonicity may expound a structural contrast between extensive transitive clause with *–self* as Complement and intransitive clause with *–self* as Qualifier.

(11) CLAUSE STRUCTURE: (i) transitive – tonicity neutral // ∧ he / **asked** him/self //; intransitive – tonicity marked // ∧ he / asked him/**self** // (= 'he himself asked').

Again these can be reversed to give a marked information point. For the appositional // **he** asked him//**self** //, compare (6.1) above.

179

System (8) can be generalized to extend to compound sentences with marked tonality (one tone group): unmarked information point // ˄ he / said he was / **com**ing // contrasts with marked // ˄ he / **said** he was / coming //. In group structure, however, tonicity has distinct functions, both in the verbal group and in the nominal group, which should perhaps be regarded as forming separate systems.

> (12) CONTRAST (VERBAL GROUP): (i) non-contrastive – tonicity
> neutral // ˄ he / hasn't been / **asked** //; (ii) contrastive
> – tonicity marked // ˄ he / hasn't / **been** asked //.

The contrastive term requires tonic *does/do, did* in present and past positive active (note that non-tonic *does/do, did* are non-contrastive: // ˄ he / did / **ask** //, with tonicity neutral, is non-contrastive marked positive); and non-reduced forms where these items carry the tonic: // ˄ he / **has** asked // beside // ˄ he's / **asked** //. In verbal groups with three or more words there is a sub-system of "contrastive":

> (13) FOCUS OF CONTRAST: (i) polarity contrast – tonic on finite
> element // ˄ he // **has** been / asked // (= 'it's not that he
> hasn't'); (ii) tense contrast – tonic on non-finite element // ˄
> he's **been** asked // (= 'it's not that he's going to be').

But the factors determining this choice are complex, and other variables, such as voice, may be involved; sometimes it is difficult to show that the exponents are not simply in free variation.

In the nominal group tonicity expounds a structural contrast which is too complex to be dealt with here; it has been fully described elsewhere (Lees, 1963). It is generalized here into a single system, merely as an indication that it must be included in any discussion of the role of intonation:

> (14) HEAD STRUCTURE (NOMINAL GROUP): (i) simple Head
> – tonicity
> neutral // army / **offi**cer //, // home / **help** //; (ii)
> compound Head – tonicity marked // **shop** as/sistant //, //
> **cheque** / book // or // **shop** assistant //, // **cheque** book
> //.

Either of these may of course be reversed, by the superimposition of system (8), to give a marked information point: // **ar**my / officer // (= 'not air force'), // cheque / **book** // (= 'not a single cheque'). Ambiguity thus arises in a form such as // **pa**per / bag //, which may be either compound head with neutrally tonicity (= 'bag for paper') or simple

Head with marked tonicity (= 'bag made of paper (and not, as you thought, of polythene)'); // **pa**per bag //, however, can only be the former: a post-tonic simple Head remains strong.

The systems so far discussed have been for the most part those expounded by tonality and tonicity, with only occasional reference to systems expounded by tone. The remainder of the paper will be concerned with the latter. These will be considered on an assumption of neutral tonality and neutral tonicity: one clause one tone group, with tonic on final lexical item. They are, in general, in free combination with the systems described above; no attempt is made here to state the restrictions on such combination or to exemplify all possibilities.

Tone-expounded systems in the clause are, it is suggested, most usefully to be regarded as secondary systems of MOOD; that is to say, they are referable to the primary terms of the mood system – affirmative, interrogative and imperative. Mood is defined as the selection of values for the Subject-Predicator complex; the terms of the system, with their exponents, are as follows: affirmative – Subject precedes Predicator; interrogative – Subject follows first word of Predicator; imperative – Predicator present but Subject absent (*you* in imperative *you go* is not considered as Subject). The full implications of this system, and the explanation of problematical structures, lie outside the scope of this paper; for the purpose of displaying the role of intonation the generalized statement given here will suffice. The mood system is a system of the independent clause; dependent clauses, which are affirmative or, occasionally, interrogative in form, are not subject to this system: their principal tone choices have already been mentioned in connection with compound sentences, systems (1)–(4) above.

The treatment will be polysystemic; the value of the tones varies with, and depends on, the choice of mood. Affirmative clauses are considered first.

(15) RESERVATION: (i) unreserved – tone 1 //1 ∧ I'd / **like** / to //; (ii) reserved – tone **4** // **4** ∧ I'd / **like** / to // (= 'but I daren't').

Tone **4** is the tone of which the native speaker feels 'there's a "but" about it'; it is in fact very frequent on clauses which are not final in the sentence, often followed by a linked clause with *but*, and in clauses with marked tonicity: compare (5) and (9) above. It also enters, but **only** non-finally, into a sub-system which is not a subsystem of mood but operates in initial dependent clauses and in the first tone group of clauses with marked (double) tonality, where it is often associated with marked

Theme. This sub-system has already been stated as (3) above, but it may be useful to repeat it here to show its operation in clause structure:

(3.1) THEMATIC CONTRST: (i) theme unmarked – tone 4 //4 **John** //1 **al**ways / helps //, // 4 ^ at / **Christ**mas we // 1 stay at / **home** //, // 4 **lit**erature I // 1 **like** //; (ii) Theme confirmatory – tone 3 (in place of tone 4); (iii) Theme contrastive – tone **4** (in place of tone 4).

All three can be regarded as in contrast with tone 1 in neutral tonality, in which the Theme is "given": //1 John / **al**ways / helps // and so on.

(16) COMMITMENT: (i) neutral – tone 1 //1 ^ it's / **poss**ible // (= 'I don't know'), //1 ^ he / **does** //; (ii) uncommitted – tone −3 //−3 ^ it's **poss**ible // (= 'I don't care') //−3 ^ he / **might** do // ; (iii) committed – tone 5 // 5 ^ it's / **poss**ible // (= 'so what?'), // 5 ^ he / **will** do // (= 'you ought to know that').

This system is largely restricted to a clause standing alone as a simple sentence, and the marked terms are usually associated with rather short clauses.

(17) AGREEMENT: (i) neutral – tone 1 // 1 ^ I'll be / back to/**morr**ow //; (ii) confirmatory – tone 3 // 3 yes I'll be / back to/**morr**ow //; (iii) contradictory – tone 2 // 2 but I'll be / back to/**morr**ow // (= 'what are you fussing about?').

Note that (16) has tone −3, so that any pretonic strong syllables are low; (17) has tone 3, with mid-pretonic: the pitch of *back* is likely to be as high as, or higher than, that of the fi nal point of the rise on *tomorrow*.

It is possible that there is a distinction between tone 2 in (17) and tone 2 in the next system:

(18) SENTENCE FUNCTION: (i) statement – tone 1 //1 **John** has //; (ii) question – tone 2 //2 **John** has //.

But I have not been able to find convincing evidence of a distinction, and ambiguity does arise: //2 **John** has // – 'has he?' 'no, I'm asking you: has he?' It seems in any case rare for tone 2 affirmative clauses to be used as questions in British English, although minor clauses on tone 2 are regularly questions (cf. below).

(19) INFORMATION POINT: (i) major unmarked – tone 1 with tonicity neutral //1 ^ I / saw / John on the / **train** //; (ii) major

marked – tone 1 with tonicity marked //1 ∧ I / saw / **John**
on the / train //; (iii) major plus minor – tone 13 //13 ∧ I
/saw / **John** on the / **train** //.

This system is related to (7) and (8), but with the specification of tone
these three terms can be brought together as a system of the affirmative
clause. Here the system has an additional value, in that the term represented
by tone 13 is in high probability correlation with the "echo-subject"
structure: // 13 ∧ it's a / good / **shop** / **that** one //, and its variant *it's
a good shop is that one*. This yields a distinct system:

> (20) CLAUSE STRUCTURE: (i) transitive – tone 1 //1 ∧ they've/ left the
> / **oth**ers //; (ii) intransitive with echo-subject – tone 13 //13
> ∧ they've / **left** the / **oth**ers //.

The second of these is ambiguous, since it could be transitive with "major
plus minor" information point; the first is not. Tone 13 also occurs in
minor clauses consisting of two nominal groups, where its occurrence
allows us to recognize a "transitive" structure of Complement plus Subject by analogy with the echo–Subject: //13 nice / **chap** / **John** //.

In spite of the exponential parallelism, tone 53 does not stand to tone
13 in quite the same relation as does tone 5 to tone 1 (system (16)
above). In the first place, tone 53 contrasts with tone 13 in echo subject
and in minor "transitive" clauses as well as in other structures; in the
second place tone 53, though it could still be regarded as expounding
"commitment", tends to imply eagerness to help rather than the superior-
ity or even censure that are often associated with tone 5. Since moreover
there is no third term here it seems better to recognize a new system:

> (21) COMMITMENT (WITH MAJOR PLUS MINOR INFOR-
> MATION POINT):
> (i) neutral – tone 13 //13 **John** could / **tell** you //, // 13 ∧
> it's a / good / shop / **that** one //; (ii) committed – tone 53
> //53 **John** could / **tell** you //, // 53 ∧ it's a / good / **shop** /
> **that** one //.

Finally, the varieties of tone 1 yield three systems in affirmative clause as
follows:

> (22) KEY: (i) neutral – tone 1 //1 ∧ I / don't/ **know** //; (ii) strong
> – tone 1 + //1 + ∧ I / don't / **know** // (= 'stop asking
> me!'); mild – tone 1– //1– I / don't / know // (= 'sorry!').

> (23) FORCE: (i) neutral – tone 1 //1 ∧ he / simply / doesn't under/
> **stand** //; (ii) insistent – tone –1 //–1 ∧ he / simply /
> doesn't under/**stand** //.

The "insistent" tone −1 is that with uneven or "spiky" pretonic, each pretonic foot starting on a low pitch and rising steeply. (This tone is pedagogically very useful for demonstrating the rhythm of English speech.)

(24) CO-ORDINATION (LINKING): (i) neutral – tone 1 //1 ∧ I had the / jack the / king and the / **ace** //; (ii) listing – tone …1 //…1 ∧ I had the / jack the / king and the / **ace** //.

Each listed item rises slightly from mid-pitch, beginning with the strong syllable, and with optional pauses in between. If the listed item contains more than one foot, pre-final strong syllables are level, at a pitch level with or above that reached by the end of the final foot; for example, *two* and *a* in //…1 ∧ I want / two / oranges and a / **lem**on //.

In interrogative clauses the value of intonation contrasts depends on a distinction into two types: WH- interrogative and yes/no interrogatives. The WH- interrogatives, which will be considered first, resembles the affirmative in having tone 1 as a generally "neutral" term.

(25) KEY: (i) neutral – tone 1 //1 where are you / **go**ing //; (ii) mild – tone 2 with tonicity neutral //2 where are you / **go**ing // (= 'may I ask?').

Here the mild key represents a question with, as it were, request for permission to ask; it is less peremptory, more distant and more polite. Within "mild key" there is a further sub-system of "involvement"; this system, however, operates only marginally with WH- interrogatives, the marked term being rare in this type; it is therefore presented as (29) below.

If the tonic falls on the WH- group, the meaning of tone 2 is different:

(26) RELATION TO PREVIOUS UTTERANCE: (i) unrelated – tone 1; (ii) echo question – tone 2 with tonicity marked (tonic on WH-group) // 2 **where** are you / going //.

The echo question is a request for repetition of something unheard, forgotten or disbelieved.

A sub-system cutting across (25) and (26) operates within each of the tone 2 terms:

(27) SPECIFICATION OF QUERY: (i) unspecified – tone 2, tonicity neutral or marked; (ii) specified – tone **2**, tonicity neutral //2 what are you / **look**ing for // or marked // 2 **what** are you / looking for //.

Tone **2** is the sharp fall-rise; the rise takes place on a new foot if one is present (on *looking for* in the second example), otherwise on a new syllable (on *for* in the first example). If the tonic consists of one syllable, only this syllable is falling-rising: //2 **why** //. This term means 'that's what I'd like to ask about' and occurs characteristically when that clause contains an item that is "new" (as opposed to "given"), such item carrying the falling segment of the tonic: // 2 what's the / **bas**ket / for // (= 'why have you got a basket with you?').

The yes/no interrogative, on the other hand, has tone 2 as its "neutral" tone:

(28) KEY: (i) neutral – tone 2 //2 are you going to / **tell** me //; (ii) strong – tone 1 //1 are you going to / **tell** me // (= 'I want to know').

Strong key here implies a question with demand for an answer; sometimes demand for a satisfactory answer, hence approaching a request. The choice of key is bound up with the form of the verbal group: a 'pleading' item such as *won't you*, for example, is unlikely to occur with tone 1.

System (27) operates here as with WH- interrogatives: //2 d'you / want a / **bis**cuit // specifies *biscuit* as the point at issue and is more likely to occur when the biscuits are not already on display. Cutting across this is a further system:

(29) INVOLVEMENT: (i) neutral – tone 2 //2 are you coming / **with** us //; (ii) involved – tone –2 //–2 are you coming / **with** us //.

Involvement may mean a desire to affect the decision, thus implying suggestion or encouragement, or may imply some judgement such as 'you ought (not) to', 'you should have told me'. The combination of the marked terms of (27) and (29) is the most infrequent variant: // –2 are you coming / **with** us // might imply 'I thought you were going on your own (27), and it would have been better if you had done (29)'. (29) also operates with WH- interrogatives (see (25) above), but rather infrequently (that is, the marked term is infrequent) except with clauses which could be suggestions: // –2 why don't you / take a / **taxi** //.

Two further systems are found only with yes/no interrogatives:

(30) COMMITMENT: (i) neutral – tone 2 //2 is he / **sure** of it //; (ii) uncommitted – tone –3 // –3 is he / **sure** of it // (= 'not that I care'); committed – tone 5 //5 is he / **sure** of it // (= 'because if not, then . . .').

This system is closely parallel to (16). The "committed" type often begin with *yes but* or end with *though*; the uncertainty is a cause of concern, by contrast with the "uncommitted" where concern is disclaimed.

(31) SENTENCE FUNCTION: (i) question – tone 2; (ii) statement
      (strong assertion) – tone **4** //4 is he / **sure** of it // (= 'of course he is').

This system is marginal; the tone **4** term seems to occur in children's speech and in loud-reading but rarely in conversation among adults – it may represent a survival or a dialectal form.

Finally, yes/no interrogatives with co-ordinate groups display a distinct choice in which the co-ordinate items may be in one of two contrasting relations, with marked tonality in each case:

(32) CO-ORDINATION TYPE: (i) alternative question – tone sequence
      2(...)1 //2 would you like / **tea** or //1 **coff**ee //
      (= 'which?'); (ii) list question – tone sequence 2(...)2 //2
      would you like / **tea** or //2 **coff**ee // (= 'yes or no?').

The same choice appears with co-ordinate clauses:

(32.1) //2 ∧ shall I / **write** or shall I //1 **phone** you //; //2 ∧ shall
        I / **write** or shall I // 2 **phone** you // ∧

The second term in each case may be an unfinished alternative question: = "or what?" An interrogative clause with co-ordinate groups may, on the other hand, have neutral tonality, in which case the choice is expounded as follows:

(32.2) alternative question – tone 1 //1 would you like / tea or /
        coffee //; list question – tone 2 //2 would you like / tea or
        / **coff**ee //.

The first term is subject to system (24): it may have tone...1, in which case it is unambiguously an alternative question. With tone 1 (neutral) it tends to be ambiguous, or at least to be treated as such by the humorist, who may answer simply: "yes".

In imperative clauses, it seems necessary to consider negative imperative as being distinct from positive imperative, at least as regards "key". In positive imperative tone 1 is perhaps "neutral":

(33) KEY: (i) neutral – tone 1 //1 wait for / **me** //; (ii) mild – tone
      3 //3 wait for / **me** //.

The choice is, however, affected by another factor: if the final element is new, tone 1 is more likely: //1 take the/ **train** //, //1 come for / **dinn**er

//; if given, tone 3: //3 leave your / **coat** //, //3 keep the / **change** //. This is the neutral variety of tone 3, with mid-pretonic; here, uniquely, pretonic and tonic may occur on a single foot or even a single syllable: //3 hur-**ry** //, //3 ru-**un** // (compare (40) below).

In negative imperative, tone 1 is marked as "strong":

(34) KEY: (i) neutral – tone 3 //3 don't be / **late** //; (ii) strong
– tone 1 //1 don't be / **late** //.

In both positive and negative, system (22) operates as a sub-system of the tone 1 term, although, especially in negative imperative, its marked terms seem less frequent than in affirmative clauses.

The remaining systems in imperative operate with both positive and negative; the marked terms thus contrast with tone 1 or with tone 3.

(35) REQUEST TYPE: (i) neutral – tone 1 or 3; (ii) warning – tone
–3 //–3 ∧ be / **careful**//, //–3 don't / **move** //.

(36) INFORMATION POINT: (i) major – tone 1 or 3; (ii) major plus
minor – tone 13 //13 **wait** for / **me** //, // 13 **don't** be /
late //.

Tone 13 here thus has the additional function of showing the verbal element as a major information point with the Complement or Adjunct as minor: //13 **leave** the / **oth**ers //; this is especially common in the negative, where the tone 1 tonic falls on *don't*. The tonic marking of the finite verbal element relates to the polarity of the request (cf. (13) above); in the negative, and the marked positive with *do*, this tone is often a plea and is accompanied by creaky voice quality: //13 **do** hurry / **up** //.

The marked exclusive imperative with *you*, as in *you go* (exclusive by contrast with inclusive imperative *let's go*), is distinguished from affirmative by the fact that *you* in imperative clause is always a strong syllable; it may or may not be tonic; // **you** / go // contrasts with // you / **go** //. In affirmative it may also be tonic, but if it is not it is weak: // **you** / go // contrasts with // ∧ you / **go** //. There is thus ambiguity when (and only when) *you* is tonic; such a clause could be either affirmative or imperative. If affirmative, however, it is likely, because of marked tonicity, to have tone **4**: //**4 you** / say so //, whereas in imperative it will be more likely to have tone 1, 3 or 13 as above. Likewise ambiguity arises with tonic *you* between negative imperative and interrogative: //don't /
you / go //; here interrogative is likely to have tone 2 and imperative (see next paragraph) tone **4**.

(37) FORCE: (i) neutral – tone 1 or 3; (ii) compromising – tone **4**
//**4** tell him the / **truth** // (= 'at least do that'), //**4** don't let

him / **have** it // ('whatever else you do'); insistent – tone 5
//5 tell him the / **truth** // ('why not?'), //5 don't let him /
have it // (= 'that's the solution, obviously').

The "compromising" term is clearly related to affirmative "reserved",
system (15), but not identical; tone **4** in imperative implies 'do this whatever else you (don't) do' and is often accompanied by *at least*. A special
use of this term is that with tonic *you* in negative imperative: //**4** don't
/ **you** / do it // (= 'whoever else might' or 'let someone else'). Thus
while tone **4** suggests that this is all that is being asked, tone **5** by contrast
implies 'I make no concession'. It is perhaps worth noting in this connection that the use of *please* in imperative clauses, both initially and
finally, is subject to a great deal of variation both in tone and in tonality;
a more detailed study would need to take account of this.

Finally in imperative clause:

> (38) SENTENCE FUNCTION: (i) command – tone 1 or 3; (ii) question
> – tone 2 //2 tell him the / **truth** // (= 'shall I?').

"Minor" clauses, those with no predicator, which lie outside the mood
system, are subject to systems (15)–(24) as are affirmative clauses. There
are, however, one or two additional points to be made about them.

Minor clauses on tone 2 regularly have the sentence function of question; a clause such as //2 ∧ on the / **train** // may be selecting with equal
likelihood either in system (17) or in system (18). A minor clause consisting of, or containing, a WH- group is subject to (25)–(27); if, however,
it consists of only one foot, such as / **who** //, the distinction between
(26) and (27) is neutralized. Thus while //2 **which** / book // is echo
question and //2 which / **book** // is "mild key", //2 **who** // may be
either.

A minor clause on tone –**3** may be either, as affirmative, "uncommitted" (17): //–3 per/**haps** //, or, as imperative, warning (35): //–3 **care**-
ful //. On tone 5 it is usually operating in (16): //5 **cer**tainly //; there
is, however, a sub-system here:

> (39) EXCLAMATION KEY: (i) neutral – tone 5 //5 **won**derful i/dea
> //; (ii) strong – tone **5**, often with breathy voice quality //**5**
> **won**derful i/dea //.

This system may be found associated with some clauses having imperative form with exclamatory sentence function, for example //5 or **5**
look at the / **time** //.

Vocatives may operate, usually initially or finally, in major clauses: if
final, they do not take a separate tone group, although they frequently

"turn" a tone 1 into a tone 13 or a tone 2 into a tone **2**; if initial, they may take a separate tone group, usually with tone 1 or 2. When a vocative operates as a minor clause on its own, it may take any of the simple tones 1–5 including the "split" variety of tone 3 (see under (33) above). It may be worthwhile recognizing a distinct system for minor clause vocatives:

> (40) VOCATIVE: (i) command, as in (33) – tone 1 //1 **John** //, with sub-system (22); (ii) question, as in (28) – tone 2 //2 **John** //, with sub-system (27); (iii) warning, as in (35) – tone 3 //3 **John** //; (iv) mild command, as in (33) – tone 3 "split" //3 Jo-**ohn** //; (v) non-finality, as "unmarked theme" in (3.1) – tone 4 //4 **John** //; (vi) insistent command, as in (37) – tone 5 //5 **John** //; (vii) reproach, as in (39) – tone **5** //5 **John** //.

The above is an attempt to organize some of the meaningful contrasts expounded by intonation in English into the framework of a grammatical statement. It is not, as already remarked, claimed to be "complete", either at the level of phonology, where many more delicate distinctions can be recognized (O'Connor and Arnold 1961), or at the level of grammar, where in addition to contrasts expounded by the more delicate phonological distinctions (for example those in the pretonic of tone 1, which is widely variable) there are undoubtedly other meaningful uses to be stated for the distinctions here recognized (Schubiger 1958). In particular, intonation features characteristic of specific items have not been taken into account; moreover I have concentrated on those places where intonation can be shown to be independently systemic, that is, not fully correlated with other choices, but wholly or at least partially independent of them.

It is perhaps necessary to justify the introduction here of yet another form of notation; the reason for doing so was that the present form seemed simpler for the specific purpose of discussing intonation as an exponent of grammatical meaning. The contrasts which it was necessary to take into account are phonetically much less delicate than those provided for in a "tonetic" notation; the system used here reflects the general principle that only those distinctions which are shown in the grammatical description to be meaningful are represented in the phonological analysis.

In treating intonation grammatically I am not suggesting that the view of it as carrying emotive meanings is to be rejected. The response of informants to contours which they are asked to evaluate on certain scales reflects precisely the native speaker's awareness of intonation as meaningful in the language; and many of the labels used here, which like all grammatical labels are chosen on semantic criteria, add by themselves nothing to a formulation in emotive terms. What I have tried to suggest is that in many cases the patterns can be systematized into a formal grammatical statement, which enables us both to show what are the contrastive possibilities at specific places in the language and to link these with other grammatical choices. We cannot, I think, fully describe the grammar of spoken English **without** reference to contrasts expounded by intonation; many important distinctions are made in this way, including some on which others, not themselves intonational, can be shown to depend.

The danger is perhaps of not seeing the wood for the trees; it is natural that we should wish to seek 'the general meaning' of English intonation. In the previous paper (VII.8) I attempted a crude generalization of this kind. This could certainly be considerably improved upon; but with each refinement some generality tends to be lost: there is the familiar inverse relation between range of validity and precision. The results of the extensive current work in this field could well lead to a more effective synthesis; meanwhile the sort of treatment suggested here may in turn perhaps contribute to the total picture.

VII.9(1963):264–86

★ ★ ★

It has long been recognized that intonation in English performs a dual function. In the **metafunctional** conceptual framework of systemic theory, it expresses both textual and interpersonal meanings.

The interpersonal meanings are those associated with mood and modality. These are realized by the choice of tone. Thus the most obvious contrast of all, and the earliest to be described, that between falling tone and rising tone, expresses some form of 'telling' versus 'asking', sharing with the mood system (declarative, interrogative etc.) the realization of speech function; while within this, the continuously graded contrast of wide fall versus narrow fall expresses the force of the telling, that of 'strong' versus 'weak', and so on. I shall not be concerned with these interpersonal meanings here.

The textual meanings are those involved in the creation of discourse. Intonation also has a **phoric** function, that of creating cohesion with what has gone before (anaphoric), or with what is still to come (cataphoric). Delbridge's interesting experiments reported in 1970 showed how even under experimental conditions listeners were typically sensitive to intonational signals of this kind. The present paper attempts a brief summary of the textual functions of English intonation, under three headings (cf. Halliday, 1967;VII.2(1967)):

(1) tonicity. location of tonic prominence
(2) tone: choice of pitch contour
(3) tone sequences.

We will say something about each of these in turn.

1 LOCATION OF TONIC PROMINENCE

As is well known, the unmarked focus of information on the information unit in English is on the final lexical item; and this has considerable discourse potential. We have to consider the unmarked and the marked forms separately, since they differ in this respect.

1.1 Unmarked tonicity

This realizes an information structure in which the news line is that of (Given +) New, that is, an element New as culminative, optionally preceded by an element Given. The listener's attention is directed towards the culmination; what comes before may or may not hark back to something that has preceded in the discourse. So for example in

//1 how about / going to see the / Moscow / **circus** //1 ^ it's
sup/posed to be / very / **good** //

whereas the first clause is entirely New, the anaphoric *it* of the second clause is assigned a Given status. There may be a rhythmic signal of this "givenness"; for example, in the agnate form.

//1^ it's supposed to be / very / **good** //

the rhythm suggests that the "givenness" also extends across the modalized Predicator *supposed to be*.

1.2 Marked tonicity

Whereas anything **preceding** the focal element may be Given, and hence phoric in the discourse, if there is lexical material **following** the focus, this is thereby explicitly **signalled** as Given. Hence marked tonicity has a clearly defined discourse function. So, for example, in

//1 nobody'd / ever / **tried** / working the / whole / programme
/ out in / detail //

the marked focus not only has an effect on the focal item itself, giving it an added feature of assertion, contrast etc. depending on what tone it is, it also determines the discourse value of what follows. Here, we know that the entire segment *working the whole programme out in detail* is Given; its post-tonic status enables us to know that this meaning – and possibly this exact wording, though not necessarily so – is already in the air. Asked to guess what preceded it we might say something like *So what happened when they worked out all the details of the programme?*

2 Choice of pitch contour

We can construct the tonal system of English out of the basic opposition between fall and rise: falling pitch means 'polarity determinate', rising means 'polarity indeterminate'. Then the system of five tones arises as follows:

1 fall (determinate)
2 rise (indeterminate)
3 level (no decision)
4 fall–rise (seemed determinate but isn't)
5 rise–fall (seemed not determinate but is).

This means that tones other than those with a (terminal) fall are essentially phoric. Tones 1 and 5 are self-sufficient; they do not presume any surrounding discourse. But tones 2, 3 and 4 all presuppose further text. They do so, however, in a variety of different ways.

2.1 Tone 2 (rising)

Here "polarity indeterminate" typically means 'you tell me whether or not'; in other words, I want an answer – so I'm asking you a question. The direction of presumption is thus cataphoric: the answer will follow.

There are two subsidiary functions of tone 2. One is the famous "high rising tone" (HRT) of Australian English, with its sense of 'got it? is that what you want to know? – come again if not satisfied' (see Guy and Vonwiller, 1984); this is an ordinary tone 2, and also cataphoric – though silence is an acceptable answer. The other is the meaning of 'contradiction': 'you were wrong, so I'm challenging you'; this one is anaphoric to a preceding assertion, as in

//1˄ you were / going to / let me / copy / all your / **games** //
– //2 I never / **said** that //

Both of these are ordinary rising tones, perhaps with additional voice quality features, or with pitch range realizing a particular "key".

2.2 Tone 4 (falling-rising)

The sense of this is: 'it seemed, or seems, determinate; but . . .'; there is some reservation or contrast. The contrast may be either anaphoric or cataphoric, that is, either with an assertion preceding or with one (by the same speaker) to follow; for example,

//1 ∧ you / have to / leave them a / fixed de/**posit** //
– //4 ∧ it / doesn't say / anything a/bout that / **here** //
//4 ∧ I / may be i/**magining** / things but I //1 can't help / feeling / someone's / **watching** us //

The reservation is the sense of 'whatever else (may be the case)'; the exact nature of the reservation is typically left in the air, so that the listener has to construct the discourse for himself. For example,

//4 ∧ I / don't want / **all** of it //

– to which the listener might respond by *you could just have a half if you'd like,* showing that he had understood the fall-rise as signaling 'but that doesn't mean I don't want any'.

2.3 Tone 3 (level; realized phonetically as low rising, to distinguish clearly from a fall)

Here the sense is 'neither determinate nor indeterminate', so the message to hand is unfinished, contingent or partial. That is to say, there may be a cataphoric presumption of a following 'and', or at least some additional information without which the message is incomplete:

//3 ∧ I'll / just / water the / **plants** and //1 then I'll be / **with** you //
//3 ∧ you take / three / **tablets** //1 every / four / **hours** //

Alternatively the tone 3 message may be leaning backwards, rounding off some preceding information: a final circumstantial element in the clause, for example,

//13 ∧ he / seems to have / lost his / **appetite** with / all this / moving a/**round** //

(where the sense is 'New but secondary'), or a reminder following what would otherwise be a marked focus (where the sense is 'Given but important'):

//13 ∧ I / **never** for/get a / **face** //

And in some registers tone 3 is simply used to break up what would otherwise be unmanageably long chunks of information, especially in reading aloud:

//3 each / **volume** con //3 tains a col/**lection** of more than //3
three hundred and / fifty / **artefacts** from //3 various / **sites**
//1 scattered through/out the Pa/**cific** //

3 TONE SEQUENCES

Consideration of the essentially phoric function of the non-falling tones leads naturally into the fi nal topic, that of the textual significance of particular sequences of tones (cf. Elmenoufy, 1969). Here we shall consider just the tone sequences 3–1 and 4–1; comparing these with tone 1 used by itself. The semantic variation may be displayed in the form of a paradigm:

(i) //1 ∧ I / like / **milk** // 1 ∧ I / don't like / **cheese** //
(ii) //3 ∧ I / like / **milk** but I //1 don't like / **cheese** //
(iii) //4 ∧ al/though I / like / **milk** I //1 don't like / **cheese** //
(iv) //1 ∧ de/spite my / liking for / milk I / don't like / **cheese** //

Here, each of (i)–(iii) contains two information units. In (i), no relationship is set up between them. In (ii), the two are presented as equal, but the first is shown to be not the end of the story. In (iii), the two are unequal: the first, which is dependent, functions as a condition on the second. Finally in (iv) there is only one unit of information.

It will be observed that in the above paradigm the tactic (logical) structure covaries with the informational (textual) structure:

	tactic	informational	
(i)	two unrelated clauses	tone sequence	1 + 1
(ii)	one paratactic clause complex	"	3 + 1
(iii)	one hypotactic clause complex	"	4 + 1
(iv)	one clause	single tone 1	

This brings out the association between the textual and the logical systems. Each traverses a gamut from 'two units, unrelated', through 'two units, related and equal' and 'two units, related and unequal', to 'one unit'; in one instance the unit is a quantum of information, in the other it is an element in a tactic construction (cf. Martin, 1983). The unmarked combination is that of terms of the same degree, as set out in the paradigm above. The speaker may, however, select marked alternatives in which textual and logical options are recombined, with tension set up between them; for example

//4 ˄ they / don't / **die** //1 ˄ they / don't / **grow** //

'they just sit there'; cf.

//4 ˄ I / like / **milk** //1 ˄ I / don't like / **cheese** //

'that's all there is to it'; likewise

//1 ˄ although he / said /**yes** //1 ˄ he / meant / **no** //
//1 ˄ although I / like / **milk** //1 ˄ I / don't like / **cheese** //

So the tone sequence 3–1 and 4–1 create textual structures which are intermediate between 1–1 and 1: neither is the information all of a piece, nor is it two pieces each complete in itself. When the listener hears a tone 3 or a tone 4 he listens out for something to satisfy the expectancy set up by the "non-fall". There must be some context in which the rising pitch movement is resolved, its relevance being established by its relation to something else. Under heading (2) above, we saw how tone relates to the discourse, through conversational structures such as question and answer (and part of the fascination of the Australian HRT has been the difficulty of interpreting exactly what its discourse context is). Under (3) we showed how tone is related to the grammar, through the logical structure of the clause complex. Thus the structure of information as New plus Given, and the choice between information that is self-contextualizing and information that is not, are both realized in English through the phonological system of intonation; hence the very great significance of intonation as a resource for carrying forward the discourse (cf. Fawcett, 1981).

VII.10(1985):287–92

Additional readings

On Grammar (Volume 1) – 2(1961):55, 78, 90–1; 4(1966):114; 7(1970):192–3; 8(1979):205-7; 10(1985): 262-4, 269-70

Linguistic Studies of Text and Discourse (Volume 2) – 1(1964):19; 2(1977):27–9, 32–6; 7(1992):204–5; 8(1994):232–3, 255

On Language and Linguistics (Volume 3) – 12(1997):265

The Language of Early Childhood (Volume 4) – 2(1975):50–1; 4(1974):106–7; 7(1975):162, 177, 184-9; 10(1984):233; 13(1975):297

The Language of Science (Volume 5) – 3(1998):70-71

Computational and Quantitative Studies (Volume 6) – 5(1992):77-8; 7(1993):135; 10(1995):221

Studies in English Language (Volume 7) – Introduction(2005):xxxvi; 2(1967): 57–70, 106–7; 3(1968):139–40; 4 (1969):155-6, 161; 5(1970):192–5; 7(1985): 213–5, 218; 8(1963):237–86; 10(1985):287–92

Language and Education (Volume 9) – 4(1979):71–3; 6(1996):101; 7(1960):158–9

Language and Society (Volume 10) – 2(1971):63

Chapter Nine

LANGUAGE TEACHING, LEARNING
AND DEVELOPMENT

Summary

M.A.K. Halliday suggests that language development is three things: learning language, learning through language, and learning about language. Because language learning is learning how to mean, it is all the more important for language teaching to be informed by a description of language that takes meaning into account. Whether one is learning his mother tongue or a second language, the learning experience should be an enriching one as the learner becomes aware of the rich meaning potential of language. Almost all learning takes place through language, and while a child does not need to know about language to learn language, the better informed the language teacher is about language, the more successful the learning is likely to be.

Selected readings

On Language and Linguistics (Volume 3)

THE DEVELOPMENTAL PERSPECTIVE

When in the early 1970s, through working with teachers engaged in initial literacy, I began investigating the earliest phases of language development in children, I was struck by a number of features of the child's "emergence into meaning", and of early semiotic encounters which seemed highly significant for the way language had evolved. I will refer here to six of these features: (1) "Meaning and moving": the correlations between linguistic and physical development; (2) "Protolanguage": the emergence of a "child tongue" before the mother tongue begins to take over; (3) "Microfunctions": the functional contexts of the protolanguage;

(4) "Macrofunctions": the strategy guiding the transition from protolanguage to mother tongue; (5) "Grammar last": the way the protolanguage (which has no level of grammar in it) is deconstrued and then reconstrued as a three-level system of "semantics/ grammar/phonology"; (6) "Telling": the development of the concept of imparting information, as the latest phase of all. The next few paragraphs deal with each of these in turn.[3]

1 Learning language is not learning sounds and words; nor is it learning to name and to refer. Rather it is, as I put it in the title of an earlier book, "learning how to mean". Meaning (acting semiotically) develops along with doing (acting materially) as interdependent modes of human behaviour; and both depend on interaction with the physical and social environment. We find various stages in a child's semiotic development, associated with the development of bodily postures and movement. (i) Premeaning: exchanging *attention*. This takes place from birth: it goes with moving the head and body, flexing the limbs, "pre-reaching". The two activities, material and pre-semiotic, are combined when the baby activates the whole body, including the organs of speech, accompanied by smiling and gurgling, in phase with the directed attention of its mother or other member of its "meaning group".[4] (ii) First steps in meaning: exchanging *signs* (see below, (2) for definition). This takes place from around four months; it goes with lifting the head, aligning the body, rolling over, reaching and grasping an object. The sign (which may be realized, say, as a high-pitched squeak) is gaining attention and/or showing curiosity, "I want to be together with you", "I want to know what's going on" (meaning as interpersonal or experiential intentionality). (iii) Protolanguage: exchanging *sign systems*. This takes place typically in the second half of the first year; it goes with crawling, mobility from one place to another. (The systems are described in (3) below.) (iv) Language: exchanging *words-in-structures* (lexicogrammar). This takes place typically early in the second year; it goes with walking, bipedal movement. It is only at this fourth stage that grammar begins to develop.

2 The protolanguage, or child tongue, is a semiotic of a type that has evolved in many species, perhaps all those with a certain level of primary consciousness (that exemplified by dogs in Edelman's discussion). Its elements are signs in the classical sense: that is, *meaning/expression pairs*, such that there is a redundancy between the two (the expression "realizes" the meaning, e.g. a particular miaow "means" 'I want milk'). (Note that the meaning here is non-referential; there is no "naming" involved.) Looking back at the protolanguage from the vantagepoint of (adult-like) language we can say that it has a semantics and a phonology (or kinology: the

expression may be any combination of vocal and gestural) but no (lexico-) grammar.[5] The meanings develop around a small number of motifs: "I (don't) want, (don't) give me" (instrumental); "do this for/with me" (regulatory); "let's be together, you-&-me" (interactional); "I'm curious about/(don't) like that" (personal), and may extend also to "let's pretend" (imaginative) and perhaps "what's that?" (heuristic – this is already transitional into language). The mode of expression children use in their protolinguistic signs is highly variable. Some prefer the gestural mode, others the vocal, others some mixture of the two. The origin of vocal expressions may be imitation of the child's own natural sounds (sighing, crying), imitation of adult sounds, or pure invention; they seem to adults to range over a wide phonetic space, but they appear quite stable once one describes them in terms of vocal postures rather than of articulatory categories. The critical feature of the protolanguage is that it is a system of social signs; the impetus – the semiotic energy – comes from the child, but the signs, and sign systems, can only be construed in interaction with the child's "others", the meaning group, who are (unselfconsciously, of course) tracking the child's development by exchanging meanings with him throughout his waking hours.

3 The glosses used in the previous paragraph (instrumental, regulatory, interactional, personal, imaginative, heuristic) are semiotic contexts in which meaning first develops in the form of **contrast**: that is, as a network of systems, in the technical sense of this term in systemic theory – sets of options within a given material–semiotic situation, like 'I want'/ 'I don't want', or 'that's an interesting object'/'that's my favourite toy' (again, all adult language glosses are misleading because they imply referential meanings). A typical synchronic cross-section of a protolinguistic system is that of Hal at twelve to thirteen and a half months (Figure 1).[6] The overall system, of course, is in constant flux – typically expanding, although individual signs may drop out or change into something different; the optimum interval for such cross-sectional overviews seems to be about six weeks. As a developing system of this kind the protolanguage may continue to function for the child for six to eight or nine months or even more; but it then gets transformed, more or less rapidly, into a system of the adult kind, the "mother tongue". There is no clear evidence that any other species take this step.

Meanwhile the protolanguage provides the conditions for the emerging consciousness of self. Let us represent the microfunctions schematically as in Figure 2. This theorizes that meaning – semiotic activity – develops out of the child's sense of contradiction between the two primary modes of experience, the material (what goes on "out there") and the conscious

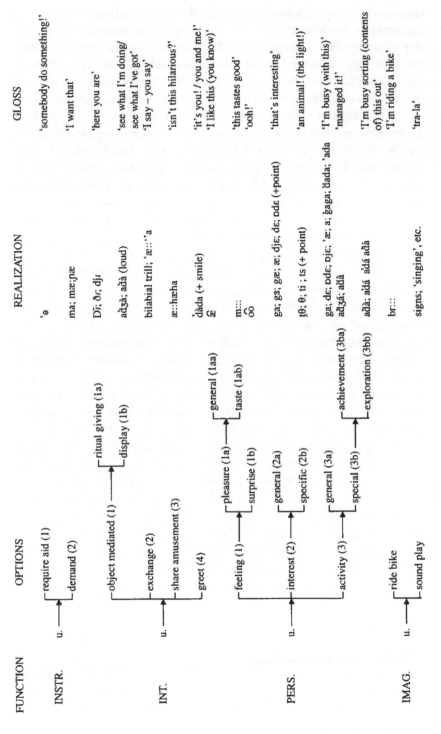

Figure 1 Hal's protolanguage at 12 to 13 ½ months (From Clare Painter, *Into the Mother Tongue*, London: Pinter 1984)

(what goes on "in here"). In construing a sign, the child is projecting one mode through the intermediary of the other – construing conceptual order out of perceptual chaos (as Edelman says, "the world . . . is an unlabelled place" (p. 99)). The projection of the material by the conscious transforms this impact between inner and outer experience into meaning. There are thus two variables involved. The projection may take the form either of 'this is how I want things to be' ("active") or of 'this is how things are' ("reflective"); the domain that is being projected may be either 'you and me' ("first/second person") or 'the rest of reality' ("third person"). The intersection of these two variables defines the "self" simultaneously (1) as source of projection and (2) as distinct (a) from the "other" (me from you) and (b) from the perceived environment. The transition from child tongue to mother tongue depends epigenetically on this social-semiotic construction of selfhood.

4 When children begin to move from protolanguage into language, typically when they are some way into the second year of life, the same underlying principles are extended to serve as the guiding strategy for the transition. It has been known for a long time that some form of opposition between demanding and describing is characteristic of the first phase of language (mother tongue) development;[7] we have been able to show (i) that this is systematically realized (construed) in the form of the expression, perhaps typically by intonation, voice quality or some combination of the two, and (ii) that it does not emerge "out of the blue" but is derived by generalizing from the microfunctional profile of the protolanguage. I labelled the opposition "pragmatic/mathetic", to suggest 'language to act with' as against 'language to learn with'. Initially, in this phase, each utterance of the child is **either** one **or** the other: either 'this is the way I think things are' (objects, properties, processes like

form of projection / domain of experience	active (what should be)	reflective (what is)
1st/2nd person (you & me)	regulatory 'do for me!'	interactional 'you + me together'
"3rd person" (all else)	instrumental 'give me!'	personal 'I like/wonder'

Figure 2 Microfunctions of protolanguage: semiotic origins

201

moon, big ladder, green light, bird gone), or 'this is the way I want things to be' (demands for goods or services, like *down!* ('I want to get down'), *mummy come!, more drink!*). The latter always demand a response; their pragmatic function is made entirely clear. The former do not; they may be self-addressed or other-addressed, but if addressed to another then that person must be someone who is sharing or has shared the experience. The child is describing, or annotating, but not yet telling – the meaning is mathetic (construing experience), not informative, and the child has still no concept of language as information.

5 Now for the first time the child has developed a "grammar": that is, a purely abstract level of semiosis "in between" the meaning and the expression. The sign-based system of the protolanguage has been deconstrued and reconstrued as a tristratal semiotic comprising semantics, lexicogrammar and phonology. It should be emphasized that "lexicogrammar" is a single stratum, with a continuum from grammar (small closed systems with very general domains) to lexis (open-ended sets with very specific domains); it makes no sense to say that lexis develops before grammar. Children may take variable lengths of time to construe complex syntagms; but as soon as their utterance is being construed as a word, by the same token it is also functioning grammatically.

How does this grammaticization of the system of meaning come about? The strategy seems to be the fundamental principle of semogenesis, namely that of decoupling – the dissociation of associated variables. This can take place in many different contexts; here is the instance I myself first observed, a few days after the child in question had taken his first steps in walking. He had at the time, as part of his protolanguage, three signs that had become specialized to the three people in his meaning group, 'mummy', 'daddy', 'anna'; these were not yet referring, but were person-specific interactional, and were said always on a high level tone (not used in other expressions), as in Figure 3(a). Within a period of two or three days he deconstrued this system and reconstrued it as in Figure 18.3(b). The person-specific signs have now become names, while the interactional component has been grammaticized as a modal opposition of greeting (acknowledging presence) or seeking (overcoming absence). In other words, the child now has a proto-grammar consisting of two systems, one realized lexically, the other phonologically; the two systems are dissociated, hence freely combinable, and each utterance must select in both. In the event, it was another three months before the child followed up this development; but in this one move he had underpinned a semiotic of a fundamentally different kind.[8] This is the semiotic that embodies Edelman's "higher-order consciousness"; it has a new and

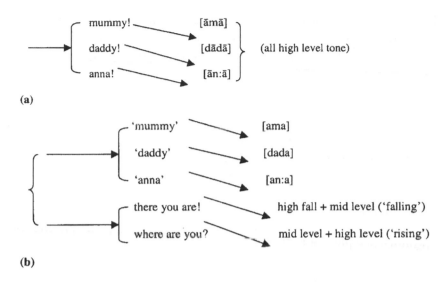

(a)

(b)

Figure 3 (a) System of person–specific interactional signs, with complex realization (articulation + intonation); (b) system (a) reconstrued as two simultaneous systems: one referring (now as "proper names"), realized by articulation; the other addressing (greeting or seeking), realized by intonation

distinctive kind of network, a lexicogrammar, at the core. (If the form of a grammar was genetically programmed, why would children first construe a semiotic of another kind, in which there is no trace of grammar at all?)

6 The final step to be taken in developing language in this specifically human sense is that of reconstruing the strategic opposition of "pragmatic/mathetic" into a new "metafunctional" form of organization. I shall return to this in the section of the paper that follows; but a brief account needs to be given from the developmental perspective. We can summarize under four headings. (i) The **opposition between** pragmatic and mathetic develops into the grammar of mood and modality: grammar in its guise of ***enacting interpersonal relationships*** of all kinds, from rapidly alternating dialogic roles to ongoing patterns of familial, institutional and socio–economic hierarchy. (ii) The **experiential content** of both mathetic and pragmatic develops into the grammar of processes, things and properties (transitivity, systems of nominal categorization): grammar in its guise of ***construing experience***, both that of the collective, embodied in the grammatical system, and that of the individual, embodied in the ongoing instantial selections. (iii) The child now

develops the grammar of **relations between** processes (and other phenomena): grammar in its role of building up commonsense logic, construed as 'and', 'or', 'is', 'so', 'then', 'says', 'thinks' and so on (formal logic and mathematics are designed descendants of these). (iv) At the same time the child develops the grammar for construing itself: that is, for *engendering text*, as a parallel "virtual" universe that is made of meaning, and that has its own structure as metaphor for the structures it is imposing on the material world.

Once these two principles, the stratal and the metafunctional, have been established as semiotic foundations, the child has the potential for expanding his resources of meaning to an indefinite extent – of which, at present at least, we are not aware of any limitations. (This is not to say there cannot be any limitations). As part of this process, completing the transition into the mother tongue, the child has developed the power of "information": using language to tell people things that they do not already know. In other words, meaning has become a **way of sharing experience**, instead of just a way construing experience that has been or is being shared. This is a rather late development, which typically is not consolidated until the grammatical framework is in place: information does not exist until it is created by language, so "telling" involves both the interpersonal resources for exchanging (declarative and interrogative mood) and the experiential resources for creating the "commodity" that is being exchanged.

Thus it seems to me that what we have learnt about the ontogenesis of language – how the individual child develops the semiotic potential of the human species, in tandem with the development of the biological potential – is not only compatible with, but mutually supportive of, the theory of neuronal group selection as the neurobiological basis of consciousness, specifically higher-level consciousness or "mind". The epigenetic trajectory, in which the child follows the evolutionary path in dependence on and interaction with the (sociosemiotic and material) environment; the progression through primary symbolization and protolanguage; the late "slotting in" of lexicogrammar, turning a simple semiotic (sign system) into a stratified one; the simultaneous emergence of the metafunctions of construing experience and enacting interpersonal relations; and the progression from annotating shared experience to telling experience that was not shared (information) – all these resonate very positively with Edelman's evolutionary theory. Let me turn now to some considerations of language as higher-order consciousness with particular reference to its metafunctional character as action and reflection: as the semiotic resource with which human beings simultaneously enact their social processes and construe the experience of themselves and their environment.

Notes

3. These features emerge in the course of the study reported in Halliday (1975b). Subsequent research by Clare Painter (1984, 1989) and by Jane Oldenburg (1986) has added considerable further insights into children's protolanguage and the transition to mother tongue.
4. Margaret Bullowa used to say that when she was a medical student in Boston in the 1930s they were taught that babies were born unable to see or hear effectively and that they did not begin to "communicate" until about eighteen months old (i.e. with the onset of the mother tongue). This so obviously contradicts the experience of daily life that it seems hard to believe. It was from work beginning in the 1960s that a picture of the ontogenesis of meaning began to emerge; see Bullowa (1979) for a collection including respresentative samples of her own work and that of Trevarthen, Junker and others.
5. The emergence of grammar (as always, in the sense of 'lexicogrammar' – what we call "grammar" and "lexis" (lexicon, vocabulary) are simply the two poles of the continuous stratum of "wording") is the critical factor in the development of higher-order consciousness; homo sapiens = homo grammaticus. See Halliday (1978a, 1979b); Painter (1984, 1989); Oldenburg (1986).
6. This figure (cf. others in the studies referred to here) brings out the fact that the protolanguage is not dependent on the mother tongue; indeed one cannot tell from the protolanguage what the child's mother tongue is going to be. Cf. Qiu (1985) on protolanguage in (later to be) Chinese-speaking children.
7. See Lewis (1951) for an earlier account.
8. See Halliday (1975b, 1992, 1993a) for further discussion of this point.

III.18(1995):397–404, 429–30

The Language of Early Childhood (Volume 4)

Bernstein (1970) has shown that educational failure is often, in a very general and rather deep sense, language failure. The child who does not succeed in the school system is one who has not mastered certain essential aspects of language ability. In its immediate interpretation, this could refer to the simple fact that a child cannot read or write or express himself adequately in speech. But these are, as it were, the externals of linguistic success, and it is likely that underlying the failure to master these skills is a deeper and more general failure of language, some fundamental gap in the child's linguistic capabilities.

This is not a lack of words; vocabulary seems to be learnt very easily in response to opportunity combined with motivation. Nor is it, by and large, an impoverishment of the grammar: there is no real evidence to show that the unsuccessful child uses or disposes of a narrower range of syntactic options. (I hope it is unnecessary to add that it has also nothing to do with dialect or accent.) Rather it would appear that the child who, in Bernstein's terms, has only a "restricted code" is one who is deficient in respect of the set of linguistic models that we have outlined above, because some of the functions of language have not been accessible to him. The "restriction" is a restriction on the range of uses of language. In particular, it is likely that he has not learnt to operate with language in the two functions which are crucial to his success in school: the personal function, and the heuristic function.

In order to be taught successfully, it is necessary to know how to use language to learn; and also, how to use language to participate **as an individual** in the learning situation. These requirements are probably not a feature of any particular school system, but rather are inherent in the very concept of education. The ability to operate effectively in the personal and heuristic modes is, however, something that has to be learnt; it does not follow automatically from the acquisition of the grammar and vocabulary of the mother tongue. It is not, that is to say, a question of which words and structures the child knows or uses, but of their functional significance and interpretation. In Bernstein's formulation, the child may not be oriented towards the meanings realized by the personal and heuristic functions of language. Restricted and elaborated code are in effect, as Ruqaiya Hasan (1969) suggests, varieties of language function, determining the meanings that syntactic patterns and the lexical items have for the child who hears or uses them.

To say that educational failure is linguistic failure is merely to take the first step in explaining it: it means that the most immediately accessible cause of educational failure is to be sought in language. Beyond this, and underlying the linguistic failure, is a complex pattern of social and familial factors whose significance has been revealed by Bernstein's work. But while the limitations of a child's linguistic experience may ultimately be ascribed – though not in any simple or obvious way – to features of the social background, the problem as it faces the teacher is essentially a linguistic problem. It is a failure in the child's effective mastery of the use of language, in his adaptation of language to meet certain basic demands. Whether one calls it a failure in language or a failure in the use of language is immaterial; the distinction between knowing language and knowing how to use it is merely one of terminology. This situation is not easy even to diagnose; it is much more difficult to treat. We have tried here to shed some light on it by relating it to the total set of demands, in terms of the needs of the child, that language is called upon to serve.

The implication for a teacher is that his own model of language should at least not fall short of that of the child. If the teacher's image of language is narrower and less rich than that which is already present in the minds of those he is teaching (or which needs to be present, if they are to succeed), it will be irrelevant to him as a teacher. A minimum requirement for an educationally relevant approach to language is that it should take account of the child's own linguistic experience, defining this experience in terms of its richest potential and noting where there may be gaps, with certain children, which could be educationally and developmentally harmful. This is one component. The other component of relevance is the relevance to the experiences that the child will have later on: to the linguistic demands that society will eventually make of him, and, in the intermediate stage, to the demands on language which the school is going to make and which he must meet if he is to succeed in the classroom.

We are still very ignorant of many aspects of the part language plays in our lives. But it is clear that language serves a wide range of human needs, and the richness and variety of its functions is reflected in the nature of language itself, in its organization as a system: within the grammatical structure of a language, certain areas are primarily associated with the heuristic and representational functions, others with the personal and interactional functions. Different bits of the system, as it were, do different jobs; and this in turn helps us to interpret and make more precise the notion of uses of language. What is common to every use of language is that it is meaningful, contextualized, and in the broadest sense social; this is brought home very clearly to the child, in the course of his day-to-day experience. The child is surrounded by language, but not in the form of grammars and dictionaries, or of randomly chosen words and sentences, or of undirected monologue. What he encounters is "text", or language in use: sequences of language articulated each within itself and with the situation in which it occurs. Such sequences are purposive – though very varied in purpose – and have an evident social significance. The child's awareness of language cannot be isolated from his awareness of language function, and this conceptual unity offers a useful vantage point from which language may be seen in a perspective that is educationally relevant.

IV.12(1969):278–80

Studies in English Language (Volume 7)

'The Teacher Taught the Student English': An Essay in Applied Linguistics[1]

How can linguistics help the language teacher? This question has been asked so often in recent years that we tend to regard it as settled, although the actual answers given might range anywhere from a carefully constructed study programme, at one end of the scale, to a weary and negative "It can't" at the other.

If we offer a positive answer, it will probably focus on the description and comparison of the languages involved, rather than on anything to do with language method. Linguistics has not had much to say on language teaching methods. Yet a teaching method is not an easy notion, and the distinctions of principle that are invoked sometimes seem very elusive. The attention may be on the teacher, on the learner, or on the language; we may try to classify in terms of the psychology of the language learner, the relative emphasis placed on different language skills, the type of instructional materials; there are so many possible angles of vision. But this is just the sort of situation where linguistics might be able to help.

I propose to adopt, here, a very simple procedure for considering the application of linguistics to language teaching method. This will be to consider, in turn, a number of different grammatical descriptions of a single English sentence. The sentence is

The teacher taught the student English.

This sentence can be analysed in various ways, to each of which, I shall suggest, corresponds a particular philosophy of language teaching.

In each analysis: (a) is the description of the sentence in terms of features, abbreviated to include only those that are relevant to the discussion – this is the basic description, representing the meaning of the sentence in grammatical terms; (b) is the structural description, which is derived from (a) and shows the configuration of structural elements through which the meaning is expressed; (c) is an example of another sentence having the same features and the same structure; and (d) is a paraphrase, designed to bring out what the sentence means if it is analysed in this way.

Let us start with Description No. 1.

Description No. 1

(a) material process, action; non-middle, active; benefactive

| the teacher | taught | the student | English |

(b)	Actor	Process	Beneficiary	Goal
(c)	Peter	gave	Paul	a silver penny

(b) Actor — Process — Beneficiary — Goal
(c) Peter — gave — Paul — a silver penny

(d) 'The teacher imparted English to the student.'

If we adopt this analysis, we are seeing the language teaching process as a kind of transaction: as the handing over of some commodity to a recipient. Viewing the process in this way, we are likely to feel that the recipient is merely circumstantial to it; essentially, the process involves a giver and a gift – the teacher, and the language. The student's role in the transaction is then largely an incidental one, except that presumably the giver wishes to please the recipient, so the goods must be of the highest possible quality and also nicely packaged and wrapped.

So we give him the best English. We give him only the best, and of course it is our own idea of what is the best, not his, for it is rare for a giver to be able to operate with the recipient's scale of values rather than his own. We give him Shakespeare and T. S. Eliot, even if what he would value most highly is the motor mechanic's manual; and we wrap it up in the best critical scholarship we have, sometimes barely disguising our feeling that it is really too good for him. It would be worse, of course, to give him the motor mechanic's manual if what he wanted was T. S. Eliot; but this does not often happen. Either way, the gift is an act of charity, and the student is invited to take it, or leave it. It is the language that is under focus of attention – that is the "goal" of the process, in grammatical terms.

Compare this with Description No. 2.

Description No. 2

(a) material process, action; non–middle, active; range–specific

	the teacher	taught	the student	English
(b)	Actor	Process	Goal	Range
(c)	Peter	beat	Paul	at tennis

(d) 'The teacher instructed the student in English.'

Here we have a different model of the language teaching process. The teacher is now doing something to the student rather than to the language: he is involving him in some kind of joint activity. The student has become a participant.

At the same time, it is still the teacher, as "actor", who sets the pace. The actor determines the nature of the process in question and the respective roles of the two participants, as winner and loser, or as teacher and learner. The student is no longer merely circumstantial; he is an essential element in the process. But his participation is subject to an external agency; something is happening to him, in which his own role, though necessary, is a passive one.

The language has now become what I am referring to as the "range", a kind of delimitation of the scope of the process: the cognate object, in an extended sense. The teacher taught the student; and the relationship was with respect to English. English was the particular form taken by the teaching process, just as tennis was the form taken by Peter's defeat of Paul.

If this is the image of the language teaching process (and it corresponds to the situation in some schools, especially where there is a teacher of strong personality who takes the same class for a number of subjects), the language becomes, as it were, a means of expressing the relationship between teacher and student. This approach favours classroom drills and exercises, and plenty of tests; the teacher is working on the student – instructing him, in fact – and something should be seen to be happening. The student provides the responses. These may often be choral responses, especially in those countries where it is easier to achieve participation in this way.

(If we wanted to be very sophisticated, we might introduce a further grammatical distinction between two types of goal-directed action, to each of which would correspond a different version of the 'instructional' approach, the one more one-sided, the other more reciprocal. In the former, the student is required to memorize rules and paradigms and vocabulary lists, and his performance is purely repetitive. In the latter, he performs quasi-creative tasks such as question-answering, substituting and transforming; here the student is hitting the ball back, not just imitating strokes, so that there is a real game being played. The danger is precisely that it is a game; it may become self-defining and self-justifying, with little relation to the student's deeper understanding of language or to his actual and intended patterns of living.)

Here, then, we encounter two somewhat different conceptions of the language teaching process, suggested by two possible analyses of a sentence that is used to describe it. One is that of consigning a commodity; the other is that of manipulating a person. But a language is not primarily a commodity, so in the first approach what is offered is usually something else; typically, literature, especially "good" literature of a bygone age. This has been referred to as "the literature fallacy" in language teaching. And language learning does not primarily take place by manipulation; rather, it is an active and voluntary process. Nevertheless if there is more than one way of analysing a sentence it is likely that no one description tells the whole truth, and it would be a mistake to suppose that these approaches to language teaching have nothing whatever to recommend them simply because by themselves they do not satisfy our notion of what "learning" is or of what "a language" is.

Let us go on to consider Description No. 3.

Description No. 3

(a) material process, action; middle, causative; range-specific

the teacher	taught		the student	English
Initiator	Process		Actor	Range
Peter	got ... to take up		Paul	Carpentry

(b) Initiator / (c) Peter rows as above

(i.e. Peter got Paul to take up carpentry)

(d) 'The teacher caused the student to learn (study) English.'

This puts the matter in a rather different light. Here, the student is doing the job: he is learning English, and the teacher is helping him to achieve this desirable end. The term "causative" should not, of course, be taken to imply coercion; it includes the sense of 'enable' as well as 'make'. We might have introduced the distinction between enabling and making into our grammatical analysis here; but we do not really need it, as it is a well-known fact that it is impossible to make anyone learn anything if they do not want to.

This view of language learning suggests programming and mechanization: the use of a full battery of audio–visual and other "aids". The student is the actor in the process; he is doing the work. The teacher comes in as a helper, an enabler; and in this context he brings with him all the modern techniques and facilities that are available for the purpose.

Here we are probably much closer than in the earlier versions to the outlook of many language teachers today. They would think primarily in terms of the student, and would see their own role as that of guiding and helping him in his task. The question that we have not considered up to now, however, is what the nature of the learner's task actually is. This has just been taken for granted.

There is one assumption common to all three descriptions of the sentence that have been given so far. We assumed at the start, and have continued to do so, that the clause to be analysed belonged to the class of "material process" or "action" clauses. But not all clauses are of the action type; there are other types of process recognized in language. As teachers we may well be inclined to regard teaching as a form of action, if only because it leads to exhaustion. But where *teach* is analysed as 'cause to learn' it may not follow that we regard learning in the same light.

211

Certainly *he is studying English* could be a clause of action. But *learning English* does not mean the same thing as *studying English*; and *teach* is related to *learn* rather than to *study*. Suppose that we analyse *teach* as 'cause to learn' but treat *learn* as a mental rather than a material process, interpreting it as 'come to know'. This may be represented by Description No. 4, where "cognizant" is simply the equivalent of "actor" (in No. 3) in the context of a mental process. Both No. 3 and No. 4 are "middle" in voice – there is only one inherent participant instead of two: and No. 4 is perfective in aspect.

This description retains from No. 3 the notion that teaching someone means enabling him to learn. But it treats learning as something different from the acquiring of skill in action. Learning a language, in this account, is not like learning to drive, or learning bricklaying or acrobatics: it is a mental exercise involving the acquisition of knowledge.

Description No. 4

(a) material process, cognition; middle, causative, perfective; range-specific

	the teacher	taught	the student	English
(b)	Initiator	Process	Cognizant	Range
(c)	Peter	primed	Paul	with history

(d) 'The teacher enabled the student to come to know English.'

In the approach to language teaching that corresponds to this description, the focus is again on the learner. The student is the key participant in the process, and the teacher is present as helper and guide. What is the student envisaged to be doing? He is enlarging his mental powers by the acquisition of new knowledge. And since the teacher is helping him in the process, the teacher's role is to supply the required knowledge in doses of suitable size and strength.

The joker here is the word *knowledge*. It has often been pointed out that there is a difference between knowing a language, in the sense of being able to speak and understand and read and write it, and knowing about a language – knowing its rules, and being able to write up a grammatical description of it or compile a dictionary. The view of the learning process that is embodied in Description No. 4 fails to make this distinction. It corresponds, in other words, to what is now labelled "the linguistics fallacy" in language teaching (it used to be called simply "teaching grammar"), namely the tendency to teach about the language – that is, to teach linguistics – on the assumption that this is a means of teaching the language.

This is a very old approach. It was no doubt taken over from the teaching of classics, which is a rather different kind of task, especially in the context of today. Its use in modern language teaching was described, and denounced, a hundred years ago by one of the pioneers of language teaching theory, François Gouin (1896). But it continues to flourish, and indeed gains new life each generation as new linguistic theories come along. There are shifts in emphasis and in ideas about language; but whether the emphasis is on the facts of the language or on the principles behind them, and whether the grammar is 'old' or 'new', whether Nesfield, Fries or Chomsky, the basic approach is the same. Learning a language is regarded as a process of acquiring knowledge, of coming to know something, like studying history or mathematics.

But when we talk of "knowing a language" we are not really talking about a knowledge of facts or principles. Even if mastering a language seems to belong to the class of mental processes rather than to that of actions, it may still be rather different from mastering a subject, whether mathematics or history. This was hinted at in Description No. 3, where "learn" was interpreted as 'acquire a skill', only there the skill was assumed to be a skill in action. We can suggest another description of the text sentence, one which retains the notion of acquiring a skill – or rather a set of skills – but which treats these as skills of a special kind, not of action but of verbalization.

In this analysis, knowing a language means having the ability to speak and understand and read and write it. These could be interpreted as mental processes; but if so they are mental processes of a different kind, with a strong component of 'doing' in them. Their unique status is reflected in the fact that there is often a special clause type in the grammar for expressing them, centring around verbs like *say*, *tell*, *ask* and *understand*. Let us call these processes of verbalization. Knowing a language is being able to verbalize; this is expressed in the grammatical description by the presence of the feature "verbalization" instead of "mental process: cognition".

In Description No. 5, as in No. 4, *teach* is analysed as 'cause to learn'. But whereas in 4 "learn English" is interpreted as 'come to know English', in 5, where the process is one of speaking, understanding etc. rather than one of knowing, "learn English" does not mean 'come to speak English', it means 'come to be able to speak English'. This version expresses the complex notion that teaching a language means helping the student to master the ability to verbalize. Here is Description No. 5 (where "speaker" is the equivalent of actor in the special context of verbalization). A notable feature of this description is that it applies rather specifically to language teaching, and treats it as unique. It is not easy to find a clause having the same features and structure in which Peter is not already teaching Paul a language. We might manage to draw a parallel from technical or from inspired linguistic powers, such as *Peter trained Paul in the language of the law courts*, or *Peter induced Paul to woo the poetic muse*. But these would hardly make the illustration any clearer; so here we leave item (c) out (p. 304, VII.11(1976)).

In Description No. 5, a language is treated as a potential. To know a language is to possess that potential, to learn a language is to acquire it; and the process of teaching a language is one of helping the student to build it up for himself. The language potential, however, is represented as different in kind from other human skills; if we wanted to characterize it briefly, we could call it a **meaning potential**. To know a language is to have mastered the ability to mean.

Description No. 5

(a)   verbal process; middle, causative, perfective; range-specific; potential

the teacher	taught	the student	English
Initiator	Process	Speaker	Range

(b)

(d)   'The teacher enabled the student to become a speaker (etc.) of English.'

This will be the last of our excursions into the grammar of the language teaching process. We have not attempted to justify or explain the analyses in detail; nor have we given more than a fragment of the full description, but only as much as was needed to show up the similarities and the differences. In moving from one description to the next, we have readily changed more than one feature at a time, ignoring other combinations and selecting just those which seem to suggest real interpretations of the language teaching process. But each of the five descriptions presents a possible and defensible account of the English sentence *The teacher taught the student English*. Certain aspects of its syntax may be brought out more systematically in one version than in another; but no version can be dismissed as wrong, and all have something to recommend them from a grammatical point of view.

This sentence is, perhaps, something of a syntactic oracle. Now, up to a point, the same is true of all sentences; but this, it seems, is one of the more versatile ones. It is probably the simplest and most typical expression of the process of language teaching that one could find in English. Yet it represents this process in a way which makes it look something like conveying goods to someone, something like moulding or working on him, something like helping him acquire a skill, and something like supplying him with knowledge; while at the same time being unique, differing in some respect from processes of all other types.

If the linguistic representation of the language teaching process is so many-sided, it may be that the process which it describes is many-sided too. This would not be an unreasonable view. If I had to choose just one of these five interpretations, and no other, I suppose I should choose the last, on the grounds that it approximates more closely than any of the others to my own conception of language teaching and language learning, and that the most fruitful practices seem to be associated with this approach: those where the teacher attempts to structure the language learning, within the limits of the teaching conditions and the resources available, in ways which impose certain demands on the student's abilities – demands such as on the one hand to relate, albeit often very indirectly, to the student's own language learning goals, and on the other hand to stretch his abilities fully in all the areas of verbal imitation and exploration that are relevant to his needs.

It is quite likely, however, that really effective language teaching is not tied methodologically to any one interpretation of the teaching process or of the learning process. Learning a language is a complex and demanding task which needs to be understood not only in psychological but also in sociocultural terms; it is not by any means the same task to all learners, and in a class of thirty students there will probably be thirty different ways or styles of learning. It would be surprising if any one conception of the process was equally suited to all.

Seen in this light, all the descriptions of our text sentence may have something of the truth in them. We are not of course expecting to derive a general principle for the classification and evaluation of language teaching methods from the grammar of one English sentence (that would be "linguistics as magic" all over again). What the grammatical exploration does is to offer a way of looking at the language teaching process. At the same time, it offers a way of looking at a sentence; and that is something which a language teacher will always need to do, whatever his conception of his task.

Note

1. This paper is based on a talk given to the Karachi University English Teachers' Association, Karachi, Pakistan. My thanks are due to Dr S. Ali Ashraf, Head of the Department of English, University of Karachi, for help and encouragement.

VII.11(1976):297–305

Language and Education (Volume 9)

IMPLICATIONS FOR PRACTICE

With any academic discipline (turning to question 4), there is always a problem of "implications for educational practice": what do you teach, out of the huge accumulation of knowledge, and how does your teaching relate to the theorizing of the practitioners in the field? Experience in science education and maths education shows how big a problem this is even in these subjects.

The relationship is even more complex in the human sciences, and especially in the sciences of human behaviour. What implications does one draw from sociology, psychology and linguistics? Whatever else, you don't draw your content from them. Traditionally (that is, for the past hundred years or so), the answer has been: from psychology you get the basic theory and practice of education, and from sociology and linguistics you get nothing. This dominance of psychology over sociology in the theory of education reflects Western obsession with the individual, and the conviction that learning is an individual rather than a social process. It would help if we had a more balanced contribution from these two disciplines – especially in countries where different cultures mix (which means all English-speaking countries, now).

From linguistics, of course, it is not true that nothing has been drawn; there is a long tradition of taking content from linguistics, in the form of 'school grammar', the version of classical and medieval linguistic scholarship that went into the making of humanist descriptive grammars. It is not a bad grammar; but it is not very useful in school. It is formal; rigid; based on the notion of rule; syntactic in focus; and oriented towards the sentence. A more useful grammar would be one which is functional; flexible; based on the notion of resource; semantic in focus; and oriented towards the text. Hence the recurrent cycle of love and hate for it: 'we thought it would help children to write; it doesn't, so we abandon it; they still can't write, so we take it up again', and so on.

When I say that no implications have been drawn from linguistics, I'm not intending to denigrate classroom grammar, where linguistics has supplied the content of the teaching. But by "educational implications" I understand not the content but the theory and practice of the educational process. I think linguistics is of central importance here, and yet this aspect of its value is still very largely ignored.

In working with our Language Development Project I have suggested that language development is three things: learning language, learning through language, and learning about language. Again, perhaps, by making it sound like a slogan I may stop people from listening to what it means; but, again, I mean it to be taken seriously. Let me take up the last part first.

Learning about language is, of course, linguistics; this refers to the importance of the study of language (as an 'object') in school. This does not have to be grammar; when *Language in Use* was written, at a time when grammar was 'out', the authors found no difficulty in devising 110 units for work on language in secondary school without any reference to grammar at all. Now, I think, we are reopening the question of 'a grammar for schools'. I think it will be possible to develop a school grammar that is interesting and useful; I have some idea of what it might be like, but I don't think we have one yet. But even given an ideal grammar, it would be only one part of the "learning about language" that needs to go on in school.

Learning through language refers to the fact that almost all educational learning (as well as much learning outside school) takes place through language, written and spoken. This notion came into educational parlance as "Language Across the Curriculum". A child doesn't need to know any linguistics in order to use language to learn; but a teacher needs to know some linguistics if he wants to understand how the process takes place – or what is going wrong when it doesn't. Here therefore linguistics has the role of a background discipline, such as psychology and sociology. I think it is probably as important as they are, and needing about the same emphasis in teacher education. Of course, not all branches of linguistics are equally important (that is true of any background subject); but it is not too difficult to identify those that matter.

Learning language means construing the mother tongue – and before that the 'child tongue', the protolanguage with which an infant first exchanges meanings with those around him. There is a special branch of linguistics – child language studies, or "developmental linguistics" – that is concerned with how children learn their mother tongue; it has made enormous strides in the past 20 years, probably more than any other branch of the subject; and its findings are of tremendous importance for education. For one thing it has shown that children take certain steps in their semantic development – that is, control certain meanings and meaning relationships – well before they have been thought to do in cognitive-psychological representations of the learning process. Since, presumably, a child's semantic system does not run ahead of his cognitive system (I don't even know what that would mean, I suspect that these are merely two different ways of looking at the same thing), we may have to revise some of the prevalent notions about cognitive development.

More important: by supplementing the cognitive model with a semantic one (which relates meaning to its 'output' in words and structures, sounds, and writing) we get a much more rounded picture of the nature of learning, and the relation of learning to environment.

I have always been an 'applied linguist': my interest in linguistics is in what you can do with it. But there must be something to apply. Applied linguistics is not a separate domain; it is the principles and practice that come from an understanding of language. Adopting these principles and practices provides, in turn, a way in to understanding language. In this perspective, you look for models of language that neutralize the difference between theory and application; in the light of which, research and development in language education become one process rather than two. But this means selecting, refining, adapting; and being prepared to hasten slowly. The one difficulty I have always had in working with teachers is that they so often expect immediate results; the latest findings translated there and then into effective, not to say magical, curriculum design, or classroom processes. Now, I think we can often make intellectual, research applications of our latest findings right there, on the spot (partly because no one will get hurt if they turn out not to work). But for shaping what we do, with children, or adult learners, I think we have to depend more on the indirect, oblique and thoughtful application of the accumulated wisdom of the past. I get worried by the fashions in language teaching, which are sometimes only a half-baked application of ideas about language which themselves were only half-baked in the first place.

IX.16(1981):336–9

Language and Society (Volume 10)

A FUNCTIONAL APPROACH TO LANGUAGE AND LANGUAGE DEVELOPMENT

In the last part of this paper we shall suggest a number of specific topics which might be explored, both inside and outside the school, as a way of finding out for oneself more about the nature of language and its place in the life of social man. These are related to the general perspective outlined in Section 2 (X.3(1974):70-5), that of the individual as seen through the lens of his membership of 'society' – that is, in the context of other individuals; with his language potential being understood as the medium by which the relationships into which he enters are established, developed and maintained. This means that we are taking a functional view of language, in the sense that we are interested in what language can do, or rather in what the speaker, child or adult, can do with it; and that we try to explain the nature of language, its internal organization and patterning, in terms of the functions that it has evolved to serve.

First of all, therefore, we should look briefly into the question of linguistic function, and say a little about it, both in regard to what language is and in regard to how it is learnt by a child. Let us take the latter point first, and consider a functional approach to the question of how the child learns his mother tongue. This process, the learning of the mother tongue, is often referred to as "language acquisition". This seems rather an unfortunate term because it suggests that language is some kind of a commodity to be acquired, and, although the metaphor is innocent enough in itself, if it is taken too literally the consequences can be rather harmful. The use of this metaphor has led to the belief in what is known as a "deficit theory" of language learning, as a means of explaining how children come to fail in school: the suggestion that certain children, perhaps because of their social background, have not acquired enough of this commodity called language, and in order to help them we must send relief supplies. The implication is that there is a gap to be filled, and from this derive various compensatory practices that may be largely irrelevant to the children's needs. Now this is a false and misleading view of language and of educational failure; and while one should not make too much of one item of terminology, we prefer to avoid the term "language acquisition" and return to the earlier and entirely appropriate designation of "language development".

In the psychological, or psycholinguistic, sphere, there are two main types of approach to the question of language development. These have been referred to as the "nativist" and the "environmentalist" position. Everyone agrees, of course, that human beings are biologically endowed with the ability to learn language, and that this is a uniquely human attribute – no other species has it, however much a chimpanzee or a dolphin may be trained to operate with words or symbols. But the nativist view holds that there is a specific language-learning faculty, distinct from other learning faculties, and that this provides the human infant with a ready-made and rather detailed blueprint of the structure of language. Learning one's mother tongue consists in fitting the patterns of whatever language he hears around him into the framework which he already possesses. The environmentalist view considers that language learning is not fundamentally distinct from other kinds of learning; it depends on those same mental faculties that are involved in all aspects of the child's learning processes. Rather than having built in to his genetic make-up a set of concrete universals of language, in this view what the child has is the ability to process certain highly abstract types of cognitive relation which underlie (among other things) the linguistic system; the very specific properties of language are not innate, and therefore the child is more dependent on his environment – on the language he hears around him, together with the contexts in which it is uttered – for the successful learning of his mother tongue. In a sense, therefore, the difference of views is a recurrence of the old controversy of nature and nurture, or heredity and environment, in a new guise.

Each of these views can be criticized, although the criticisms that are actually made often relate to particular models of the learning process that have no necessary connection with a nativist or environmentalist position. For example, it is sometimes assumed that an environmentalist interpretation implies some form of behaviourist theory, an essentially stimulus–response, associationist view of learning; but this is totally untrue. Equally, the nativist view is by no means dependent on the notion that learning proceeds by fitting items into the marked slots which nature provided and running the machine to test whether the match is appropriate. The differences between nativist and environmentalist are differences of emphasis, among other things in their ideas concerning the essential character of language, where they stem from two rather different traditions. Broadly speaking, the nativist model reflects the philosophical-logical strand in the history of thinking about language, with its sharp distinction between the ideal and the real (which Chomsky calls "competence" and "performance") and its view of language as "rules" – essentially rules of syntax. The environmentalist represents the ethnographic tradition, which rejects the distinction of ideal and real, defines what is grammatical as, by and large, what is acceptable, and sees language as relations based on meaning, with meaning defined in terms of function. To this extent the two interpretations are complementary rather than contradictory; but they have tended to become associated with conflicting psychological theories and thus to be strongly counterposed one against the other.

One argument often put forward in support of a nativist approach must be dismissed as fallacious; this is the theory of the unstructured input, according to which the child cannot be dependent on what he hears around him because what he hears is no more than bits and pieces – unfinished or ungrammatical sentences, full of hesitations, backtracking, unrelated fragments and the like. This idea seems to have arisen because the earliest tape recordings of connected discourse that linguists analysed were usually recordings of intellectual conversations, which do tend to be very scrappy, since the speakers are having to plan as they go along and the premises are constantly shifting, and which are also largely insulated from the immediate situation, so that there are no contextual clues. But it is not in fact true of the ordinary everyday speech that typically surrounds the small child, which is fluent, highly structured, and closely related to the non-verbal context of situation. Moreover it tends to have very few deviations in it; I found myself when observing the language spoken to, and in the presence of, a small child that almost all the sequences were well formed and whole, acceptable even to the sternest grammatical lawgiver. Of course the fact that the notion of unstructured input is unsound does not disprove the nativist theory; it merely removes one of the arguments that has been used to support it.

More important than the grammatical shape of what the child hears, however, is the fact that it is functionally related to observable features of the situation around him. This consideration allows us to give another account of language development that is not dependent on any particular psycholinguistic theory, an account that is functional and sociological rather than structural and psychological. The two are not in competition; they are about different things. A functional theory is not a theory about the mental processes involved in the learning of the mother tongue; it is a theory about the social processes involved. As we expressed it in the first section, it is concerned with language between people (interorganism), and therefore learning to speak is interpreted as the individual's mastery of a behaviour potential. In this perspective, language is a form of interaction, and it is learnt through interaction; this, essentially, is what makes it possible for a culture to be transmitted from one generation to the next.

In a functional approach to language development the first question to be asked is, 'what are the functions that language serves in the life of an infant?' This might seem self-contradictory, if an infant is one who does not yet speak; but the paradox is intentional — before he has mastered any recognizable form of his mother tongue the child already has a linguistic system, in the sense that he can express certain meanings through the consistent use of vocal sounds. There are, perhaps, four main reasons for putting the question in this form.

1. We can ask the same question at any stage in the life of the individual, up to and including adulthood; there have in fact been a number of functional theories of adult and adolescent language.
2. It is much easier to answer the question in respect of a very young child; the earlier one starts, the more clear-cut the functions are (whereas with an approach based on structure, the opposite is the case; it is in general **harder** to analyse the structure of children's speech than of adults).

3. We can reasonably assume that the child is functionally motivated; if language is for the child a means of attaining social ends – that is, ends which are important to him as a social being – we need look no further than this for the reasons why he learns it.
4. A functional approach to language, if it includes a developmental perspective, can throw a great deal of light on the nature of language itself. Language is as it is because of what it has to do.

To these we might add a fifth, though this is not so much a reason for asking the question as an incidental bonus for having done so. One of the problems in studying the language of a very young child is that of knowing what is language and what is not. We can answer that, in a functional context, by saying that any vocal sound (and any gesture, if the definition is made to include gesture) which is interpretable by reference to a recognized function of language is language – provided always that the relationship of sound to meaning is regular and consistent. The production of a sound for the purpose of practicing that sound is a means of **learning** language, but is not itself an instance of language. The production of a sound for the purpose of attracting attention **is** language, once we have reason to assert that 'attracting attention' is a meaning that fits in with the functional potential of language at this stage of development.

Looking at the early stages of language development form a functional viewpoint, we can follow the process whereby the child gradually 'learns how to mean' – for this is what first-language learning is. If there is anything which the child can be said to be acquiring, it is a range of potential, which we could refer to as his *meaning potential*. This consists in the mastery of a small number of elementary functions of language, and of a range of choices in meaning within each one. The choices are very few at first, but they expand rapidly as the functional potential of the system is reinforced by success: the sounds that the child makes do in fact achieve the desired results, at least on a significant number of occasions, and this provides the impetus for taking the process further. As an example, Nigel, whose language I studied in successive six-weekly stages from the age of nine months onwards, started apparently with just two functions and one or two meanings in each. At 10½ months, when he first had a recognizable linguistic system, he could express a total of 12 different meanings; these were derived from four clearly identifiable functions (the first four in the list below) and included, among others, what we might translate as 'do that right now!', 'I want my toy bird down' and 'nice to see you; shall we look at this picture together?' By 16½ months, when he was on the threshold of the second phase of language development, the move into English (or whatever language is going to be the mother tongue), he had six functions and a total of 50 meanings that he could, and regularly did, express.

In studying Nigel's progress I used as the framework a set of functions which I had worked out – before he was born – in the course of discussion with my colleagues in the Programme in Linguistics and English Teaching. Teachers taking part in the trials of the materials which were being produced by the Programme had often felt the need for more information about how children learn language, with the emphasis on use rather than on structure; and the Home Office Children's Department Development Group, on behalf of those of the teachers who were from approved schools (as they were then), had called a conference on "Language, Life and Learning", at which I put forward an outline of what language means to the pre-school child, as understood in terms of what be is able to do with it. This involved a set of seven initial functions, as follows:

1. Instrumental ('I want'): satisfying material needs
2. Regulatory ('do as I tell you'): controlling the behaviour of others
3. Interactional ('me and you'): getting along with other people
4. Personal ('here I come'): identifying and expressing the self
5. Heuristic ('tell me why'): exploring the world around (and inside one)
6. Imaginative ('let's pretend'): creating a world of one's own
7. Informative ('I've got something to tell you'): communicating new information.

These headings served as a useful basis for following the developmental progress of an infant, whose early vocal sounds, although still prelinguistic in the sense that they were not modelled on the English language, were used effectively for just these purposes – to obtain goods or services that he required (instrumental), to influence the behaviour of those closest to him (regulatory), to maintain his emotional ties with them (interactional), and so on. The meanings that he can express at this stage – the number of different things that he can ask for, for example – are naturally very restricted; but he has internalized the fact that language serves these purposes, and it is significant that for each of them he has one generalized expression, meaning simply 'I want that' or 'do that!' etc., where the interpretation is given by the situation (e.g. 'I want that spoon' or 'go on singing'), as well as a number of specific expressions, very few at first but soon growing, and soon becoming independent of the presence of the object or other visible sign of his intent.

So by adopting a functional standpoint we can go back to the beginning of the child's language development, reaching beyond the point where he has started to master structures, beyond even his first words, if by "words" we mean items derived from the adult language; and taking as the foundations of language those early utterances which are not yet English or French or Swahili or Urdu but which every parent recognizes as being meaningful, quite distinct from crying and sneezing and the other non-linguistic noises the child makes. At this stage, the child's utterances cannot readily be 'translated' into the adult language. Just as we cannot adequately represent the sounds he makes by spelling them, either in the orthography of the mother tongue or even in phonetic script, because the system which these symbols impose is too detailed and specific, so also we cannot adequately represent the meanings the child expresses in terms of adult grammar and vocabulary. The child's experience differs so widely from that of the adult that there is only a very partial correspondence between his meanings and those that the adult is predisposed to recognize. But if his utterances are interpreted in the light of particular functions, which are recognizable to the adult as plausible ways of using language, it becomes possible to bridge the gap between them – and in this way to show how the infant's linguistic system ultimately evolves and develops into that of the adult, which is otherwise the most puzzling aspect of the language development process. By the time he reached the age of 18 months, Nigel could use language effectively in the instrumental, regulatory, interactional and personal functions, and was beginning to use it for pretend-play (the 'imaginative' function), and also heuristically, for the purpose of exploring the environment. Now for the first time he launched into English, making rapid strides in vocabulary and grammar; and it was very clear from a study of his speech that his principal motive for doing so was the use of language as a learning device.

In order for language to be a means of learning, it is essential for the child to be able to encode in language, through words and structures, his experience of processes of the external world and of the people and things that participate in them.

X.3(1974):75–81

★ ★ ★

The work of the (originally Nuffield, later Schools Council) Programme in Linguistic and English Teaching spanned the period from 1964 to 1971, and provided the background of thinking, experience and practical endeavour that lies behind the perspective adopted here. It is in the light of this experience that 'language and social man' assumes relevance as an approach to language in an educational context.

Language has for a long time been a depressed area in our educational system; and only a serious concern with language on the part of teachers, a concern that is enlightened, imaginative and humane, can restore it to the central place which it ought to occupy if we are tackling the problem of educational failure at its deepest level.

Lately there has been a considerable amount of research effort that is relevant to this theme, often following up earlier ideas that had been neglected; and reference has been made to some of the important books and papers that have appeared. But the basic discussion of how these ideas may be translated into practice will be found in the two sets of materials produced by the Programme: *Breakthrough to Literacy* (Longman, 1970) for primary schools, and *Language in Use* (Edward Arnold, 1971) for secondary schools.

The title *Breakthrough to Literacy* referred to the child's breakthrough from speech into the new medium of writing. But it is a breakthrough also in another sense: a breakthrough in the whole concept of language in the primary school. The ideas behind it are embodied in the Teacher's Manual, which can be read on its own as a thoughtful discussion of the question of literacy. It was very encouraging that, at the end of the project, the ILEA set up their Centre for Language in Primary Education, and that the person appointed to take charge of it was David Mackay, leader of the *Breakthrough* team.

It is not unreasonable to claim for *Language in Use* a breakthrough of another kind, this time at the secondary level. This takes the perspective of 'language and social man' and gives it a concrete expression in the form of study units for the exploration of language by pupils within the secondary school range. The accompanying volume *Exploring Language* (Edward Arnold 1971) has been referred to at many points, and provides the best discussion of language in an educational context that has yet appeared.

There is another breakthrough still to come, in the training of teachers, who have so far been left to fend almost entirely for themselves as far as language is concerned. Perhaps we may look forward to a time when language study has some place in the professional training of all teachers, and the central place in the relevant specialist courses, especially those relating to English and to literacy ('teaching of reading'). "Language study" is not meant to imply a diluted version of academic linguistics – a subject which has often been defined much too rigidly in the university context; but, rather, a serious exploration of language from different angles, ignoring the artificial boundaries which universities (like schools) tend to interpose between one discipline and another. The exploration of language cannot be neatly classified as natural science, social science, humanity or fine art; it takes something from each of these world views. If we claim that language has a key place in the processes of education, this is not only for the obvious reason that it is the primary channel for the transmission of knowledge, but much more because it reflects, as nothing else does, the multi-level personality of man.

X.3(1974):128–9

Additional readings

On Grammar (Volume 1) −12(1987):323–4, 349–51

On Language and Linguistics (Volume 3) − 10(1993):228–30; 13(2001):273–4; 14(1973):300; 17(1992):378–9, 384

The Language of Early Childhood (Volume 4)

The Language of Science (Volume 5) − 6(1989):178; 7(1997):197

Language and Education (Volume 9)

Language and Society (Volume 10) − 2 (1971):63–4; 3(1974):118; 5(1975):175–6, 193–5; 6(1975):212–3; 7(1973):223–30

Chapter Ten

LINGUISTIC COMPUTING

Summary

Over the years, there have been various attempts at computing with language, ranging from attempts at machine translation in the 1950's, through the 'artificial intelligence' phase of the 60's and 70's, during which researchers tried to tackle more specific computational tasks like building parsers, and question-&-answer or expert systems. By the 80's, advances in computer technology had introduced the possibility of using the computer as a tool for linguistic research, both for testing grammatical descriptions, and for building large-scale corpora for carrying out linguistic research.

More recent attempts to push the envelope still further have relocated language at the centre of the computing process. No longer just the object of computing, language is becoming the means for achieving what computer scientists refer to as intelligent computing. However, before natural language can become the instrument for computing, there first needs to exist a theory of language which serves as the basis for a more realistic account of language as a system rich in meaning potential.

Systemic-functional theory provides a form of semantic representation which captures the full complexity of natural language, thereby enabling advances in data fusion, fuzzy reasoning, and the ability to construe the context of situation by inference from the text.

Selected reading

Computational and Quantitative Studies (Volume 6)

It is the privilege of an old person to be allowed to look back in time – even perhaps in a context such as this, when addressing specialists in computing. Computing is, after all, one of the most future-oriented of all present-day human activities! But it happens to be just forty years since I had my first encounter with computational linguistics.

This was in an early project in machine translation, which was the main purpose that was envisaged for linguistic computing at the time. I was Assistant Lecturer in Chinese at Cambridge; and I was delighted at being asked to be a member of the Cambridge Language Research Unit, along with Margaret Masterman, who directed it, R. H. Richens, plant geneticist, and A. F. Parker- Rhodes, whose extensive interests ranged from botany to mathematical statistics. That was a fairly brief excursion, since I left Cambridge shortly afterwards; but since then I have had further encounters from time to time, as the field of linguistic computing has developed and expanded to its present high-energy state. Of these the most notable, for me, were the times I spent working with Sydney Lamb, first at Berkeley then at Yale, in the 1960s, and then later, in the 1980s, working with William Mann and his group at the Information Sciences Institute of the University of Southern California.

Looking back over this period, I seem to see a change of direction taking place roughly every fifteen years. The first turning point, of course, was the idea of computing with language at all; we can date this in round figures from 1950, when the idea of using a computer to translate from one language to another began to be taken seriously.

The approach was essentially mathematical, in that machine translation was seen as a problem to be solved by applying to language the same logical methods that had gone into the design of the computer itself. There was, at least among mainstream researchers, no serious concern with language as a distinct type of phenomenon, one which might need to be investigated theoretically in terms of its own systemic traits.

Then in and around the mid-1960s a significant transformation took place. Language came more sharply into focus; it began to be treated as a phenomenon *sui generis*, with linguistics replacing logic as the theoretical point of departure from which to engage with it. In Russia, and perhaps in Japan, this transformation was fairly gradual; but in North America and western Europe it was more catastrophic, because 1965 was the year in which the US Air Force officially pronounced machine translation a failure and withdrew the funding from the major translation projects. American researchers who continued computing with language carried on their activities under other headings; taking over "artificial intelligence" as a unifying concept, they addressed some more specific computational tasks that were not tied directly to translating, such as parsing, abstracting, question-answering or expert systems and the like. Terry Winograd's major contribution *Understanding Natural Language* belongs to this time; so does the earliest work in computing our own system networks (forming paradigms, implementing realizations and so on) which was done by Alick Henrici at University College London (see Winograd 1972; Henrici 1966 [Halliday and Martin 1981]).

The third turning point came around 1980, when a new generation of computers made it possible to build systems that approached somewhat closer the complexity of natural language. Computational linguists now had at their disposal the necessary speed, memory and processing power that made parsing and generating look like more realistic goals. Before that time, computational grammars had remained fairly simple: limited to "toy" domains, syntactically constrained, and accommodating only rather gross distinctions in meaning; whereas one could now begin to conceive of "writing the grammar of a natural language in computable form", with account taken of considerations from linguistic theory. For linguists this meant that the computer now became, for the first time, a tool for linguistic research, a means of finding out new things about language: it made it possible on the one hand to test grammatical descriptions (which were becoming too complex to be tested manually) and on the other hand to build a large-scale corpus – not only to assemble and manage it but to access it and interrogate it from many different angles. Two very large systemic grammars of English for text generation were developed during this period: the Penman "Nigel" grammar built up by Christian Matthiessen under William Mann's direction at I.S.I., and the "Communal" grammar compiled by Robin Fawcett at the University of Wales (Matthiessen and Bateman 1992; Fawcett *et al.* 1993).

Fifteen years from 1980 brings us up to 1995; so are we now moving through another turning point? I suspect we may be, in that the status of language – that is, its general relationship to computing – is once again undergoing a major shift. It seems that language is being relocated at the very centre of the computing process itself. In order to explore this further, I would like to refer explicitly to the notion of "computing meanings" that I used in the title of my talk. But first let me say what I do not mean. I am not referring here to the rather overworked concept of the "information society". It is no doubt true, as we have been being told for the past two decades, that the exchange of goods-&-services is rapidly being overtaken by the exchange of information as the dominant mode of socio-economic activity; and this is certainly relevant, since information is prototypically made of language. But it is relevant as the **context** of the change I am referring to; it is not the nature of the change itself.

What I have in mind is what Professor Sugeno calls "intelligent comput-ing", which he defines as computing that is based on natural language. In Sugeno's view, if we want to move forward to the point where the computer becomes truly intelligent, we have to make it function, as people do, through the medium of language. And this critically alters the relationship of language to computing.

Let me then briefly return to the past, and use the concept of "com-puting meanings" to track the shifting relationship between the two. In the 1950s, there was no direct engagement between them at all; it was taken for granted that translating meant selecting from lists of possible formal equivalents – that it was an engineering job, in other words. The prevailing metaphor was that of a code: as Warren Weaver conceived of it, a Russian text was simply an English text with different coding con-ventions. There was no conception of language as the systemic resources that lay behind a text; hence no need to construct any kind of theoretical model of language. This is not to imply that nothing of value was achieved; on the contrary, there was a great deal of essential analytical work, especially in lexis and morphology: see for example Delavenay's (1960) *Introduction to Machine Translation*. But meaning was taken as given, rather than problematized; this was not yet "computing with meanings".

In the second phase, language emerged as a computable object, need-ing to be modelled in its own right; the concept of "a grammar", a description of a language as written by a linguist, came to be accepted – or at least tolerated as a necessary nuisance. But such a descriptive gram-mar had no direct place in the computing process; the computational grammar was purely procedural, a program for parsing strings of words. (There was little text generation during this phase; one of the few such projects was the systemic generator developed in Edinburgh by Anthony Davey (1978).) On the other hand, as implied by the label "computa-tional linguistics" which came into favour during this period, these were computing operations performed on language; the way the strings of words were manipulated was designed to establish what they meant. There had clearly been a move in the direction of computing with meanings.

It was in the third phase, after about 1980, that developments took place which the phrase "computing with meanings" could more accu-rately describe. By this time computational grammars came to take the form of descriptive, or "declarative", representations, and researchers sought to develop generalized forms of representation suited to their computational needs. It was accepted that these had to accommodate large-scale grammars with reasonable detail and complexity, not just the dedicated and simplified grammars of the earlier phase. The move from procedural to declarative, and the shift in scale and in depth of focus, changed the relationship once again: the value of a piece of wording was, for the first time, being interpreted in terms of *agnation*, its locus in the total meaning potential of the language. It would seem accurate now to characterize computational linguistic operations as operations on meaning.

Perhaps I could gloss this with a story from personal experience. Back in the 1960s, the working assumption was, "If we can't compute your grammar, your grammar must be wrong". This was not, let me make it clear, arrogance on the part of individual computer specialists; simply a conviction that the computer defined the parameters of human understanding. To me it seemed that the constraints set by current technology, and even more those set by current theories of logic, at that particular moment in human history, were quite irrelevant for evaluating models of grammar; this was the main reason why I moved away from the scene, for the second and (as I thought) the final time. So when in 1980 William Mann came to see me – I was working at U.C. Irvine – and asked me to write a systemic grammar of English for his forthcoming text generation project (the "Penman" I mentioned earlier), I challenged him on this point: how much would I have to "simplify" (that is, distort) the grammar in order to make it computable? Bill Mann's answer was, "If I can't compute your grammar, I'll have to learn how". He later added an interesting comment: "I don't always understand why linguists describe things the way they do; but I've come to realize they always have a reason". It was clear then that the relationship of language to computing had moved on.

There is a serious point underlying this little anecdote. Of course we, as grammarians, had to learn to write our descriptions in computable form: that is, to make them fully explicit. This was an important exercise, from which we learnt a great deal. But to make them explicit is not the same demand as to make them **simple**. Language is not simple; it is ferociously complex – perhaps the single most complex phenomenon in nature; and at least some of that complexity had to be accounted for. To take just one example: what was referred to under the general label "constituency" is not a single, undifferentiated type of structure (like a "tree"), but a highly variable array of different meaning-making resources, with highly complex interrelations among them. Unfortunately the linguists themselves had made the problem worse: the prevailing ideology, at least in America, but also perhaps in western Europe and in Japan, was the structuralist one deriving out of Bloomfield via Chomsky; and this was highly reductionist, in that, in order for natural language to be represented as a formal system, much of the rich variation in meaning had to be idealized out of the picture. But not only was it reductionist – it was also authoritarian: for linguists of this persuasion, the standard response to anyone who disagreed with them was, "Either your grammar is a notational variant of my grammar, or else your grammar is wrong". So computer scientists who ventured across the frontier into linguistics, in that second phase, might reasonably conclude that a natural language could be modelled as a well-formed system conforming to a recognizable mathematical-type logic. This period in mainstream linguistics was an age of syntax, in which a grammar could be reduced to an inventory of well-defined structural forms.

But by the time of what I am calling the third phase, the orientation of linguistics had changed. Much more attention was now being paid to semantics, both by linguists working from within the Chomskyan paradigm and by those who had remained outside it. Thus the concept of "computational linguistics" already implied something closer to "computing meanings"; it implied a system that fully engaged with natural language, parsing and generating text in operational contexts. Machine translation once again figured prominently on the agenda, as the four components of a speech-to-speech translation program fell into place: recognition + parsing + generation + synthesis were all seen to be possible, and such systems now began to appear on the market – not perhaps doing all that was claimed for them, but performing adequately for a limited range of tasks. The general encompassing term was now "natural language processing".

But these continue to appear as two distinct activities: computing, and language processing. There is still the awkward disjunction between computing in general, and meaning. Computational linguistics, or natural language processing, or generation and parsing, are separate operations from computing in the general sense. And this has some strange consequences. I recently visited Japan, to attend the international conference on fuzzy systems chaired by Professor Sugeno. There were many interesting exhibits, from industry and also from LIFE, the Laboratory for International Fuzzy Engineering, which was just coming to the end of its own life cycle. One of the latter was FLINS, the Fuzzy Natural Language Communication System; this was a question-answering system incorporating an inference engine, which reasoned by taking the special case, assigning it to a general class and inferring a course of action therefrom. One very interesting feature of this system was the use of traditional proverbs to state the general proposition – this being precisely the function that proverbs had in our traditional societies. (My grandmother had a proverb for every occasion.) But what struck me particularly was that their inferencing procedures, which involved both symbolic and fuzzy matching, were totally insulated from their language processing; they had simply bought ready-made commercial systems for parsing and generating text. In other words, reasoning and inferencing were being treated as non-linguistic operations – although they were being entirely carried out through the medium of language. Notice what this implies: that there is no semantic relationship – no systematic relationship in meaning – between, say, the proverbial expression *more haste less speed* and (the verbal component of) an instance to which it relates as a general proposition, for example *Don't be in a hurry to overtake; it only slows you down. More haste less speed!*

This seems to be a scenario in which linguistics and computing inhabit two different worlds. Natural language is being seen as something to be separately processed, rather than as an inherent part of the computing process itself. And this is the difference, it seems to me, between the third phase and the subsequent fourth phase which we may now be entering. With "intelligent computing", the boundary between computing in general and natural language processing rather disappears: all computing could involve operating with natural language. Computing then becomes synonymous with computing meanings.

"Intelligent computing" is an important concept which could have very far-reaching consequences; so I would like to consider it here in a little more detail. As I mentioned earlier, Sugeno defines this as computing based on natural language; he also sometimes expresses it in simplified terms as "computing with words". Lotfi Zadeh, the founder of "fuzzy logic", used this same formulation in his talk at the conference, remarking that computing with words "enhances the ability of machines to mimic the human mind, and points to a flaw in the foundations of science and engineering". He also observed that, while human reasoning is "overwhelmingly expressed through the medium of words", people are only taught to compute with numbers – they are never taught how to compute with words. Commenting on the formulation "computing with words", Zadeh glossed "computing" as "computing and reasoning", and "words" as "strings of words, not very small".

We need to reformulate that last expression, in two steps as follows:

(1) for *words* (or *strings of words*), read *wordings*: words in grammatical structures, i.e. lexicogrammatical strings of any extent;
(2) for *wordings*, in turn, read *meanings*, again in the technical sense; that is, semantic sequences of any given extent.

Note that, in reformulating in this way, we are not questioning Sugeno's concept; we are recasting it in terms of semiotic practice. People reason and infer with **meanings**, not with wordings. (They don't store wordings, as is easily demonstrated when they repeat the steps along the way.) To put this in more technical terms: reasoning and inferencing are semantic operations.

Thus, if they are performed computationally, this will be done on semantic representations. But, at the same time, such semantic representations are related systemically to the lexicogrammatical ones. In other words, the meanings are **construed** in wordings. When people reason through talk, they are actually reasoning with **meanings**; but these meanings are not a separate "cognitive" universe of concepts or ideas – they are patterns of semantic (that is, linguistic) organization brought about, or "realized", by the wordings. They are reasoning in language, even though not, strictly speaking, in words.

There are in fact two noticeable disjunctions needing to be overcome, in the move into the intelligent computing phase. One is this one between language and knowledge, or rather between meaning and knowing, or meaning and thinking. Natural language processing systems typically operate with one kind of representation for language, a "grammar", and another, very different kind of representation for knowledge – a separate "knowledge base"; and the two different representations have then to be made to interact (see Figure 11.1). If we reconceptualize the knowledge base as a *meaning base* – as another level in the representation of language – the problem becomes more easily manageable: instead of two systems, one inside language and one outside (the grammatical and the conceptual), there is only one system, language, with two levels of representation, the grammatical (lexicogrammatical) and the semantic (see Figure 11.2) (cf. Halliday and Matthiessen 1999, 2000).

The second disjunction I have in mind is that between the *instance* and the *system* of which it is an instance. The grammar of a natural language is represented systematically: **either** conventionally, as a set of structures, **or**, in a systemic grammar, as a network of options – language as semiotic potential. On the other hand, reasoning and inferencing are operations performed on (representations of) *instances*. Now, any instance is meaningful only by virtue of its **place** in, and its derivation from, the total *systemic potential*. But in computational reasoning and inferencing, the instances are typically presented as unrelated to the overall system of the language. They are handled as "discourse", with the implication that discourse is process, without any system behind it. If we reconceptualize discourse as "text" – as the instantiation of an underlying system – the

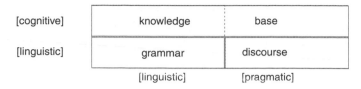

[cognitive]	knowledge	base
[linguistic]	grammar	discourse
	[linguistic]	[pragmatic]

Figure 11.1 The cognitive model

[semantic]	semantic system	semantic instance (text as meaning)	
[lexico-grammatical]	grammatical system	grammatical instance (text as wording)	[linguistic]
	[system (potential)]	[text (instantial)]	

Figure 11.2 The semantic model

problem of reasoning and inferencing may also become more easily manageable.

Each of these disjunctions corresponds to a major duality in Western thinking, enshrined in contemporary philosophy and philosophical linguistics. The first is the duality between language and mind, which is institutionalized in today's dichotomy between linguistics and cognitive science; the second is the duality of langue and parole, which in turn is institutionalized in today's dichotomy between linguistics and pragmatics. (See Ellis 1993, esp. chapter 5, and Matthiessen 1993a & b, 1998 for relevant discussions.) These dualities are taken over into our intellectual pursuits – such as computational linguistics – without being problematized or even brought to conscious attention. But there are alternative strategies available, as I have remarked. Instead of two systems, one inside language (the grammatical) and one outside language (the conceptual, or cognitive), it is possible to operate with one system, language, having two related levels of representation, the (lexico)grammatical and the semantic; and instead of two classes of phenomena, one of langue (grammar) and one of parole (discourse), it is possible to operate with one phenomenon, language, having two degrees or phases of instantiation, that of system and that of text. The "knowledge base" becomes a "meaning base", which can then be described in a framework that is homologous to the grammar; and each instance of wording or meaning can be described by reference to the overall potential of the system.

In this way the boundaries are redrawn as boundaries within language itself. The frontier between language and cognition becomes a **stratal** boundary between grammar and semantics, or wordings and meanings; while the frontier between langue and parole becomes an **instantial** boundary between the system (of grammar or semantics) and the instance (of wording or meaning). I shall suggest later that the two dimensions of **stratification** and **instantiation** can be used to define a matrix for locating computational linguistic representations. Meanwhile, a consequence of redrawing these frontiers as boundaries internal to language is that both of them become indeterminate, or "fuzzy". Since they are theoretical constructs for explaining, and managing, what is now being conceived of as a single unified semiotic system, namely language, this is not really surprising. But they are fuzzy in different ways.

Instantiation is a cline, modelling the shift in the standpoint of the observer: what we call the "system" is language seen from a distance, as semiotic potential, while what we call "text" is language seen from close up, as instances derived from that potential. In other words, there is only one phenomenon here, not two; langue and parole are simply different observational positions. But we can also position ourselves at an intermediate point along this cline, moving in from one end or from the other. I think that the critical intermediate concept, for our purposes, is that of **register**, which enables us to model contextual variation in language. Seen from the instantial end of the cline, a register appears as a cluster of similar texts, a **text type**; whereas seen from the systemic end, a register appears as a **sub-system**. Computationally it is possible to exploit these two complementary perspectives (see Figure 11.3).

Stratification is a relationship of a different kind. The boundary between semantics and grammar is a true boundary; these are two distinct levels, or **strata**, within the content plane of natural language, and they have different realms of **agnation** – that is, the organization of grammatical space

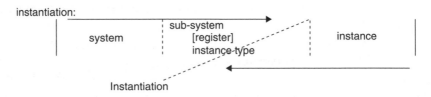

Figure 11.3 Instantiation

stratification:

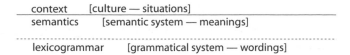

context	[culture — situations]
semantics	[semantic system — meanings]
lexicogrammar	[grammatical system — wordings]

Figure 11.4 Stratification

differs from the organization of semantic space (Martin and Matthiessen 1991). But we can draw this boundary at different places, shifting it "up or down" according to the task in hand. Furthermore, having defined the relationship between semantics and grammar in this way, we are then able to extend the same concept (known as **realization**) so as to model the relationship of language to the context of situation, interpreting the context also as a semiotic system (see Figure 11.4). Thus by deconstructing the two dualities and overcoming the disjunctions they set up, we gain additional freedom of movement on both the dimensions involved.

How is this relevant to the issue of "intelligent computing"? This concept, as defined by Sugeno and by Zadeh, involves using natural language as the "language" of the computer: natural language as the computational metalanguage. But this inevitably raises questions of representation. It is sometimes forgotten that the orthographic system of every (written) language already involves a large number of highly complex decisions about meaning – what meanings are to be distinguished, how they are to be interrelated, and so on; to take a very clear example, in the English writing system, if a semantic contrast is realized by the order of elements it will be registered in writing (*you can go/can you go*), whereas if it is realized by intonation or rhythm it is not (thus *you can go* represents a wide range of different kinds and degrees of emphasis, different modalities and so on). Since these decisions were taken a long time ago, without conscious reflection, we tend simply to forget about them; but the differences in meaning that are obscured in this way could be critical to the computational process. Even if we have a speech-recognition system which can accept spoken input, however, this does not eliminate the problem. Using natural language as metalanguage does not mean plucking isolated instances out of the air, as can be done with simple command control or question-answering systems. It means locating each instance within a defined realm of meaning potential, from which it derives its value in the given computational context – in other words, relating the instance to the system, or to some specified register or subsystem; and this requires engaging with the language in theoretical terms.

We cannot just take language for granted as something we know all about in terms of common sense (which usually means, in practice, in terms of how our teachers used to talk about language in primary school). Intelligent computing will make stringent demands on the full range of complexity of natural languages; otherwise they would be of little use for the purpose. Therefore, it will require theoretical tools for describing and managing that complexity.

In other words, it will require what I have been calling a **grammatics**: a model of language which uses grammar as its underlying logic. Let me recall here Zadeh's reference to the "flaw in the foundations of science and engineering", and ask what Zadeh meant by this remark. The flaw, as Zadeh saw it, was that mathematics ruled, and that events were "quantized rather than granular": features that were characteristic of what he called "hard computing". We were now moving into an era of "soft computing", in imitation of human thinking which is "granular", a granule being defined as "a group of points with a fuzzy boundary". In other terms, "computational intelligence" (the analysis and design of intelligent systems, human-like in that they are based on approximate reasoning) takes over from "artificial intelligence" (which Zadeh characterized as analysis and design of physical systems); just as, in the industrial revolution, machine power augmented and transformed human muscular strength, so in the information revolution machine intelligence augments and transforms the power of the human brain (Zadeh 1995). Terano observed, in the same context (1995), that there is no mathematical model for macroscopic information processing; it is too "ill structured". What then replaces mathematics in this new context? – the answer has to be, I think, **grammar**. When language comes to function not just as the **object** of computing but as its **instrument**, the intellectual foundation may have to shift, from mathematical logic to grammatical logic. Mathematics and grammar are both semiotic systems; but they constitute different, and in a sense complementary, kinds of logic: the logic of numbers and the logic of wordings and meanings – linguistic logic, in Sugeno's formulation.

As mathematics enables us to manage the complexity of numbers, so the grammatics enables us to manage the complexity of language. (And also, perhaps, to celebrate it! – we are often reminded of the aesthetic appeal of mathematics, but the aesthetic appeal of grammar has scarcely begun to be recognized, though it is certainly no less than that of numbers.) This means theorizing about language with an orientation towards working systems, in data fusion, contextual simulation and other such operations; not only mapping out the complexity but finding ways of ordering and operationalizing it. If I was seeking a research grant, I might dream up a "total language complexity management system".

In fact, of course, it will not be total; there are aspects of the complexity of language which we must be able to ignore, as irrelevant to the tasks in hand. So what are the aspects of linguistic complexity that do need to be taken into account, in practice, if one is computing with natural language? Here is a first guess, very tentative, in summary form. The first five points have been discussed already; the sixth and seventh remain to be explained.

1 **words** function by being organized into **wordings** (lexicogrammatical patterns);
2 **wordings**, in turn, construct semantic patterns, or **meanings**;
3 **meanings** relate systematically to features of the **context**;
4 particular **instances** of wording / meaning derive their value from their place in the **system** (relationships within the system network, or **agnation**);
5 the **system** accommodates **sub-systemic variation** (variation in **register**);
6 the **system** is organized **metafunctionally** (into zones of semantic space, which determine both the form of the grammar and its relationship to the context);
7 **meaning** involves three dimensions of history: **evolution** of the system, **unfolding** of the individual text, **development** of the human infant into adulthood (phylogenesis, logogenesis, ontogenesis).

I shall first discuss point no. 6; then, on the basis of 1–6, suggest a possible architecture for a linguistic module that might be used in intelligent computing. Finally I shall return to point no. 7, adding one further dimension to the total picture.

Let me return briefly to the notion of lexicogrammar (which we usually refer to simply as "grammar", for short). A grammar is a purely abstract semiotic construct that evolves as a distinct level, or **stratum**, in between the content and the expression; by "purely abstract" I mean that it has no direct interface with material phenomena (whereas the "lower" stratum, that of spoken or written expression, interfaces with the human body, and the "higher" stratum of the content, that of semantics, interfaces with human experience and human social processes). A stratified system of this kind – one with a grammar in it – has the special property that it can **constitute**; unlike simple sign systems, which reflect meanings that are already given, a stratified system **creates** meaning. It creates meaning, of course, in contexts of function; and because the meanings

Table 11.1 The metafunctional components of meaning

metafunction	gloss
ideational:	construing experience (the "knowledge base")
experiential	construing categories
logical	construing relations among categories
interpersonal	enacting personal and social relationships (the "action base")
textual	creating flow of meaning (the "text, or discourse, base")

are then non-randomly related to features of these contexts, it can also create the contexts themselves.

The functional contexts of language fall into two major types; and the semiotic function that language is performing differs as between the two (see Table 11.1). On the one hand, language constitutes human experience; and in this aspect, its function is to *construe*: language **imposes order on** the world that lies around us, and that is located within ourselves. On the other hand, language constitutes human relationships; and in this aspect, its function is not to construe but to *enact*: language **brings about** our ongoing social interaction. The grammar integrates these two modes of meaning in such a way that every *instance* – everything we say or write, listen to or read – "means" in these two ways at once. These major functional types are referred to in systemic theory as *metafunctions*.

This interdependence of the two metafunctions, the *experiential* (or *ideational*, to give it its more inclusive name) and the *interpersonal*, has been central to the evolution of language, and to its persistence as a metastable system, constantly changing in interaction with its environment. The ideational mode of meaning comes closest to "meaning" in the everyday sense of the term ('content', especially 'referential content'). It is language as the **categorizing** and logical **construing of human experience**: that is, language taking over the material processes and conditions of human existence and transforming them into meanings. We usually become aware of this semiotic transformation only when we consider designed scientific or technical knowledge, where we have a clear sense of the semiotic energy involved (for example in writing a theoretical discussion such as the present one!). But all knowledge is like this. To "know" anything is to have transformed it into meaning; and what we call "understanding" is the process of that semiotic transformation.

The integration, by the grammar, of ideational and interpersonal meanings calls into being a third functional component, the *textual* metafunctions, which creates a flow of meanings, a semiotic current by which the other components are activated in conjunction. We refer to this process, or more often to its output, by the name of "discourse". In commonsense terms, what makes it possible for humans to develop and use language, in the contexts of daily life, is that every linguistic act (every *act of meaning*) involves both talking about the world and acting upon those who are in it; and that this conjunction is achieved by creating a semiotic flow of events that parallels, and in some respects mimics, the material flow which constitutes its environment.

By a "linguistic module" for intelligent computing, I mean an operational map of the terrain, such that any step in the process of computing meanings can be located and defined within an overall theoretical framework. Such a module could be initially constructed as a simple matrix intersecting stratification and instantiation. For the purpose of illustration, I shall ignore the expression plane, and consider just the strata of lexicogrammar, semantics and context. On the instantiation cline, I shall include just the one intermediate category of "sub-system/type". This gives a framework consisting of nine cells, but with those of the centre column represented in two aspects (see Table 11.2).

Each of the nine cells defined in this way is in turn occupied by a structure of an analogous kind. If we take as prototypical the bottom left-hand cell (column "system", row "lexicogrammar", i.e. the lexicogrammatical system), this structure takes the form of another matrix, this time with the vectors of metafunctions and rank. The metafunctions are common to semantics and grammar; shown here in their grammatical "order" (logical; experiential, interpersonal, textual). The ranks are the

Table 11.2 Instantiation/stratification matrix

STRATI-FICATION \ INSTANTIATION	system	sub-system / instance type	instance
context	culture	institution / situation type	situations
semantics	semantic system	register / text type	[text as] meanings
lexico-grammar	grammatical system	register / text type	[text as] wordings

structural units of the grammar (clause, phrase, group, word; each with its associated complex – clause complex, etc.).

The form of entry, in each cell of this inner matrix, is that of a system network. What this means is that the grammatical system of the given language is represented *paradigmatically*, in the form of a network of options, or alternative possibilities: either positive or negative, either past or present or future, either indicative or imperative, and so on; each set of options accompanied by its realizations. The grammar is thus presented synoptically, as a resource. Operationally, the activity of meaning consists in tracing paths through this network; either "left to right", in the case of production (speaking or writing), or "right to left" in the case of understanding (listening or reading). The network is open-ended: the more we know, or find out, about the grammar, the further we can extend it in delicacy, or depth of detail. Current systemic grammars of English in computational form have about a thousand sets of options (*systems*, in the technical sense).

The form taken by these inner matrices – the vectors involved, and the representational mode – will differ from one to another of the cells of the outer matrix. Table 11.3 gives a sketch of the overall organization of the content. Despite the architectural metaphor, and the solid lines separating the rows and the columns, this is not a building with rigid walls and floors; it is a multidimensional elastic space, within which are constituted the whole of human experience and social processes.

The left-hand middle cell is the semantic system. This we are not yet capable of modelling as a whole; we can, however, specify its internal organization, which is closely analogous to the function/rank matrix of the grammar but with its own distinctive categories – a "rank scale" of structural units such as, possibly, text, subtext, semantic paragraph, sequence, figure, element; and metafunctional regions defined in topological fashion, construing the activity patterns and ideological motifs of the culture (clusters relating to technology, to social hierarchy, to the sphere of activities of daily life, and so on). As with the lexicogrammar, these are represented paradigmatically, as networks of "meaning potential".

The left-hand upper cell is taken up with contextual networks: it contains a theory of the **possible semiotic situations** that collectively constitute a culture – taxonomies of institutions and of doings and happenings, manifested as possible clusterings of values of field, tenor and mode. Consider as an example the generalized institution of professionalism, with (as field) the thematic systems of medicine, the law, technical education and the like; (as tenor) the paired interactive processes involving professional and client, such as doctor and patient, lawyer and client,

Table 11.3 Instantiation/stratification matrix, with glosses

STRATI-FICATION	INSTANTIATION system	sub-system instance type	instance
context	the culture" == social-semiotic system:network of social semiotic features constituting the systems-&-processes of the cltures; defined as potential clusters of values of field, tenor, mode	networks of regions of social semiotic space a set of like stitua- tions forming a situation type	instantial values of field, tenor and mode; particular social semiotic situation events, with their organization
semantics	"the semantic system": networks of ideational, interpersonal and textual meanings; their construction as texts, subtexts, parasemes, sequences, figures and elements	networks of topological regions of semantic space a set of like texts (meanings) form- ing a text type	semantic selection expressions (features from passes through semantic networks), and their representation as meanings particular texts, with their organization
lexicogrammar	"the grammatical system": metafunction rank < networks >	networks of typological regions of lexicogram -matical space a set of like texts (wordings) forming a text type	lexicogrammatical selection expressions (features from passes through grammatical networks), and their manifestation as wordings particular texts, spoken or written, with their organization

teacher and student; (as mode) the mixed patterns of spoken and written communication that constitute a professional exchange. Such clusterings are highly solidary, with strong coupling among the various components; in other cases, the couplings will be looser and less mutually constrained.

Thus the left-hand column as a whole is the **potential**: the total semiotic resources of the culture, represented systemically as networks. Stratifying it – sorting it out into doings (level of context), meanings (level of semantics) and wordings (level of lexicogrammar) – is a way of managing its complexity: splitting up meaning by dispersing it into a spectrum, to use Firth's metaphor from forty years ago (1957b). The right-hand column represents the **instantial**: a particular event (doing) involving some linguistic activity (meaning/wording). Here too we take account of the stratal organization. Typically in computational work the wording is represented in ordinary orthography; this has served well enough up to now, but it imposes arbitrary constraints which may need to be overcome. (For example, for input to a speech synthesizer the wording needs to include information concerning intonation and rhythm.) Semantic representations of the instance – the instance as meaning – are still quite unsatisfactory, and there is much work to be done in this respect. Likewise for the instantial **situation**: we tend to work with informal word-pictures, like the stage directions in the printed edition of a play; but the basic concept of situation as instance has advanced very little in recent decades. The sense of "context" is usually taken to include the situation **before** (and sometimes also **after**) what is selected as the instance of meaning / wording, on the grounds that, while we can "freeze" instances over as many frames as we like, there will always be a precursor and a sequel; and this is also taken to include the "co-text", the **text** preceding and following that which is under focus. (Note that the **instance** is the event itself. We may have a **record** of it, say on video, and then a replay or performance of it; but then the performance itself becomes the substantive event, the "original" being now an event of the second order.)

It may be helpful to distinguish recording from describing. When we **describe** an instance, we relate it across the row from right to left: that is, to our representation of the **system** at that stratum. This is a theoretical operation, different from the sort of running commentary that is sometimes offered by way of description. The form taken by such a description, in a systemic grammar, is called a "selection expression"; this states which of the features in the system network have been selected in the instance in question. The selection expression thus gives an account of the total **agnation** of the instance – how it relates to other possible instances. This is based on the **paradigmatic** principle, referred to earlier: the significance of a semiotic event lies in what it might have been, but was not.

Let me introduce here some snatches of a constructed text, in order to illustrate some of the points being raised. Items [in square brackets] represent "doings"; other text represents wordings; the interactants are a driving instructor and her pupil.

[Driving instructor and pupil in car; on public roads, in urban traffic; pupil driving]

[Pupil takes corner rather too fast]
Instr:You should have braked before turning. O.k.; go left here.
[Pupil again takes corner too fast]
Instr: Now what did I tell you just now?
Pupil: Sorry! You said I had to slow down at corners.

[Bus pulls out in front]
Instr: Brake!!
[Pupil stops car]

[On three-lane highway; pupil repeatedly changes lanes]
Instr: Don't be in a hurry to overtake; it'll only slow you down. More haste less speed!

[Bus appears from cross street; pupil swerves and misses it]
Instr:Why didn't you brake?
[Pupil slows down and draws into kerb]
Instr:You can't stop here – go on!
Pupil: But you told me to stop the car!

Consider for example the urgent command *Brake!!* This is a piece of wording, in orthographic representation; its locus is in the right-hand bottom corner cell. Moving up the column, we might give it a semantic representation along these lines: 'you = learner / listener = responsible person / agent + cause / stop + car + I insist'. Moving up to the top row, we might characterize the situation as: (preceding situation) [pupil driving, instructor sitting beside; a bus crosses in front]; (following situation) [pupil hits foot brake; car slows and stops]. Starting again from the instance of wording *Brake!!*, but now moving across the row to the left-hand column, we map the traversal in the form of a selection expression showing that this piece of wording realizes the following features, among others: (clause:) polarity: positive; mood: imperative: jussive; process type: material: action; voice: middle; (verbal group:) finiteness: non-finite; tense: neutral, and so on – the number of features depending on the **delicacy** (depth in detail) of our grammatics. The left-hand bottom cell itself, as already remarked, is the locus of (our representation of) the lexico-grammatical system as a whole.

The situation, in any given instance, will be one of a set of similar situations, constituting a "situation type". Of course, all such sets are fuzzy;

we determine their boundaries according to the task in hand, assigning some "membership function" to non-core, borderline cases: if the situation type is characterized as "driving lessons", such a peripheral instance might be one where the trainee is learning to drive a bus, or a train, where the instructor is an amateur rather than a professional, and so on. Likewise, the text, in any given instance, will be one of a set of similar texts — we refer to it as a "text type". Such "types" share common features; this is what enables us to make predictions in the way we do all the time in daily life, both from the text to the situation and from the situation to the text.

Descriptively, the type is the instantial manifestation of a subsystem, shown in our middle column in Table 11.2 as *register*. A "sub-system" is a complex category, not definable as a subset. It is not simply the full system network with some of its arteries sealed off. Some systemic options may be effectively ruled out, especially at the level of context; people do not mix up their patterns of cultural activity — or if they do (if, for example, the instructor and the pupil start playing chess in the middle of the driving lesson), this **constitutes** a change of register. But semantically, and even more lexicogrammatically, sub-systems are characterized mainly in terms of probabilities. Seen from the "system" end, a register is a **local** resetting of the **global** probabilities that characterize the system as a whole. So, for example, in instructional situations direct imperative may take over as the most favoured selection of mood, as in *Brake!!*; but that does not mean closing off the other moods: the instructor also uses wordings such as declarative *You should have braked*, interrogative *Why didn't you brake?*, or indirect, projected imperative as in *I told you to brake*. Subsystemic variation is thus a selective highlighting of features of the overall system. (At the level of the grammar, where we are able to model the system as a whole, subsystemic variation in register can be represented in these terms, as further, largely quantitative patterning superimposed upon it. But at the level of the semantics, it may be that each register will be modelled, initially at least, in its own terms, following the usual practice of domain-specific representations.)

Let me now return to the points enumerated earlier (as "aspects of linguistic complexity" to be accounted for), and add brief illustrations by making reference to the "driving instruction" mini-text.

(1) Words are organized into wordings (lexicogrammatical patterns). We can represent these patterns in structural terms, so as to show the grammar "at work" in the construction of meaning. Table 11.4 shows part of the structural make-up of *You should have braked before turning.*

Table 11.4 The grammar at work (showing metafunctions)

	You	should	have	braked	before		turning
logical	α. (primary clause)				xβ (secondary)		
	clause nexus: hypotactic / enhancing : temporal						
experiential	Actor	Process			Conjunction		Process
	clause: material				clause: material		
interpersonal	Subject	Finite	Predicator				Predicator
	Mood		Residue				Residue
	clause: finite : declarative/ modulated : high / neutral key				clause: non-finite		
textual (1)	Theme	Rheme			Theme		Rheme
	clause: unmarked theme				clause: structural theme		
textual (2)	Given ⟵			New ⟵			New
	information unit: complex (major + minor focus)						

(2) Wordings construct meanings (semantic patterns). Notice that when reasoning about 'what did I do wrong?', the pupil *rewords* you *should have braked before turning* as *(you said) I had to slow down at corners.* These two wordings could be related through the grammar, showing rather complex patterns of agnation. But the pupil is reasoning with meanings, not with wordings; and it is probably more effective to relate them at the semantic level. Thus, *you / I* are dialogic alternants for the same interactant, the pupil, functioning in both cases as (i) Actor/Agent, (ii) Subject and (iii) Theme: semantically, as the doer, as the one held to account, and as the point of origin of the message. Secondly, *should have . . . ed* and *had to . . .* are both high value obligations; the former relating to a past event, the latter relating to the situation in general (*had to* is projected into a past tense form by "sequence of tenses" following *said*). Thirdly, in *brake | slow down*, one process has been replaced by another one designating its intended effect. Fourthly, in *before turning | at corners* a spatial process defined by temporal location has been replaced by a spatial location in which this process takes place.

(3) Meanings relate to features of the context. We may represent the context as a construction of three variables: field, tenor, and mode. The *field* is 'what is going on': the nature of the social process, as institutionalized in the culture. The *tenor* is 'who are taking part': the role and status relationships of the interactants. The *mode* is 'what the text is doing': the rhetorical functions and channels assigned to language in the situation. By modelling the context in these terms we can display the "resonance"

between contextual and linguistic features: typically, the field is realized in ideational meanings, the tenor in interpersonal meanings and the mode in textual meanings.

There is a note to be added at this point. The critical factor here is the modelling of language in "stratal" terms, such that the concept of a *semiotic system* comes to include not only meanings but also the environment in which meanings are exchanged. It seems likely that, in intelligent computing, the "knowledge base" of artificial intelligence will be replaced by a "meaning base", and the external world of referents by a world located at the interface between semiotic and material events (this is the meaning of "context"). In this way particular operations in meaning, such as reasoning from a general to a particular case, inferring the situation from instances of discourse, or deriving information from a variety of different sources, may be located and managed within an overall conceptual framework.

(4) Instances derive value from their place within the system. For example, the features enumerated above in the selection expression for the wording *Brake!!* are all represented paradigmatically in the system network for the grammar of English (cf. Matthiessen 1995). See Figure 9.1 [in VI.9(1995):212] to see a network for the English verbal group, incorporating about 70,000 alternatives. Each instance of a verbal group may be represented as a pass through this network, showing the option selected at each of the possible choice points. Thus *[you] should have braked!* is "finite: modal: high / oblique / obligation; secondary tense: past; contrast: event / (force:) neutral; polarity: positive; voice: active"; agnate to:

— You should **brake!** [secondary tense: past | neutral]
— You shouldn't have **braked!** [polarity: positive | negative]
— You could have **braked!** [modal value: high | low]
— You **should** have braked! [contrast | location: event | auxiliary]
— You didn't **brake**. [polarity; deixis: modal | temporal] etc. etc.

The pupil understands the meaning of the particular instance, as spoken by the instructor, from its location in this multidimensional grammatical space.

(5) The system accommodates variation in register. We could characterize the context of the driving lesson, as institution, in something like the following terms:

Field: Learning, under instruction; a skill: (mechanical operation: driving a car).

Tenor: Instructor: professional (power = knowledge: can give orders);
   learner: client (power = authority: can withdraw custom).
Mode: Spoken; instructional: action-oriented; mainly monologic.

The corresponding register is likely to foreground ideational meanings to do with the field, such as active processes of locomotion with explicit agency; interpersonal eanings to do with the tenor, such as imperatives, or declaratives modulated by obligation; and textual meanings to do with the mode, such as clausal information units with learner as theme and focus on the process or the vehicle. (Compare what was said about "resonance" under (3) above.)

(6) The system is organized metafunctionally. The different components of the meaning are integrated by the grammar into a single wording, as illustrated in Table 11.4. The multiple layers of structure (whose actual difference is rather greater than appears when they are represented in this unified compositional format) are displayed so as to suggest how this integration is achieved. Each structural layer contributes one band of meaning, which we could bring out informally in a hybrid grammatico-semantic commentary:

You should have **braked** before **turning**

Ideational: logical:

> sequence of two processes linked by temporal succession, the subsequent process made dependent on (i.e., construed as conditioning environment of) the prior one;

Ideational: experiential:

(1) material process: action: 'make + stop / slow'; active participant 'the learner'; time: past;
(2) material process: action: 'make + turn'; same active participant;

Interpersonal:

(1) statement of unfulfilled obligation: high (strong); force: neutral (moderate); person held accountable: 'the listener';
(2) [meanings carried over from (1)];

Textual:

(1) theme 'you (learner/listener)'; focus 'brake (action)';
(2) theme: prior location in time; focus 'turn (action)';
(1 & 2) message complete: one information unit, with major + minor focus.

(7) Meaning involves three dimensions of history, a point to which I said I would return at the end. Up to now I have freeze framed both the instances and the systemic categories, taking them out of history; it is useful to hold them still while we examine them. But, of course, semiotic processes, just like material processes, take place in time. There is always a diachronic dimension. Meaning has a history; and when computing with meanings, one may need to take account of the axis or dimension of time. The problem is, that there is more than one dimension of time involved – more than one distinct kind of history. In terms of the matrix I have been using, each of the two outer columns has a separate history of its own.

On the one hand, the system has a history: a language *evolves*. Its evolution is that of what Edelman (1992) refers to as higher-order consciousness: the evolution of the human brain. On the other hand, the instance also has a history: a text *unfolds*. Its unfolding is the individuation of the (in principle unique) semiotic act. The evolution of the system is "phylogenesis"; we refer to the unfolding of the text as "logogenesis" (see Figure 11.5). When we locate ourselves, as observers, in between the system and the text, we adopt one orientation or the other; so register, as noted already, appears either as variation in the system or as similarity in text type. There are thus two historical perspectives on register variation in language. On the one hand, a register is something that evolves, as a distinct subsystem (say, the language of science); on the other hand, a register is something that unfolds, as an accumulation of related text (say, the discourse of science; with "intertextuality" throughout – all scientific texts in English as one macrotext unfolding since the time of Newton and beyond) (see Figures 11.6 & 11.7). This dual historical perspective sets the parameters for any particular instance. If we consider reasoning, then the individual speaker (or "meaner") is typically reasoning within these historically determined limits: to take the same trivial (though not so trivial) example of the driving lesson, within the limits of the language of driving instruction as it has evolved, and of a particular sequence of driving instruction texts as these have unfolded.

But this, in turn, directs us on to a third dimension of history, that of "ontogenesis": the development of the meaning subject from birth through childhood and adolescence into the adult state. The individual human being has his/her own history, which is neither evolution nor unfolding but growth, maturation and eventual decay. This history of *development* defines a third set of limits within which the act of meaning is located (see Figure 11.8). (I have presented these historical parameters as "limitations" on the semiotic processes involved. But it is better,

Figure 11.5 Phylogenesis and logogenesis

Figure 11.6 Two angles on register

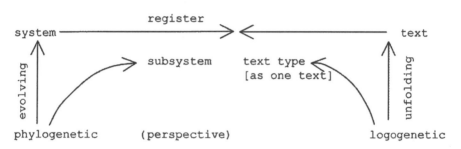

Figure 11.7 Historical angles on register

I think, to see them as enabling rather than constraining. What sets limits on the production and interpretation of discourse is simply the set of conditions that makes such discourse possible in the first place.)

It might seem that the developmental, ontogenetic perspective is the least relevant to intelligent computing; but I am not so sure. Every instance embodies some aspects of developmental history; what is important here is not the difference between one human being and another (the significance of this I think is often exaggerated) but rather what is common to the developmental history of the group, the paths traversed by all members in building up their meaning potential (Halliday 1975/2004; Painter 1984). This particular historical dimension is important because the development of language proceeds epigenetically, broadly recapitulating the trajectory of its evolution; and the discourse of adult life tends to comprise meanings from each phase along the way. If I may project our driving instruction text back into the history of the child, to the time when he is given his first wheeled vehicle to propel himself on, here is a brief sample of the instructions that might be offered:

These examples are constructed so as to illustrate the one most significant movement that underlies the development of the typical adult discourse of the age of information: the progression from the general, through the abstract, to the metaphorical. Generalization (the move from

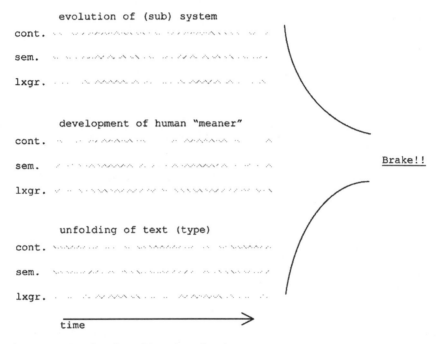

Figure 11.8 The three histories of an instance

(age)
1 Don't go too fast! You'll hit something.
2 You shouldn't go so fast. If you go too fast, you won't be able to stop.
5 You'd better slow down! The faster you go, the harder it is (the longer it takes) to stop.
9 It's important to keep at a low speed. Faster speed makes stopping much more difficult.
13+ Low speed maintenance is essential. Braking distance increases more rapidly at high speeds.

"proper" to "common" meanings) is the condition of entry from infant protolanguage into the mother tongue; abstractness is the gateway into the literate discourses of primary education; and metaphor (in the grammatical sense, particularly in the form of nominalization) is the gateway into the technical languages of adolescent and adult life – in which every text tends to contain meanings from all these developmental phases. But there are other reasons for stressing the ontogenetic perspective. It challenges the rather one-sided subjectivity that is characteristic of mainstream thinking in cognitive science, and the disjunction between "speaker models" and "hearer models", offering instead an intersubjective view in which what is being modelled is the relationship of interactants one to another – this is after all where meanings are made: the semogenic process is inherently dialogic rather than monologic. And, finally, the ontogenetic approach engages with current interest in learning and learning models. I have been pressing for some time now (without any success!) for a project of research in which the computer builds up its grammar the way a child does. I think we have enough evidence to do this, in English at least, and probably in other languages besides; and the experience would teach us a great deal about computing with meanings.

What I have been trying to address here are the problems of managing the complexity of language. If language is taking on a new role in relation to computing, which is what Sugeno and Zadeh have suggested, we cannot ignore that complexity, or idealize it out of the picture, because it is precisely the complexity of language that makes it operationally effective. Up to the present, language has been represented in the computer through the intermediary of designed systems, forms of representation based on a logic that is itself derivative of language. But this involves a fairly massive loss of information, a serious semiotic seepage over a wide area. It is now being suggested that language itself will become the primary computational resource; this should not only help to preserve the level of information but also make it possible to exploit the positive features of natural language – its multiplicity of functions, its elasticity, its systematic variation and so on. These are highly relevant to specific tasks of the kind that Sugeno has identified, such as data fusion (integrating information from language with that from numbers, symbols, images and non-linguistic sounds), fuzzy reasoning (as in his example of playing Go) and construing the context of situation by inference from the text. But even if the metalinguistic role is taken over directly by natural language, this still involves some form of representation. (It is useful to recall that ordinary orthography is ultimately a representational device, even if "written language" has now evolved into a system in its own right.) In particular, if, as I have suggested, computing with words really means computing with meanings, some form of *semantic* representation becomes crucial. I have not tried to tackle this problem here (cf. Halliday and Martin 1993, chapter 2, for some relevant discussion; also Halliday and Matthiessen 1999). What I have attempted, in the latter part of this chapter, is to outline a conceptual framework in which to locate representations of meaning – by reference one to another, and to whatever is "above" and "below". At least I have found it helpful for myself, in trying to follow the sometimes tortuous paths through computational linguistics. It is easy to lose one's way in the labyrinth of language.

VI.11(1995):239–67

Additional reading

Computational and Quantitative Studies (Volume 6)

Chapter Eleven

MARKEDNESS

Summary

When it comes to the distinction between marked and unmarked, there are cases where the options are skew with one option more frequent, and thus quantitatively unmarked. Where the options are equally probable – neither is the "unmarked term". Besides being quantitatively unmarked, an option may be simpler and therefore identified as being formally unmarked.

Among observations related to marked vs. unmarked options, Halliday notes that children typically sequence their learning of the grammar, beginning with quantitatively unmarked options. Also, he notes how grammatical systems in Chinese typically include an option which is "unmarked" in the sense that it simply allows one to avoid choosing between either alternative, where the option is not simply a choice between A or B, but rather choosing among A, B, or neither.

Selected readings

The Language of Early Childhood (Volume 4)

FEATURE 15

Learning a semiotic system means learning its options **together with their relative probabilities**, and so building up a quantitative profile of the whole. This concept is familiar in linguistics with regard to word frequencies: it is accepted that speakers have a rather clear sense of the relative frequency of the words in their mother tongue; for example, in English, that *go* is more frequent than *walk*, and *walk*, in its turn, is more frequent than *stroll*. But remarkably little attention has been paid to probabilities in the grammar.

Grammatical probabilities are no less part of the system of a language; and they are more powerful than lexical probabilities because of their greater generality. Children construe both kinds from the very rich evidence they have around them. By five years of age, a child is likely to have heard between half a million and a million clauses, so that, as an inherent aspect of learning the principal grammatical systems of the language, he has learnt the relative probabilities of each of their terms. An important corollary of this is that children are able to sequence their learning of the grammar, beginning with those options that stand out as being the more frequent. The longitudinal data suggest clearly that this is what they do, and examples will be found throughout.

It is necessary here to distinguish between quantitatively unmarked (more frequent) and formally unmarked (simpler). In most cases, the two coincide; thus in polarity (positive/negative), positive is unmarked in both respects, so if children learn the positive first (as they do) this might have to do as much with its formal simplicity as with its frequency. A case where the two are reversed is the system of mood in questions: here the interrogative is quantitatively unmarked while the declarative is formally unmarked – **as a question** (both on rising tone), *do you like it?* is very much more frequent in adult speech than *you like it?*, as can be attested from Svartvik and Quirk (1980). There is a time, of course, when children have not yet developed the 'question' feature at all; but when they do, they use the interrogative form for some time before introducing the declarative as a marked alternative to it.

It is conceivable that grammatical frequencies in natural languages follow a fairly regular pattern, such that the options in the most general grammatical systems display one or the other of two probability profiles: either equiprobable (for example, number: singular/plural), or noticeably skew, perhaps by about one order of magnitude (for example, polarity: positive/negative; Halliday and James 1993). This would be the quantitative analogue of the distinction between systems having no unmarked term and those having one term unmarked. If this was so, it would have significant consequences for a learner, because a semiotic of this kind would be learner-friendly in a way that one displaying all possible probability profiles would not.

IV.15(1993):342–3

Computational and Quantitative Studies (Volume 6)

Halliday had formulated the hypothesis that grammatical systems fell largely into two types: those where the options were equally probable – there being no "unmarked term", in the quantitative sense; and those where the options were skew, one term being unmarked. This was based on figures he had arrived at in the 1960s, by counting manually 2,000 instances each of a number of sets of systemic options across texts of different genres in modern English. If we assume a binary system (and it should be emphasized explicitly that **not** all systems are binary), this means that in an "equi" system, each term would occur with roughly the same frequency, while in a "skew" system one term would be significantly more frequent than the other. In his small-scale manual counting Halliday had found that the difference in frequency of the options in a skew system tended to be approximately one order of magnitude. In order to formulate a hypothesis in terms of probabilities he expressed this as

equi systems: 0.5 : 0.5
skew systems: 0.9 : 0.1

In other words, the prediction was that general grammatical systems would not be distributed evenly across the probability scale, with all values from 0.5 : 0.5 to 0.99 : 0.01, but that they would be distributed bimodally into these two probability profiles – with some approximation to these two values. A similar pattern would be predicted for ternary systems, except that it should be possible to find more than one type within the skew. We expect this overall picture to be generally true, although the exact distribution of probabilities may vary among different genres.

VI. 6(1993):96-7

* * *

I myself first became interested in grammatical frequencies in a crude and simplistic fashion many years ago in the course of my work as a language teacher – although, if I pursue this even further, the reason for my interest in such information as a teacher was that I had felt the need for it in the first place as a learner. Faced with the task of learning, from scratch, as a young adult, a language very distant from my own, or from any language I had had experience of before, I was constantly wanting to know what people actually said in this language. When I had to master very basic systems of mood, aspect, phase and so on that were unlike anything in English, I wanted to know which of a set of alternatives was the most likely – I did not know the term "unmarked" at that time, but what I was looking for was some guidance about which, if any, was the unmarked term. A few years later, when I started to teach that same language, although I had by then acquired some feeling for its patterns of discourse, I found it frustrating that I could not offer the students reliable information of the kind that I myself would have liked to have.

In other words, I wanted to know the probabilities that were associated with these grammatical choices. Given, for example, a particular grammatical system, say that of *aspect*, with terms *perfective/imperfective*, what was the relative probability of choosing one or the other in a Chinese clause (Chinese was the language I was teaching)? This is a considerable problem for a speaker of a western European language, for two reasons. On the one hand, the aspect system itself is unfamiliar; there is some form of grammatical aspect in English – its exact nature is disputed; but on any interpretation it is not the dominant temporal system in the clause, which is tense, whereas in Chinese the dominant temporal system is that of aspect. On the other hand, there is the problem of the nature of the unmarked term. Grammatical systems in Chinese typically embody an alternative which is "unmarked", not in the sense of being the default or most frequent choice (it often will be that too), but in the sense that it is a way of opting out – of not choosing either of the terms. So the aspect system is not simply "either perfective or imperfective" but "perfective, imperfective or **neither**". Speakers of European languages are much less accustomed to systems of this kind; and again, it would be helpful to know the relative probability of choosing one way or another.

VI.7(1993):131–2

Studies in English Language (Volume 7)

All text in spoken English is organized in information units, and the information unit is structured as a configuration of 'given' and 'new' elements. The realization of this structure involves intonation and rhythm, the upper reaches of the phonological hierarchy; the details have been described in a number of studies.[24] One information unit is realized as one complete tone contour, or "tone group"; broadly, the 'new' element is then realized as the tonic element in the tone group, that which contains the primary stress. Anything which follows this is necessarily 'given'. So, in an example such as

(21) **all** the examination papers are to be marked out of two hundred

where the tonic element consists of the single word *all* at the beginning of the tone group, it is possible to reconstruct quite a number of features of the preceding conversation, because everything following the word *all* must fall within the 'given' element in the information unit.

On the other hand, what precedes the tonic element may be 'given' but is not necessarily so. Here is a typical passage, shown with information units bounded by // and 'new' elements in bold type:

(22) // **my** side of the road // was **completely blocked** // and
unfortunately // I **went into a four wheel skid** // before
coming up to this **Mini** // and at **that** time // I **didn't
know how to deal with** a four wheel skid//[25]

In *before coming up to this Mini*, the tonic is at *Mini* and what precedes is given; whereas in *I went into a four wheel skid*, the tonic is at *skid* but all except *I* is informationally new.

For the present purpose it will be useful to note just one further detail of the system, namely the distinction between unmarked and marked information structure. In the unmarked instance, the new element comes last in the information unit; this has certain consequences which again may be brought out by an example:

(23.1) **George** takes his wife to the movies
(23.2) George **takes** his wife to the movies
(23.3) George takes **his wife** to the movies
(23.4) George takes his wife to the **movies**

These presuppose, respectively, contexts such as the following:

(24.1) I don't know any man who takes his wife to the movies
(24.2) Does George approve of his wife going to the movies?
(24.2') Does any man approve of his wife going to the movies?
(24.3) Who does George take to the movies then?
(24.3') Does George go all by himself to the movies?
(24.3") Most people go to the movies by themselves

That is to say, for (23.1) we must have an environment such as (24.1), in which the taking, the wife and the movies are all recoverable. (23.2) presupposes just the wife and the movies; and we can actually specify the nature of a clause (23.2') corresponding exactly to the environment (24.2') and differing from (23.2) (i.e. having *George* within the 'new'), but this requires reference to rhythm.[26] Similarly, (23.3) presupposes the movies only (with, again, variants (23.3') and (23.3")). However – and this is the point – (23.4) presupposes nothing. It is not necessarily the 'answer' to anything at all; it may just be the beginning of a discourse.

259

This is the sense in which it is unmarked. The unmarked form is unique in that it does not require that any element should be recoverable. Thus the unmarked form is very different from the marked forms in its textual function, its significance for the construction of discourse.

While therefore there is some tendency for the 'given–new' structure of information to be reflected in the sequence of elements in the clause, in that in the unmarked form of the information unit the 'new' element occurs in fi nal position, this is true only to a very limited extent. In the fi rst place, even in the unmarked form there may be no 'given' element preceding the new; and in the marked forms the order is actually partly reversed, with at least some of the given component occurring after the new. In the second place, the domain of 'given–new' structure is not the clause but the information unit, which is coextensive with the clause only under 'good reason' conditions; it is often shorter and sometimes longer than a clause, so that even where an information unit is structured in the unmarked form, as given followed by new, this does not by itself specify any ordering of clause constituents. The mapping of information structure onto clause structure is a distinct relation with its own signifi-cance as a semantic variable.

This is important to the present discussion, since it establishes that first position in the English clause does not express the function 'given'. Yet at the same time first position in the clause is structurally significant. In fact, it expresses something else, something which is also concerned with the organization of a text but is nevertheless a distinct structural func-tion. First position (and note that this does mean first position in the clause, and not in the information unit) expresses the function of 'theme'. What the speaker puts first is the theme of the clause, the remainder being the 'rheme'. While Given–New is a structure not of the clause but of the information unit, and is realized not by sequence but by intona-tion, Theme–Rheme on the other hand is a structure of the clause, and is realized by the sequence of elements: the theme comes first.

Notes

24. For a detailed textual study see Afaf Elmenoufy (1969).
25. Elmenoufy (1969); vol. 2, p. 119. For the tone group, see Elmenoufy (1969) vol. 1, parts I and II. Cf. Daneš (1960).
26. (23.2) // ˄ George / takes . . . // with *George* weak;
    (23.2') // George / **takes** . . . // with *George* salient.
    Likewise (23.3) // ˄ George takes his / **wife** . . . //;

(23.3') // ∧ George takes his / **wife** ... //;
(23.3") // George / takes his / **wife** ... //

VII.5(1970):193–5, 203

Additional readings

On Grammar (Volume 1) – 8(1979):207; 11(1984):305, 320–1; 12(1987):326; 14(1998): 376–7
Linguistic Studies of Text and Discourse (Volume 2) – 1(1964):10; 2(1977):28–38; 7(1992):199–200, 205
On Language and Linguistics (Volume 3) – 9(1992):206
Computational and Quantitative Studies (Volume 6) – 2(1962):22–3; 3(1991):48; 4(1991):68; 5(1992):81, 88, 91; 6(1993):101–2
Studies in English Language (Volume 7) – 1(1967); 2(1967); 3(1968); 4(1969); 7(1985): 220–31; 8(1963):249–61; 9(1963):264–86; 10(1985):288–9
Studies in Chinese Language (Volume 8) – 1(1959); 3(1956); 7(1984):330–2

Chapter Twelve

METAFUNCTIONS

Summary

Language is organized around a small number of discrete systemic clusters of systems with strong interconnections within each cluster, but weak associations outside the cluster with the rest of the grammar. These clusters correspond to what Halliday refers to as the ideational (logical and experiential), interpersonal and textual components or "metafunctions". The three metafunctions operate in parallel with the other two. A clause is the complex realization of options from these three functional-semantic components: ideational, interpersonal and textual.

Each metafunctional component produces its own distinct dimension of structure, with experiential meaning, i.e. the 'construing experience' function, realized as the structural configuration of process, participant(s), circumstance(s); textual meaning, i.e. the 'creating discourse' function, in terms of theme and information structures; and interpersonal meaning, i.e. the 'enacting social relationships' function, in structural terms closer to the syntactic tradition, i.e. Subject, Predicator, Complement(s), Adjunct(s).

Selected readings

On Language and Linguistics (Volume 3)

5 METAFUNCTION: THE GRAMMAR AT WORK

When children learn their first language, they are doing two things at once: learning language, and learning **through** language. As they learn their mother tongue, they are at the same time using it as a tool for learning everything else. In this way language comes to define the nature of learning.

Most obviously, perhaps, when we watch small children interacting with the objects around them we can see that they are using language to construe a theoretical model of their experience. This is language in its *experiential* function; the patterns of meaning are installed in the brain and continue to expand on a vast scale as each child, in cahoots with all those around, builds up, renovates and keeps in good repair the semiotic "reality" that provides the framework of day-to-day existence and is manifested in every moment of discourse, spoken or listened to. We should stress, I think, that the grammar is not merely **annotating** experience; it is *construing* experience – theorizing it, in the form that we call "understanding". By the time the human child reaches adolescence, the grammar has not only put in place and managed a huge array of categories and relations, from the most specific to the most general, but it has also created analogies, whereby everything is both like and unlike everything else, from the most concrete to the most abstract realms of being; and whatever it has first construed in one way it has then gone on to deconstrue, and then reconstrue metaphorically in a different semiotic guise. All this takes up an enormous amount of semantic space.

But from the start, in the evolution of language out of protolanguage, this "construing" function has been combined with another mode of meaning, that of *enacting*: acting out the interpersonal encounters that are essential to our survival. These range all the way from the rapidly changing microencounters of daily life – most centrally, **semiotic** encounters, where we set up and maintain complex patterns of dialogue – to the more permanent institutionalized relationships that collectively constitute the social bond. This is language in its *interpersonal* function, which includes those meanings that are more onesidedly personal: expressions of attitude and appraisal, pleasure and displeasure, and other emotional states. Note that, while language can of course **talk about** these personal and interactional states and processes, its essential function in this area is to act them out.

This functional complementarity is built in to the basic architecture of human language. It appears in the view "from above", as distinct modes of meaning – construing experience, and enacting interpersonal relationships. It appears in the view "from below", since these two modes of meaning are typically expressed through different kinds of structure: experiential meanings as organic configurations of parts (like the Actor + Process + Goal structure of a clause); interpersonal meanings as prosodic patterns spread over variable domains (like the distinction between falling and rising intonation). Most clearly, however, it appears in the view "from round about" – that is, in the internal organization of the lexicogrammar itself. When the grammar is represented paradigmatically, as networks of interlocking systems, the networks show up like different regions of space: instead of being evenly spread across the whole, the networks form clusters, such that within one cluster there are lots of interconnections but there is rather little association between one cluster and another.

This effect was apparent when the "Nigel grammar" (the systemic grammar of the English clause used in the Penman text generation project) was first represented in graphic form. When it had reached a little under one thousand systems, it was printed out in network format in about thirty large "tiles", which when assembled covered one entire wall of the office. The most obvious feature was that the systems bunched into a small number of large dense patches. One such patch was made up of experiential systems; another was made up of interpersonal systems. What this meant was that the meaning potential through which we construe our experience of the world (the world around us, and also the world inside ourselves) is very highly organized; and likewise, the meaning potential through which we enact our personal and social existence is very highly organized; but between the two there is comparatively little constraint. By and large, you can put any interactional "spin" on any representational content. It is this freedom, in fact, which makes both kinds of meaning possible – but only via the intercession of a third.

There was in fact a third systemic cluster: those systems concerned with organizing the clause as a message. This is an aspect of what subsequently came to be called "information flow"; but that term suggests that all meaning can be reduced to "information", so I prefer the more inclusive term "discourse flow". These are the systems which create coherent text – text that coheres within itself and with the context of situation; some of them, the thematic systems, are realized in English by the syntagmatic ordering of elements in the clause. Others are realized by a variety of non-structural devices described by Hasan and myself (1976) under the general heading of "cohesion". I labeled this third component of meaning simply the *textual*.

It turned out that one needed to recognize a fourth functional component, the *logical*; this embodies those systems which set up logical-semantic relationships between one clausal unit and another. Grammatically, they create *clause complexes*; sequences of clauses bonded together tactically (by parataxis and/or hypotaxis) into a single complex unit, the origin of what in written language became the sentence. These systems extend the experiential power of the grammar by theorizing the connection between one quantum of experience and another (note that their "logic" is grammatical logic, not formal logic, though it is the source from which formal logic is derived). Seen "from below", they are very different from experiential systems, because their realization is iterative rather than configurational: they form sequences of (most typically) clauses into a dynamic progression; but seen "from above" they are closest in meaning to the experiential, and there is a lot of give-and-take between the two. It was important, therefore, to be able to bring together the logical and the experiential under a single heading; this was what I referred to as the *ideational* function.

The overall meaning potential of a language, therefore, is organized by the grammar on functional lines. Not in the sense that particular instances of language use have different functions (no doubt they have, but that is a separate point), but in the sense that language evolved in these functional contexts as one aspect of the evolution of the human species; and this has determined the way the grammar is organized – it has yielded one dimension in the overall architecture of language. Since "function" here is being used in a more abstract, theoretical reading, I have found it helpful to give the term the seal of technicality, calling it by the more weighty (if etymologically suspect) term *metafunction*. This principle – the metafunctional principle – has shaped the organization of meaning in language; and (with trivial exceptions) every act of meaning embodies all three metafunctional components.

III.Introduction (2003):15–8

* * *

2 LANGUAGE AS MEANING POTENTIAL

I have always spoken of a language as a *meaning potential*; that was the motif behind the idea of a *system network*, which is an attempt to capture this potential. We try to construct networks for all the strata of language – perhaps concentrating particularly on the lexicogrammar since that is, as it were, the source of energy, the semogenic powerhouse of a language, but making it explicit that all strata participate in the overall construction of meaning. In a sense this central question underlies all the other questions we ask, at least at the present imperfect state of our knowledge: how do people mean? What is the real nature of this semogenic power, and how does it come to be attained by language ± or, if you prefer, how is it that it comes to be attained by human beings through the forms of their various languages? I have always felt it important to try to view a language as a whole, to get a sense of its total potential as a meaning-making resource. This is not to imply that a language is some kind of a mechanical construct all of whose parts come together in a perfect fit, any more than if you try to see a human body as a whole you are conceiving of it as an idealized machine. Indeed it is precisely because the human body is not a mechanical assemblage of parts that it is important to view it paradigmatically as well as syntagmatically (to view it panaxially, if you like); and the same consideration applies to language.

In trying to construe, and to maintain, this general perspective on language as a semogenic resource, I have found it helpful to keep in focus the mutually constructive sets of relationships that I referred to as **metafunctions**: the ideational, whereby language construes human experience; the interpersonal, whereby language enacts human relationships; and the textual, whereby language creates the discursive order of reality that enables the other two. This gives some substance to the notion of meaning potential. Language construes experience by transforming it into the experience of meaning; it enacts interpersonal relationships by performing them as acts of meaning; in this way the world of semiosis unfolds alongside the material world, interpenetratingly. The semogenic power of language derives from, and depends on, its constantly reasserting its connection with the material conditions of existence; the concept of metafunction allows us to interpret where, and how, these connections are being made.

I might perhaps mention here various more specific problems on which the metafunctional frame of reference has helped to throw some light, because these also relate to my general theme. One is the question of grammatical agnateness: how do we establish systematic patterns of predictable meaning relationship? Structural proportionalities provide evidence, but the underlying proportions are systemic, and located within metafunctionally defined regions of the grammar – which enable us to set up proportionalities such as these, from the region of modality in English:

I think [they're away]	:I don't think [they're here]
::it's possible [they're away]	:it's not certain [they're here]
::they must [be away]	:they can't [be here] . . .

A second question is that of the relation of such patterns of agnateness to functional varieties – to variation in register, and hence to context of situation. And a third question, or set of questions, arises when we adopt a developmental perspective, seeing how small children build up their potential for meaning. The metafunctional framing makes it possible to approach these questions by setting up environments within the grammar, which can be (a) interrelated one to another and (b) related to the dia-typic and diachronic environments within which the grammar is deployed and within which it is learnt.

III.12(1997):248–50

The Language of Early Childhood (Volume 4)

FEATURE 9

Perhaps the most important single principle that is involved in the move from protolanguage into mother tongue is the ***metafunctional*** principle: that meaning is at once both doing and understanding. The transition begins with an opposition between utterance as action (doing) and utterance as reflection (understanding); I have referred to this as the opposition of two ***macrofunctions***, "pragmatic/mathetic". This is trans-formed, in the course of the transition, into a combination whereby every utterance involves both choice of speech function (that is, among different kinds of doing) and choice of content (that is, among different realms of understanding). In the grammar of the mother tongue, each clause is a mapping of a "doing" component (the ***interpersonal*** meta-function) and an "understanding" component (the ***experiential*** meta-function) (see IV:9(1983); Oldenburg-Torr 1987; Painter 1984, 1989).

We can summarize this as shown in Table 2. In stage 1, content$_x$ and content$_y$ do not overlap and there are no combinations of prosody$_a$ with content$_y$ or prosody$_b$ with content$_x$. Stage 2 shows the beginning of clause and group structures, the grammar's construction of processes and entities. In Stage 3 the mood is now also grammaticalized, the non-declarative then evolving into imperative versus interrogative.

The child has now established the metafunctional principle, that meaning consists in simultaneously construing experience and enacting interpersonal relationships. The mood system is part of the interpersonal grammar: here the meaning is 'what relationship am I setting up between myself and the listener?'. The transitivity system is part of the experien-tial grammar; here, the meaning is 'what aspect of experience am I rep-resenting?'. From now on (subject, obviously, to specific localized constraints), any content can combine with any speech function. But the more significant aspect of the metafunctional principle, for learning the-ory, is that in language (as distinct from protolanguage) it is the **combi-nation of the experiential and the interpersonal** that constitutes an act of meaning. All meaning – and hence all learning – is at once both action and reflection.

267

Table 2 Stages in development of the metafunctional principle

Stage	Examples			
1 (early transition)				
Either:	Doing ("pragmatic")		more meat	"I want more meat!"
	$\downarrow$ [prosody$_a$ + content$_x$]			
Or:	Understanding ("mathetic")		green car	"That's a green car."
	$\downarrow$[prosody$_b$+ content$_y$]			
2 (mid-transition)				
Doing	$\downarrow$ prosody$_a$ $\Big\}_+$ any		mummy book	"I want mummy's book!"
Understanding	$\downarrow$ prosody$_b$ $\quad$ content		mummy book	"That's mummy's book."
3 (late transition)				
Mood system (speech functions)	$\Big\{$ Non–declarative Declarative	Transitivity system (Process types)	$\Big\{$ Material Mental Relational	

We shall see later (feature 16) that the metafunctional principle also implies a third component of meaning, simultaneous with the other two.

...

Let us return to the notion of a learning gateway. Under feature 7 (IV.15(1993):332-3) I referred to what is undoubtedly the single most critical step in learning language, and arguably the most critical step in the entire experience of learning, namely, the move into grammar, and suggested that, since this step involves leaping over many generations of semiotic evolution, children have to find a magic gateway through which to pass.

This move into grammar is a unique event in the life of any individual. But the evidence suggests that the gateway principle has a more general application in language learning. There are numerous smaller steps that have to be taken; and it seems to be the case that, most typically, each critical step in learning language is taken first of all in the interpersonal metafunction – even if its eventual semiotic contexts are going to be primarily experiential.

These terms are being used here in their technical sense in systemic theory, as outlined under feature 9: the interpersonal is the "active" principle, whereby language enacts interpersonal relationships; the experiential is the "reflective" principle, whereby language construes experience. Here, in fact, it would be appropriate to introduce the more general term *ideational*, encompassing the *logical* as well as the experiential mode of meaning. It appears that we can recognize a generalized *interpersonal gateway*, whereby new meanings are first construed in interpersonal contexts and only later transferred to ideational ones, experiential and/or logical.

We can identify a number of such "interpersonal occasions" when the meaning potential has been extended in this way, as shown in the following five examples: (1) imparting unknown information, (2) extending into new experiential domains, (3) developing logical–semantic relations, (4) learning abstract terms, and (5) moving into grammatical metaphor.

Imparting unknown information
This is the step discussed in the previous section, that of learning to "tell". Painter (1989: 52) recorded the context in which Hal first learnt to impart unshared experience (that is, give information previously unknown to the listener): she heard a noise from the next room, after which the child ran up to her crying "Bump! Bump!": 'you weren't there to see, but I hurt myself, and I need your sympathy'. We naturally think of information as something inherently experiential, and so, eventually, it will turn out to be, but its origins seem to be interpersonal.

Extending into new experiential domains
Oldenburg-Torr (1990) described how Anna, at 2;0, learnt about the principle of sharing. Hasan (1986) cited part of an extended text in which Kristy's mother talks to Kristy, 3;9, about dying. In the first instance the semantic domain is itself largely interpersonal; in the second, however, it is entirely experiential, but the way in is through interpersonal meanings – Kristy has been upset by observing the death of a moth, and she needs new knowledge for comfort and reassurance.

Developing logical–semantic relations
The logical component of natural languages included, as a central motif, the grammar's construal of logical–semantic relations, among which

cause and condition play a critical part. Such logical–semantic relations are part of the ideational grammar, but, again, they are first built up, it seems, in interpersonal contexts. Phillips (1986) showed how Nigel, at 1;7 to 2;7, developed the potential for hypothetical meanings; examples such *as if you walk on the railway line the train would come and go boomp! and knock you over* (you = 'I, me'), *if you* (= 'I') *make it fall on the floor how will Daddy be able to cut it?* are typical of the warnings and threats in which these meanings first appear – modelled for children by adults saying such things to them, like 'don't touch that because it's hot', 'if you don't stop that . . .!', and so on. Hasan's (1992) exploration of rationality in everyday talk shows the same principle at work in the age range 3;6 to 4;0.

Learning abstract terms
It seems likely that abstract meanings are first understood when children come to terms with strongly interpersonally oriented expressions such as 'you're a nuisance', 'that's not fair'. Thus, Nigel at 1;10 learnt to use right and wrong in expressions such as *that not right* (when someone misquoted a verse he knew), *that the wrong way to put your bib* (when it kept falling off the chair), *that not the right record to put on* (when he wanted a different one) (Halliday 1984). Cloran's (1989) account of the social construction of gender contains many instances of interpersonal abstractions being foregrounded in discussions between parents and children aged 3;6 to 4;0. The abstract conceptualization of experience is still a source of difficulty at this age, but it is necessary for the move into literacy (cf. feature 18, IV.15(1993):346), and once again, the gateway seems to be through the interpersonal metafunction.

Moving into grammatical metaphor
Likewise, when at a later stage children begin to develop the principle of grammatical metaphor, this appears to have been first construed in interpersonal contexts. Children learn to "unpack" expressions such as *if you'd just keep quiet for a moment* (= 'keep quiet!'); compare examples in Cloran (1989: 135) such as "*I don't think Nana wants her blind cord chewed*". Butt (1989) showed that rhetorical strategies of this kind may themselves become the object of discussion with the child concerned. Such exchanges probably serve as models for subsequent unpacking of ideational metaphors based on nominalization, for example, *in times of engine failure* 'whenever an engine fails' (scc feature 20, IV.15(1993):348-9).

. . .

FEATURE 16

We now return to the metafunctional principle (cf. features 9 and 12) and consider a third metafunction, the *textual*, which is the resource for creating discourse. I have suggested that learning consists in expanding one's meaning potential, and up to this point, meaning potential has been defined in terms of the ideational (experiential plus logical) and interpersonal metafunctions. The interpersonal component of the grammar is that of "language as action"; this builds up into a rich array of speech functions, modalities, personal forms, keys, and various dimensions of force and attitude by which the speaker enacts immediate social relationships and, more broadly, the whole pattern of the social system with its complexity of roles, statuses, voices, and the like. The experiential component of the grammar is that of "language as reflection"; this expands into a theory of human experience, construing the processes of the "outside world", as well as those of inner consciousness, and (in a related but distinct "logical" component) the logical–semantic relations that may obtain between one process and another. Together these make up a semiotic resource for doing and for understanding **as an integrated mode of activity**.

The intersection of these metafunctions defines a multidimensional semantic space. This becomes operational through being combined with a further component, the *textual*. From about mid-way through the transition from protolanguage to mother tongue, children begin to create discourse; that is, text that is open-ended and functional in some context of situation. This means that they develop a further set of grammatical resources, learning to structure the clause as a piece of information (a "message"), and also learning to construct semantic relationships above and beyond those construed by the grammatical structure – but still using lexicogrammatical resources: patterns of conjunction, ellipsis, coreference, synonymy, and the like (for an informative case study, see Nelson and Levy 1987). An early example of a child learning to structure the clause as a message is the following from Nigel at 1;8 (IV:7(1975)). Walking past some road repair work, his mother had exclaimed at the noise made by the pneumatic drill. "Big **noise**", said Nigel when they reached home. He often said this as a comment on one of his own raucous yells. "Who makes a big noise?" his mother asked. But this time Nigel was not talking about himself. "**Drill** make big noise", he said, giving a marked intonation prominence on the appropriate word *drill*.

These resources constitute a distinct metafunctional component, by which the language creates a semiotic world of its own: a parallel universe, or "virtual reality" in modern terms, that exists only at the level of meaning but serves both as means and as model, or metaphor, for the world of action and experience (see Matthiessen 1992 for the source of this important insight). Children learn to navigate in this universe, producing and understanding discourse that "hangs together" (coheres with itself) as well as being contextualized by events on the non-symbolic plane. This step is a prerequisite for construing any kind of theoretical knowledge, because all theories are themselves semiotic constructs, and theory building is a semiotic process.

IV.15(1993): 335–6, 338–41, 343–4

Computational and Quantitative Studies (Volume 6)

Part 2 Metafunctions of natural languages

2.1 IDEATIONAL, INTERPERSONAL AND TEXTUAL

The **grammar** of every natural language, such as Japanese, or English, has two primary functions:

(1) It **construes** human experience: making sense of what we perceive as "reality", both the world outside us and the world of our own inner consciousness.

(2) It **enacts** social and personal relationships: setting up both immediate and long-term interaction with other persons, and in this way establishing each one's identity and self-awareness.

In systemic functional theory these are called **metafunctions**: (1) **ideational** and (2) **interpersonal**. There is also a third metafunction, the **textual**, whereby the grammar gives substance to the other two:

(3) It **creates** discourse: formulating a distinct "semiotic reality" in which (1) and (2) are combined into a single flow of meaning, as spoken or written text.

This flow of discourse is sometimes called "information flow"; we can use this term, provided we avoid any suggestion that language evolved as the communication of information.[2]

To put this in other terms: the grammar of a natural language is both (1) a way of thinking (a "theory" of human experience) and (2) a way of doing (a form of social "praxis"). Furthermore, neither of these can occur without the other; every grammatical construct embodies **both** ideational **and** interpersonal meanings. It is the intersection of these two that is (3) formed by the grammar into discourse.

As an example, consider a clause such as the following, from everyday spoken English:

Don't tease your baby sister!

(1) Ideationally, it construes a form of action, 'tease', verbal and/or non-verbal; with two human participants, one 'doing' the other 'done to'; the latter as 'young female sibling' to the former; . . .
(2) Interpersonally, it enacts a negative command 'don't!', the speaker demanding compliance from the listener; peremptory, to take immediate effect; . . .
(3) Textually, it creates a coherent message, with a discursive movement from the speaker-oriented theme 'I want you not to (tease)' to the listener-oriented focus of information on the 'other' (third party) [the last shown by the intonation, not marked in writing]; . . .

These features are brought out in the grammatical analysis of the clause, as shown in Figure 10.1. (For the metafunctional analysis of the clause and other features of the grammar of English referred to in this chapter, see Halliday 1985/1994.)

	don't	tease	your baby sister
ideational	Process: material/verbal		Goal/Target
interpersonal	Mood: negative	Residue	
		Predicator	Complement
textual: theme information	Theme: interpersonal	topical	Rheme
	Focus		→

Figure 10.1

2.2 MEANING AND CONTEXT; CONTEXT OF DISCOURSE, AND CONTEXT OF SITUATION

It is customary in natural language processing, especially in the context of text generation, to make a distinction between "meaning" as constructed in the grammar and "inference" from "knowledge of the world". Thus, in the case of the example above, it would be said that we assume the addressee must be not more than (say) 25 years old, because the third party is a baby and we know that siblings cannot normally be more than 25 years apart.

But there is no clear line between "meaning" and "knowing/inferring". We might suggest, rather, that this "knowledge" is part of the **meaning** of *sister* and of *baby* – which must be taken together with the meaning of the grammatical relationship that is here constructed between the two (one of Classifier + Thing in the nominal group), as well as that between *baby sister* and *your*. There seems no need to postulate two separate realms of cognition, one semantic (within language), the other conceptual (outside language).

In any case, the third party in this instance may not be an infant; she might be middle-aged, the clause being addressed jokingly to an older sibling who still thought of her as a baby. She might even be the older of the two, being treated as if she were a baby; the possibilities are open. But they are open because we have taken the clause out of its context.

The "context" of an utterance, however, is an essential aspect of its meaning. Decontextualized words and clauses have a place in grammar books and dictionaries, but seldom in real life. (Of course, they are not really "decontextualized" – rather, citation is a very special type of context.) Our grammatics would engage with this clause in its **context of situation**, consisting of (say) a mother with two daughters, one aged about four years old and the other around one year; and in its **discursive context**, which might be something like the following:

> Child: Do you want that balloon? Well you can't have it; it's mine!
> Baby: [*cries*]
> Mother: Now look what you've done! Don't tease your baby sister; you
>   make her cry.

Of course, we can also construct the context from the text. The grammatical analysis should show that it is part of the meaning of this clause that it enables us to construct a discursive and situational context such as the above. It should also show that other contextual possibilities exist – but under more closely specified conditions: the possibilities are clearly ordered, such that a type of situation like that illustrated above is the most likely, or "default" choice. (For the relation of text and context, see Hasan 1980b; Halliday and Hasan 1985.)

2.3 FIGURE, PROPOSITION/PROPOSAL, MESSAGE; SEQUENCES; ELEMENTS
Let me now say a little more about the metafunctional components of the grammar; looking at them, this time, from a functional semantic viewpoint ("from above", instead of "from below").

(1) Ideational. The central organizing unit here is a *figure*. A figure construes a "quantum" of experience, categorizing it as (a) material, (b) mental, (c) verbal or (d) relational. (The experience may be purely fictitious or imaginary, of course!) Grammatically, this is formed as a *configuration* consisting typically of (i) a process, (ii) a small number of participating entities, and perhaps (iii) one or two circumstantial elements. For examples, see Figure 10.2.

Each component within the figure is an *element*. Prototypically, in English, the grammar construes the figure as a *clause* and the elements as (i) [process] verbal group, (ii) [participating entity] nominal group, and (iii) [circumstance] adverbial group or prepositional phrase.

Two or more figures may combine to form a *sequence*, as in Figure 10.3. Prototypically, the grammar construes a sequence as a *clause complex*. [Note that it is important to stress the "prototypically" throughout; the grammar always has alternative strategies for construing sequences, figures, and the various types of element within a figure. Cf. Figures 10.4 and 10.5.]

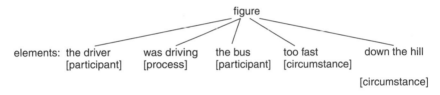

Figure 10.2

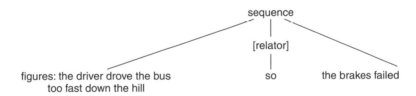

Figure 10.3

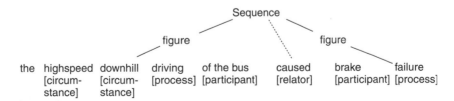

Figure 10.4

nominal group:	the driver's	highspeed	downhill	driving	of the bus
	Deictic	Epithet	Classifier	Thing	Qualifier

clause:	the driver	was driving	the bus	too fast	down the hill
	Actor	Process: material	Goal	Manner	Location

Figure 10.5

(2) Interpersonal. Here the central organizing unit is a **proposition** or a **proposal** (i.e. one move in an exchange). The proposition/proposal enacts a "speech function", either (a) statement or question [proposition], or (b) offer or command [proposal]. Grammatically, this is formed as a **predication**, which is something that can be argued over – confirmed, disputed, rejected etc.; containing (i) some element that is held responsible (typically, the addressee 'you' in commands, the speaker 'me' in offers, and some third party – the grammatical "Subjects" – in statements and questions); (ii) a predicating element and (iii) other residual elements, some of which are potential "Subjects" and others are not.

In most languages the speech functions are marked prosodically in some way: e.g. "annotated" by a particle, as in Japanese *ka*, Chinese *ma*, *ba*, etc.; "clustered" into two parts, as in English (Mood + Residue; see Figure 10.1); "re-predicated", as in English and Chinese (*it is . . ., isn't it?*; *shi bushi . . .?*); and/or realized by intonation contour. The different speech functions are often further accompanied by expressions of the speaker's attitude (judgements, emotions etc.), e.g. *for God's sake please don't . . .!*

Typically the grammar construes the proposition/proposal as a **clause**, and the elements as (i) [predicator] verbal group, (ii) [subject, and potential subjects] nominal group, and (iii) [other residual elements] adverbial group or prepositional phrase.

The details given here are those of English. But the significant point is that, in all languages, the grammar constructs the **figure** and the **proposition/proposal** **simultaneously**, in such a way that the two are mapped on to each other as a single, unitary **clause**. The clause is the main gateway between the grammar and the semantics.

If two (or more) clauses are combined in one **clause complex**, so as to form a **sequence**, then (1) each clause construes a **figure**, but (2) depending on the type of sequence, not every clause may function as **proposition/proposal**. A "paratactic" sequence is one in which each predication does achieve propositional status, e.g.

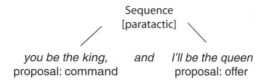

A "hypotactic" sequence is one in which only one predication achieves propositional status, e.g.

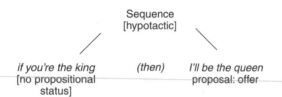

(3) Textual. The central organizing unit here is a ***message***. This is a complex notion, with a great deal of variation among different languages; what is common to all, however, is that the message creates the discursive flow, turning the progression of figures/propositions into ***text***. The account here relates specifically to English.

In English, the "flow" is a blend of two discursive currents, one ***thematic***, the other ***informational***; there are various ways of modelling this, in grammatical terms – my own preference is to model it as two separate movements with partial association between them. Let me use the analogy of a television camera. (a) The "thematic" movement is the **siting** of the camera, locating the **operator** of the camera at a particular angle. (b) The "informational" movement is the **focusing** of the lens, bringing some object into the **viewer's** focus. The "operator" of the camera corresponds to the speaker; the "viewer" corresponds to the listener. (It is of course the operator who **selects both** the thematic angle **and** the informational focus.) (On the grammatical category of "theme", see Hasan and Fries 1995, Matthiessen 1992).

Grammatically, in English, the thematic movement is construed as a ***clause***, with the "theme" as the initial element; the informational movement is organized as a distinct unit, the ***information unit***, which is formed as an ***intonation contour*** (technically, a "tone group") with the *focus* taking the form of ***tonic prominence***. These two movements provide a complex periodicity to discourse; the typical phasing of the two yields a regular kind of "wave shape" with each clause moving from an initial theme (the "siting" or location of the message) to a final point of focus (the "news-point" of the message), as shown in Figure 10.1. But the association between "theme" and "focus" – between the ongoing siting of the camera and the ongoing focusing of the lens – is fluid, not fixed; so the resulting wave shape may be indefinitely varied.

A summary of the principal categories is given in Figure 10.6.

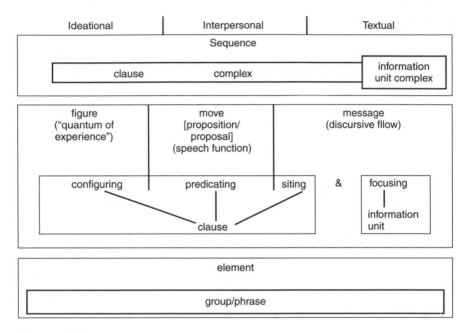

Figure 10.6
Note: categories enclosed in ⌈inner boxes⌉ are the typical realizations in grammar of the semantic categories shown above them.

VI.10(1995):215–22

Additional readings

On Grammar (Volume 1) – 1(1970); 14(1998):382; 15(1996):390–2
On Language and Linguistics (Volume 3) – 13(2001):277–8
Computational and Quantitative Studies (Volume 6) – 9(1995):200–2
Language and Society (Volume 10) – 5(1975):183–4

Chapter Thirteen

QUANTIFYING LANGUAGE

Summary

M.A.K. Halliday makes the case that our discourse will pattern itself according to the probability profile of the grammar. In other words, quantitiative properties of systems are part of our semiotic make-up, and thus need to be built into the grammatics.

Probabilities are associated with choices in the grammar. Incorporation of grammatical probabilities demands a paradigmatic model of grammar, which specifies the options available to the speaker. Taking the grammatical system of Aspect in Chinese as an example, one could investigate the relative probability of choosing between perfective and imperfective. With advances in corpus building, such quantitative questions may more realistically be pursued.

Selected readings

On Grammar (Volume 1)

10.7 The problem of "redundancy" is complex, and needs treating separately and at length; but the term has become a commonplace in description and a brief reference may be made here. The name is assigned to a number of varied phenomena, none of which is related in any clear way to the quantifiable redundancy of information theory.[100] These include relations of formal categories to exponents in form, of formal and phonological features to exponents in substance, and of formal features to context. Moreover, in some instances the so-called "redundancy" is simply put in by the method of description and has no relevance to the language at all.

"Redundancy" is assigned to what is displayed as multiple exponence: either in form, where more than one formal item is said to be the exponent of one grammatical category, or in substance, where a distinction is carried by what is said to be more than one phonetic feature. But neither of these is at all clearcut. Formal redundancy "occurs" where there is concord, but no criteria are available for identifying the two prerequisites of concord: that there is "more than one" exponent as opposed to "one", and that these are exponents of "the same" category.[101] Discontinuous morphemes, for example, may sometimes be clearly recognizable, though at others it is impossible to say "how many" exponents are present;[102] but the question is irrelevant, since where the description does recognize concord this concord is itself the exponent of a distinct category of relation that is different from the category of which the form is exponent, and that has its own formal meaning.[103] Redundancy in substance appears when formal or phonological distinctions are related to contrastive features.[104] Here precisely the same problem arises, since it is not possible to give rigorous criteria for deciding what is "one" phonetic feature and what is "more than one".[105] Each time a new parameter or a further degree of differentiation is introduced into the phonetic statement, all its precursors are thereby made "redundant".

In extreme cases this "redundancy" becomes completely artificial, since it is simply inserted by the description. This happens when a contrast (or system) is assigned to a unit lower than that to which it is appropriate, and may result therefore from overemphasis on the lowest unit. This tends to happen more in phonology, when the phoneme is made to carry contrasts appropriate to a higher unit; one of the merits of prosodic phonology is that it avoids this error.[106] But it is not unknown in grammar, where it may also arise from the use of morphological instead of syntactic criteria for classes.[107] In such cases "redundancy" can only refer to the loss of power in the grammar brought about by such a description: it already follows from the theory that the "appropriate" unit for the assignment of any feature is the highest unit that can carry it without requiring the statement to be made twice. The best description therefore can be thought of as that which minimalizes artificial "redundancy". But at the same time those instances where what is called "redundancy" is an artificial product of the description are not essentially different from, but are merely extreme cases of, the "multiple exponence" in form and substance to which the same name is applied.[108]

What is of doubtful validity here is the implication that there are formal contrasts carried by "one" exponent and others carried by "more than one", with a meaningful distinction between the two. Even if "multiple exponence" in form can be validly identified, it is itself formally meaningful; and it is arbitrary to postulate "one feature" as the norm of exponence in substance. The use of the term "redundancy" is unfortunate for two reasons. On the one hand it implies that some features, by contrast to others,[109] can be recognized as carried by something more than what "would be enough" – to the extent even of suggesting that one may judge which of a number of exponents is "the" non-redundant one.[110] On the other hand, even if it is possible to devise some theoretically valid criteria for "redundancy" of this kind, its relation to the redundancy of information theory is extremely complex and it would be better not to call it by the same name. The redundancy of information theory is of considerable interest to linguistics in the study of the information carried by grammatical *systems*; but this, as far as I know, has not yet been seriously attempted. The quantification of systems, rather than the appraisal of features as contrastive or idle, which rests on a very partial interpretation of the redundancy of information theory, seems the more useful role for the concept of redundancy in linguistics.

Most, if not all, of the points made in this section can be brought together under Chomsky's observation that "a linguistic theory should not be identified with a manual of useful procedures, nor should it be expected to provide mechanical procedures for the discovery of grammar".[111] The point is a familiar one to British linguists, who have for some time stressed the theoretical, as opposed to procedural, character of their own approach.[112] But is it true that "it is unreasonable to demand of linguistic theory that it provide anything more than a practical evaluation procedure for grammars"?[113] This it must do. But it can be asked to do more: to provide a framework of logically interrelated categories (so that it can be evaluated as a theory, and compared with other theories) from which can be derived methods of description, whether textual, exemplificatory or transformative–generative, which show us something of how language works.

Notes

100. Hockett's statement of the link between the two (1958: 87), "In everyday parlance, this word means saying more than is strictly necessary ... In modern information theory, the term has much the same meaning, but freed from the connotation of undesirability, and theoretically capable of precise quantification", may I think be taken as underlying the uses of the term referred to in this section. In my view this formulation reduces a potentially powerful concept to a status where it is neither rigorous nor useful in linguistics.

101. Harris recognizes this in his use of the "broken morpheme" (1951: 165–7).

102. For example in the contrast between *l'oeil* and *les yeux*, or between *have gone* and *were going*. If, in Old English, a nominal group consisting of a noun alone may carry four case/number distinctions, one with adjective and noun six and one with deictic, adjective, and noun seven, how can any two case/number forms be considered exponents of "the same" category when they occur in different structures?

103. Harris states this distributionally (1951: 205). Hill (1958: 477) rejects the redundancy of concord in Latin, on the grounds that it "sorts out the members of the sentence element or construction for us", but accepts it in Bantu "where there are repeated suffixes of agreement but in which the members of the same sentence element are continuous". Quite apart from the arbitrary choice of assignment of redundancy, this is simply a shift of criteria: Bantu concord is still the exponent of a relation (since not all contiguous items are members of the same sentence element). But even if concord and contiguity were completely mutually determined, the problem would still not arise, since there would then be no valid reason for not treating the whole complex as a single exponent.

104. Cf. Hill's statement of the English affricates (*op. cit.*: 44): "In the system we have adopted, therefore, affrication has not been mentioned, since /c/ is distinguished from /t/ by its position, and the affrication is redundant". Ebeling (1960: 30) rightly rejects redundancy in substance: "A choice of one of the equivalent features as relevant and the other as redundant is in such cases arbitrary and, therefore, senseless".

105. They might perhaps be acoustic, so that all but one of the formants which distinguish [a] from [i] would be redundant?

106. By assigning contrasts where they belong. Cf. for example Carnochan (1952: esp. 94); and all works by linguists of the School of Oriental and African Studies, London, some of which are referred to throughout this paper. Cf. also Robins (1957 a & b).

107. If polarity in English, which belongs to the group, is assigned to the word, or morpheme, "redundancy" arises: one can ask unreal questions such as "is the negative in *didn't go*, in contrast to positive 'went', carried by the *did* or the *n't* or the *go*"? If the category of number is assigned to the unit "word" in any language that has a nominal group which can select only one number at a time, there will be artificial "redundancy" whether there is concord, negative concord or no concord at all, the "redundancy" of complementary distribution. Again, as in phonology: Cantonese, for example, has pairs of syllables in which in final position short vowel plus long nasal consonant contrast with long vowel plus short nasal consonant. If these are phonemicized as for example /a: n/, /an:/, /a/ contrasts with /a:/ and /n/ with /n:/; if as /aan/, /ann/, /a/ contrasts with /n/ in penultimate position, but /an/ and /aann/ are absent: "redundancy" in either case. If the contrast is referred to an element in the structure of a higher unit, it can be stated as a single contrast of relative duration.

108. Another use of this same "redundancy" which has not been mentioned here is contextual redundancy. This is used, for example, by Bull (1960: 16): "Unless a language is needlessly redundant, there is little or no likelihood that any tense system uses the point tensor formulas"; p. 27: "English is extremely redundant. It almost always defines the axes while Mandarin is extremely parsimonious. It defines the axes only to avoid confusion". In other words, the form is said to have reflected more of the context than it need have done. This has the merit of having nothing whatever to do with the redundancy of information theory. What it **has** to do with is not yet clear; but it does pose interesting problems for contextual description and for comparison and typology.

109. In fact, all description of language is the description of this "redundancy". A language without it would presumably have to have only one sound, variable in duration, and only one unit with either no structure or no class. Language activity is a progression of events in environments; and as soon as we have stated the event (as one among a defined number of possible events, this number being always less than the **total** number of possible events in that language – *class*) and the environment (this being defined as not the same as **all** other environments – *structure*) there is "redundancy".

110. An extreme instance is found in Hill (1958: 26n.), where we are told that every audible exponent of /+/ is redundant, the one contrastive exponent being inaudible. Cf. Haas (1957: 37).

111. Chomsky (1957: 55n.).

112. Cf. Firth (1955: 93, 99; 1957a: 1).

113. Chomsky (1957: 52).

I.2(1961):70–2, 92–4

On Language and Linguistics (Volume 3)

8 PROBABILITY

Let me come back for a moment to the question of size: how big is a language? We had reached a figure of the order of half a billion different verbs. It is quite likely, of course, that any one we might generate at random, say *couldn't have been going to go ŏn cringing*, or *ought **nòt** to have been getting telephoned*, has never before been either spoken or written; but it is still part of the meaning potential of the language. To put this in perspective: adults conversing steadily in English would be likely to use between 1,000 and 2,000 verbs in an hour; taking the lower figure, that would mean that half a billion occurrences (instances) would need about half a million hours of conversation. Now, if we collected half a billion clauses of natural speech (not inconceivable today), and processed it (still a little way off!), we would probably find that about half of them had one of the verbs *be*, *have* or *do*. We already know a good deal about the relative frequencies of lexical items, and something about those of the most general grammatical systems: for example, the negative will account for about 10 per cent of the total, the rest being positive; about 90 per cent of finite verbs will have primary tense or modality only, with no secondary tense, and within those having primary tense the past and present will account for over 45 per cent each, the future about 5–10 per cent. So if we combine the relative frequency of the verb *cringe* with the relative frequency of the grammatical features selected in that example above, we could work out how much natural conversation we would have to process before it became more likely than not that such a form would occur. And it would be a very large amount.

These issues will be brought up in Volume 6 of this series. The point here is, that these quantitative features are not empty curiosities. They are an inherent part of the meaning potential of a language. An important aspect of the meaning of negative is that it is significantly less likely than positive; it takes up considerably more grammatical energy, so to speak. The frequencies that we observe in a large corpus represent the systemic probabilities of the language; and the full representation of a system network ought to include the probability attached to each option in each of the principal systems (the figure becomes less meaningful as we move into systems of greater delicacy, because the entry condition of the choice becomes too restrictive). We have not yet got the evidence to do this; but until it can be done, grammars will not have come of age.

What this is saying is that, to give a realistic estimate of the meaning potential of a language – of its semiotic power – we need to include not only the options in meaning that are available but also the relative contribution that each of these options makes. We take a step in this direction when we locate the options in system networks, according to their entry conditions: a system way down in the delicacy scale will have a relatively small domain of operation (for example, clausal substitute polarity transfer in English, as in *I think not/I don't think so*, which figures only in a certain type of projected clause nexus). But the relative contribution to the meaning potential also depends on these quantitative factors: a system whose options are very skew makes less contribution than one whose options are more or less equiprobable; and a system that is accessed only via a chain of low probability options makes less contribution than one that is accessed in a majority of selectional environments. Thus semiotic power is not simply a product of the number of choices in meaning that are available; their different quantitative profiles affect their semogenic potential – and therefore affect the meaning potential of the linguistic system as a whole.

Finally, we do not yet know how many systems it takes, on the average, to generate a given number of selection expressions. In other words, we do not know what is a typical degree of association among systems having a common point of origin – say, the systems of the English clause. The estimate given earlier of the total number of possible verbal groups did take account of the interdependence among the various systems; as already remarked, that network is unusual in the degree of freedom the various systems have to combine one with another – it took less than thirty systems to specify all the options available to any one verb. We can of course define the outer limits of possible association among systems. Stipulating that all systems are to be binary (they are not, of course; but it makes it easier), then given a network of n systems, (a) if all are dependent on each other (i.e. they form a strict taxonomy), there will be $n + 1$ possible selection expressions; whereas (b) if all are independent, the number of possible selection expressions will be 2^n. Compare four systems associated as in (a) and as in (b) in Figure 6.

The networks written for the two major text generation projects in English that have used systemic grammar – the NIGEL grammar developed by Christian Matthiessen for William Mann's PENMAN project at the University of Southern California, and Robin Fawcett's GENESYS grammar used in his COMMUNAL project at Cardiff University – each

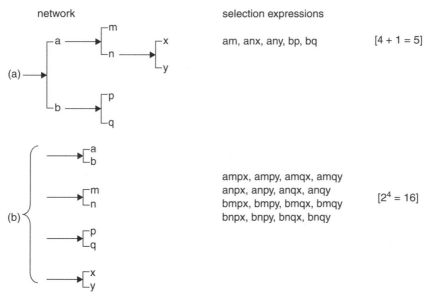

Figure 6

had of the order of a thousand systems. Clearly they did not specify anything like two to the thousandth different selection expressions! The more systems there are in a network, the more densely they will be associated. When I wrote the prototype NIGEL grammar, consisting of 81 systems of the clause, Mann's off-the-cuff estimate was that it defined between half a billion and a billion selection expressions. This seems reasonable.

But such figures don't really matter, because we are far from being able to measure the size of a language in any meaningful way. All we can say is that a language is a vast, open-ended system of meaning potential, constantly renewing itself in interaction with its ecosocial environment. The phenomenon of "language death", so familiar in our contemporary world where the extinction of semiotic species matches the extinction of biological species as a by-product of our relentless population growth, is one where the community of speakers is no longer able to sustain this kind of metastable adaptation, and their language as it were closes down (see Hagège 2000). If a language no longer creates new meanings, it will not survive.

III.Introduction(2003):23–6

★ ★ ★

3 How big is a language? Some quantitative features
of human meaning potential

Language may be defined as a "meaning potential": a system-&-process of **choice**, choice which typically goes on below the threshold of attention, but can be attended to and reflected on under certain circumstances – most typically, though not exclusively, associated with the evolution of writing. We model this as a system network, showing (a) the sets or options, (b) their interconnections, and (c) their realizations. Text, spoken or written, is the effect (process/product) of repeated passes through the network, manifested as a (typically continuous) flow of activity – pulmonic, glottalic and articulatory, in the case of spoken text. The system network models the potential, the process of selection, and the "output"; like all such theoretical models in linguistics, it is an abstract representation, not an attempt to model neural processes. In protolanguage, such selection takes place in a single pass. But in language the networks are layered, or **stratified**, in the way this concept was developed by mid-century linguists following Saussure, for example scholars such as Trubetzkoy, Martinet, Hjelmslev and Firth:[9] there is a **content** network, which generates words-in-structures, and an **expression** network, which generates speech sounds. The content network is further stratified into the **semantic** (we often refer to this as ***discourse-semantic***) and the ***lexicogrammatical***; this step, referred to above in the developmental context, turns language into a dynamic open system with an indefinitely large semantic potential (cf. the discussion in the final section of the paper below). An example of a partial lexicogrammatical network of English is given in Figure 4.

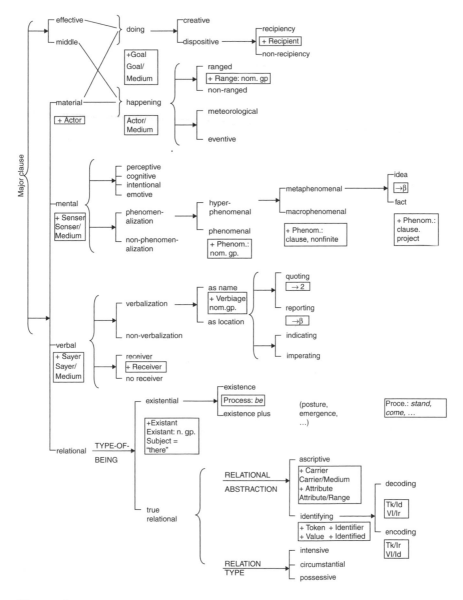

Figure 4

How big is a language? We can conceptualize the content plane as a kind of semantic space, multidimensional and elastic, which is capable of expanding to some indefinite extent. But if we think of it in digital terms, it can be quantified as the number of options that might be represented in a network of grammatical systems. Such networks are partially ordered: some systems are mutually independent (not associated), for example the primary systems of transitivity and mood: others are taxonomically associated, access to one being dependent on selection within another (e.g. if indicative, then either declarative or interrogative). If we pretend for the moment that all systems are binary, then given any set of n systems forming a network, if they form a simple taxonomy the number of possible options is just n + 1 (one system, two options; six systems, seven options; fifteen systems, sixteen options and so on); if they are all independent, then the number of possible options is 2^n (one system, two options; six systems, 64 options; fifteen systems, $2^{15} = 32,768$ options, and so on). Systems in a grammatical network fall, obviously, somewhere in between the two extremes: the most general at each rank (clause, phrase, group) tend to be independent, but as one moves in delicacy towards the ones that are more localized the degree of ordering naturally increases.

Let us take as an example the English verb, or rather verbal group. This may be finite or non-finite; let us first select "finite". We then have three primary or deictic tenses, past, present, and future; two voices, active and passive; two polarities, positive and negative, each with an unmarked and a marked variant; and two degrees of contrast, or focal stress, neutral (non-contrastive) and contrastive; thus:

$$3 \times 2 \times 4 \times 2 = 48 \text{ possibilities}$$

But instead of temporal deixis (primary tense), we could have selected modal deixis; and here there are 24 possible options (three values, high, median and low; two angles, neutral and oblique; and four types, probable, usual, ready, and obliged), so instead of three choices of deixis we now have 27. There are also two forms of the passive, so not two voices but three; and with all these options there are twelve possible secondary tenses. If we calculate again:

$$27 \times 3 \times 4 \times 2 \times 12 = 7,776 \text{ possibilities}$$

However, if we choose contrastive focus, there are (1) various keys, or tonal options – let us recognize the principal set of eight; and (2) various possible loci – the exact number depends on other choices, but we can average it at two; so in the system of contrast instead of two options we recognize $1 + (8 \times 2) = 17$: non–contrastive, or contrastive in any of eight ways at either of two locations. Furthermore we could have chosen non–finite (no verbal deixis) as an alternative initial state, and that would give the further option of two aspects, perfective and imperfective, so the 27 becomes 29. We now have.

$$29 \times 12 \times 3 \times 4 \times 17 = 70{,}992 \text{ possibilities}$$

Here, then, without double negatives, special third person forms, ellipses, more subtle modalities and tense variants – let alone the causative, inceptive, durative and other phases construed as verbal group complexes – we are getting towards 100,000 forms: all of these with one and the same lexical verb. But the network which specifies all these options is relatively simple (see Figure 5); this huge set of possibilities arises from the intersection of a fairly small set of fairly simple choices. That is what the grammar of a language is like.

When I wrote the initial English clause grammar for the Penman artificial intelligence (text generation) project, at the Information Sciences Institute of the University of Southern California in 1980, it was a network consisting of 81 systems. When it had been installed into the program, I asked the project director, Professor William Mann, how many different selection expressions (clause types) he thought the network would specify. His estimate was somewhere in the order of 10^9 – say between half a billion and a billion. I am not claiming that my grammar got it right – far from it! My point is that this figure is entirely reasonable as an output for the clause grammar of a natural language. 10^9 is less than 2^{30}; it needs only 29 independent binary choices to yield that number of possibilities. The grammar was then extended by Christian Matthiessen, who worked with the Penman project for a number of years; the existing network has around 1,000 systems. Likewise the systemic grammar being developed by Robin Fawcett at the University of Wales: this differs descriptively in various aspects, but there are also about one thousand systems in the network.

Needless to say these networks do not contain any single point of entry into 29 independent binary systems. The actual organization is much richer: more complex, and also more indeterminate. The relations among the systems within the grammar – the patterns of grammatical **agnation** – involve not only simultaneity and dependence but also disjunct and conjunct entry conditions, such as "if both term x in system a and term y in system b are selected, then there is selection among terms within p, q, r in system c". Since it represents the grammar in paradigmatic form, the network construes these complex patterns of agnation.

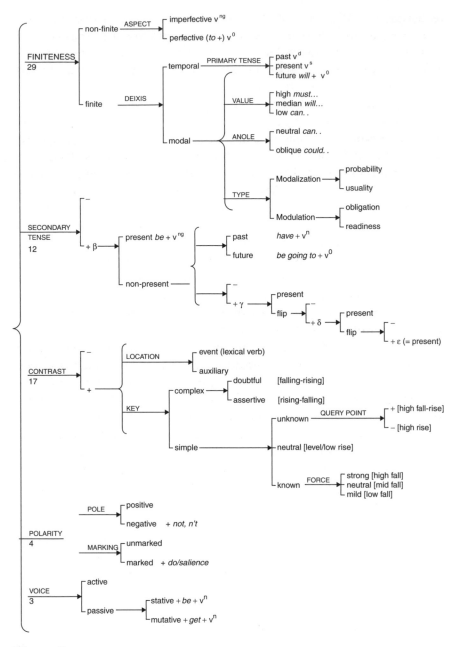

Figure 5

What the network does not display, however, are degrees of partial association between systems, because this depends on the probabilistic nature of the systems themselves.

When the grammarian says, for example, that every clause in English is (selects for) either positive or negative polarity, this means "with a certain measure of probability": a global, system-internal probability but one that is susceptible to local, environmental conditioning. The global probability might be "positive, 0.9; negative, 0.1"; but in certain contexts, such as sets of regulations, these probabilities might become equal, or even get reversed. Each instance – every clause that is actually spoken, or written, in English – modifies the probabilities of the system; these can therefore change in the course of time. Under typical conditions they change very gradually; but there may be more or less catastrophic moments, as in creolization and decreolization, or language death. Sometimes a probability profile will become increasingly skew, with one option tending towards zero and then perhaps disappearing altogether, like *thou* in the English second person system *thou/you*. But by and large the quantitative structure of a grammar seems to remain relatively stable from one generation to the next.

We seek to build such probabilities into the grammatics; they can be readily embodied in the representation of a system network. In the 1980 Penman grammar I attached to each system the values of either 0.5: 0.5 or 0.9: 0.1, interpreting it as either equiprobable or significantly skew; these values derived from some small-scale frequency studies I had carried out many years earlier, which suggested that at least the most general ("least delicate") systems in the grammar tended towards one or other of these two profiles (considering just those systems that could be represented as binary). Now that we have access to very large corpuses it becomes possible to test such a hypothesis; thus, using a sample of 18 million words (about 1.5 million clauses) of written English, Zoe James and I found that the relative frequency of simple past:present (primary tense) was 51:49 per cent; that of positive:negative (polarity) was 88:12 per cent. We interpret these figures as the manifestation of inherent probability within the system.[10]

These are global probabilities; they are of course subject to conditioning of various kinds. (1) Probabilities vary **locally** with the register (functional variety of a language; cf. further below): so, for example, while our provisional figures for the system of English verbal deixis were as in Figure 6, showing future having a very low probability (less than 0.6 per cent of primary tenses overall), when we examine the register of weather forecasting we find – no surprise! – that future leaps to the front as the

Figure 6 Probability profile of English "verbal deixis" system

favoured tense. (2) Probabilities vary *transitionally* throughout the unfolding of a text ("logogenetically"): thus, Fawcett's GENESYS grammar referred to above presents the probabilities as shifting when one re-enters the system network. (3) Thirdly, probabilities vary *conditionally* according to selection in other systems: Fawcett's "preference re-setting rules" in fact operate Figure 6 Probability profile of English "verbal deixis" system not only on subsequent passes but also in the course of a single pass. All these may be seen as systematic aspects of the grammar of a natural language.[11]

It is important to stress that these quantitative properties of systems are part of the grammar of an individual, similarly to the options themselves and their realizations. I am not talking here about predicting particular sayings, which are the outcome of a complex mixture of system-internal, contextual (i.e. environmental) and random factors falling within the individual's subjective experience. It is of no great theoretical interest to try to predict what you or I are going to say next (even though in practice we are doing this with each other all the time). But it is part of our semiotic make-up, our higher-level consciousness, that our discourse as a whole will pattern quantitatively according to the probability profile of the grammar. This feature of discourse is one of the principal factors enabling children to learn their mother tongue. (It is of course a feature of the lexicogrammatical system as a whole; grammar and vocabulary are simply the two complementary aspects of a single stratum.)

By the same token, the quantitative changes referred to earlier take place in the grammar of the individual, as the "unit of selection", the locus of the evolution of the language. It may be that major categorical shifts in the system of a language take place primarily in the course of inter-generational transmission; we see the developmental cycle biologically as one of growth, maturity, senescence and eventual death, with growth (meaning "getting bigger") coming to an end in late adolescence, and we tend to assume that semiotically also maturity means stability – the adult's meaning potential stays the same, until it begins to decay. But the mature system is not impervious to change. I myself am aware of various changes that have taken place in my own grammar of English during my adult lifetime – including three or four within the verbal group, starting (and perhaps remaining) as changes in relative frequency but still restructuring the system in subtle and significant ways. This is the "instantiation" effect referred to earlier, whereby each instance (which means, in this context, each utterance received by and produced by the individual) perturbs the probabilities of the system: rather as each day's weather perturbs the probabilities of the climatic system, except that in a semiotic system, as opposed to a physical one, this effect takes place in three time dimensions – three "histories" at once, the **social-semiotic process** ("the language" as observed from a distance), the **individual brain** (the neuronal group networks), and the **text** ("the language" as observed from close at hand).

A language is a semogenic system: it is a system which creates meaning. This is a system of fourth-order complexity: it is physical; also biological (with added **life**); also social (with added **value**);[12] and also semiotic (with added **meaning**). All other human semiotic systems derive their specific potential for meaning from the general potential opened up by language. Such a system has three distinct histories: evolutionary (the phylogenetic evolution of human language, as particular languages), developmental (the ontogenetic growth of the individual's neurosemiotic potential) and individuating (the logogenetic unfolding of discourse, as particular texts). Let me briefly contextualize the preceding discussion, the probabilistic nature of the system, in terms of these three histories; then in the section that follows I will note some qualitative feature of language that will put this part in perspective. The examples, as elsewhere, relate to English.

Any piece of discourse unfolds as a flow of meaning, a complex interplay of the predictable and the unpredictable. From the standpoint of the **instance**, this means a construction of "given" and "new" in relation to the text itself and its environment ("context of situation"). From the standpoint of the **system**, it means its overall pattern of information and redundancy. If the bimodal hypothesis of the quantitative typology of systems turns out to be valid (it may not be), this would mean that the well-recognized marking principle in grammar has a quantitative basis, in that systems (again taking the binary as prototypical) are of two types: either both terms are equally (un)marked, with probabilities roughly equal at 0.5:0.5, or else one of the two is marked, with the probabilities skew at roughly 0.9:0.1. By reference to the mathematical theory of information these values define two critical cusps: (1) at 0.5:0.5, H (information) = 1, R (redundancy) = 0; (2) at 0.9:0.1, H = R = 0.5.

Type (1), with zero redundancy, is maximally efficient mathematically – but not socially; one needs redundancy to allow for noise. With type (2), redundancy and information balance out. It seems that discourse unfolds as the interplay of grammatical systems of these two logogenetic profiles: the equiprobable, like past/present tense (and probably singular/plural [number], material/mental/relational [process type], intransitive/transitive), and the skew, like positive/negative polarity (and probably active/passive [voice], declarative/interrogative [mood], final/non-final focus [information]). It would also seem, ontogenetically, that a system having these properties would be maximally accessible to a learner; whereas one with no redundancy, or the same level of redundancy throughout, or with the degree of redundancy scattered randomly across all possible values, would be much more difficult for a learner to model progressively. In phylogenetic time, a probabilistic system of this kind achieves metastability: it is constantly being modulated, in dynamic interaction with the (material and semiotic) environment.

In all three dimensions of its history, the general tendency of a system of this kind is towards growth; the meaning potential is constantly tending to expand. (1) The system tends to *evolve* towards increasing semantic complexity: this clearly happened in the evolution of language itself, with the accumulating experience that constituted the human condition; we cannot observe this, but we can observe it happening with particular languages when that condition changes, which means that new semiotic resources (new registers) evolve in tandem with new material practices. (2) The *development* of each individual's language is another history of expansion, as successive areas of semantic space are colonized and existing ones filled out with greater delicacy; but this is in turn rests on a critical epigenetic progression, from (i) generalization, around age one to two [non-referring → "proper" (individual) reference → "common" (class) reference → taxonomic (class of classes) reference], through (ii) abstractness, around age four to six [concrete (perceptual) reference → abstract reference], to (iii) metaphor, around age nine to thirteen [primary construal → secondary construal of experience] (cf. Section 4 below). (3) The *unfolding* of a particular text, dialogic or monologic, is itself a form of growth as new instantial meanings are being created; we are most easily aware of this in technical discourse because this is the process whereby meanings come to be technicalized, but it happens all the time in the spontaneous exchanges of everyday encounter, as interactants engage in semiotic challenge and display. In all these histories, meanwhile, the past is always present; the system continues to accommodate the foundations of the construction of experience; the individual's grammar continues to embody the elements that first appeared (including even some protolin-guistic ones); and the instances of discourse continue to incorporate a significant repertory of ready–worded "snatches", semiotic fragments from earlier instances of text. The old is then ongoingly recontextualized within the ambience of the new, and this too is a part of the fundamental semogenic process.

Notes

9. Sydney Lamb did a great deal to clarify the nature and significance of stratifica-tion in language. An early paper (1964) relates stratification to other theoretical concepts in linguistics. Lamb's recent thinking on the question may be found in Lamb 1999. Cf. also Martin's discussion in chapter 2 of Halliday and Martin (1993a).
10. See Halliday and James (1993) for a detailed account of this investigation. Halliday (1993a) gives further general background.
11. See Fawcett (1994), Fawcett and Tucker (1990), Fawcett, Tucker and Lin (1993).
12. Edelman uses "value" in a different – though related – sense: it is a feature of primary consciousness that it categorizes by value that accrues on the basis of experience (as distinct from genetic programming); see Edelman (1992: pp. 90 ff).

III.18(1995):404–13, 430

Computational and Quantitative Studies (Volume 6)

One consequence of the development of the modern corpus is that we can now for the first time undertake serious **quantitative** work in the field of grammar. Quantitative studies require very large populations to work with. This is obvious in lexis, where the underlying principles of the frequency distribution of lexical items have been known for quite some time (since the groundbreaking studies by Zipf (1935), in fact): if we want to investigate any words other than those of highest frequency in a language, we need text data running at least into millions of words, and preferably into hundreds of millions. Even to study the most frequent words, once we start investigating their collocational patterns, we need very large samples of text. It might be argued that grammatical patterns do not demand text data on that scale, because they will typically occur more often. That is true of the broadest, primary categories, like singular and plural in the English noun, or positive and negative in the verb.

But the finer, more delicate our categories become the less frequently each instance will occur; and even with the broader categories, since many of the ones we are likely to be most concerned with are categories of the clause and above, it will require a rather large sample (if we are thinking in terms of the number of words) to yield a sufficiently large number of occurrences. Consider for example the clause nexus, a structure of two clauses related by expansion or projection: Nesbitt and Plum were able to retrieve 2,733 instances from a corpus of 100,000 words. If we want to compare the grammar of different registers, the functional varieties of a language, in quantitative terms (for example, the different proportions of active and passive in different registers of Modern English), then it is clearly going to require a very large corpus of data to produce reliable results.

I myself first became interested in grammatical frequencies in a crude and simplistic fashion many years ago in the course of my work as a language teacher – although, if I pursue this even further, the reason for my interest in such information as a teacher was that I had felt the need for it in the first place as a learner. Faced with the task of learning, from scratch, as a young adult, a language very distant from my own, or from any language I had had experience of before, I was constantly wanting to know what people actually said in this language. When I had to master very basic systems of mood, aspect, phase and so on that were unlike anything in English, I wanted to know which of a set of alternatives was the most likely – I did not know the term "unmarked" at that time, but what I was looking for was some guidance about which, if any, was the unmarked term. A few years later, when I started to teach that same language, although I had by then acquired some feeling for its patterns of discourse, I found it frustrating that I could not offer the students reliable information of the kind that I myself would have liked to have.

In other words, I wanted to know the probabilities that were associated with these grammatical choices. Given, for example, a particular grammatical system, say that of *aspect*, with terms *perfective/imperfective*, what was the relative probability of choosing one or the other in a Chinese clause (Chinese was the language I was teaching)? This is a considerable problem for a speaker of a western European language, for two reasons. On the one hand, the aspect system itself is unfamiliar; there is some form of grammatical aspect in English – its exact nature is disputed; but on any interpretation it is not the dominant temporal system in the clause, which is tense, whereas in Chinese the dominant temporal system is that of aspect. On the other hand, there is the problem of the nature of the unmarked term. Grammatical systems in Chinese typically embody an alternative which is "unmarked", not in the sense of being the default or most frequent choice (it often will be that too), but in the sense that it is a way of opting out – of not choosing either of the terms. So the aspect system is not simply "either perfective or imperfective" but "perfective, imperfective or **neither**". Speakers of European languages are much less accustomed to systems of this kind; and again, it would be helpful to know the relative probability of choosing one way or another.

Of course, every learner will carry over into the new language some predictions based on the experience of his or her mother tongue, and maybe also of other languages that he or she knows. Some of these predictions will hold good: I would imagine that the ratio of positive to negative clauses is substantially the same in all languages – although it would be nice to know. But some of them will not hold good; and there will be some cases where the learner has no idea what to predict at all. And this is often where one begins to reflect on these matters; as long as the predictions work, they tend to remain unconscious. But there was another question which kept arising in my work as a teacher, especially in preparing for conversation classes; and this was something I found quite impossible to predict: was the probability of a choice in one system affected by a choice in another? Could I combine freely, say, negative polarity with perfective aspect; or different voice-like options (the Chinese *bǎ* construction, for example) with interrogative as well as with declarative mood?

When I wrote my first sketch of a grammar of Chinese (1956), I attached probabilities to most of the primary systems. These were, obviously, in a very crude form: I used the values 0+, ½-, ½, ½+, 1-. The values were derived mainly from my own knowledge of the language, backed up from two sources: a small amount of counting of grammatical options in modern Chinese dramatic texts; and the work that I had subsequently been doing on a text in early Mandarin, the fourteenth-century Chinese version of the *Secret History of the Mongols*, in which I had counted every instance of those grammatical categories that I had been able to resolve into systems. One reason for doing all this counting had been to try to establish the extent of the association between different systems: to find out, for example, whether it was possible to predict the number of instances of negative interrogative by intersecting the probabilities of negative (versus positive) with those of interrogative (vs declarative). On the basis of this quantitative work, although obviously I was able to access only very minute samples from the modern language, I adopted the principle that frequency in text instantiated probability in the system.

Any concern with grammatical probabilities makes sense only in the context of a paradigmatic model of grammar, one that incorporates the category of *system* in its technical sense as defined by Firth.[1] The system, in Firth's system-structure theory, is the category which models paradigmatic relations: just as a *structure*, in Firth's specialized use of the term, is a deep syntagm, so to speak, so a system is a deep paradigm. The system, as Firth put it, "gives value to the elements of structure": it specifies the oppositions, or sets of alternatives, to which a defined place in structure provides the condition of entry. Firth's own application of these concepts was largely confined to phonology; but, if we want to give a brief illustration from grammar, using modern terms, we could say that the element "Finite operator" in the structure of the English verb (verbal group) is given value by the systems of *verbal deixis* (temporal/modal) and *polarity* (positive/negative) which originate there. This concept of the system enables us to show that, under given conditions, the speaker is selecting one, and only one, from among a small closed set of possibilities; and therefore it makes sense to talk about the probability of choosing one or the other. What I hoped to do was to model each system not just as "choose *a* or *b* or *c*", but as "choose *a* or *b* or *c* with a certain probability attached to each". In other words, I was positing that an inherent property of any linguistics system is the relative probability of its terms.

I have often encountered considerable resistance to this idea. People have become quite accustomed to lexical probabilities, and find no difficulty in accepting that they are going to use *go* more often than *grow*, and *grow* more often than *glow* (or, if you prefer a semantically related set of words, that they will say *go* more often than *walk* and *walk* more often than *stroll*). They do not feel that this constitutes any threat to their individual freedom. But when faced with the very similar observation that they are going to use active more often than passive, or positive more often than negative, many people object very strongly, and protest that they have a perfect right to choose to do otherwise if they wish. And of course they have; that is exactly the point that is being made. They could choose to use negative more often than positive, just as they could choose to use *stroll* more often than *walk* – but they won't. The resistance seems to arise because grammar is buried more deeply below the level of our conscious awareness and control; hence it is more threatening to be told that your grammatical choices are governed by overall patterns of probability.

Before being able to pursue these studies any further with Chinese, however, I changed the focus of my work and found myself professionally involved with English. So again I started counting things, this time using an early version of a system-based grammar of the language worked out first in collaboration with Jeffrey Ellis and Denis Berg, and subsequently elaborated together with John Sinclair, Angus McIntosh and others at the University of Edinburgh in the early 1960s. I collected a small sample of four different registers of English, just big enough to yield a total of 2,000 occurrences of whatever category provided the entry condition to the systems I wanted to study. For example, in order to count instances of indicative/imperative mood, I had to have 2,000 independent clauses, because it is here that the choice is made: each independent clause selects one or the other. But to compare declarative with interrogative I had to count 2,000 indicative clauses, because it is the indicative clause that is either declarative or interrogative. The reason for settling on a figure of 2,000 occurrences was the following: first, I estimated it needed about 200 occurrences of the less frequent term to ensure a reasonable degree of accuracy; and second, that the less frequent term in a binary system seemed to occur about 10 per cent of the time. So if I restricted the counting to binary systems, 2,000 instances tended to yield around 200 occurrences of the less frequent term in the system.

The systems that I was interested in were mainly clause systems, although this did not imply that every clause would select in the system in question: each system would have its origin in some specific class of the clause (but a very large class, like the "indicative" referred to above). So from each of four registers (a science magazine, a novel, a conversation and a play) I took samples that would be large enough to yield 500 instances of whatever category was required. The systems I investigated were nine in all. The first eight were: (1) voice (active/passive); (2) transitivity (transitive/intransitive), (3) tense (simple/complex), (4) theme (unmarked/marked), (5,6) mood (indicative/imperative, and, within indicative, declarative/interrogative), (7) polarity (positive/negative), (8) nominal deixis (specific/non-specific). The ninth was the system of tone, one of the systems of intonation in English; here there is a separate unit as point of origin of the system, namely the tone group, and five terms (falling/rising/level (low rising)/fall–rise/rise–fall). For this I used a recorded conversation containing about 1,500 tone groups.

Such samples were of course extremely small, much too small for serious quantitative work; and in any case I was far from confident in the grammatical categories I was using as the basis, because these had not yet been put to the test – indeed one of my main reasons for doing this kind of close analysis of the data was to test the validity of the categories themselves when applied to natural, including spoken, texts. At this time a very sharp distinction was being drawn in linguistics between the system and the instance (the text), or between competence and performance; and quantitative effects were dismissed as "merely perfor-mance features", so very few people were interested in this sort of study (and there was certainly no question of anyone publishing the results!). However it seemed to me that these were important issues, very relevant to our overall understanding of language itself; and that some interesting patterns seemed to emerge. One which I reported on at the time was this. There seemed to be certain systems where the frequency of the terms was more or less equal: given a binary system (and as already noted I had confined the counting to systems that could be represented as binary, apart from the system of tone), this meant a ratio of about fifty: fifty, or (in terms of probabilities) of 0.5 : 0.5. There were then other sys-tems where the frequency was unequal. But these latter were not distrib-uted across the whole range of possible values. They seemed to tend – again, very roughly – towards a skewing by about one order of magnitude, a "ten to one" ratio. This I represented as 0.9 : 0.1. The former type were those where, from the point of view of frequency, there was no unmarked term; the latter were those in which one of the terms was unmarked.

I did not attach much weight to this observation, for obvious reasons: the whole procedure was far too unreliable. But I did wonder about whether such a pattern would make sense. We can imagine two possible alternatives: one, that the probability profiles of different systems might be randomly distributed across all possible values, from equiprobable to highly skew; the other where the skew systems might cluster around a particular value, but not at 0.9 : 0.1 – say at 99 to 1, or 3 to 1. It seemed easy to suggest that, in some vague sense, 99 to 1 would be too much skewed to be useful in the grammar of a language, while 3 to 1 would not be clearly enough distinguishable from even probabilities; but such an explanation would hardly stand up by itself. At the time, I was just beginning to investigate child language development, as a result of work-ing with primary school teachers on an educational programme con-cerned with initial literacy; and since I had first faced up to the issue as a language learner, it seemed natural to try to look at it in developmental terms. I had not yet begun to make any direct observations of my own on how children learn their mother tongue; but later when I came to do this, I was struck by the way they respond to the more frequent options in the grammar and use these first, bringing in the less frequent ones by a later step. In other words, children seem to learn language as a probabi-listic system; they are surrounded by large quantities of data, probably at least a hundred thousand clauses a year, and they are sensitive to relative frequency as a resource for ordering what they learn to say. (I am not suggesting they do any of this consciously, of course!) From this point of view, one could hypothesize that a semiotic in which the probabilities associated with various sets of options, or systems, were distributed randomly all the way from 0.5 : 0.5 to 0.99 : 0.01 would be virtually impossible to learn. One in which there was some kind of bimodal distribution, on the other hand, would be much more accessible to a learner. This did not in itself favour one particular profile over another, for systems of the type which were skew; but it did suggest that they might very well tend to cluster around just one set of values.

Among the systems I had counted at the beginning was tense. What I was counting here was not the opposition of past and present, or past and non-past; it was that of "simple tense" versus "complex tense". This was based on analysis of the English tense system different from that favoured by the structuralist linguists, which had only past and present tense (rejecting the traditional notion of future) and combined these with "continuous" (or "progressive") and "perfect" as forms of aspect. My own analysis was more in harmony with the traditional concept of tense, and as interpreted in semantic terms by Reichenbach (1947). In this view, tense (past/present/future) is a potentially iterative system, construing a "serial time", in which there is a primary tense choice of past, present or future relative to the moment of speaking, and also the option of then making a further choice, where the time frame of the primary tense is taken as the reference point for another tense selection of past, present or future – a secondary time system that is relative to the primary one. So as well as simple past *took*, simple present *takes* and simple future *will take*, there is the possibility of **past** in past, *had taken*, **present** in past, *was taking*, and **future** in past, *was going to take*; likewise past in **present** *has taken*, **present** in present *is taking*, **future** in present *is going to take*; and past in **future** *will have taken*, **present** in future *will be taking*, **future** in future *will be going to take*. This second time choice can then serve as reference point for a third, and so on. In this analysis, a verb form such as that in *I hadn't been going to tell you* is "future in past in past"; that in *he was going to have been looking after things for us all this time* is "present in past in future in past". In all, sequences of up to five tense choices have been observed to occur (see Matthiessen 1983, 1996).

Both this and the structuralist form of analysis can be used to throw light on the English tense system, and each will illuminate a different facet of it. The reasons for using the iterative form of analysis would take too long to go into here, particularly as they require illustration from discourse – this analysis treats tense more as a discourse feature. The relevance to the present discussion is that, when interpreted in this way, tense becomes an instance of a very general kind of system found in language: the kind of system that embodies an iterative option, a choice of "going round again". Another example of this would be projection (direct and indirect speech and thought), where we can say not only *Henry said that the day would be fine* but also *Mary reported that Henry had said that the day would be fine, Peter forgot that Mary had reported that Henry had said that the day would be fine*, and so on. Such systems obviously require very large samples for counting the relative frequency of sequences of different lengths; the only one I had tried to count was tense, which is less demanding because it is a system of the verb (verbal group) and so each tense form, however complex, remains within the limits of one clause. Comparing simple tense forms (primary tense only) with complex tense forms (primary plus secondary), I found that there was the same general pattern of skew distribution: simple tenses were about ten times as frequent as complex ones. In other words, having made one choice of tense, you can go round and choose again; but you are much more likely not to – and roughly in the same proportion as you are more likely to choose positive than negative or active than passive. This kind of iterative system is something that would appear highly prominent to a child learning the language; and it seems to provide a kind of prototype or model of a skew system, as being a system having one option that is highly marked (much less frequent than the other).

So while my original interest in the quantitative aspect of grammatical systems had been an educational one – its importance for learning and teaching languages – in the course of working on texts, first in Chinese and then in English, I had become aware of the different information loading that different systems can carry. Now, in the late 1950s I had had the privilege of working alongside Margaret Braithwaite, together with A. F. Parker-Rhodes and R. H. Richens, in the pioneering Cambridge Language Research Unit, one of the early projects concerned with machine translation (see Léon 2000). In this context it became necessary to represent grammatical features in explicit, computable terms. I wanted to formalize paradigmatic relations, those of the system; but I did not know how to do it – and I totally failed to persuade anyone else of this! The emphasis at that time – and for many years to come – was on formalizing syntagmatic relations, those of structure, which seemed to me less central to the task. One of the lines of approach that I tried to explore was through Shannon and Weaver's (1963 [1949]) information theory. This had already been rejected by linguists as being of no interest; partly because Shannon and Weaver's own incursions into language had been purely at the orthographic level (what they meant by the "redundancy of English" was the redundancy of the system consisting of twenty-six letters and a space), but partly also because of the current obsession with structure. Information theory has nothing to say about constituent structure; information and redundancy are properties of systems. But it does provide a very valuable measure of the information content of any one system.

A binary system whose terms are equiprobable (0.5 : 0.5) has an information value of 1 ($H = 1$); redundancy is $1-H$, so it had a redundancy of 1-1, which is zero. Redundancy is therefore a measure of the skewness of a system; the greater the skewness (departure from equiprobability), the lower the value of H (information) and consequently the higher the redundancy. (This is, of course, "information" and "redundancy" in these specific mathematical senses, without any implication that one or other is to be avoided!) The original Shannon and Weaver formula for measuring information was

$$- \Sigma \, p_i \, . \log_n p_i$$

where n is the number of terms in the system (so $\log_2$ if the system is binary) and p_i is the probability of each. I used a table of the values of $p_i \log_2 p_i$ for $p = 0.01$ to $p = 0.99$, in order to calculate the information of grammatical systems with different degrees of skewness. But when I reported on this it aroused no kind of interest; and when I came to count the frequencies of the systems referred to above, in texts in English, I did not have enough confidence in the figures (or in my own interpretation of them) to pursue the question of information and redundancy any further.

Meanwhile in the 1960s the foundations were being laid for an eventual breakthrough in our understanding of linguistic systems, both qualitatively and quantitatively: namely the beginning of corpus-based linguistics. The "corpus" had been the brainchild of two leading specialists in English linguistics: Randolph Quirk, in Britain, and Freeman Twaddell in the United States. By the middle of the decade the "Brown Corpus", at Brown University in Providence, and the Survey of English Usage at University College London were making available bodies of text data that were sufficiently large to allow valid quantitative studies to be carried out. A groundbreaking piece of work was Jan Svartvik's *On Voice in the English Verb*, in which Svartvik used the text resources of the Survey of English Usage to investigate the use and significance of the passive in written English. Since that time a steady output of research has come from these corpus projects, the high point of this achievement being the "Quirk grammar". At the same time other corpus studies were being undertaken; for example in lexis, by John Sinclair and his colleagues in Birmingham, and in grammar by Rodney Huddleston and the members of the "scientific English" project in my own department at University College London. Work of this kind clearly demonstrated the value of this general approach to the study of language.[2] By the 1970s the corpus was well established as a research resource, and was being extended into the domain of language education, both as a resource for foreign-language learning (for example the "Leuven Drama Corpus" compiled by Leopold Engels at the Catholic University of Leuven), and as a theoretical basis for work in initial literacy (e.g. the "Mount Gravatt Corpus" developed by Norman Hart and R. H. Walker at Mount Gravatt College of Advanced Education in Brisbane).

As far as quantitative studies were concerned, the corpus entirely transformed the scene. On the one hand, samples of text were becoming available that were large enough for reliable statistical investigation into features both of vocabulary and of grammar. On the other hand, these texts were now in machine-readable form, so that step by step, as appropriate software was developed, it was becoming possible to handle such large bodies of data in a way that would have been impossible with any form of manual processing. Meanwhile one critical contribution to these studies came from the sophisticated methodology for quantitative analysis developed by William Labov, together with Gillian Sankoff and David Sankoff, in their investigation of socially conditioned variation in the phonology and morphology of urban speech. This has been adapted to systemic-functional corpus studies in syntactic and semantic variation, where (unlike Labov's work) what is being investigated is systematic variation in patterns of meaning, on the plane of content rather than the plane of expression.

These studies are well known, and I have discussed them in a similar context elsewhere (VI.3, 5). What follows is a very brief summary. Plum and Cowling used the corpus of interviews from Barbara Horvath's *Sydney Social Dialect Survey* to study variation in the system of temporal and modal deixis in the English verbal group, and within temporal deixis the system of past/present/future primary tense. They examined 4,436 finite clauses, and found that 75 per cent selected temporal deixis and 25 per cent modal; while of those selecting temporal deixis, leaving out a very small proportion of futures, they found 57 per cent selecting past and 43 per cent selecting present. These were from texts in one particular register: spoken interviews in which the respondents were asked to recall their childhood experiences in primary school, especially the games they used to play. Examining the data for systematic variation within the population, Plum and Cowling found no significant variation in the choice of tense versus modality; but, within tense, they found significant variation among three social groups: relatively, the middle class favoured past tense in their narratives (70 per cent : 30 per cent), the lower working class favoured present tense (65 per cent : 35 per cent), while the upper working class fell in between, but closer to the middle-class figures (60 per cent of clauses past).

Using a different corpus, spoken interviews with dog fanciers discussing the breeding and showing of dogs, Nesbitt and Plum examined a sample of 2,733 clause nexuses to investigate the internal relationship between two systems within the grammar: interdependency (parataxis/hypotaxis) and logical-semantic relations (expansion/projection, and their sub-types). Here the question concerned the intersection (mutual conditioning) of the two sets of probabilities: were the two systems independent, or were they associated in some way? It would take too long to summarize their findings here (cf.VI.3–5); but let me mention one of them. In the intersection of interdependency with projection (the combination of "parataxis/hypotaxis" with "locution/idea" which defines the four categories traditionally referred to as "direct and indirect speech and thought"), they found that there was a strong association of parataxis with locution ("direct speech") and of hypotaxis with idea ("indirect thought"); both "indirect speech" and "direct thought" were highly marked combinations. In other words, there was a strong conditioning of the probabilities within the grammar itself; and it remained constant whichever system was taken as the environment of the other.

On a considerably larger scale, since the mid-1980s Ruqaiya Hasan has been conducting research into conversation between mothers and children, where the children were just below school age (3½–4 years). Her aim has been to investigate how children's patterns of learning are developed through ordinary everyday interaction in the home, and to explore the consequences of this early semantic experience for their subsequent learning in school. Using a population of 24 mother-child dyads, structured by social class (12 "higher autonomy professions", 12 "lower autonomy professions") and sex of child (12 boys, 12 girls), Hasan and her colleagues collected over 60,000 clauses of natural conversation of which they analysed over one-third in terms of a detailed network of semantic features. Subjecting the results to a cluster analysis brought out some highly significant correlations between the social factors of class and sex on the one hand and the orientation towards certain patterns of semantic choice on the other. For example, while all mothers used a great deal of reasoning, middle-class and working-class mothers tended to favour different kinds of grounding for their explanations; while

305

mothers of boys differed from mothers of girls in the ways in which they elaborated on their answers to their children's questions (Plum and Cowling 1987; Nesbitt and Plum 1988; Hasan and Cloran 1990; Hasan 1992).

Let me take up one final point before moving to the second part of the chapter. In 1980 William Mann, director of the "Penman" artificial intelligence project at the University of Southern California Information Sciences Institute, asked me to write a grammar for use in text generation by computer. I constructed a network, on systemic principles, for the grammar of the English clause, based on the work I had been doing since the mid-1960s; there were 81 systems in the network (Appendix, p. 268 ff. this volume). Whenever possible I represented these as binary systems and added probabilities to them, using just the two values of 0.5 : 0.5 and 0.9 : 0.1 that I had arrived at earlier. This network was then implemented computationally by their programmer Mark James. The network was of course designed to be used under the control of some higher-level system, a "knowledge representation system" of some kind; but for testing it was operated randomly. When let loose in this way it produced garbage, as such grammars always will until sufficiently constrained. But when it was operated still randomly but with the probabilities taken into account, Mann's comment was that, while it still produced garbage, the garbage now looked as if it might bear some distant resemblance to English. That may not sound to you very encouraging! – but that remark did more than anything else to persuade me to reactivate my interest in probabilities (see Mann 1985; Matthiessen 1985; Bateman and Matthiessen 1991).

I thought again about this bimodal effect, of probabilities tending towards either 0.5 : 0.5 or 0.9 : 0.1, and formulated it as a hypothesis about the typology of grammatical systems: that they fall into one or other of these two types, the "equi" and the "skew", with the "skew" having a value of very roughly nine to one, or one order of magnitude in our decimal scheme of things. Then, wondering again about this nine to one, I looked once more into the Shannon and Weaver formula for calculating information. We saw that, at 0.5 : 0.5, $H = 1$, $R = 0$. What, I wondered, was the point at which information and redundancy exactly balance out ($H = 0.5$, $R = 0.5$)? – the property of 50 per cent redundancy that Shannon and Weaver had originally assigned to "English" (meaning by that the English writing system, based on the relative frequencies of the twenty-six letters of the alphabet and the space). It turns out that, in a binary system, the probability profile where information and redundancy match one another, at 50 per cent each, is almost exactly

0.9 : 0.1. To give the exact probabilities to two places of decimals: at probabilities of 0.89 : 0.11, H (information) = 0.4999. In other words, the particular distribution of probabilities to which these skew systems seemed to conform was that where there is 50 per cent redundancy in the system. This could perhaps begin to suggest an explanation for this kind of phenomenon in the grammar – if it turned out to survive under adequate large-scale scrutiny. To investigate it properly, it was necessary to have access to a sufficiently large corpus of modern English.

Notes

1. For the discussion of "system" and "structure" as fundamental theoretical concepts see Firth 1957a.
2. For a general perspective on corpus studies in English see Svartvik 1992. For examples of corpus-based lexicogrammatical studies in the 1960s, cf. Svartvik 1966; Sinclair *et al.* 1970; Huddleston *et al.* 1970.

VI.7(1993):130–43, 156

Additional readings

On Grammar (Volume 1) – 6(1966):166, 168–9; 13(1992):352–68
On Language and Linguistics (Volume 3) – 5(1987):122; 12(1997):253; 18(1995): 425–6
Computational and Quantitative Studies (Volume 6) – 1(1956):8–9, 13–9; 3(1991); 4(1991); 5(1992); 6(1993); 7(1993); 8(2002); 10(1995):235–8
Studies in Chinese Language (Volume 8) – 3(1956):209–48
Language and Education (Volume 9) – 15(1994):310–6

Chapter Fourteen

SEMANTIC SYSTEM

Summary

A semantic system is a system of meaning which is distinguished from other semiotic systems by the fact that it is founded on grammar. It is a system of meaning of a natural language, a system of wordings. The semantic system is one of three levels, or strata, which together comprise the whole linguistic system. Between the semantic system above and the phonological and morphological realization below is the lexicogrammar. A semantic system is organized into three main functional components. The three components are: ideational, including logical and experiential; interpersonal; and textual.

Selected readings

On Grammar (Volume 1)

In principle, the domain of a semantic description may be anything from 'the whole language' down to a single text. At one end of the scale, I have found it useful to set up a semantic system relating to just one dialogue of 35 words long; this was a child–adult dialogue, and the purpose was to explore what meaning potential the child must have in order to be able to construe such a discourse (see I.11(1984):313). Geoffrey Turner's (1973) semantic networks define a rather broader range of texts, such as mother–child control patterns in specific experimental situation types. More general again is Ruqaiya Hasan's (1983) 'message function' network, which describes spontaneous interaction between children and parents, for the purpose of investigating the development of children's learning patterns. At the other end of the scale, J. R. Martin's (1983, 1992) conjunction networks are like grammatical networks in that they are set up for the language as a whole.

When we describe semantic systems, we are saying what it is that 'preselects' the grammatical categories: what choices in meaning call on what features in the grammar for their realization. It is by this process that the grammatical categories are defined; when this is done, there is no need to gloss them further. Once the semantic system is made explicit, it can only be misleading to attach separate semantic descriptions as glosses to the categories of the grammar.

At the same time, if the semantic system is set up only for a restricted domain, some particular register variety, then the meanings of any grammatical categories that figure distinctively in that variety will appear thereby less ineffable. For example, we have no general definition of 'future' as a category of English grammar; its effability measure is decidedly low. But when this category figures in the register of weather reporting and forecasting, the semantics of that variety makes only limited demands on it, for realizing the meanings that are engendered by that particular context. The category of 'future in the register of weather forecasting' is much less resistant to being glossed than the general category of 'future in English'.

This interpretation of semantic systems is a kind of functional semantics, and it derives from the twentieth century functional semantic traditions of Boas, Sapir and Whorf, of Malinowski and Firth, and of Mathesius and the Prague school. These were three groups of scholars with very different orientations, but their work was complementary in significant ways. While each had a well-rounded view of language, they emphasized, respectively, the ideational, the interpersonal and the textual aspects of meaning.

For Malinowski, language was a means of action; and since symbols cannot act on things, this meant a means of **inter**action – acting on other people. Language need not (and often did not) match reality; but since it derived its meaning potential from use, it typically worked. For Whorf, on the other hand, language was a means of thought. It provided a model of reality; but when the two did not match, since experience was interpreted within the limitations of this model it could be disastrous in action – witness the exploding petrol drums. Mathesius showed how language varied to suit the context. Each sentence of the text was organized by the speaker so as to convey the message he wanted at that juncture, and the total effect was what we recognize as discourse. Their work provides the foundation for a systematic functional semantics which enables us to bridge the gap between the context of culture and the language, and between the context of situation and the text. This is how we can become aware of the meaning of grammatical categories.

I.11(1984):310–1

Linguistic Studies of Text and Discourse (Volume 2)

1 THE SEMANTIC SYSTEM

1.1 Initial assumptions

First, and least controversially, let us assume that the semantic system is one of three levels, or strata, that constitute the linguistic system:

Semantic (semology)
Lexicogrammatical (lexology: syntax, morphology and lexis)
Phonological (phonology and phonetics).

These are strata in Lamb's "stratificational" sense.

Second, let us assume that the semantic system has the four components experiential, logical, interpersonal and textual. The first two of these are closely related, more so than other pairs, and can be combined under the heading of "ideational" (but see 1.3 below):

Third, let us assume that each stratum, and each component, is described as a network of options, sets of interrelated choices having the form "if *a*, then either *b* or *c*". Variants of this general form include: "if *a*, then either *x* or *y* or *z* and either *m* or *n*; if *x*, or if *m*, then either *p* or *q*; if both *y* and *n*, then either *r* or *s* or *t*" and so on. The description is, therefore, a paradigmatic one, in which environments are also defined paradigmatically: the environment of any option is the set of options that are related to it, including those that define its condition of entry. The description is also open-ended: there is no point at which no further sub-categorization of the options is possible.

Fourth, let us assume that each component of the semantic system specifies its own structures, as the "output" of the options in the network (each act of choice contributes to the formation of the structure). It is the function of the lexicogrammatical stratum to map the structures one on to another so as to form a single integrated structure that represents all components simultaneously. With negligible exceptions, every operational instance of a lexicogrammatical construct in the adult language – anything that realizes text – is structured as the expression of all four components. In other words, any instance of language in use "means" in these various ways, and shows that it does so in its grammar.

Fifth, let us assume that the lexicogrammatical system is organized by rank (as opposed to by immediate constituent structure); each rank is the locus of structural configurations, the place where structures from the different components are mapped on to each other. The "rank scale" for the lexicogrammar of English is:

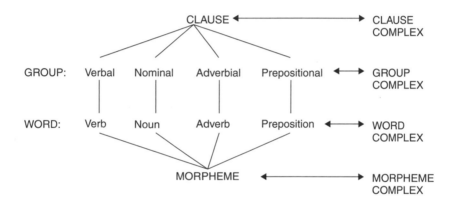

Complexes are univariate (recursive) structures formed by paratactic or hypotactic combinations – co-ordination, apposition, modification and the like – at the rank in question; a clause complex may be formed for example by two clauses in co-ordination. All other structures are multivariate (non-recursive). A "sentence" is defined as a clause complex. See Huddleston (1965), Hudson (1967 and 1971), and Sinclair (1972).

1.2 Structural configurations

It follows from the above that each type of unit – clause, verbal group, nominal group, etc. – is in itself a structural composite, a combination of structures each of which derives from one or other component of the semantics.

A clause, for example, has a structure formed out of elements such as Agent, Process, Extent; this structure derives from the system of transitivity, which is part of the experiential component. Simultaneously it has a structure formed out of the elements Modal and Propositional: this derives from the system of mood, which is part of the interpersonal component. It also has a third structure composed of the elements Theme and Rheme, deriving from the theme system, which is part of the textual component. For example:

		the Grays	retired	to their beds
Experiential	TRANSITIVITY	Medium	Process	Location: locative
Interpersonal	MOOD	Modal	Propositional	
Textual	THEME	Theme	Rheme	

It is not the case that the same constituent structure (same bracketing) holds throughout, with only the labels differing. This is already clear from this example: the thematic and modal structures are simple binary ones, whereas the transitivity structure is not. In any case, the representation just given is oversimplified; the Modal constituent includes the finite element in the verb, and consists of Subject plus Finiteness, yielding an analysis as follows:

Clause:	the Grays	'did	retire'	to their beds
(1)	Medium	Process		Location: locative
(2)	Modal		Propositional	
	Subject	Finite		
(3)	Theme	Rheme		

There may be differences at other points too; in general it is characteristic of lexicogrammatical structures that the configurations deriving from the various functional components of the semantic system will differ not only in their labelling but in their bracketing also.

The logical component is distinct from the other three in that all logical meanings, and only logical meanings, are expressed through the structure of "unit complexes": clause complex, group complex and so on. For example:

Clause complex:	the Grays stopped maligning the hippopatamuses	and retired to their beds
Logical: (co-ordination)	(Clause) A ⟶ (Clause) B	

1.3 Functional components of the system

The grouping of semantic components differs according to the perspective from which we look at them.

From the standpoint of their realization in the lexicogrammatical system (i.e. "from below"), the logical component, since it alone is, and it always is, realized through recursive structures, is the one that stands out as distinct from all the others.

From the standpoint of the functions of the linguistic system in relation to some higher-level semiotic that is realized through the **linguistic** semiotic (i.e. "from above"), it is the textual component that appears as distinct, since the textual component has an enabling function in respect of the other components: language can effectively express ideational and interpersonal meanings only because it can create text. Text is language in operation; and the textual component embodies the semantic systems by means of which text is created.

From the point of view of the organization within the semantic system itself (i.e. "from the same level"), the experiential and the logical go together because there is greater systemic interdependence between these two than between other pairings. This shows up in various places throughout the English semantic system (the general pattern may well be the same in all languages, though the specifics are different): for example, the semantics of time reference, of speaking ("X said –"), and of identifying ("A = B") all involve some interplay of experiential and logical systems. To illustrate this from the semantics of speaking, the **process** 'say' is an option in the transitivity system, which is experiential; whereas the **relation** between the process of saying and what is said – the "reporting" relation – is an option in the logical system of interclause relations. The picture is something like the following.

Table 1 sets out the principal semantic systems arranged by function and rank, showing their functional location in the semantic system and their point of origin in the lexicogrammar.

Functional components of semantic systems,
seen from different vantage points:

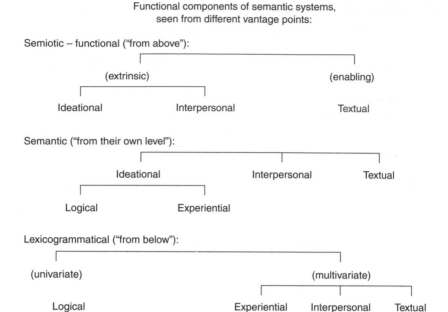

Semiotic – functional ("from above"):

| | (extrinsic) | | (enabling) |
| Ideational | Interpersonal | | Textual |

Semantic ("from their own level"):

| Ideational | Interpersonal | Textual |
| Logical | Experiential | |

Lexicogrammatical ("from below"):

| (univariate) | | | (multivariate) | |
| Logical | | Experiential | Interpersonal | Textual |

Table 1 Functional components of the semantic system

IDEATIONAL		INTERPERSONAL		TEXTUAL
LOGICAL	EXPERIENTIAL			(COHESION)
	STRUCTURAL			NON-STRUCTURAL
	1. CLAUSE STRUCTURE			
expansion	clause: transitivity, modulation; polarity	clause: mood, modality	clause: theme	reference
identity				
projection	verbal group: types of process; tense	verbal group: person, polarity	verbal group: voice; contrast	substitution/ ellipsis
(paratactic and hypotactic)	nominal group: types of participant; class, quality, quantity, etc.	nominal group: person ('role')	nominal group: deixis	conjunction
	adverbial group: prepositional group: typres of circumstance	adverbial group: prepositional group comment	adverbial group: prepositional group: conjunction	lexical cohesion: reiteration, collocation
		2. INFORMATION STRUCTURE		
		information unit: key	information unit: information distribution and focus	

(left margin label: Complexes at all ranks (clause complex, etc.))

(vertical label between interpersonal columns: connotations of attitude etc.)

II.2(1977):23–8

Language and Society (Volume 10)

From a sociolinguistic viewpoint, the semantic system can be defined as a functional or function-oriented meaning potential; a network of options for the encoding of some extra-linguistic semiotic system or systems in terms of the two basic components of meaning that we have called the ideational and the interpersonal. In principle this higher-level semiotic system may be viewed in the tradition of humanist thought as a conceptual or cognitive system, one of information about the real world. But it may equally be viewed as a semiotic of some other type, logical, ideological, aesthetic – or social. Here it is the social perspective that is relevant, the semantic system as realization of a social semiotic; in the words of Mary Douglas (1971: 389),

> If we ask of any form of communication the simple question what is being communicated? the answer is: information from the social system. The exchanges which are being communicated constitute the social system.

Information from the social system has this property, that it is, typically, presented in highly context-specific doses. Whereas a logical semantics may be a monosystem, a social semantics is and must be a polysystem, a set of sets of options in meaning, each of which is referable to a given social context, situation type or domain.

The semantic system is an interface, between the (rest of the) linguistic system, and some higher order symbolic system. It is a projection, or realization, of the social system; at the same time it is projected on to, or realized by, the lexico-grammatical system. It is in this perspective that the sociolinguistic conditions of semantic change may become accessible.

X.4(1975):153

* * *

2.5 THE LINGUISTIC SYSTEM

Within the linguistic system, it is the ***semantic system*** that is of primary concern in a sociolinguistic context. Let us assume a tristratal model of language, with a semantic, a lexicogrammatical and a phonological stratum; this is the basic pattern underlying the (often superficially more complex) interpretations of language in the work of Troubetzkoy, Hjelmslev, Firth, Jakobson, Martinet, Pottier, Pike, Lamb, Lakoff and McCawley (among many others). We can then adopt the general conception of the organization of each stratum, and of the realization between strata, that is embodied in Lamb's stratification theory (Lamb 1971, 1974).

The semantic system is Lamb's "semological stratum"; it is conceived of here, however, in functional rather than in cognitive terms. The conceptual framework was already referred to in 1.3 above [X.5(1975):173-4], with the terms *ideational*, *interpersonal* and *textual*. These are to be interpreted not as functions in the sense of uses of language, but as functional components of the semantic system – *metafunctions* as we have called them elsewhere (Halliday 1974). (Since in respect both of the stratal and of the functional organization of the linguistic system we are adopting a ternary interpretation rather than a binary one, we should perhaps explicitly disavow any particular adherence to the magic number three. In fact the functional interpretation could just as readily be stated in terms of four components, since the ideational comprises two distinct subparts, the experiential and the logical; but the distinction happens not to be very relevant here.)

What are these functional components of the semantic system? They are the modes of meaning that are present in every use of language in every social context. A text is a product of all three; it is a polyphonic composition in which different semantic melodies are interwoven, to be realized as integrated lexicogrammatical structures. Each functional component contributes a band of structure to the whole.

The ideational function represents the speaker's meaning potential as an observer. It is the content function of language, language as about something. This is the component through which the language encodes the cultural experience, and the speaker encodes his own individual experience as a member of the culture. It expresses the phenomena of the environment: the things – creatures, objects, actions, events, qualities, states and relations – of the world and of our own consciousness, including the phenomenon of language itself; and also the 'metaphenomena', the things that are already encoded as facts and as reports. All these are part of the ideational meaning of language.

The interpersonal component represents the speaker's meaning potential as an intruder. It is the participatory function of language, language as doing something. This is the component through which the speaker intrudes himself into the context of situation, both expressing his own attitudes and judgements and seeking to influence the attitudes and behaviour of others. It expresses the role relationships associated with the situation, including those that are defined by language itself, relationships of questioner–respondent, informer–doubter and the like. These constitute the interpersonal meaning of language.

The textual component represents the speaker's text-forming potential; it is that which makes language relevant. This is the component which provides the texture; that which makes the difference between language that is suspended *in vacuo* and language that is operational in a context of situation. It expresses the relation of the language to its environment, including both the verbal environment – what has been said or written before – and the non-verbal, situational environment. Hence the textual component has an enabling function with respect to the other two; it is only in combination with textual meanings that ideational and interpersonal meanings are actualized.

These components are reflected in the lexicogrammatical system in the form of discrete networks of options. In the clause (simple sentence), for example, the ideational function is represented by transitivity, the interpersonal by mood, and the textual by a set of systems that have been referred to collectively as "theme". Each of these three sets of options is characterized by strong internal but weak external constraints: for example, any choice made in transitivity has a significant effect on other choices within the transitivity systems, but has very little effect on choices within the mood or theme systems. Hence the functional organization of meaning in language is built in to the core of the linguistic system, as the most general organizing principle of the lexicogrammatical stratum.

X.5(1975):183–4

★ ★ ★

The semantic system is organized into a small number of components – three or four depending on how one looks at them – such that **within** one component there is a high degree of interdependence and mutual constraint, whereas **between** components there is very little: each one is relatively independent of the others.

The components can be identified as follows:

1 ideational (language as reflection), comprising
  (a) experiential
  (b) logical
2 interpersonal (language as action)
3 textual (language as texture, in relation to the environment).

When we say that these components are relatively independent of one another, we mean that the choices that are made within any one component, while strongly affected by other choices within the same component, have no effect, or only a very weak effect, on choices made within the others. For example, given the meaning potential of the interpersonal

317

component, out of the innumerable choices that are available to me I might choose (i) to offer a proposition, (ii) pitched in a particular key (e.g. contradictory-defensive), (iii) with a particular intent towards you (e.g. of convincing you), (iv) with a particular assessment of its probability (e.g. certain) and (v) with indication of particular attitude (e.g. regretful). Now, all these choices are strongly interdetermining; if we use a network mode of representation, as in systemic theory, they can be seen as complex patterns of internal constraint among the various subnetworks. But they have almost no effect on the ideational meanings, on the **content** of what you are to be convinced of, which may be that the earth is flat, that Mozart was a great musician, or that I am hungry. Similarly, the ideational meanings do not determine the interpersonal ones; but there is a high degree of interdetermination **within** the ideational component: the kind of process I choose to refer to, the participants in the process, the taxonomies of things and properties, the circumstances of time and space, and the natural logic that links all these together.

X.9(1978):256–7

Additional readings

On Grammar (Volume 1) – 8(1979):196–218; 11(1984):310–1; 15(1996):397
Linguistic Studies of Text and Discourse (Volume 2) – 2(1977):45–52
On Language and Linguistics (Volume 3) – 15(1972):323–54
The Language of Early Childhood (Volume 4) – 4(1974):90–8, 109–12; 5(1978): 115–25; 13(1975):281–94
Computational and Quantitative Studies (Volume 6) – 9(1995):198–200
Language and Education (Volume 9) – 17(1988):345–6
Language and Society (Volume 10) – 4(1975):131–3, 143–4, 153, 158, 164–6; 5(1975):186–95

Chapter Fifteen

SEMIOTICS

Summary

A semiotic system is a system of meaning, the means by which meanings are created and exchanged. Because it is too is a systemic resource for making and exchanging meaning, language is a semiotic system. Language is the instantiation of an indefinitely large meaning potential through acts of meaning which simultaneously construe experience and enact social relationships. Language is a particular kind of semiotic system which is based on grammar, characterized by both a stratal organization and functional diversity. Both this stratal organization and metafunctional diversity in language combine to form what M.A.K. Halliday refers to as a semiotic of higher-order consciousness, the basis for the human activity of meaning.

Selected readings

On Language and Linguistics (Volume 3)

1 SYSTEMS OF MEANING

A language is a system of meaning – a *semiotic* system. Here, as in all my writing, "semiotic" means 'having to do with meaning (*semiosis*)'; so a system of meaning is one by which meaning is created and meanings are exchanged. Human beings use numerous semiotic systems, some simple and others very complex, some rather clearly defined and others notably fuzzy. A language is almost certainly the most complicated semiotic system we have; it is also a very fuzzy one, both in the sense that its own limits are unclear and in the sense that its internal organization is full of indeterminacy.

319

What other kinds of system are there? I shall assume there are three: physical, biological and social. One way to think of these is as forming an ascending order of complexity. A physical system is just that: a physical system. A biological system, on the other hand, is not just that; it is a physical system (or an assembly of physical systems) having an additional feature, let us say "life". A social system, in turn, is an assembly of biological systems (life forms) having a further additional feature – which we might call "value": it is what defines membership; so, an assembly of life forms with a membership hierarchy. So a social system is a system of a third order of complexity, because it is social and biological and physical. We could then think of a semiotic system as being of a fourth order of complexity, being semiotic and social and biological and physical: meaning is socially constructed, biologically activated and exchanged through physical channels.

But this picture has to be reconciled with another: that of the two orders of phenomena which make up the world which we inhabit. Here "semiotic" contrasts with "material": phenomena of matter, and phenomena of meaning. George Williams puts it like this:

> Evolutionary biologists . . . work with two more or less incommensurable domains: that of information and that of matter . . . These two domains will never be brought together in any kind of the sense usually implied by the term "reductionism". You can speak of galaxies and particles of dust in the same terms, because they both have mass and charge and length and width. You can't do that with information and matter. Information doesn't have mass or charge or length in millimetres. Likewise, matter doesn't have bytes. You can't measure so much gold in so many bytes. It doesn't have redundancy, or fidelity, or any of the other descriptors we apply to information. This dearth of shared descriptors makes matter and information two separate domains of existence, which have to be discussed separately, in their own terms.
>
> (Williams 1995: 43)

But "information" is, I think, a special kind of meaning – the kind that can be measured (in bytes, as Williams says). Most higher-order meaning, it seems to me, cannot be measured, or at least cannot be quantified; it can sometimes be graded in terms of value. So I will prefer the opposition of "matter" and "meaning", the realm of the material and the realm of the semiotic.

The four types of system then appear as different mixes of the semiotic and the material, ranging from physical systems, which are organizations of material phenomena, to semiotic systems, which are organizations of meaning. (I am using "semiotic" in both these taxonomic contexts, but not, I think, with any danger of ambiguity.) Biological systems are largely material – except that they are organized by genes, and at a certain point in evolution by neurons, which are semiotic phenomena; and with social systems the meaning component comes to predominate. But even semiotic systems are grounded in material processes; and on the other hand in post-Newtonian physics quantum systems are interpreted as systems of meaning. Meaning needs matter to realize it; at the same time, matter needs meaning to organize it.

Human history is a continuing interplay of the material and the semiotic, as modes of action – ways of doing and of being. The balance between the two is constantly shifting (presumably the "information society" is one in which the semiotic mode of exchange predominates over the material). This is the context in which language needs to be understood.

Of all human semiotic systems, language is the greatest source of power. Its potential is indefinitely large. We might characterize it as matching in scope all our material systems – always able to keep up with the changes in the material conditions of our existence. But putting it like that over-privileges the material: it spells a technology-driven view of the human condition. Language is not a passive reflex of material reality; it is an active partner in the constitution of reality, and all human processes however they are manifested, whether in our consciousness, our material frames, or in the physical world around us, are the outcome of forces which are both material and semiotic at the same time. Semiotic energy is a necessary concomitant, or complement, of material energy in bringing about changes in the world.

Whether or not language matches the scope of all other human *semiotic* systems must be left open to question. Some people claim that it does; they would say that anything that can be meant in any way at all can also be meant in language. In this view, the scope of *semantics* (the meaning potential of language) is equivalent to the whole of human semiosis. I am not so sure. Some semiotic systems may be incommensurable with language; witness the sometimes far-fetched attempts to represent the meaning of a work of art in language (but, again, cf. O'Toole 1994). But while the question is important, and deserves to be tackled much more subtly and fundamentally than this rather simplistic formulation suggests, it is not necessary for me to try and resolve it here. All that needs to be said in the present context is that other human semiotics are dependent on the premise that their users **also** have language. Language is a prerequisite; but there is no need to insist that language can mean it all.

The crucial question is: how does language achieve what it does? What must language be like such that we are able to do with it all the things that we do?

2 TYPES OF COMPLEXITY IN LANGUAGE

The simplest account of a semiotic system is as a set of **signs**, a "sign" being defined as a content/expression pair, like "red means 'stop!' " A set of such signs is turned into a system by means of closure:

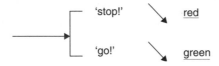

When we represent it like that we can see that it is not complete: we do not know how we get into the system. There must be a condition of entry: let us say "control point":

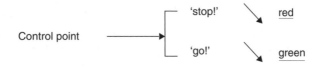

This states the domain of the system. At control point, the system is entered: one or the other option must be chosen. Other than at control point, the system cannot be entered. Note that 'control point' is itself a semiotic feature, though no doubt realized materially, like 'stop!' and 'go!'

Some semiotic systems are minimal, like this one (as presented here). A language, obviously, is not; it is vastly more complicated. The question is: how? In what ways is a language more complex than a minimal system of signs? We need to spell out the kinds of additional complexity which could transform a simple sign system into a language. The system is "thickened" along a number of different dimensions. If we posed the question in these terms, with the thought that language could be built up by expansion from a simple system of signs, we might recognize four dimensions along which such expansion would be taking place:

1. Signs may be combined, to form larger signs [syntagmatic complexity].
2. Signs may be uncoupled, to create new pairings [realizational complexity].
3. Signs may be layered, one cycling into another [stratificational complexity].

4. Signs may be networked, in relations of dependence [paradigmatic complexity].

We shall not remain within this schema – it is a builder's perspective, rather than an architect's; but it will serve to provide a way in.

2.1 Signs may be combined

We do not usually make just one meaning and stop there, like a traffic light. Meanings follow quickly one after another, each setting up a new context for the next. In this way, larger meanings are built up out of combinations of smaller ones: minimal signs – words, or even parts of words, like *I/you* realizing the contrasting roles of 'speaker' and 'addressee' in a dialogue – combine to make up larger signs, realized as a clause, or a paragraph, or an entire text like a public speech, a novel or a scientific treatise. These are all "signs", in the sense that they are units, or unities, of meaning.

2.2 Signs may be uncoupled

We are not bound by a fixed one-to-one mapping between a content and an expression. A given content may come to be realized by a different expression, or a given expression may realize a new content; and in this way new signs are being created, since variation of this kind tends to open up new meanings – new pairings are unlikely to take on if they are not in some way expanding the total resource. Then, putting this feature together with the last means that the domain of the content is not limited by the form of the expression: thus, in English, the content 'POLARITY: positive/negative' is typically realized as a small fragment attached to a word, the *n't* in *did/didn't*; but its domain is an entire clause.

2.3 Signs may be layered

We are not restricted to a single semiotic cycle. The expression of one content comes to be, at the same time, the content of another expression. So, for example, in English the content 'RESPONSE POLARITY: negative' is realized by the expression *no*; the content *no* is realized by the expression /alveolar nasal consonant + half-close back rounded vowel/ (or some other vowel, according to the dialect). How many cycles of content + expression we need to recognize is in the last resort a theoretical decision; but there must be at least these two: (i) meaning to wording, (ii) wording to sound.

2.4 Signs may be networked

We do not construct meaning out of sign systems that are unrelated to each other. Systems are organized together in the form of networks, in such a way that some are dependent on others for their condition of entry. To come back to the traffic lights: there may be a set of options 'keep straight'/'turn left'/'turn right': but if so, this is obviously dependent on selecting the option 'go!' at 'control point'; the feature 'go!' becomes the entry condition to this further option. Some sets of options, on the other hand, may share the same entry condition but be independent of each other. It is this organization in system networks that makes it possible for a language to expand its meaning potential more or less indefinitely.

When we observe the way very small children develop their powers of meaning, we can see all these different kinds of complexity emerging. Children's first language-like semiotic system, which I labeled "protolanguage" when I observed and described it thirty years ago, begins as a collection of simple signs. These signs soon come to be organized into minimal systems, like 'I want'/'I don't want'; and these show the beginning of further organization in clusters, on a functional basis; but they are not yet combined, nor are they yet layered or uncoupled. All these types of complexity, including the network, develop together as the necessary condition for the move from protolanguage to mother tongue. Not that they have somehow to be put in place in advance, as this formulation might imply; rather, they are essential features of our evolved human semiotic, and children take them up as they come to construe language in its new, post-infancy form.

It is through this "thickening" of its meaning-making resources that human language has evolved. What has been called the "architecture" of language is the organization of these resources within a space defined by a small number of interrelated vectors, those of stratification, metafunction, and the two compositional axes (syntagmatic and paradigmatic); all, in turn, predicated on the vector of instantiation (the relation between an instance and the system that lies behind it) which is based on memory and is a feature of all systematic behaviour.

In some ways "architecture" is a misleading metaphor, because it is too static; if we want a spatial metaphor of this kind we might perhaps think more in terms of town planning, with its conception of a spatial layout defined by the movement of people, or "traffic flow". The organization of language is likewise defined by the movement of meanings, or **discourse flow** (I use this term in preference to "information flow" for various reasons, one of which was mentioned in Section 1 above).

III.Introduction(2003):2–7

★ ★ ★

Systemic theory is more like language itself – a system whose stability lies in its variation. A language is a 'metastable' system; it persists because it is constantly in flux. This does not mean that we cannot characterize a particular language, but that our characterization of it has to incorporate this feature. Similarly we can state certain essential characteristics of systemic theory (cf. Fawcett 1983). Let me try to enumerate some of those that are most central to our present theme.

1 A language is not a well-defined system, and cannot be equated with "the set of all grammatical sentences", whether that set is conceived of as finite or infinite. Hence a language cannot be interpreted by rules defining such a set. A language is a semiotic system; not in the sense of a system of signs, but a systemic resource for meaning – what I have often called a **meaning potential** (Halliday 1971). Linguistics is about how people exchange meanings by 'languaging'.

Part of the synoptic representation of a semiotic system is an account of its structure, the organic part-whole relationships that are known in linguistics as constituency. Because of the historical association of linguistics with writing – linguistics begins when a language is written down, and so made accessible to conscious attention; so grammar evolved as a grammar of written language – constituency has tended to occupy the centre of attention; so much so that my early (1961) paper 'Categories of the theory of grammar' was entirely misread (by Paul Postal 1964) as a theory of constituent structure, and the same mistake was made by Terence Langendoen in his book *The London School of Linguistics* (1968), which makes no reference at all to Firth's concept of system. In systemic theory, constituency is treated as a small, though essential, part of the total picture; and it is treated in a specific way, using ranks (which are the folk-linguistic notion of constituency, incidentally, and also that which is embodied in writing systems) instead of immediate constituents for the bracketing, and functions instead of classes for the labelling. These are not arbitrary choices; there are good reasons why philosophical theories of language, which tend to be formal and sentence-oriented, use maximal bracketing and class labels, whereas ethnographic theories, which tend to be functional and discourse-oriented, use minimal bracketing and functional labels.

What distinguishes systemic theory is that its basic form of synoptic representation is not syntagmatic but paradigmatic; the organizing concept is not structure, but system (hence the name). Since language is a semiotic potential, the description of a language is a description of choice. The various levels, or strata, of the semiotic 'code' are interrelated networks of options. The constituent structure is the realization of these options, and hence plays a derivative role in the overall interpretation.

2 Closely allied to this is the fact that constituent structure at the "content" level is part of an integrated lexicogrammar (as distinct from a syntax with lexicon attached) seen as natural, i.e. non-arbitrary. There are two distinct, though related, aspects to this non-arbitrariness, one functional the other metafunctional. (i) Every structural feature has its origin in the semantics; that is, it has some function in the expression of meaning. (This is unaffected by whether semantics and lexicogrammar are treated as one stratum or as two.) (ii) The different types of structure tend to express different kinds of meaning, as embodied in the metafunctional hypothesis; and constituency is simply one type of structure, that which typically represents the experiential metafunctions – the reflective component in our meaning potential. But whereas our experience is largely organized into particulate forms of representation, our interpersonal meanings – the active component – are expressed more prosodically, as field-like structures; and the texture is provided by periodic, wave-like patterns of discourse, in which prominence is achieved by beginnings and endings (of clauses, paragraphs and so on). Like the water I was contemplating at Niagara Falls, language is at once particle, wave and field (cf. Pike 1959); and depending on which kind of meaning we want to be foregrounded, so our representation of its structure needs to adapt to the appropriate mode.

3 The heart of language is the abstract level of coding that is the lexicogrammar. (I see no reason why we should not retain the term "grammar" in this, its traditional sense in linguistics; the purpose of introducing the more cumbersome term *lexicogrammar* is simply to make explicit the point that vocabulary is also a part of it, along with syntax and morphology.) A lexicogrammar is not a closed, determinate system; and this fact has three consequences for systemic theory and practice. First, grammar cannot be modelled as new sentences made out of old words – a fixed stock of vocabulary in never-to-be-repeated combinations. On the one hand, we process and store entire groups, phrases, clauses, clauses complexes and even texts; this is a crucial element in a child's language development. On the other hand, we constantly create new words, and even now and again new morphemes. The higher the rank, the more likely a given instance is to be in some sense a first occurrence; but there is nothing remarkable about that. Secondly, and closely related to the last point, the lexicogrammatical system of a language is inherently probabilistic. It has been readily accepted that the relative frequency of words is a systematic feature of language, but this principle has not

generally been extended to grammatical systems; yet it is a fundamental property of grammar that, at least in some systems, the options are not equiprobable, and this can be built in to the representation of a grammatical network. The principle is an important one because it is likely that one of the significant differences between one register and another is difference of probabilities in the grammar (this again is to be expected, since it is clearly true of the vocabulary – different registers display different lexical probabilities). Thirdly, grammar is indeterminate in the sense that there are often two or more possible grammatical interpretations of an item, each of which relates it to a different set of other items, thus making a particular generalization of a paradigmatic kind. This may affect anything from an entire system – transitive and ergative interpretations of English transitivity would be a case in point – to a single instance, where alternative analyses can be suggested for some item in a particular text.

4 A fourth assumption of systemic theory is that language is functionally variable; any text belongs to some register or other. (Dialect variation is also functional, of course, as the symbolic vehicle of social structure; but the term "functional variety" refers to register). The different kinds of situation that collectively constitute a culture engender different kinds of text; but if we understand the semiotic properties of a situation we can make predictions about the meanings that are likely to be exchanged, in the same way that the interactants make predictions and in so doing facilitate their own participation. The notions of field, mode and tenor, together with the subsequent distinction into personal and functional tenor, provided an initial conceptual framework for characterizing the situation and moving from the situation to the text; and much current work in systemic theory is directed towards the construction of an adequate model of register and genre, taking into account the context of situation, the rhetorical structure of the text and the higher-level semiotics that make up the context of culture. This is an essential step in any adequate interpretation of language as a social semiotic, within the tradition that I referred to above as 'ethnographic' as opposed to 'philosophical' linguistics; but it also has important educational applications, for example in the development of children's writing (Martin and Rothery 1980/1). In general, as remarked above, differences among different registers are likely to be found in the relative weightings assigned to different systems: the orientation towards different metafunctions and different options in semantics. In some instances, however, more clear-cut distinctions emerge; for example the different kinds of complexity associated respectively with speech and writing.

5 Systemic theory accepts the Saussurean concept of how the system is represented by the observed *actes de parole*. But, as I see it at least, this has to be interpreted as Hjelmslev interpreted it; first in the framework of system and process, where the process (text) **instantiates** the system, and secondly, with a distinction between instantiation and realization. The latter refers to the stratal organization of the system (and therefore also of the process) whereby the expression is said to **realize** the content.

To take the latter point first: we assume that language is stratified. The number of strata ("levels", in Firth's terminology) that we recognize, and the kind of relationship between strata, will tend to depend on the questions we are asking and the problems we are trying to solve. For example, for certain purposes we may want to work with the Hjelmslevian model of content and expression, the only stratal boundary being the Saussurean line of arbitrariness; this is a way of pushing the grammar so far towards the interface as to incorporate the semantics within it. For other purposes, such as the study of language development, especially the move from protolanguage to language, we may want to interpret the lexicogrammar as a third, purely abstract, level of coding that gets 'slotted in' between the two interface levels of semantics and phonology. We may want to add other, higher-level strata to accommodate a theory of register, or to represent the knowledge base in a text generation program. It is the basic concept of stratification that is important.

Secondly, whereas Saussure, in separating *langue* from *parole*, drew the conclusion that linguistics was a theory of *langue*, systemic theory follows Hjelmslev in encompassing both. For a linguist, to describe language without accounting for text is sterile; to describe text without relating it to language is vacuous. The major problem perhaps is that of interpreting the text as process, and the system as evolution (its ontogenesis in the language development of children): in other words, of representing both the system and its instantiation in dynamic as well as in synoptic terms. Dynamic models of semiotic systems are not yet very well developed, and this is one of the problems that theorists of language now have to solve.

6 It is a general feature of semiotic systems that they develop and function in a context, and that meaning is a product of the relationship between the system and its environment – where that environment may be another semiotic system. For language, the context of the system is the higher-level semiotics which it serves to realize; hence it is the stratal representation that allows us to interpret the context of the system (Malinowski's "context of culture"). It is in this sense that semantics is an interface ("interlevel", in earlier terminology), namely when we are

considering it as the relationship between lexicogrammar and some higher-level semiotic. The context of a text, on the other hand, is Malinowski's "context of situation": the configuration of semiotic processes that are constitutive of its rhetorical structure and shape its ideational, interpersonal and textual characteristics. Systemic theory has always been explicitly contextual, in both these senses, offering contextual explanations for such problems as how children learn language from what goes on around them and how language provides a grid for the construction of models of experience.

7 Finally, given the tradition to which it belongs, it is to be expected that those using systemic theory have tended to take a particularist rather than a generalist position with regard to linguistic categories. In part, this has been to avoid claiming universality for categories such as "cases", or phonological features, that seemed far too specific to bear such a theoretical load, but equally, perhaps, from the knowledge that, while no one is likely to question the identity of all languages at a sufficiently abstract level, for most purposes for which linguistic theory is used it is **differences** among languages that need to be understood – while in those applications where only one language is concerned, the universality or otherwise of its categories is irrelevant.

I am not suggesting for a moment that these observations are acts of faith to which all 'systemicists' subscribe; but that it is an inclination to adopt viewpoints such as these that leads people to explore the potential of systemic theory. What is perhaps a unifying factor among these who work within this framework is a strong sense of the social accountability of linguistics and of linguists. Systemic theory is designed not so much to prove things as to do things. It is a form of praxis. I have often emphasized that language, both in its nature and in its ontogenetic development, clearly reveals a dual function; it is at once, and inseparably, a means of action and a means of reflection. Linguistics, as metalanguage, has to serve the same twofold purpose. Systemic theory is explicitly constructed both for thinking with and for acting with. Hence – like language, again – it is rather elastic and rather extravagant. To be an effective tool for these purposes, a theory of language may have to share these properties with language itself; to be non-rigid, so that it can be stretched and squeezed into various shapes as required, and to be non-parsimonious, so that it has more power at its disposal than is actually needed in any one context.

Systemic theory, then, is a way of thinking about language and of working on language – and through language, on other things. But it is also a symbolic system; and, as every infant knows, symbols do not affect things, only people. Thus 'applying' linguistics is using a linguistic theory to act on people. But thinking about language is also, of course, thinking about people, since there is no language other than is people's acts of meaning; so that action and reflection in linguistics are not very clearly separated activities. Just as, in the evolved adult language, mood and transitivity are mapped into a single clause, so that one cannot mean in one way without also meaning in the other, so in reflecting on how people communicate we are likely to be also acting on their communicative processes. It seems to me that this is a perspective which most systemicists share.

III.8(1985):192-8

The Language of Science (Volume 5)

Higher order consciousness is semiotic consciousness; it is this which transforms experience into meaning. From my point of view in this paper, with its focus on language, higher order consciousness depends on two critical steps by which language evolved. One I have already introduced: that of functional diversity, or **metafunction**: the principle that 'meaning' is a parallel mode of activity (the semiotic, alongside and in dialectic relation with the material) which simultaneously both construes experience and enacts the social process. The other critical step is stratal organization, or **stratification**.

Primary semiotic systems – those of other species, and the "protolanguage" of human infants before they embark on the mother tongue – are not stratified; they are inventories of signs, without a grammar. Such systems cannot create meaning; their contexts are 'given' constructs like 'here I am', 'let's be together', 'I want that' (which we distort, of course, by glossing them in adult language wordings). Language, the semiotic of higher order consciousness, is **stratified**: it has a stratum of lexicogrammar 'in between' the meaning and the expression (Halliday and Martin 1993, Chapter 2). The "signified" part of the original sign has now evolved into a meaning space, within which the meaning potential can be indefinitely expanded (Figure 3.2). Such a system can **create** meaning; its text-forming resources engender a discursive flow which is then modified (rather like the airstream is modified, on the expression plane, by articulation and intonation) so that it becomes at the same time both interactive (dialogic) and representational.

In the primary semiotic, "content" is formed directly at the interface with the experiential world – hence it is 'given', as described above. In the higher order stratified semiotic, meaning is created across a semiotic space which is defined by the **semantic** stratum (itself interfacing, as

stratal \ metafunctional	ideational	interpersonal	textual
semantic			
lexicogrammatical			

Figure 3.2 The 'meaning space' defined by stratification and metafunction

before, with the world of experiential phenomena) and the **lexicogram-matical** stratum, a new, purely abstract level of semiotic organization which interfaces only with the two material interfaces. The semiotic energy of the system comes from the lexicogrammar.

This 'thick', dimensional semiotic thus creates meaning on two strata, with a relation of **realization** between them: the semantic, and the lexicogrammatical – analogous to Hjelmslev's "content substance" and "content form" within his "content plane". If we focus now on the ideational function, we can represent the outline of the way experience is construed into meaning in the grammar of English along the following lines:

	semantic		lexicogrammatical
rank:	sequence (of figures)	realized by	clause complex
	figure	"	clause
	element (of figure)	"	group/phrase
types of element:	process	realized by	verbal group
	participating entity	"	nominal group
	circumstance	"	adverbial group or prepositional phrase
	relation	"	conjunction

For example: *the driver drove the bus too rapidly down the hill, so the brakes failed* (Figure 3.3).

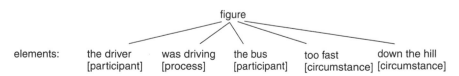

		figure			
elements:	the driver	was driving	the bus	too fast	down the hill
	[participant]	[process]	[participant]	[circumstance]	[circumstance]

Figure 3.3 Construal of experience

331

Thus the grammar, in a stratified system, sets up categories and relationships which have the effect of transforming experience into meaning. In creating a formal distinction such as that between verb and noun, the grammar is theorizing about processes: that a distinction can be made, of a very general kind, between two facets: the process itself, and entities that are involved in it.

But, as remarked above, since the grammar has the power of construing, by the same token (that is, by virtue of being stratified) it can also deconstrue, and reconstrue along different lines. Since stratification involves mapping meanings into forms, 'process' into verbal and 'participant' into nominal, it also allows remapping – say, of 'process' into a nominal form: the previous clause could be reworded as a nominal group *the driver's overrapid downhill driving of the bus*. The experience has now been retransformed – in other words, it has undergone a process of metaphor. A stratified system has inherent metaphoric power.

V.3(1998):53–5

Computational and Quantitative Studies (Volume 6)

The general term for referring to systems of meaning is **semiotic** systems. Note that the word "semiotic" here means 'having to do with meaning' rather than 'having to do with signs'; and that the term "system" always covers **both system and process** – both the potential and its output. Thus a semiotic system is a **meaning potential** together with its **instantiation** in acts of meaning.

One special kind of semiotic system is a **semantic** system; this is the meaning system of a natural language (HAL). What distinguishes a semantic system from semiotic systems of other types is that a semantic system is founded on a **grammar**, a system of **wordings** (words together with associated structural patterns); it is the presence of a grammar that gives language its unique potential for creating meaning.

In order to explore this further, let me first set up a simple evolutionary typology of systems:

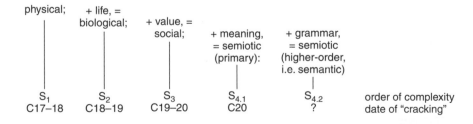

Semiotic systems are of a fourth order of complexity, in that they are at once semiotic **and** social **and** biological **and** physical. The bottom line of the figure shows the approximate date of "cracking the code" of these systems (bringing them within the domain of "scientific" inquiry).

Semiotic systems first evolve in the form of what Gerald Edelman calls "primary consciousness" (see e.g. his (1992) *Bright Air, Brilliant Fire*). They evolve as inventories of *signs*, in the classical sense of this term: that is, content/expression pairs. We find a system of this kind (a "primary semiotic", $S_{4.1}$) developed by human infants in the first year of their lives. (I have referred to this system as "protolanguage"; see Collected Works Vol. 4.) Such a system has no grammar. The more complex type of semiotic system is that which evolves in the form of what Edelman calls "higher order consciousness". This has a grammar; and it appears to be unique to adult (i.e. post-infancy) human beings, who learn it as "mother tongue" from early in the second year of life. It is this higher-order semiotic that we commonly refer to simply as "language", and we give names to its different varieties: "Japanese", "Chinese", "English" and so on.

Certain features of the protolanguage, the primary semiotic, persist into adult life, for example expressions of pain, anger, astonishment or fear ("interjections" like *ouch!, oy!, wow!*). On the other hand, human adults also develop numerous non-linguistic semiotic systems: forms of ritual, art forms etc.; these have no grammars of their own, but they are parasitic on natural language – their meaning potential derives from the fact that those who use them **also** have a grammar. Thus all human semiotic activity, making and exchanging meanings, from early childhood onwards, depends on natural language.

What, then, is a *grammar*? And how does it reshape a semiotic system? A grammar is a purely abstract semiotic construct (that is, having no direct interface with material phenomena) that evolves as a distinct "stratum" **in between** the content and the expression. Hence a semiotic system with a grammar in it is said to be "stratified".

A system of this kind – that is, a higher-order semiotic organized around a grammar – has a unique property that is critical from our point of view in this present context: it has the potential for **creating** meaning. A primary semiotic (such as a human infant's protolanguage) "means" by a process of reflection: its meanings are **given**, from elsewhere. These are meanings such as 'here I am!', 'I'm in pain', 'let's be together', 'that's nice!'. By contrast, a stratified system – a language in the adult sense – can **constitute**: it does not **reflect** meaning, it **creates** meaning. It creates meaning in contexts of function; and because the meanings are non-randomly related to features of the context, it can also create the contexts themselves. For example: the grammar of English construes a particular class of phenomena as 'flash' + 'lightning', as in *there was a flash of lightning*, or *lightning flashed*. Now, if I say *there was a flash of lightning*, there may be a thunderstorm going on outside the building. On the other hand, I may just be telling you a story – or even presenting a paper about language.

The functional contexts of language fall into two major types; and the semiotic function that language is performing differs as between the two types. On the one hand, language constitutes human **experience**; and in this aspect, its function is to *construe* – language **imposes order on** the world that lies around us, and within our own bodies. On the other hand, language constitutes human **relationships**; and in this aspect, its function is not to construe but to *enact* – language **brings about** our ongoing social interaction. The grammar integrates these two modes of meaning into a single structure, such that every instance – everything we say or write, listen to or read – "means" in these two ways at once. (In the process of doing this, it creates a third functional context of its own; I will come back to this in a moment.) Thus, I cannot give you a command (interpersonal function) without tying that command to some domain of experience, such as driving a car; and I cannot talk about driving a car (experiential) unless combining it with some interpersonal act, such as giving a command. Even if the driving instructor shouts out one single word, such as *Brake!*, this carries a full grammatical load in both these functional contexts. We refer to these major functional types as *metafunctions*; such a system is said to be metafunctionally *diversified*.

This interdependence of the two metafunctions, the experiential (or *ideational*, to give it its more inclusive name) and the interpersonal, is central to the evolution of language, and to its persistence through constant change in interaction with its environment. The ideational mode of meaning corresponds to what people usually think of as "meaning" in the ordinary sense: that is, 'content', especially 'referential content'. It is language as the categorization of human experience: language taking over the material processes and conditions of human existence and transforming them into meanings. We usually become aware of this *semiotic transformation* only when we think of systematic, scientific or technical knowledge, where we have a clear sense of the semiotic energy involved (for example in writing a theoretical paper); compare Lemke's (1984) observation that "a scientific theory is a system of related meanings". But all knowledge is like this. To "know" anything is to have transformed it into meaning; and what we call "understanding" is the process of that transformation.

But how does this transformation take place? The explanation lies in the metafunctional diversity. Experience is construed (understood, known) in the course of, and by means of, being acted out interpersonally; and in the same way, interpersonal relations are enacted in the course of, and by means of, being construed ideationally. And, as I noted a moment ago, the two are integrated together, and activated, by a third component of the grammar – a third metafunction, which we call the **textual** – which creates a flow of meaning, a semiotic current, that we know as **discourse**. It is this metafunctional diversity in the grammar that has enabled human language to evolve as the form of higher-order consciousness. In commonsense terms, what makes it possible for humans to develop and use language, in the contexts of daily life, is that every linguistic act (every **act of meaning**) involves both talking about the world and acting upon those who are in it. Both these sets of phenomena may of course be purely imaginary; that in itself is the best demonstration of the constitutive power of language.

VI.9(1995):198–202

Language and Society (Volume 10)

3.3 Socio-semantics of language development
A child learning his mother tongue is learning how to mean; he is building up a meaning potential in respect of a limited number of social functions (see 1.7, X.5(1975):178-9). These functions constitute the semiotic environment of a very small child, and may be thought of as universals of human culture.

The meanings the child can express at this stage derive very directly from the social functions. For example, one of the functions served by the child's "proto-language" is the regulatory function, that of controlling the behaviour of other people; and in this function he is likely to develop meanings such as 'do that some more' (continue or repeat what you've just been doing), and 'don't do that'. How does he get from these to the complex and functionally remote meanings of the adult semantic system?

These language-engendering functions, or 'proto-contexts', are the origin at one and the same time both of the social context and of the semantic system. The child develops his ability to mean by a gradual process of generalization and abstraction, which in the case of Nigel appeared to go somewhat along the following lines. Out of the six functions of his proto-language (instrumental, regulatory, interactional, personal, heuristic and imaginative), he derived a simple but highly general distinction between language as a means of doing and language as a means of knowing – with the latter, at this stage, interpretable functionally as 'learning'. As he moved into the phase of transition into the adult system, at around 18 months, he assigned every utterance to one or another of these generalized functional categories, encoding the distinction by means of intonation: all 'learning' utterances were on a falling tone, and all 'doing' utterances on a rising tone. As forms of interaction, the latter required a response (increasingly, as time went on, a **verbal** response) while the former did not.

From the moment when this semantic principle was adopted, however, it ceased to satisfy, since Nigel already needed a semiotic system which would enable him to do both these things at once – to use language in both the learning mode and the doing mode within a single utterance. Without this ability he could not engage in true dialogue; the system could not develop a dynamic for the adoption and assignment of semiotic roles in verbal interaction. At this point, two steps were required, or really one complex step, for effectively completing the transition to the adult system. One was a further abstraction of the basic functional opposition, such that it came to be incorporated into his semantic system, as the two components of "ideational" and "interpersonal"; in the most general terms, the former developed from 'learning' function, the latter from the 'doing' function. The other step was the introduction of a lexicogrammar, or syntax, making it possible for these two modes of meaning to be expressed simultaneously in the form of integrated lexicogrammatical structures.

The term "socio-semantics of language development" refers to this process, whereby the original social functions of the infant's protolanguage are reinterpreted first as *macro-functions*, and then as *meta-functions*, functional components in the organization of the semantic system. These components, as remarked earlier (see 2.5, X.5(1975):183-4), are clearly seen in the adult language; the options show a high degree of mutual constraint within one component but a very low degree of constraint between components. At the same time, looked at from another point of view, what the child has done is finally to dissociate the concept of 'function' from that of 'use'; the functions evolve into components of the semantic system, and the uses into what we are calling social contexts or situation types. For a detailed treatment of this topic see Halliday (1975b).

X.5(1975):193–5

* * *

3. LANGUAGE AS SOCIAL SEMIOTIC

3.1 Variation and social meaning

The distinction between language as system and language as institution is an important one for the investigation of problems of language and society. But these are really two aspects of a more general set of phenomena, and in any interpretation of the 'sociolinguistic order' we need to bring them together again.

A significant step in this direction is taken by variation theory. We have said that a feature of language as **institution** is that it is variable: different groups of speakers, or the same speakers in different task-roles, use different dialects or registers. But this is not to imply that there is no variation in the **system**. Some linguists would deny this, and would explain all variation institutionally. Others (myself among them) would argue that this is to make too rigid a distinction between the system and the institution, and would contend that a major achievement of social dialectology has been to show that dialect-like variation is a normal feature of the speech of the individual, at least in some but possibly in all communities. At certain contexts in the language a speaker will select, with a certain probability, one among a small set of variants all of which are equivalent in the sense that they are alternative realizations of the same higher-level configuration. The conditions determining this probability may be linguistic or social or some combination of the two. To know the probability of a particular speaker pronouncing a certain variant (say [t], glottal stop or zero) at a certain point in the speech chain (say word-final), we take the product of the conditioning effects of a set of variables such as: is the word lexical or structural? does the following word begin with a vowel? is the phrase thematic? is the speaker angry? and is his father a member of the working class? (This is, of course, a caricature, but it gives a fair representation of the way these things are.)

So variation, which we first recognize as a property of language as institution (in the form of variation **between** speakers, of a dialectal kind), begins to appear as an extension of variation which is a property of the system. A 'dialect' is then just a sum of variants having a strong tendency to co-occur. In this perspective, dialectal variation is made out to be not so much a consequence of the social structure as an outcome of the inherent nature of language itself.

But this is one-sided. In the last analysis, the linguistic system is the product of the social system; and seen from that angle, dialect-like variation **within** an individual is a special case of variation **between** individuals, not the other way round. The significant point, however, is that there is no sharp line between this externally conditioned, so-called "sociolinguistic" variation that is found in the speech of an individual **because** it is a property of language as institution, and the purely internally conditioned variation that occurs within a particular part of the linguistic system (e.g. morphophonemic alternation). Conditioning environments may be of any kind; there is ultimately no discontinuity between such apparently diverse phenomena as (i) select [ʔ] not [t] before a consonant and (ii) select [ʔ] not [t] before a king. This explains how it comes about that all variation is potentially meaningful; any set of alternants may (but need not) become the bearer of social information and social value.

3.2 Language and social reality

Above and beyond "language as system" and "language as institution" lies the more general, unifying concept that I have labelled "language as social semiotic": language in the context of the culture as a semiotic system.

Consider the way a child constructs his social reality. Through language as system – its organization into levels of coding and functional components – he builds up a model of the exchange of meanings, and learns to construe the interpersonal relationships, the experiential phenomena, the forms of natural logic and the modes of symbolic interaction into coherent patterns of social context. He does this very young; this is in fact what makes it possible for him to learn the language successfully – the two processes go hand in hand.

Through language as institution – its variation into dialects and registers – he builds up a model of the social system. This follows a little way behind his learning of grammar and semantics (compare the interesting suggestion by Sankoff (1974) that some patterns at first learnt as categorical are later modified to become variable), though it is essentially part of single unitary process of language development. In the broadest terms, from dialectal variation he learns to construe the patterns of social hierarchy, and from variation of the 'register' kind he gains an insight into the structure of knowledge.

So language, while it represents reality **referentially**, through its words and structures, also represents reality **metaphorically** through its own internal and external form. (1) The functional organization of the semantics symbolizes the structure of human interaction (the semiotics of social contexts, as we expressed it earlier). (2) Dialectal and "diatypic" (register) variation symbolize respectively the structure of society and the structure of human knowledge.

But as language becomes a metaphor of reality, so by the same process reality becomes a metaphor of language. Since reality is a social construct, it can be constructed only through an exchange of meanings. Hence meanings are seen as constitutive of reality. This, at least, is the natural conclusion for the present era, when the exchange of information tends to replace the exchange of goods-and-services as the primary mode of social action. With a sociological linguistics we should be able to stand back from this perspective, and arrive at an interpretation of language through understanding its place in the long-term evolution of the social system.

3.3 Methodological considerations
It has been customary among linguists in recent years to represent language in terms of rules. In investigating language and the social system, it is important to transcend this limitation and to interpret language not as a set of rules but as a **resource**. I have used the term *meaning potential* to characterize language in this way.

When we focus attention on the processes of human interaction, we are seeing this meaning potential at work. In the microsemiotic encounters of daily life, we find people making creative use of their resources of meaning, and continuously modifying these resources in the process.

Hence in the interpretation of language, the organizing concept that we need is not structure but **system**. Most recent linguistics has been structure-bound (since structure is what is described by rules). With the notion of system we can represent language as a resource, in terms of the choices that are available, the interconnection of these choices, and the conditions affecting their access. We can then relate these choices to recognizable and significant social contexts, using socio-semantic networks; and investigate questions such as the influence of various social factors on the meanings exchanged by parents and children. The data are the observed facts of 'text-in-situation': what people say in real life, not discounting what they think they might say and what they think they ought to say. (Or rather, what they **mean**, since saying is only one way of meaning.) In order to interpret what is observed, however, we have to relate it to the system: (i) to the linguistic system, which it then helps to explain, and (ii) to the social context, and through that to the social system.

After a period of intensive study of language as an idealized philosophical construct, linguists have come around to taking account of the fact that people talk to each other. In order to solve purely internal problems of its own history and structure, language has had to be taken out of its glass case, dusted, and put back in a living environment – into a "context of situation", in Malinowski's term. But it is one thing to have a 'socio-' (that is, real life) component in the explanation of the facts of language. It is quite another thing to seek explanations that relate the linguistic system to the social system, and so work towards some general theory of language and social structure.

X.9(1978):259–63

Additional readings

On Grammar (Volume 1) – 8(1979); 15(1996)
Linguistic Studies of Text and Discourse (Volume 2) – 2(1977); 5(1987):150–2
On Language and Linguistics (Volume 3) – 4(1977):93,113–5; 5(1987):116–24, 131–7; 6(1990):147–51, 171; 9(1992); 10(1993); 13(2001):275–7; 16(1992); 17(1992); 18(1995)
The Language of Early Childhood (Volume 4) – 1(1998); 4(1974); 5(1978):140–3; 7(1975); 9(1983):212–26; 11(1991); 13(1975); 15(1993)
The Language of Science (Volume 5) – 2(1998):43–4; 4(1999); 8(1993):216–25
Language and Education (Volume 9) – 5(1988)
Language and Society (Volume 10) – 5(1975):179–86, 196

Chapter Sixteen

STRUCTURE AND RANK

Summary

The fundamental categories for the theory of grammar are unit, structure, class and system. Language is patterned activity, and units are pattern carriers. Rank is the scale on which the units are ranged. Rankshift occurs when a given unit is transferred to a lower rank. A structure is made up of ordered elements. Sequence is one formal exponent of the more abstract notion of order. Delicacy has to do with the depth of detail, ranging along a cline from least delicate at one end, i.e. primary, to those small infinities at the opposite "where distinctions are so fine that they cease to be distinctions at all", i.e. secondary.

Structural types include configurational, prosodic and periodic. While experiential meaning is well accounted for in terms of a configuration of discrete parts, including process, participant and circumstance, interpersonal meaning is more often prosodic, involving intonation, and textual meaning tends more toward the periodic, with the flow of discourse understood less in terms of clumps of constituents than wave-like movements.

Selected readings

On Grammar (Volume 1)

2 GRAMMAR

2.1 Grammar is that level of linguistic form at which operate closed systems.[16,17] Since a system is by definition closed, the use of the term "closed" here is a mnemonic device; but since "system" alone will be used as the name of one of the four fundamental grammatical categories (see I.2(1961):52–5) it is useful to retain "closed system" when referring to the system as the crucial criterion for distinguishing grammar from lexis.

A closed system is a set of terms with these characteristics:

(a) The number of terms is finite: they can be listed as A B C D, and all other items E . . . are outside the system.
(b) Each term is exclusive of all the others: a given term A cannot be identical with B or C or D.
(c) If a new term is added to the system this changes the meaning of all the others.[18]

Any part of linguistic form which is not concerned with the operation of closed systems belongs to the level of lexis. The distinction between closed system patterns and open set patterns in language is in fact a cline; but the theory has to treat them as two distinct types of pattern requiring different categories. For this reason General Linguistic theory must here provide both a theory of grammar and a theory of lexis, and also a means of relating the two. A description depending on General Linguistic theory will need to separate the descriptions of the two levels both from each other and from the description of their interrelations. This paper is primarily concerned with the theory of grammar, though reference will be made to lexis at various points.

2.2 The fundamental categories for the theory of grammar are four: *unit*, *structure*, *class* and *system*. These are categories of the highest order of abstraction: they are established, and interrelated, in the theory. If one asks: "why these four, and not three, or five, or another four?", the answer must be: because language is like that – because these four, and no others, are needed to account for the data: that is, to account for all grammatical patterns that emerge by generalization from the data. As the primary categories of the theory, they make possible a coherent account of what grammar is and of its place in language, and a comprehensive description of the grammars of languages, neither of which is possible without them.

Each of the four is specifically related to, and logically derivable from, each of the others. There is no relation of precedence or logical priority among them. They are all mutually defining: as with theoretical categories in general, "definition" in the lexicographical sense is impossible, since no one category is defined until all the others are, in the totality of the theory.[19] The order chosen here for exposition is therefore simply that which seemed the easiest: namely the order in which they are listed above.

The relation of these categories to each other and to the data involve three distinct scales of abstraction, those of *rank*, *exponence* and *delicacy*;

these are considered separately (see I.2(1961):55-9) but have also to be referred to in connection with the categories. In discussing these I have used the terms "hierarchy", "taxonomy" and 'cline' as general scale–types. A hierarchy is taken to mean a system of terms related along a single dimension which must be one involving some form of logical precedence (such as inclusion).[20] A taxonomy is taken to mean a special type of hierarchy, one with two additional characteristics: (i) there is a constant relation of each term to the term immediately following it, and a constant reciprocal relation of each to that immediately preceding it; and (ii) degree is significant, so that the place in order of each one of the terms, stable as the distance in number of steps from either end, is a defining characteristic of that term.[21] A cline resembles a hierarchy in that it involves relation along a single dimension; but instead of being made up of a number of discrete terms a cline is a continuum carrying potentially infinite gradation.

2.3 In this view of linguistics description is, as already emphasized, a body of method derived from theory, and **not** a set of procedures. This has one important consequence. If description is procedural, the only way of evaluating a given description is by reference to the procedures themselves: a good description is one that has carried out the right procedures in the right order, but for any more delicate evaluation external criteria have to be invoked. Moreover, every language has to be treated as if it was unknown, otherwise procedural rules will be violated; so the linguist has to throw away half his evidence and a good few of his tools.

A theory on the other hand provides a means for evaluating descriptions without reference to the order in which the facts are accounted for. The linguist makes use of all he knows and there is no priority of dependence among the various parts of the description. The best description is then that which, comprehensiveness presupposed, is maximally grammatical: that is, makes maximum use of the theory to account for a maximum amount of the data. Simplicity has then to be invoked only when it is necessary to decide between fewer systems with more terms and more systems with fewer terms; and since both information theory and linguistic intuition favour the latter even this preference might be built in to the theory.[22]

3 UNIT

3.1 Language is patterned activity. At the formal level, the patterns are patterns of meaningful organization: certain regularities are exhibited over certain stretches of language activity. An essential feature of the stretches over which formal patterns operate is that they are of varying extent.

Abstracting out those of lexis, where the selection is from open sets, we find that the remaining, closed system, patterns are associated with stretches that not only are of differing extent but also appear as it were one inside the other, in a sort of one-dimensional Chinese box arrangement. Since language activity takes place in time, the simplest formulation of this dimension is that it is the dimension of time, or, for written language, of linear space: the two can then be generalized as "progression" and the relation between two items in progression is one of "sequence".

But there is a danger here. It is obvious that **absolute** measurements of linear progression belong to language **substance** (where one may be interested in the number of seconds, or possibly even the number of inches, occupied by an utterance). What is less obvious is that the whole dimension of progression in fact belongs to substance, and that the stretches which carry grammatical pattern – or rather the members of that abstract category that we set up to account for these stretches – have to be ranged on a dimension of which linear progression is only a manifestation in substance: a dimension we may call "order".[23] By implication, this allows that in any given instance sequence may **not** manifest order, or that order may have other manifestations; even if this never happens, the distinction is necessary until such time as it is shown that the theory does not need to make provision for its happening. In fact it does happen: sequence is a variable, and must be replaced in the theory by the more abstract dimension of order.[24]

3.2 The category set up to account for the stretches that carry grammatical patterns is the *unit*. The units of grammar form a hierarchy that is a taxonomy. To talk about any hierarchy, we need a conversational scale; the most appropriate here might seem that of size, going from "largest" to "smallest"; on the other hand size is difficult to represent in tables and diagrams, and may also trap one into thinking in substantial terms, and a vertical scale, from "highest" to "lowest", has advantages here. For the moment we may use both, eventually preferring the latter. The relation among the units, then, is that, going from top (largest) to bottom (smallest), each **consists of** one, or of more than one, of the unit next below (next smaller). The scale on which the units are in fact ranged in the theory needs a name, and may be called *rank*.

"Consists of", like "unit" and "rank", also belongs to the theory: its realization in form varies between and within languages, and is stated of course in description.[25] The possibilities are sequence, inclusion and conflation. Thus if in a given instance a unit of one rank consists of two units of rank next below, these may appear in form as one following, interrupting, or overlaying the other.

Three further points about the rank relation need to be clarified. First, the theory allows for downward **rankshift**: the transfer of a (formal realization of a) given unit to a lower rank. Second, it does not allow for upward rankshift. Third, only whole units can enter into higher units. Taken together these three mean that a unit can include, in what it consists of, a unit of rank higher than or equal to itself but not a unit of rank more than one degree lower than itself; and not, in any case, a part of any unit.[26]

3.3 The number of units in the hierarchy is a feature of the description. It varies from language to language, but is fixed by the description for each language, or rather for each describendum or "état de langue". The possibility of there being only one is excluded by the theory, since a hierarchy cannot be composed of one member. It is, however, theoretically possible to conceive of a language having only two, and an artificial language could be constructed on these lines (whereas it would not be possible to construct an artificial language having only one unit). English grammar, as far as it has been studied to date, seems to require five, though further, statistical, work on grammar might yield at least one more.

No special status, other than that[27] presupposed by rank, is assigned by grammatical theory to any one unit. Since in any case only two, as a minimum, are required, only two would be available for special status. As it happens we can assign special status to two grammatical units by reference to other levels on a "more / less" basis. There will always be one unit which, more than any other, offers itself as an item for contextual statement because it does the language work in situations: so it might as well always have the same name: **sentence**. There will be another unit, always lower in rank, which more than any other (but again **not exclusively**) enters into another type of pattern and thus offers itself as an item for lexical statement;[28] this we may as well always call the **word**. So, in grammatical theory, all languages have at least two units; in description, all languages have sentences and all languages have words – but the "sentenceness" of the sentence and the "wordness" of the word do not derive from the theory of grammar.

Various names are available for those above, below or in between when they turn up. For English, for the two units between sentence and word the terms **clause** and **phrase** are generally used. It is at the rank of the phrase that there is most confusion – because there are here the greatest difficulties – in the description of English; one reason is that in English this unit carries a fundamental **class** division (see I.2(1961):49-52), so fundamental that it is useful to have two names for this unit in order to be able to talk about it: I propose to call it the **group**, but to make a **class**

345

distinction within it between *group* and *phrase*. Below the word, English has one unit, called by the general name for the unit of lowest rank, the *morpheme*.[29]

So in the description of English the sentence[30] consists of one or more complete clauses, the clause of one or more complete groups, the group of one or more complete words and the word of one or more complete morphemes. The descriptive meaning of "consists of", and the possibilities of rankshift (including recursive rankshift), are stated as and where applicable. One distinction that is often useful is between a member of a unit that consists of only one member of the unit next below and one that consists of more than one; the former may be called *simple* and the latter *compound*, but if this is done the terms must be kept rigorously to this, and no other, use.[31]

3.4 The theory requires that each unit should be fully identifiable in description. This means that, if the description is textual, every item of the text is accounted for at all ranks, through the various links of the *exponence* chain which involve, of course, the remaining theoretical categories. If the description is exemplificatory, exactly the same is implied, except that the description proceeds from category to exponent instead of from exponent to category.

It will be clear from the discussion in the next sections that there can be no question of independent identification of the exponents of the different units, since criteria of any given unit always involve reference to others, and therefore indirectly to all the others. A clause can only be identified as a clause if a sentence can be identified as a sentence and a group as a group, and so on up and down the line. For this reason description is not and can never be unidirectional: it is essential to "shunt", and "shunting" is a descriptive method that is imposed on description by theory.

4 STRUCTURE

4.1 The unit being the category of pattern-carrier, what is the nature of the patterns it carries? In terms once again of language as activity, and therefore in linear progression, the patterns take the form of the repetition of like events. Likeness, at whatever degree of abstraction, is of course a cline, ranging from "having everything in common" to "having nothing in common". The commonplace that no two events are ever identical, that the same thing can never happen twice, is of no relevance whatever to linguistics; as soon as description starts, however little the generalization involved, absolute identity is a necessary hypothesis, which is then built into the theory, as one endpoint of the likeness cline. Likeness, including absolute identity, is of course redefined for each level and each category.

In grammar the category set up to account for likeness between events in successivity is the ***structure***.[32] If the relation between events in successivity is ***syntagmatic***, the structure is the highest abstraction of patterns of syntagmatic relations. The scale used for talking about it, and for its graphic display, will most naturally be the orthographic scale: to those of us brought up on the roman alphabet this happens to run horizontally from left to right, which is enough reason for adopting this version of the scale. But, as in the case of the unit, it must be stressed that linear progression itself is a feature of substance. A structure is made up of ***elements*** which are graphically represented as being in linear progression; but the theoretical relation among them is one of ***order***. Order may, but does not necessarily, have as its realization ***sequence***, the formal relation carried by linear progression; sequence is at a lower degree of abstraction than order and is one possible formal exponent of it.[33]

4.2 A structure is thus an arrangement of elements ordered in ***places***. Places are distinguished by order alone: a structure XXX consists of three places. Different elements, on the other hand, are distinguished by some relation other than that of order: a structure XYZ consists of three elements which are (and must be, to form a structure) place-ordered, though they can be listed (X, Y, Z) as an inventory of elements making up the particular structure.[34] A structure is always a structure **of a given unit**.

Each unit may display a range of possible structures, and the only theoretical restriction is that each unit must carry at least one structure that consists of more than one place.[35] Each place and each element in the structure of a given unit is defined with reference to the unit next below. Each place is the place of operation of one member of the unit next below, considered as one occurrence. Each element represents the potentiality of operation of a member of one **grouping** of members of the unit next below, considered as one item–grouping.[36] It follows from this that the lowest unit has no structure;[37] if it carried structure, there would be another unit below it.

4.3 In description, structures are stated as linear arrangements of symbols, each symbol (occurrence) standing for one place and each different symbol (item) standing for one element. Since elements of structure "exist" only at this degree of abstraction, the relation "stands for" means simply "is shorthand for", like that of an initial: " 'U' stands for 'United'." In a few cases traditional names exist which can usefully serve as names for elements of structure, with the initial letter as the descriptive symbol. In the statement of English clause structure, for example, four elements are needed, for which the widely accepted terms ***subject***, ***predicator***, ***complement*** and ***adjunct*** are appropriate.[38] These yield four distinct symbols, so that S, P, C, A would be the inventory of elements of English clause structure. All clause structures can then be stated as combinations of these four in different places: SAPA, ASP, SPC, ASPCC, etc. For one type of group we have the names *modifier*, *head*, *qualifier*, giving an inventory M, H, Q: here, if the total range of possible structures is H, MH, HQ, MHQ, these possibilities can be stated in a single formula, where parentheses indicate "may or may not be present", as (M) H (Q).[39]

In other cases, no names come ready to hand; names can be imported or coined, or arbitrary symbols chosen – colours, for example, have advantages over letters in presentation, though there are not enough of them and they have to be redefined in description for each unit. It is tempting sometimes to derive the symbols from the name given to the grouping of members of the unit next below which operates at the given element (as if one were to put V instead of P because what operates at P is the verbal group); but it is important to avoid identifying this grouping, which belongs to a different category as well as a different rank, with the element itself – therefore if this method is to be used at all it must be used all the time and a statement made to cover it.[40]

There are some instances where an element of structure is identified as such solely by reference to formal sequence: where the element is **defined by** place stated as absolute or relative position in sequence. It is useful to indicate that here sequence is so to speak built in to structure, and this can be shown by an arrow placed over the symbols for the elements concerned. For example, in English clause structure it is a crucial criterion of the element S that it precedes $\vec{P}$ in sequence: structures can be stated as S$\vec{P}$CA, SA$\vec{P}$A, AS$\vec{P}$, etc.[41] This displays the contrast between this situation, where S is crucially defined by position relative to P, and realized sequences of elements which are not, however, defined by sequence, which may be indicated by simple linearity of the symbols.[42]

4.4 In the consideration of the places and elements of structure of each unit, which of course vary from language to language and from unit to unit within a language, a new scale enters, that of *delicacy* (see I.2(1961):58-9). This is depth of detail, and is a cline running from a fixed point at one end (least delicate, or *primary*) to that undefined but theoretically crucial point (probably statistically definable) where distinctions are so fine that they cease to be distinctions at all, like a river followed up from the mouth, each of whose tributaries ends in a moorland bog. Primary structures are those which distinguish the minimum number of elements necessary to account comprehensively for the operation in the structure of the given unit of members of the unit next below: necessary, that is, for the identification of every item at all ranks. (M)H((Q)) and the various possible combinations of S, P, C, A, are primary structures: one cannot account for all words in group structure, or all groups in clause structure, with fewer than these elements or places.

Subsequent more delicate differentiations are then stated as **secondary** structures. These are still structures of the same unit, not of the unit next below; they take account of finer distinctions recognizable at the same rank.[43] Rank and delicacy are different scales of abstraction: primary group structures differ in rank from primary clause structures, but are at the same degree of delicacy; while primary and secondary clause structures differ in delicacy but not in rank.

As the description increases in delicacy the network of grammatical relations becomes more complex. The interaction of criteria makes the relation between categories, and between category and exponent, increasingly one of "more/less" rather than "either/or". It becomes necessary to weight criteria and to make statements in terms of probabilities. With more delicate secondary structures, different combinations of elements, and their relation to groupings of the unit next below, have to be stated as more and less probable.[44] The concept of "most delicate grammar", and its relation to lexis, is discussed below (see I.2(1961): 53-4 and 58-9); but the "more/less" relation itself, far from being an unexpected complication in grammar, is in fact a basic feature of language and is treated as such by the theory. It is not simply that all grammar **can** be stated in probability terms, based on frequency counts in texts: this is due to the nature of a text as a sample. But the very fact that we can recognize primary and secondary structures – that there is a scale of delicacy at all – shows that the nature of language is **not** to operate with relations of "always this and never that". Grammatical theory takes this into account by introducing a special scale, that of delicacy, to handle the improbability of certainty; this frees the rest of the theory from what would otherwise be the weakening effect of this feature of language. The category of structure, for example, is the more powerful because it can be used to state the patterns of a given unit comprehensively at the primary degree without the assumption that it has accounted for all the facts.

Notes

16. Cf. Firth (1957a: 22), and above, 1.8 n. 11; Garvin (1957); see I.2(1961):53-4, n. 60; Robins (1959).
17. "Grammar" is also the name for the study of grammar; as with "level" (above, 1.4 n. 8), it is unnecessary to distinguish between "the grammar" of a language

and "grammar" in theory and description – though a distinction is often made between "lexis" and "lexicology", the latter being the study of lexis. Again, **not** a set of discovery procedures, but a set of properties of what the linguist accounts for grammatically. The grammar of a language can only be "defined" as that part of the language that is accounted for by grammatical description.

18. The reference is, of course, in formal meaning: it is form that is under discussion. It may always happen that the addition of a new term changes the contextual meaning of at least one of the others, since terms that are formally mutually exclusive are likely to carry contextual distinctions; but this is not a property of a system. The "addition" of a new term is not of course considered as a process (though historical change is one type of instance of it): it may be displayed in any comparison of two related systems. For example, two possible systems of first and second person pronouns used by different speakers of Italian (quoted in oblique disjunct form; I = "interior to social group", E = "exterior . . ."").

1	me	me
1+	noi	moi
2I	te	te
2I+	voi	
2E	lei	voi
2E+	loro	

(The distinctions made in written Italian are ignored, since they would not affect the point.) The difference in format meaning is a function of the different number of terms: in system one *me* excludes five others, in system two only three. In contextual meaning only terms of the second group are affected.

19. Cf. Firth (1957a): "Moreover, these and other technical words are given their "meaning" by the restricted language of the theory, and by application of the theory in quoted works" (p. 2). This is true of descriptive categories too: "noun" can no more be defined in a glossary than "structure".

20. I should therefore agree with Palmer (1958) that linguistic levels do not form a hierarchy. His view is "that there are levels, but only in the widest sense, and that these are related in specific, but different, ways. The set of relationships cannot be regarded as a hierarchy, except in the loosest sense of the word". Palmer, however, appears to reintroduce procedural hierarchy when he says, "The procedure is not from phonetics via phonology to grammar, but from grammar via phonology to phonetics, though with the reminder that the phonetic statement is the basis, i.e. the ultimate justification for the analysis" (p. 240). I would rather say that there is **order** among the levels, determined by their interrelations, but (a) no hierarchy, in the **defined** sense of the word, and (b) no procedural direction. Unfortunately Palmer excludes this use of "order". "There is a stable **order** of levels . . . and, therefore, a hierarchy" (pp. 231–2, in reference to Hockett).

21. Immediate Constituent analysis, for example, yields a hierarchy that is not a taxonomy: it does not fulfil criterion (ii). (It may not always fulfil (i): cf. Hockett (1957): "There must be also at least a few utterances in which the hierarchical structure is ambiguous, since otherwise the hierarchical structure would in every case be determined by form, and order, and hence not a "primitive"" (p. 391).)

22. The theory thus leads to "polysystemic"-ness in description – both syntagmatically and paradigmatically. Syntagmatic polysystemic statement follows from the linking of classes and systems to places in structure (see I.2(1961):46-55), so that the question "how can we prove that the *b* of *beak* and the *b* of *cab* are occurrences of one and the same phoneme?" (Ebeling: 1960: 17) is regarded as an unreal one; cf. Henderson (1951: 132); Carnochan (1952: 78); Robins (1953: 96); Firth (1955: 93; 1957c: 121) and Palmer (1958: 122–4). Paradigmatically, the "simplicity" referred to here follows from the requirement of making maximum use of the category of "system" by polysystemic or "multidimensional" statement in grammar; cf. Halliday (1956: 192).

23. **Manifestation** (in substance) and **realization** (in form) are introduced here to represent different degrees along the scale of exponence (see I.2(1961):57-8). In this paper I have used **exponent** as indicating **relative** position on the exponence scale (a formal item as exponent of a formal category, and a feature of substance as exponent of a formal category or item); this departs from the practice of those who restrict the term "exponent" to **absolute** exponents in substance. As used here, *formal item* is a technical term for the endpoint of the exponence relation ("most exponential" point) **in form**: the lexical item *cat*, the word *cat* as member of the word–class of noun, the morpheme -*ing* (as class member operating at the place of an element) in word structure, etc.; it is thus already an abstraction from substance and will be stated orthographically or phonologically. In this formulation, exponence is the **only** relation by which formal category, formal item and feature of substance are linked on a **single** scale: hence the need for a single term to indicate relative position on the scale. Two defined positions on this scale can then be distinguished as "realization" and "manifestation".

24. Cf. Firth (1957a): "In these structures, one recognizes the place and order of the categories. This, however, is very different from the successivity of bits and pieces in a unidirectional time sequence" (p. 5).

25. Cf. above, 3.1 n. 23.

26. The two latter restrictions represent an important addition to the power of the **unit** as a theoretical category. The first toleration is required to account for "regressive" structures: cf. Yngve (1960: 19). As Chomsky (1957) has said, "the assumption that languages are infinite is made in order to simplify the description of these languages . . . If a grammar does not have recursive devices it will be prohibitively complex" (pp. 23, 24). Yngve makes the important distinction between "progressive" and "regressive" structures, accounting for them separately in his model. Whether or not he is right in postulating a depth limit (of about 7) for "regressive" structures, while allowing "progressive" structures to be

infinitely expanded (p. 21), they do represent very different types of "infinite-ness", and are separately accounted for in the present theory, the former with, the latter without, rankshift. This determines the nature, but does not restrict the use, of the perfectly valid arbitrary limit on delicacy which the grammar can set in each case without loss of comprehensiveness.

27. Such as the status of "being the smallest".

28. Cf. I.2(1961):49–61. The item for lexical statement is **not** to be identified on the grammatical rank scale; nor is it a **unit** at all in the sense in which the term is here used in grammar, since this use presupposes a rank scale (as well as the other terms **structure**, **class** and **system** in a system of related categories), which is absent from lexis. It is probably better to restrict the term "unit" to grammar and phonology: cf. Bazell (1953: 11) – though Bazell does not here consider lexical form.

29. So, for the description of English:

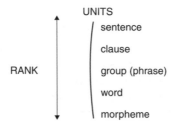

30. Statistical work on grammar may yield a further unit, above the sentence: it will then be possible to set up sentence classes, and account for sequences of them, by reference to this higher unit. Similarly in phonology we need a unit in English above the tone group to account for sequences of different tones. The grammatical and phonological "paragraph" (and perhaps 'paraphone'?) is probably within reach of a team of linguist, statistician, programmer and computer; cf. Firth (1957a): "Attention must first be paid to the longer elements of text – such as the paragraph ..." (p. 18); Harris (1952); for Hill (1958: 406), and others, this is "stylistics", but in the present theory it would come within exactly the same general framework of categories.

31. The "simple/compound" opposition is thus one of structure. It may, of course, happen that a given realization yields simple membership all the way up and down the rank scale. *Yes* may be (i.e. may be an exponent of) one sentence which is one clause which is one group which is one word which is one morpheme.

32. Cf. Robins (1953: 109); Firth (1957a, esp. 17, 30; and 1955, esp. 89, 91); Halliday (1959: 49).

33. Cf. Firth (1957a): "Elements of structure ... share a mutual expectancy in an *order* which is not merely a *sequence*" (p. 17). Since sequence is a variable, and may or may not be an exponent of structure, we find difference in sequence without difference in structure (cf. below, 4.3 n. 42), or difference in structure without difference in sequence. I am indebted to J. M. Sinclair for a recent conversational example of the latter: orthographically, *The man came(,) from the Gas Board*. Phonologically (relevant units: **tone group**, bounded by *//*, and **foot**,

by / – these are unit boundaries and have nothing to do with juncture): what was said was (tonic syllable underlined):

// 1 the / man_/ came // 1 from the / **Gas** / Board //

Grammatically, one clause, structure SP; exponent of P *came*, of S *the man . . . from the Gas Board*, being a nominal group, structure MH +Q. What might have been said was

// 1 the / man / came from the // **Gas** / Board //

Grammatically, one clause, structure SPA; exponents, S *the man*, P *came*, A *from the Gas Board*. The two are different in grammatical structure, and this difference has its exponent in phonic substance which can be stated phonologically. (That the phonological patterns, and the distinction between them, abstracted from the substance along one dimension correspond regularly (though not one / one) with the grammatical patterns, and the distinction between them, abstracted along another dimension from the same substance can be shown by the construction of other partially like clauses.) But though the difference in structure has its manifestation in substance (there **can** of course be ambiguity in substance, as in Hockett's *old men and women* (1957: 390n.), in form the difference is not realized in sequence. In sequence, *from the Gas Board* occupies the same place in both instances; in order, S and A stand in different relations to P, and *from the Gas Board* is exponent of (part of) S in the one case and of (the whole of) A in the other.

Sequence is presumably always manifested in phonic substance as linear progression; the distinction is then one of exponence, "sequence" being the name for that formal relation between formal items of which linear progression is the manifestation in phonic substance.

34. It is useful to make a distinction in the use of symbols between an inventory of elements of a structure and a structure, by the use of commas in the former. Thus, X, Y, Z is an inventory of elements, XYZ a structure composed of these elements.

35. Since a unit that carried only one-place structures would be unnecessary: if, for example, all words consist of one morpheme (i.e. the unit "word" has no structure containing more than one place), "word" and "morpheme" would be one and the same unit.

36. For the name and nature of this grouping, see I.2(1961):49–52.

37. Since the morpheme (i) is a grammatical unit and (ii) carries no grammatical structure, it has no structure. Cf. Palmer (1958: 229–30) (quoting Hockett 1955: 15):"'Morphemes are not **composed** of phonemes at all. Morphemes are indivisible units. A given morpheme is **represented** by a certain more or less compact arrangement of phonologic material . . . If we call any such representation a *morph*, then it becomes correct to say that a morph has a phonological structure – that it consists of an arrangement of phonemes.' [Hockett] recognizes that the units established at each level differ in kind, and not merely in size, from those established at other levels." The "morph" does indeed accommodate the

theoretical point (but cf. I.2(1961):65-66, n. 83), that the units differ in kind; but in accepting Hockett's view Palmer has not noted that, since they differ in kind, "size" cannot be abstracted as common to the two dimensions of abstraction for them to differ in. That is, a grammatical unit can only be exponentially coextensive (or not) with a phonological one: when it is, this is a descriptive accident for which the linguist can be thankful (cf. reference to Allen (1956) in I.2(1961):55-6, n. 64), but the grammar cannot be made to **define** the units for phonological statement (cf. the example in 4.1 n. 33 above, where two exponents of the same grammatical unit "clause" may be (systemically contrasted by being) coextensive either with one tone group or with two). And, even though we may use the categories of "unit" and "structure" both in grammar and in phonology, these are not shown to be comparable unless the two theories have the same system of primitive terms with the same interrelations.

38. As used by Hill (1958: 256). The "definitions" of these terms (i.e. the categories themselves) are of course different, since the theory differs from Hill's. Cf. I.2(1961):69-70.

39. This formulaic presentation is useful as a generalized statement of an inventory of possible structures: a list H, MH, HQ, HMQ can be generalized as (M)H(Q). This particular instance is an oversimplification, since there may be more than one exponent of M and Q: the formula would then read $(M \ldots^n)H(Q \ldots^n)$, where $\ldots^n$ allows infinite progression (not regression).

40. The real point is to avoid taking two distinct theoretical steps at once. As said I.2(1961):49-52, the relation of **class** to **structure** is such that a class of a given unit stands in one / one relation to an element of structure of the unit next above: thus, the exponent of the **element** P in the structure of the unit "clause" is the **class** "verbal" of the unit "group". We could – provided we did so consistently – replace the symbol P here by V, thus conflating two statements. But not only are there descriptive reasons for not doing so (cf. I.2(1961):51-2); it is theoretically invalid, since two sets of relations are involved (element of clause structure to unit "clause", class of group to unit "group"), and if the two steps are taken at once the crucial relation of structure to class on the rank scale is obscured.

41. If, instead, an inventory of elements is stated first, the arrow can be added (where it really belongs) in the inventory: S, $\vec{P}$, C, A. It is then no longer required in the statement of structures, since it is presupposed.

42. Cf. above, 4.1. In a Latin clause of structure SOP (O = object), sequence plays no part in the definition of the elements: so no arrow. But rearrangements of the elements, to give SPO, OSP, etc., can be usefully employed to state the more delicate distinctions beween *puer puellam amat, puellam puer amat*, etc. In English, where $\vec{SP}$ sequence is crucial to the definition of S (though various arrangements of C and A are possible), more delicate grammatical distinctions, such as those carried by intonation, must be shown secondarily.

43. For example the following two exponents of the (class) nominal (of the unit) group: *all the ten houses on the riverside* and *the finest old houses on the riverside* have the same primary structure M . . . HQ (or MMMHQ). But a more delicate

statement of M, still at group rank, shows distinct secondary structures, the first example having D_2D_bO, the second D_bOE.

44. When Hockett writes (1955: 17) "In general, then, if we find continuous-scale contrasts in the vicinity of what we are sure is language, we exclude them from language (though not from culture)", this applies (i) only to grammar and phonology, not to lexis or context (cf. Bazell 1953: 11), and (ii) only to one type of contrast, that between terms in systems. It is, indeed, a defining characteristic of a system that it cannot be a cline. But units and classes are not crucially discrete: in exponence, units display syntagmatic non-discreteness (syncretism); classes, paradigmatic non-discreteness (statable in various ways, such as multidimensional classification, assignment of an item to different classes with variable probability, etc.)

I.2(1961):40–9, 75–81

Studies in English Language (Volume 7)

2

2.1 The problem of the **clause**

It was clear to me already, when I taught my first Chinese class on 13 May 1945, that the clause was the centre of action in the grammar. At that time the clause didn't seem to exist as a general organizing category – only "compound / complex sentences" had clauses; the "simple sentence" was a sentence but not a clause. But the clause had to be introduced because it was the place, or the locus, where fundamental choices in meaning were acted out. Much of the impetus towards a "scale-and-category" grammar started from that simple observation. (See VII.Introduction(2005):xx–xxi on metafunction.)

2.2 The problem of the **system**

Categories like negative, interrogative, passive tended to be identified as isolates and then get bundled together without regard for their operational context. It seemed necessary to sort them out into their contrasting sets: to identify the system, and its terms, and to locate it at an explicit point of origin – the environment in which the selection is made, irrespective of where and how it is expressed. I needed to account for such features as:

[system]	POLARITY:	[terms]	positive/negative
"	ASPECT:	"	perfective/imperfective/neutral
"	VOICE:	"	ergative/passive/neutral
"	TRANSITIVITY:	"	intransitive/transitive

All these had the same point of origin, the "clause" – whether free or bound, and, if free, no matter whether standing alone (as "simple sentence") or in a structural relation with another (as "main clause"). Another system,

> [system] MOOD: [terms] affirmative/interrogative/imperative

was accessible to free clauses only ("affirmative" I later changed to "declarative" to accommodate to Chomskyan terminology). Thus a primary class, or any of its subclasses, could be available as the location of a systemic choice. (See VII.Introduction(2005):xx on delicacy.)

2.3 The problem of units

But other choices had different points of origin: systems such as DEIXIS, NUMBER or PERSON were associated with some smaller unit, one that had evolved out of the expansion of a word. (For this I took over Sydney Allen's term "group": hence verbal group, nominal group, adverbial group.) Other systems might have their origin in the word; for example SUBSTANCE: count/mass, or the various systems expressed by derivational morphology. But there was a limited number of such locations in a language; they corresponded to the small number of structural units needed to model constituency.

2.4 The problem of rank, and the rank scale

It was possible to identify a compositional set such as

> sentence – clause – group – word – morpheme

such that each member was the locus of a number of independent systemic choices and each could be shown to consist of whole members (one or more than one) of the unit next below. Such a "rank scale" seemed more powerful than the structuralists' "immediate constituent" analysis, where the constituent units (the "nodes") were structurally defined fragments which had no systemic value – no functional or semantic significance. The grammar of a language could be represented in terms of features, but not as a simple inventory; features were defi ned as terms in systems, and the systems sorted into independent vectors (e.g. MOOD: indicative/imperative, independent of POLARITY: positive/negative) according to the rank at which the system of options was entered. In Firthian terms, the systems "gave value" to the elements of the structure.

2.5 The problem of **structure**

But what were the "elements" of a structure? They were not strings of classes, such as nominal group + verbal group + nominal group, among which there is just a mechanical kind of solidarity, but configurations of functions, where the solidarity is organic: each element has its specific part to play within the whole. (The class is a statement of potential: if you are a nominal group, you may function either as Subject or as Complement within the clause, and you may select for NUMBER: singular/plural. Which function(s) you fulfil, and which feature(s) you select, are actualizations of this potential in a particular instance of text.)

2.6 The problem of **types of structure** (see VII.Introduction(2005): xxiii on types of structure.)

But not all structures were configurational. Some were prosodic, typified by intonation contours: graduated movements between different steadier states. Some were periodic: wave-like trajectories from an initial to a final posture. These could still be represented in constituency terms, as if they had been configurations (see VII.Introduction(2005):xx–xxi on metafunction). But there was one other type which could not: those where the elements could be iterated in logical sequences, by relations such as 'and', or 'if', or 'said'. These were generated by systems of a special type: recursive systems, which had two simultaneous choices – one the basic options, the other "stop / go", i.e. 'choose whether or not to go round again'. Thus with each rank there is the potential of expanding to a "complex" element: clause complex, group complex and so on (Huddleston, 1965). Thus in the English verbal group the tense system was recursive in this way (Ellis drew my attention to Reichenbach, 1947): the options were: (1) past / present / future, (2) stop / go, where the choice of "go" leads into tenses such as [present in present] *is doing*, [past in present] *has done*, [present in past] *was doing*, [future in past] *was going to do* and so on, up to a limit (in my own observations) of five as in:

> they'd been going to've been paying me
> it'll've been going to've been being tested

This iterative potential was a feature of the system, and was quite distinct from the structural phenomenon of rank shift, or "embedding" (see 2.7 on taxis).

2.7 The problem of **taxis** (interdependency) and **rankshift**

In the clause complex, the system of logical relations intersected with another system where the option was one of interdependency, or "taxis": in

357

any one nexus, the status of the two clauses could be either equal ("paratactic") or unequal, with one dependent on the other ("hypotactic"). Thus,

'and',	paratactic:	she's very old, and rather blind
	hypotactic:	besides being very old, she's rather blind
'so',	paratactic:	he's very old, so he needs help
	hypotactic:	he needs help, because he's very old
'said',	paratactic:	"we need help", Henry said
	hypotactic:	Henry said they needed help

The system of taxis generates an immense potential for agnation, with regular proportionalities between paratactic and hypotactic agnates – sometimes just between subsystems, sometimes extending to their individual terms. But hypotaxis was often confused with rankshift: grammars traditionally operated with an undifferentiated category of "subordinate clause", or "embedding", which lumped together these two distinct phenomena – one clause being **dependent on** another [hypotaxis], one clause being **part of** (usually something that is itself a part of) another [rankshift]. Once these were distinguished, it was possible to explain (as well as the patterns of agnation already mentioned) such things as the parallelism between expansion and projection as the two fundamental relations between clauses in a nexus, with "direct and indirect speech and thought" as paratactic and hypotactic projection; the distinction between "defining" and "non-defining" (or "describing") relative clauses, the former being rankshifted the latter hypotactic; the status of non-finite clauses in English, as a type of hypotactic clause, including those having "no verb" in them, since non-finite forms of *be* are optional:

| finite: | since you're in charge, there should be no problem |
| non-finite: | with you (being) in charge, there should be no problem |

– and so on.

2.8 The problem of the relation between **system** *and* **structure**
The recognition of highly generalized functional-semantic categories such as expansion and projection depends on being able to bring together features that turn up all around the lexicogrammatical continuum. If one takes seriously Firth's dictum of **starting from** the distinction between system and structure, one can free the description from the straitjacket of structural representations. Another example is the area of modality in

English, where regular proportions occur over widely disparate word-ings such as

it's certain they are	they certainly are	they must be	I know they are
it's likely they are	they probably are	they will be	I think they are
it's possible they are	they perhaps are	they may be	I accept they are

as well as other subsystems such as are instantiated by

it's essential you ...	you're required to ...	you must ...	I insist you ...
it's desirable you ...	you're supposed to ...	you should ...	I want you to ...

and so on. The *system* thus gradually emerges as the fundamental organizing concept for the grammar (a "deep paradigm", as I explained it in 1965). This has a further important consequence: it neutralizes the distinction between describing something and relating it to every-thing else. Once the systems are interrelated, in the form of a *system network*, then the underlying description of any item in the grammar is a *selection expression*, the set of features that delineate its path through the network; and since each feature is in systemic contrast to one or more others, the description **consists in** the statement of its patterns of agnation – of all the proportionalities into which it enters. The clause, or other item, is described by being located in its place in the total systemic potential.

VII.Introduction(2005):xv–xix

★ ★ ★

2.13 The problem of **dimensions of structure**

The problem here was to explain how the different components of mean-ing (in metafunctional terms, the experiential, interpersonal and textual meanings) were all realized at once in the structure of the clause. In the laundry card grammar I was trying to reduce them all to one dimension, deriving from the "S,P,C,A" (Subject + Predicator + Complement(s) + Adjunct(s)) which stayed closest to the syntactic tradition. This was com-plex and unsatisfactory. A much better explanation was to assume that each metafunctional component generated its own distinct dimension of structure. Experiential meaning was realized in structural configurations of process, participant(s) and circumstance(s), such as the Actor + Process + Goal of a transitive material clause: textual meaning by some form of the organization of Theme + Rheme and Given + New; while the S,P,C,A type of structure realized interpersonal meanings of mood and modality. None of these three had any kind of priority, whether analytical or historical or in terms of semantic significance: one did not "first" choose a representational content and "then" dress it up in the appropriate speech function – all choices were simultaneous. If they had to be ordered for some particular project, pedagogical, say, or computational, this was a function of the task in hand, not an inherent property of a multidimensional structure.

Daneš (1964), working within the tradition of the Prague school, interpreted the experiential dimension as "semantic structure", in contrast to the "syntactic structure" of the Subject + Predicate kind; he regarded the latter as a level of organization internal to the grammar. My own view was (and is) that both are equally "semantic" – that is, components of the grammar's overall construction of meaning; the "Subject" is as much a meaning-construing element as the "Actor", but the two construe different kinds of responsibility (Halliday 1985/1994).

2.14 The problem of *types of structure* (continued)
The logical structures realizing expansion and projection did not enter in to this multidimensional mapping because they were structures of the clause complex, not of the clause; cf. under (2.6) above. Those that did, the experiential, interpersonal and textual, could be treated as configurations of elements that could be mapped on to each other in many different ways. The same item – some nominal group – might function simultaneously as Actor, as Subject and as Theme; but any of these functions might be dissociated from the other two, or indeed all three might be realized as different items; e.g.

those bowls	we	were given	by the children	for our anniversary
Theme	Subject		Actor	

In fact, however, there was some distortion involved in representing all three dimensions as compositional structures of this kind. The constituency model, with structure set up as an organic configuration of discrete parts, worked well enough for experiential meanings, where even in a language with a high degree of fusion (e.g. of pronouns into the structure of the verbal group) the basic pattern of process and participant stands out. But the interpersonal and textual contributions to the structure were not ideally represented as clumps of constituents. Interpersonal meanings are often construed prosodically, by intonation; but even when they are lexicalized they are often spread broadly around the discourse rather than being enumerated item by item. Textual meanings, on the other hand, tend to occur periodically, setting up the flow of discourse as a series of smaller and larger wave-like movements of which the Theme + Rheme pattern of the (English or Chinese) clause is just one cycle. It was precisely this variation in the modes of meaning – the syntagmatic patterns by which the different functional components of meaning are construed – that made it possible for them to be combined in indefinitely many ways. The immense power of discourse derives from the interplay of these dimensions of discursive movement (see Hasan (1985b) on the "texture" of a text).

VII.Introduction(2005):xxii–xxiv

Additional readings

On Grammar (Volume 1) – 3(1963); 4(1966); 5(1966); 8(1979):196–218
Linguistic Studies of Text and Discourse (Volume 2) – 1(1964):7 ; 2(1977): 24–5, 27, 79–80
Computational and Quantitative Studies (Volume 6) – 2(1962):29–36
Studies in English Language (Volume 7) – 4(1969); 154–63; 8(1963):249–51

Chapter Seventeen

TEXT AND DISCOURSE ANALYSIS

Summary

The difference between a text and a clause is that a text is a semantic entity, i.e. a construct of meaning, whereas a clause is a lexicogrammatical entity, i.e a construct of wording. A text is an intersubjective event, in which speaker and listener exchange meaning in a context of situation.

Texture is what makes a text into a coherent piece of language, as opposed to simply being an unorganized string of sentences. One aspect of texture is cohesion, which deals with how successive sentences are integrated to form a whole. The other aspect of texture has to do with fit to context, or those choices based on what the speaker wants to say (Theme), and those choices related to the flow of information (Given-New).

No matter whether long or short, prose or verse, traditional or spontaneous, spoken or written, literary or conversational, all texts are meaningful, each being an instance of meaning formed through choices from the total network of meaning potential. Moreover, all texts are accessible to objective linguistic analysis through the functional and semantic categories of description for language as a whole.

Selected readings

On Grammar (Volume 1)

1 PATTERNS OF WORDING IN THE CLAUSE

Thanks to the work of our predecessors, and especially perhaps to that of outstanding figures of mid-century linguistics such as Sapir and Whorf and Bloomfield and Firth and Hjelmslev, linguists of subsequent decades have been able to extend our concerns upwards and outwards, from the syllable, through the clause, to the text.

While broadening our vision in this way we have had to ensure that we do not lose sight of the syllable when we attend to the clause, nor of the clause when we attend to the text. Being a linguist means keeping all these things in focus at once: we are trained to do this both as observers, when we listen simultaneously to the meanings, the wordings and the sounds of speech, and as theorists, when we construct representations of language as simultaneously semantics, lexicogrammar and phonology. But it is not always easy to maintain this multiple focus, because each shift of attention involves a shift in two directions, a knight's move that is a move both upwards and outwards. This same two-dimensional relationship was described by Hockett many years ago in a paper called 'Linguistic elements and their relations' (Hockett 1961), in which he discussed the different statuses of morpheme and phoneme and contrasted the two possible pathways between them.

A clause, that is to say, is not only bigger than a syllable; it is an entity of a different kind, at another level of abstraction. And it is this second relationship, that of realization, or coding, that is the critical one; the size distinction is typically associated with it, but not obligatorily – there can be a clause encoded as a single syllable. It took a surprisingly long time to clarify this two-dimensional relationship, and to accept that the relation of syllable to clause (or of phoneme to morpheme) was not simply one of part to whole, although it should have been fairly obvious seeing that the two are separated by the Saussurean line of arbitrariness. It is much harder to establish that a similar shift along two dimensions separates the clause from the text. A text is likewise – typically but not necessarily – bigger than a clause. But it is also, and more importantly, of a different level of abstraction. A text is a semantic entity rather than a formal, lexicogrammatical one; and this distinction is less easy to draw, because between the semantics and the grammar there is no such line of arbitrariness. (I shall return to this point below.)

There is a problem in discussing text, if only because a text can be such a large object: every example takes up a great deal of space. One solution to this is to write rules for generating text but never actually to generate any. Another is that once suggested by Peter Wexler when he proposed to introduce a talk with the words "This paper is about the language of this paper", so making the same entity serve both as text and as metatext. I have usually approached the problem in a different way, by using text that is so familiar that the audience can supply the missing parts for themselves, like *Mother Goose* or *Alice in Wonderland*. We need to face up to it somehow or other; there is something discouraging about a publication where the author is insisting on the importance of context but cites nothing longer than a decontextualized clause.

When text is discussed in this way, with reference made only to isolated clauses, it is perhaps being assumed that the relation of clause to text is simply one of constituency. If a text is the same kind of thing as a clause only bigger, we can reasonably use clauses as instances while making observations about text. And perhaps this approach to text in turn reflects a presemantic view of language, in which it is assumed that the linguistic system is no more than grammar and phonology; so a text must be a grammatical unit, something that consists of clauses in the same way that a clause consists of words.

Since there is no line of arbitrariness between semantics and grammar, this view is plausible. It is natural to think of text in the sense of the wordings that realize it. But it does cause some problems. The relations between the parts of a text are not such that we can set up structures whose exponents will be clause-like entities. The elements of structure of the text are more abstract; they are functional entities relating to the context of situation of the text, to its generic properties in terms of field, tenor and mode. It is not easy to explain the nature of a text if we treat a text as if it was a macrosentence, just as it was not easy to explain the nature of a sentence when a sentence was treated as if it was a macrophoneme.

I am saying this at some length (despite the fact that I have said it often enough before) because I am now going on to say the opposite, or at least what will at first sight appear to be the opposite. Having insisted that a text is **not** like a clause, I now intend to suggest that it is. It is not that I have changed my mind on the issue. The point is rather that, once we have established that texts and clauses are of different natures, the one being lexicogrammatical (a construct of wording) the other semantic (a construct of meaning), we can then go on to note that there are several important and interesting respects in which the two are alike. But the likeness is of an analogic kind; it is a metaphorical likeness, not the kind of likeness there is between, say, a clause and a word. Starting from Hockett's diagram, where one axis stands for constituency and the other for realization, we can link text to clause along the diagonal; the relationship between them is there but it is an oblique one, and this determines the kind of likeness we can expect to find.

1.1 HOW IS A TEXT LIKE A CLAUSE?
Text is the process of meaning; and a text is the product of that process. A text is therefore a semantic entity; it is given to us in clauses, but it is

not made of clauses, in the sense of being a whole of which the clauses are simply parts. So when we speak of the problem of relating clause to text as one of getting "from micro to macro", this is only one aspect of the relationship. It is true that texts are, on the whole, larger than clauses; what is more significant, however, is that they are one level of abstraction beyond the clause. The relationship is not so much one of size as one of overt to covert; the text is realized in clauses. In "scale-and-category" terminology (Halliday 1961), the relationship of clause to text is one of exponence as well as one of rank.

This has consequences for the ways in which the properties of a text are made manifest. For example, the notion that a text has "structure" would imply, if a text was a lexicogrammatical entity, that the elements of structure would be "filled" by classes of the clause (perhaps with some intermediate units) in the same way that elements of structure of the clause are filled by classes of the group. But it is difficult to specify text structures in a way which represents the text simply as a higher-rank grammatical constituent; the configurations are different in kind, and the relationship to the wording is both indirect and complex. Functional elements of text structure are not translatable into strings of clauses.

A text is therefore not "like" a clause in the way that a clause is like a word or a syllable like a phoneme. But by the same token, just because clause and text differ on two dimensions, both rank (size level) and exponence (stratal level), there can exist between them a relation of another kind: an analogic or metaphorical similarity. A clause stands as a kind of metaphor for a text. In this paper I shall refer to some well-known properties of a text, and then, drawing on some recent text-linguistic studies in a systemic-functional framework, try to show that these are paralleled in significant ways by properties of a clause that are in some sense (not always the same sense) analogous. The textual properties to be considered are the following:

1. A text has structure.
2. A text has coherence.
3. A text has function.
4. A text has development.
5. A text has character.

1.1.1 A text has structure

For at least some registers, perhaps all, it is possible to state the structure of a text as a configuration of functions (Hasan 1979). A generalized structural representation is likely to include some elements that are obligatory and others that are optional; and the sequence in which the elements occur is likely to be partly determined and partly variable.

Most of the actual formulations of text structure that have been put forward seem to relate to one broad genre, that of narrative. The original source of inspiration for these was Propp's theory of the folk tale. The structure of traditional oral narrative has been investigated in detail within tagmemic and stratificational frameworks, on foundations provided by Longacre and Gleason. A well-known representation of another kind of narrative is Labov and Waletsky's structural formula for narratives of personal experience:

> Abstract ^ Orientation ^ Complication • Evaluation • Resolution ^ Coda

Outside narrative registers, Mitchell (1957) set up structures for the "language of buying and selling" in Cyrenaican Arabic, recognizing three subvarieties having some common and some variant features:

> Market and shop transactions: Salutation ^ Enquiry as to object of sale ^ Investigation of object of sale ^ Bidding ^ Conclusion
>
> Auctions: Opening ^ Investigation of object of sale ^ Bidding ^ Conclusion

Mitchell refers to these as "stages" and comments that "stage is an abstract category and the numbering of stages does not necessarily imply sequence in time". Hasan considers that structure is a property of texts in all registers. For any register, specified at any appropriate degree of delicacy, it should be possible to state a generalized structure by reference to which any actual text can be interpreted. Her suggested formula for a particular class of transactions, retail sale in a personal service food store, is as follows:

> ((Greeting •) Sale initiation ^) ((Sale inquiry •) (Sale request ^ Sale compliance) ^) Sale ^ Purchase ^ Purchase closure (^ Finis)

Martin (1980), who uses "functional tenor", or rhetorical purpose, as the superordinate concept for characterizing registers, gives the following structural formula for the register of "persuasion":

> Set ground ^ State problem ^ Offer solution ^ Evaluate solution (^ Personalize solution)

1.1.2 A text has coherence
One of the most frequent observations made about texts that are felt to be defective in some way is that they do not "hang together": they

"lack coherence". A text has coherence; it forms a unity, a whole that is more than the sum of its parts.

Coherence is a complex property to which many factors contribute. One way to approach it is through the category of cohesion, as defined by Halliday and Hasan (1976). Cohesion is a necessary but not a sufficient condition of coherence. The different types of cohesive relation are the fundamental resources out of which coherence is built. But the mere presence of cohesive ties is not by itself a guarantee of a coherent texture. These resources have to be organized and deployed in patterned ways.

(a) Ruqaiya Hasan identifies a feature which she calls "cohesive harmony" (Hasan 1984). This is based on the recognition of cohesive chains of a lexico-referential kind. Such chains have been called "participant chains", since their most obvious manifestation is in the form of sequences such as *a little boy . . . John . . . he . . . he* which are coreferential to a narrative participant; but Hasan points out that they are not confined to participants, nor are they necessarily coreferential. They may be "identity chains" or "similarity chains"; and the element that is chained may be of any kind – participant, human or otherwise, including institutions and abstract entities; attribute or circumstantial element; event, action or relation; fact or report; or any recoverable portion of text.

What makes a text coherent is not merely the presence of such chains but their interaction one with another. In comparing texts which were judged coherent, by herself and others, with those which were not, Hasan found that in the former it was always the case that a significant majority of the tokens in each chain were functionally related with tokens in some other chain; while in the latter the ones that were related in this way were only a minority. Specifically, they were related in some experiential function – transitivity, or an extension thereof – either to each other, or identically to some third function. For example, a pair of tokens might be related to each other as Actor to Process; or by their both having the function Actor relative to some other element as Process. In other words, in order to achieve coherence there had to be not merely parallel currents of meaning running through the text, but currents of meaning intermingling in a general flow, some disappearing, new ones forming, but coming together over any stretch of text in a steady confluence of semantic force.

The following illustration (Appendix 1a) shows the difference in cohesive harmony between two stories told by children (Hasan 1980a). Hasan points out that these two texts differ hardly at all in the number and distribution of cohesive ties, or in the proportion of their lexical and referential tokens that appear in chains. Where they do differ is in the proportion of such tokens that occur in interaction with others from other chains; in other words, in the extent of cohesive harmony displayed. This has proved to be a significant element in discrimination between passages perceived as coherent and those where coherence is felt to be lacking.

(b) Another type of cohesive relationship identified by Halliday and Hasan is that of conjunction, the linking of successive elements of a text by the semantic relations of 'and, or, nor, viz, yet, so, then': additive, including alternative and appositive; adversative; causative, and termporal. These are described and illustrated, like the other cohesive systems, with reference to cohesion between adjacent sentences. But we can identify three ways in which conjunctive relations create coherence in the more extended sense.

1. James R. Martin has shown (1992) how conjunctive relations create texture in dialogue by linking sentences that are not adjacent, spanning whatever material may intervene. His interpretation of the system of conjunction, in which he modifies the version given in Halliday and Hasan, eliminating the category of "adversative" and grouping "as against" with additive and "contrary to expectation" with consequential (causal), is expressed in the network in Appendix 2. The category of "implicit", also not in Halliday and Hasan, accounts for those instances where the semantic relationship is present but there is no conjunction or textual (discourse) adjunct making it explicit. Martin's analysis of a short passage of dialogue includes instances of conjunctive relations bridging a number of intermediate turns (Appendix 2).

2. Conjunctive relations may be set up between passages of any extent. Not only a turn in a dialogue, but an episode, argument, scene or any other functional element may be "picked up" conjunctively in a succeeding portion of the text. In this way the presence of conjunctive relations creates coherence over extended passages of discourse. An example of this would be a section beginning *Because of this*, where *this* refers to the whole of some preceding argument.

3. Halliday has suggested (1975) that the "textual" properties of a text – the cohesive patterns and those of 'functional sentence perspective' – tend to be determined by the "mode", the function ascribed to the text in the given context of situation, the purpose it is intended to achieve. Thus the mode would determine the balance among the different types of cohesive resource – reference, ellipsis, conjunction, lexical cohesion; and within conjunction, the relative weight accorded to internal and external conjunctive relations and to the various semantic alternatives

within each. In this way the kind of conjunctive relations found in the text will be characteristic of the register (as defined on the dimension of 'mode') to which the text belongs.

An illustration of this principle is provided by Mary Ann Eiler (1979) in her study of expository writing by ninth graders in an American high school. She has shown how the conjunctive relation of specific instance to general principle, coded in Martin's network as:

(internal/comparative) : similarity : nonexhaustive

is the major conjunctive factor giving coherence to these texts. For example, in one part of a text there occurs the sentence

Odysseus' friends and anyone else who heard his story respected him.

Elsewhere in the same text we find:

Heroic men are very much respected and idolized.

(Either member of such a pair may come first.) There is lexical cohesion between individual items – the repetition of *respect*. There is cohesion between *Odysseus* and *heroic (men)*, with 'Odysseus' being a hyponym of 'hero'. But between the two sentences as wholes there is a conjunctive relation – itself an extension of hyponymy – such that the second one stands as a general principle of which the first one offers a specific instance; and this type of conjunction is a distinguishing feature of the sort of expository discourse she is investigating.

1.1.3 A text has function

A text unfolds in a context of situation, and has some identifiable rhetorical function with reference to that context. This is the domain of functional theories of language, insofar as these are concerned with the process ('functions of the utterance') as distinct from the system ('functional components of the grammar').

The assumption of those theories that are functional in the former sense, which we may call "process-functional theories", is that a text can be interpreted as having one or other of a small set of "rhetorical" functions – exclusively, or predominantly, or in some recognizable combination. Malinowski, starting from an ethnographic standpoint, identified the functions "pragmatic (active/narrative)/magical". Bühler, from a psychological perspective, recognized "expressive/conative/representational", with orientation respectively towards speaker, addressee and the rest of reality; to these Jakobson later added three more, having orientation towards the channel ("phatic" – inappropriately), the message ("poetic") and the code ("metalinguistic"). Britton, as an educational theorist, realigned Bühler's categories so as to group conative with representational (both being "transactional"), and added the poetic as a fourth. In the work of Desmond Morris we can even find an ethological categorization: "mood talking/grooming talking/information talking/exploratory talking".

All these apparently very divergent interpretations have in common one basic distinction: that between language as reflection and language as action – between discourse that is oriented towards the function of the representation of experience (Malinowski's narrative, Bühler's and Britton's representational, Morris' information talking) and discourse that is oriented towards the function of interpersonal behavior (Malinowski's active, Bühler's and Britton's expressive and conative, Morris' mood talking and grooming talking). There is also a partial recognition of a third orientation, towards an imaginative function (magical, poetic, exploratory).

In work on register the rhetorical function is treated as one component in the context of situation of the text. Halliday, McIntosh and Strevens (1964) proposed a tripartite framework for interpreting the register: (i) the nature of the social process in which the text is embedded – 'what is going on' (field); (ii) the interpersonal relationships among the participants – 'who are taking part' (tenor); (iii) the role assigned to the text, including both medium and rhetorical function – 'what part the language is playing' (mode). Gregory (1967) separated the rhetorical function from the medium and associated it more closely with the participant relations, referring to the latter as "personal tenor" and to rhetorical function as "functional tenor". Ure and Ellis (1979) take this one step further, recognizing four distinct categories of field, mode, formality (personal tenor) and role (functional tenor). Martin (1980) proposes to return to the rhetorical perspective and treat functional tenor, which he defines as "the purpose of the text", as superordinate to field, mode and personal tenor. His argument is that "it is the functional tenor of a text that is responsible for its structural formula" – in other words that function (in this sense) determines structure.

1.1.4 A text has development

A text is a dynamic process; it has a semantic 'flow', a development of ideational and interpersonal meanings. This flow or development is carried forward by the interaction of speaker and listener; obviously so in the case of dialogue, but so also in monologic modes where the active participation of a listener still contributes to the construction of meaning.

Even in written language the semogenic process is essentially of the same nature; researchers in writing theory now strongly insist on the part played by the imagined audience in the process of written composition.

Peter Fries refers (1981) to the "method of development" of a text. Below is one of his examples, with the relevant sections of the commentary (Appendix 3). In the paper from which this is taken, Fries is interpreting the development of a text in terms that relate it to the concepts of theme and rheme. His argument proceeds in four steps: (1) the pattern of theme–rheme organization in the clause is a function of the register; (2) the pattern in the choice of theme is a function of the method of development of the text; (3) "theme–rheme" is clearly distinct from, but also clearly related to, "given–new"; (4) the theme–rheme organization of the clause "fits into a larger pattern governing the information flow in sequences of sentences in English discourse in general".

Fries regards the theme as a "ground": "In English discourse at least there seems to be a strong tendency to set up certain information as a ground first, and then to introduce later information using that ground as a basis for evaluation and comparison". (It is reasonable to understand "information" rather broadly here; presumably the ground may be any configuration of ideational and interpersonal meanings.) So there is a movement **from** the ground, to something that is defined by it as "not ground". There is also, we may add, a complementary movement in a text, which is a movement towards rather than away from: a movement **to** what we may call the "point" (generalizing from Fries'"main point"), from something that is defined by it as "not point". Rhetorical theory has always stressed the beginning and the end: topic sentence, introductory paragraph &c. on the one hand, and culmination, climax, summation &c. on the other. But it is important to stress that this is not a single movement. A text is a kind of diminuendo – crescendo, beginning and ending with prominence; but the prominence is of two different kinds. Rather than thinking this time of a flow, a unidirectional current with a set of rapids at each end, we should perhaps change the metaphor to that of a gift, or rather an exchange, in which there is a shift of focus from donor to recipient in the course of the exchange, or rather from giving to receiving. The process begins as giving and ends as receiving; but "giving – not giving" is not the same movement as "not receiving – receiving". Moreover although the process must start with the giving – until then there is no exchange – it need not necessarily end with the receiving, which may occur quite early and be followed up in various ways.

In the development of a text, phasing out the "ground" goes along with phasing in the "point". This pattern is one that can be repeated over

371

as many levels in the hierarchy of constituents as the text has in it, from the entire text down to the individual clause.

1.1.5 A text has character

A text is an instance of a particular "register"; it has the generic features characteristic of that register, associated with a particular alignment of the features of the context of situation – the "contextual configuration", in Hasan's terms. A text is also an individual entity, having a specific character of its own distinct from that of other texts within the same register. Some texts are highly valued as individual texts, and one of the interests of text studies is the stylistic one, the attempt to understand the unique qualities of a highly valued text, and what it is that makes it highly valued.

(A) The generic character of a text is in principle predictable from its context of situation. Taking the categories of field, tenor and mode as a predictive framework, Halliday proposed that the ideational meanings of a text tend to be determined by the field, the interpersonal meanings by the tenor, and the textual meanings by the mode, suggesting that this was how listeners and readers make predictions about what is coming next – predictions that they must make if meanings are to be successfully exchanged. For illustrations of this see Halliday (1975, 1977), Halliday and Hasan (1980).

An example of a register variable is provided by Jean Ure's study of lexical density (1971). Ure shows that the lexical density of a text is a function of its level of formality, the amount of self-monitoring done by the speaker or writer; writing has a higher density than speech, with what she calls "language-in-action" having the lowest density of all. Lexical density can be defined as the number of lexical items per unit grammar (per clause, as the most natural measure), though Ure measures it as a percentage of running words; in her sample of 68 texts, comprising about 21,000 words each of speech and writing, the values range from 57 per cent (formal written) to 24 per cent (casual spoken), and all texts with a density of 35 per cent and below are dialogue. Charles Taylor (1979) has used both these measures in his study of the language of high school textbooks in New South Wales.

Robin Melrose (1979) has suggested another variable that defines the generic character of a text, one that relates to the field instead of the mode. He finds that each text will tend to be characterized by a particular "message type". Melrose distinguishes factual, phenomenal and relational message, with various subcategories; deriving these from the material, mental and relational processes of the transitivity system (Halliday 1967/68; 1975). An instance of a text with relational : attributive messages is given in Appendix 4.

According to Melrose, certain other features are associated with these message types: different patterns of theme, conjunction and lexical cohesion, and also different kinds of "message superordinate", the summative expression described by Winter (1977); the table in Appendix 4 shows Melrose's hypothesis about these.

(B) The specific character of a text is what distinguishes it from other texts of the same genre, those features which are not predictable from the contextual configuration. This has sometimes been characterized as deviation, the text creating its own rules; but "breaking the rules" is a minor and relatively insignificant form of uniqueness. What a text does is to create its own norms, its own unique selection from the resources of the system by which it is generated.

Many texts in daily life are not unique at all; the same things have been said countless times before. Such texts are often of particular interest to an ethnographer (and, one might add, to a linguist). Other texts are presumed to be unique; this class includes all those texts we think of as literature. But any text can be described and interpreted as an event that is *sui generis*. If the qualities that we perceive as specific to a text reside not merely in the particular combination of features selected but also in a special highlighting of some aspect of these, we usually try to relate this highlighting to our interpretation of the underlying theme, seeking the kind of semiotic convergence that would explain the particular impact that the text has on us.

A text is a polyphonic composition of ideational, interpersonal and textual "voices". The ideational voice provides the content: the things, facts and reports; processes, participants and circumstances; the logical relations of different kinds. The interpersonal voice provides the interaction: mood, modality, person, polarity, attitude, comment, key. The textual voice provides the organization: thematic and informational prominence; grammatical and lexical cohesion among the parts. The "character" of the text is its pattern of selections in these various voices, and the way they are combined into a single whole.

The accompanying extract from J. B. Priestley's *An Inspector Calls* (Appendix 5) is a piece of dramatic dialogue which is distinctively characterized by the foregrounding of modality. The first part is dominated by modalized assertions, which move from probability to obligation, the second part by assertions about obligations; the final speech shifts into narrative, returning at the end to the assertive mode but this time without modalities. Herein lies the movement of the play, which is concerned with social responsibility (obligation) acted out through chance (objective probability); the interplay of these modalities determines a strong narrative line leading up to a nononsense conclusion.

In this passage the linguistic system functions as a symbol within the process; this is its characteristic contribution to our interpretation of the meaning of the play.

What strikes us about these properties of a text is that all of them are also, in some sense, properties of a clause. The notion of text structure is clearly modelled on that of clause structure. A clause is a configuration of functions; so is a text.

As said at the beginning, this is not to argue that a text is a larger whole of which a clause is a part. A clause is a lexicogrammatical object, a structure of wording; whereas a text is a semantic object, a structure of meaning. The resemblance is like that of clause to syllable. A syllable is a phonological object, and therefore not part of a clause; but it has structure in the same sense.

With one difference, however: between clause and syllable runs the line of arbitrariness in language. In the realization of wording in sound, natural symbols are the exception. But there is no such line of arbitrariness separating the clause from the text. The realization of meaning in wording is largely "natural", non-arbitrary. This leads us to speculate whether the text may display the same kind of multiple structuring that is found in the clause, ideational, interpersonal and textual. The representations of text structure proposed by Hasan and others suggest that we might want to interpret a text as having, potentially at least, an ideational structure relating to its field and an interpersonal structure relating to its tenor, rather than (or as well as) a single structure deriving from the mode (functional tenor) as proposed by Martin.

Benjamin N. Colby and Lore M. Colby (1980) analyse traditional and other oral narratives in terms of "eidons", which are ideational elements of text structure set up to allow for the interpretation of the text as an ethnographic document, as a window on the culture. The theory and method are set out in Colby's study (1973) of Eskimo folk tales. The notion of the eidon Colby ascribes to Gregory Bateson's interpretation (1936) of Iatmul culture and the Naven ceremonies. Bateson talks of the "eidos" and the "ethos" of a culture, and of "eidological" and "ethological relationships" – the realization of eidos and ethos in cognitive and affective aspects of cultural behavior. Colby's interpretation of text structure is "eidological", corresponding to the ideational component in the structure

of the clause; he suggests the possibility of a parallel "ethological" interpretation corresponding to the interpersonal component in the structure
of the clause.

We should not press the analogy too far. But if it seemed useful to
set up simultaneous structures in a text along these lines we might ask
whether there is the same kind of structural variation as we find in the
clause, with the eidological structure being "particulate" (represented by
definable segments of the text) and the ethological being "field-like"
(represented by overlapping prosodies in the text). (The "wave-like"
periodic movement corresponding to the textual dimension of clause
structure has already been referred to under 1.1.4 above; cf. further
below.) (Cf. Halliday 1979a.)

To say that a text resembles a clause in having coherence is not to say
very much, since the coherence in a clause is created by its structure,
whereas coherence in a text largely depends on cohesion. Cohesion is
the resource that takes over, as it were, when grammatical structure no
longer holds (i.e. above the clause complex). We could point out that
cohesion also obtains within clauses; we find reference, substitution,
ellipsis, conjunction and lexical cohesion all operating between elements
in the same clause, for example:

M's evening speech caused more fuss than his morning one had.

C   R   L   S   E

But this is a superficial similarity. A more significant analogy can be
found with the notions of cohesive harmony and conjunctive relations
discussed in 1.1.2 above.

Ruqaiya Hasan's work showed how lexico-referential motifs enter
into a text not as isolated motifs but as interlocking chains having some
kind of regular functional relationship with each other. But these functional relationships are relationships within the clause; and this reflects
the fact that the elements in these chains themselves cannot occur as
isolated entities. Names have no place in language except in function
with other names; and the functions are defined within the structure of
the clause.

The conjunctive relations discussed by J. R. Martin (1992) are also
derived from relations with the clause. Consider a series such as the
following:

She didn't know the rules. She died.
She didn't know the rules. So she died.
She died, because she didn't know the rules.

She died because of not knowing the rules.
That she died was because she didn't know the rules.
That she died was caused by her not knowing the rules.
Her ignorance of the rules caused her death.

The same conjunctive relation, the "external causal", can be coded in very many ways. It can appear as a relationship within the clause, realized lexicogrammatically; but it can also serve to link segments of the text, at any distance and of any extent. The kind of coherence that is achieved by the presence in the text of semantic relationships of the conjunctive kind is essentially a clause-type coherence, one that is based on relations defined systematically within the transitivity system of the clause.

The notion that a text has function is again closely related to an analogous feature of the clause, also one that is coded in the lexicogrammatical system: that a clause has a speech function, realized by the mood system. The speech function of the clause – in simplest terms, as statement, question, command, offer, or a minor speech function – is represented by the grammatical categories of declarative, interrogative and so on; this is the rhetorical function of the clause, and the whole range of rhetorical functions that we assign to text are simply the "mood" of the text. (Cf. Martin (1980) for speech-functional analysis of dialogue.)

The development of the text again has its analogy in the clause. This has already been made clear from the example cited in 1.1.4, since Peter Fries used the theme–rheme structure of the clause as the source from which to derive the method of development of the text. We can generalize this still further by bringing in the notion of information structure, the given–new movement within the clause.

In its "textual" aspect, a clause has a wave-like periodic structure created by the tension between theme–rheme (where theme is the rominent element) and given–new (where new is the prominent element); the result is a pattern of diminuendo–crescendo, with a peak of prominence at each end. There is a balance of development (i) away from the theme, and (ii) towards the new. But these are separate movements. They are in phase in the unmarked, "default" case, where the theme is selected from what is given, and the news is put into the rheme. But they can also be out of phase, and this gives an alternative pattern of texture to the clause. Putting the two out of phase means locating the new (the focus of information) somewhere other than at the end of the rheme; this as it were changes the wave shape but does not disturb the essential periodicity.

This pattern is the "method of development" of the clause. It is closely analogous to what takes place in a text; not only over the whole text but also in structurally defined intermediate units within the text. The classic movement of a paragraph, beginning with a topic sentence (**from** theme to elaboration) and culmination – having a high point, unmarkedly but not obligatorily final – in a climax (from prelude **to** main point), is one of the clearest manifestations of the analogy between clause and text. It is in the clause that this movement is displayed in the most systematic and clearly motivated form.

Finally a clause can be said to have "character" in both the generic and the specific sense. If a text is typified by virtue of its being organized around the expression of processes of a particular type, the clause is the unit in which these processes are realized and categorized. The clause is the locus of the transitivity system: the system of material, mental and relational processes, together with their numerous subcategories. Thus analogous to the major types or genres of text are the major types or classes of the clause, each being characterized by the selection of a domi- nant process type.

But each clause is also a unique combination, or potentially unique combination, of features deriving from the different semantic functions, ideational, interpersonal and textual. Moreover any one or other of these may be foregrounded: the clause may display an orientation towards any one, or any combination, of the various systems and their subsystems. The extract from J. B. Priestley's *An Inspector Calls* (Appendix 5) gave an instance of a clause that is oriented towards a certain type of modality: interpersonal meanings are highlighted, with the speaker's skeptical doubting as the predominant rhetorical function. The passage cited is a unique interplay between the exploration of probabilities and the asser- tion of obligations, and so is the entire text. No one clause can recapitulate the whole; but all contribute, and some achieve a remarkable likeness – a likeness that is possible because the systems of the clause not only embody all the semantic components from which the text is built but do so in a way that allows an infinitely varied, almost text-like balance among them.

Thus the properties that we recognize in a text are also, in a trans- formed way, properties that we recognize in a clause. A clause is a kind of metaphor for a text – and a text for a clause. That this is possible is due to two things: one, that a text is not only (typically) larger than but also more abstract than a clause; two, that on the other hand there is no line of arbitrariness between clause and text as there is between clause and syllable. Hence it is not only in a formal sense that a text is like a clause. It is no accident that it is possible to illustrate so many of the relations in a text by reference to relations in a clause. The illustrations given here already contain within themselves a demonstration of this conclusion. In showing that a text has structure, coherence, function, development and character, we cannot help at the same time showing that a clause has all these things too, though in an interesting variety of different ways. Presumably this is how clauses evolved – as the most efficient means of encoding text.

SUMMARY

	TEXT	CLAUSE
Structure:	configuration of contextually motivated semantic functions	configuration of semantically grammatical functions
Coherence:	by cohesion (i) cohesive harmony: chains interrelate by function in (semantic) transitivity (ii) conjunctive relation: between messages or larger parts of text	by structure (i) names (things) interrelate by function in (grammatical) transitivity (ii) conjunctive relation: between parts of clause, as major or minor process
Function:	has "functional tenor" (rhetorical function as text)	has "speech function" (rhetorical function as speech act)
Development:	has "information flow": $\left\{ \begin{array}{l} \text{ground} - - - - > \\ - - - - > \text{point} \end{array} \right\}$	has "information structure": $\left\{ \begin{array}{l} \text{theme} - - - - > \\ - - - - > \text{focus / new} \end{array} \right\}$
Character:	generic: selects "favourite" process type as message type specific: foregrounds one or more systems	generic: selects process type specific: foregrounds selections from one or more systems

1.2 A FUNCTIONAL INTERPRETATION

We shall be able to explore the relationship between clauses and text more thoroughly by starting from a functional interpretation of the clause; so it may be helpful to comment first on functional theories of language. Functional theories of language came originally from outside linguistics; the consequence was that they were only theories of the text – they had nothing to say about the system. According to such a theory, any piece of text can be assigned a particular function, in the sense that it is oriented, exclusively or at least predominantly, towards some communicative purpose. The unit that is described in this way may be a very small piece of text, realized as one clause (the functions are then "functions of the utterance"); or it may be a larger piece constituting a recognizable semiotic event. The best-known functional schemata are two dating from around 1930, the ethnographic one of Malinowski (1935) and the psychological one of Karl Bühler (1934). Bühler's scheme is interesting because although extralinguistic in intent it is one that is explicitly derived from language – that is, from the linguistic system – in the first place: his tripartite framework of expressive, conative and representational functions denotes text that is oriented, respectively, towards speaker, addressee, and the rest of the universe – in other words the first person, second person and third person categories of the Indo-European verb. This is similar to the way in which various logical relations originally derived from natural language have been transformed into non-linguistic relations and then turned back on to language as explanations of linguistic forms.

The interest of such functional schemata for the linguist is that the functions arrived at are not in fact simply functions of the text. If they were, they would be of limited concern; but they are more than this – they are functions that are built in to language as the fundamental organizing principle of the linguistic system. We shall not be surprised at this, if we take a Hjelmslevian view of language as system and process: if we accept that language and text are one and the same thing, and that the system evolved as a means of serving human intentions through the creating of text. It is only if we set up artificial dichotomies like langue and parole, or competence and performance, that we are surprised when a system displays properties relating it to its use. Now, despite the divergencies that separate Bühler's and Malinowski's functional theories, from each other and from various subsequent schemata, divergencies that are a natural consequence of the different purposes for which they were devised (ethnographic, psychological, ethological, educational, etc.), there is one feature that strikes us as common to all of them. They all share in the fundamental opposition of action and reflection, the distinction between language as a means of doing and language as a means of thinking. The former is Bühler's first and second person function, Malinowski's active function; the latter is Bühler's third person function, Malinowski's narrative function. And the opposition is incorporated into the semantics of natural languages, in the form of what I have referred to as the "interpersonal" and "ideational" components. (The distinction between first and second person language, however, is not a systematic one; the two are simply different angles on the same interpersonality.) For all human beings, in all social groups, the environment in which they live has these two validations: it is something to be acted on, turned into food or shelter or other needs; and it is something to be thought about, researched and understood. Language has evolved to serve both these elementary functions. The reflective mode is coded directly as the ideational element in the semantic system. But since language is symbolic, one who speaks does not act on reality directly but only through the intermediary of a listener. Hence the active mode, when translated into a network of semantic systems, comes to be coded as interpersonal.

While these two functions are given to language from the outside, as it were, by its role in human situations, in order to fulfil such roles a language has to have a third semantic component, whereby it is enabled to latch on to those situations in a systematic way. There must be a relevance function, a system of meaning potential which allows a text to cohere with its environment, both the non-linguistic environment and that part of the environment which consists of what has been said before. So there is a third component in the semantics of natural language which only an immanent linguistics will discover, since it has no transcendent motivation; this is the contextualizing function – or the "textual" function, as I have called it, because it is what makes text text, what enables language to be operational in culturally meaningful environments.

Now a clause is a complex realization of all these three semantic functions. It has an ideational component, based on transitivity, the processes, participants and circumstantial elements that make up the semantics of the real world, and including the onomastic systems that classify these into nameables of various kinds. It has an interpersonal component, consisting of mood, modality, person, key and all the various attitudinal motifs that come to be organized as meaningful alternatives. And it has a textual component, the "functional sentence perspective" (thematic and news-giving systems) and the cohesive resources of reference, ellipsis and conjunction. Each of these components makes its contribution to the total make-up of the clause. What we identify as a clause is the joint product of functional-semantic processes of these three kinds.

But what is the nature of the contribution, in each case? We are accustomed to thinking of this in structural terms: that each semantic component generates its own particular tree, a configuration of parts each having a distinct function with respect to the organic whole. The ideational component generates "actor–action–goal"-type structures: configurations of Process, Medium, Agent, Beneficiary, Range, Extent, Location, Manner, Cause and so on. The interpersonal component generates so-called "modal-propositional" structures, configurations of Subject, Finite, Modality, Predicator, Complement and Adjunct. And the textual component generates thematic and informational structures, configurations of Theme and Rheme, and Given and New; as well as cohesive elements of a non-configurational kind.

We can represent all these in structural terms, using the linguist's traditional notion of structure: the simplest of all possible forms of organization, that of parts into wholes. Because this notion of constituent structure is so simple, it is natural that a linguist should want to do as much as possible with it. And it can be made to do quite a lot. But there comes a point where it ceases to be appropriate; where moulding the facts so that they fit the notion of constituency will distort them rather than just simplifying them. With a multifunctional interpretation of the clause we reach this point.

As outlined in I.8(1979), the contributions that are made by the three functional-semantic components to the form of the clause are of three rather different kinds. As far as the ideational systems are concerned, these do tend to generate part–whole structures; they are realized by organic configurations which themselves, and whose constituents, are reasonably clearly bounded, such that it can be specified where one clause element leaves off and the next one starts. But this is not nearly so true of interpersonal systems. Interpersonal systems tend to generate prosodic patterns that run all the way through the clause: not only intonation contours, though these provide a clear instance, but also reiterations of various kinds like those that are typical of modality in English, e.g. *surely ... can't ... possibly ... can ... d'you think* in:

Surely they can't possibly be serious about it can they d'you think ?

Textual systems generate patterns that differ from both of these, culminative patterns formed by peaks of prominence; and since these peaks typically appear at the beginning or the end of the clause, where there is a sequence of clauses they result in a kind of periodicity, a movement from a clause-initial peak via an off-peak medial state to a clause-final peak which is then sustained to form the initial peak of the succeeding clause. Thus a clause is at one and the same time particle, field and wave, as Pike suggested more than twenty years ago (Pike 1959), although the details of this interpretation are not quite the same as those worked out by Pike.

Now, the significance of this step in our interpretation lies not only in establishing that these three distinct patterns of realization go to make up the English clause, but also in the fact that they appear to be non-arbitrary; this is clearly important when we come to ask whether such tendencies are found in every language. The grammar of languages is a natural grammar; as I expressed it earlier, there is no line of arbitrariness between semantics and grammar as there is between grammar and phonology. If the clause is at once particle, field and wave this is because the meanings it has to express have different semiotic contours, to which these three realizational forms correspond in a natural, non-arbitrary way.

The particular nature of ideational structures reflects the relative discreteness of the phenomena of our experience. Consider *cows eat grass*: we know where the cow begins and ends, what eating is and is not, which part of reality consists of grass and which part consists of other things. Many of our perceptions are schematized into entities that are bounded in this way, and the constituent-like form of the wording reflects this fact: the word *cow* has an outline because the object cow has an outline. Of course not all experience is like this; indeed I have always tended to emphasize the unboundedness of many phenomena, the indeterminacy and the flux; and I share Whorf's view that language itself, once it has been constituted in this way, strongly influences the forms that our perceptions take. Nevertheless there is a basic fit between the discreteness of words and the discreteness of things; otherwise we should not be able to talk about the things at all, or explain contrastively those instances where the fit of words to things is less than perfect.

By contrast, the interpersonal kind of meaning is a motif that runs throughout the clause; and this is represented by lexicogrammatical or phonological motifs that are likewise strung unboundedly throughout. The speaker's attitudes and assessments; his judgements of validity and probability; his choice of speech function, the mode of exchange in dialogue – such things are not discrete elements that belong at some particular juncture, but semantic features that inform continuous stretches of discourse. It is natural that they should be realized not segmentally but prosodically, by structures (if that term is still appropriate) that are not particulate but field-like. The linguist's tree is an inappropriate construct for representing structures of this kind.

Thirdly, the undulatory movement by which textual meanings are encoded in the English clause may again be in some sense a natural form for their representation. All the patterns I have been discussing vary from language to language, as is very obvious; those of English merely provide one specific instance of something that seems to be a general tendency in the expression of meanings of each kind. The English clause, as a message, is a movement from prominence to prominence, a diminuendo that is then picked up and becomes a crescendo; but the prominence is of two different kinds. It is a movement away from a Theme, to something that we can characterize as non-Theme; that is the diminuendo aspect. It is a movement towards a New, from something that we can characterize as non-New; that is the crescendo aspect. But Theme is not the same as non-New, nor is New the same as non-Theme; there are two movements here, not one. Their relationship is less automatic than the above formulation implies, and they can be combined in other ways besides; what is described here is just the unmarked, typical form. The essential point is that the two types of prominence differ; and that they differ as speaker to listener. The Theme is speaker-oriented prominence: it is "what I am on about" (grammarians used to call it the psychological subject). The New is hearer-oriented prominence: it is "what I present as news to you". The English clause is textured by this shift in its orientation, from speaker-prominence to listener-prominence. Each clause is in this sense a kind of gift, one move in an exchange, symbolized by the change of perspective from me to you. So when Alice says:

it turned into a pig

in answer to the Cheshire Cat's question *What became of the baby?*, she begins with the Theme *it* ('I'm going to tell you about something') and ends with the New *a pig* ('here's what is news to you'). In this case, Alice has obligingly chosen as her Theme the thing that the Cat had asked her about, namely the baby, realized by the anaphoric reference item *it*; and she has kept the news, its change of state, till last. Alice is being helpful, keeping the wave pattern of the dialogue in phase. But she need not do this; the Theme is the speaker's choice, and in any case there is not always a ready-made candidate for thematic status. Compare the following instance:

"How am I to get in ?" Alice repeated, aloud.
"I shall sit here," the Footman remarked, "till to-morrow − "

The Footman, just like the rest of us, favours himself as an unmarked Theme.

So the patterns of wording in the clause, which is the basic unit of lexicogrammatical organization, display a variation that derives from the different kinds of meaning they express; and the structural shape is in each case a natural product of the semantic functions. A functional grammar is an interpretation of the primary semiotic purposes that language has evolved to serve, and of the different ways in which meanings relating to these different purposes tend to be encoded (and the patterns just described are only tendencies). When we go on to observe the developmental processes whereby young children construct their language, we gain a further insight into the steps by which grammar may have evolved on the way towards its present form.

2 FROM CLAUSE TO TEXT

Since the functions that we have called ideational, interpersonal and textual are components of the semantic system, and since a text is a semantic unit, it follows that these components will be present in the text just as they are in the lexicogrammatical entities, the wordings, by which the text is realized. In this sense, then, a clause is bound to be like a text: it originates in the same meaning potential. But to say this is to say no more than that both derive from the linguistic system – a point that is perhaps worth making, since text is still sometimes treated as if it had no source of its existence in language, but is nevertheless not saying a very great deal. The problem to be solved is how features from these semantic components are represented, on the one hand in clauses and on the other hand in texts, and with what kind of systematic relationship between the two, such that the clause can function as the principal medium through which meanings of such different kinds, and differing domains, are coded into an expressible form.

In this latter half of the paper I will suggest two different facets of the clause-to-text analogy, which correspond to the two axes of the relationship of clause to text that I referred to earlier: their relationship in size, and their relationship in abstraction. To go from text to clause involves a move along the axes both of composition (constituency) and of realization. I shall consider the size dimension first.

(A) Do we find, extending over a whole text, patterns that are like those we find in the clause? Let us take each of the three functional components in turn.

1. Ideational. Like a clause, a text has an ideational structure, with something of the same particulate kind of organization: it is possible to recognize functional constituents of a text, always allowing (as in the clause) for some variation in sequence and a certain amount of overlapping. These structural elements have been identified most clearly, perhaps, in narrative; and the researches of Pike, Longacre and their co-workers on the one hand, and of Gleason and his colleagues on the other, have provided a rich body of empirical findings about the structure of narrative in languages and cultures from every continent. Other genres have been less thoroughly studied.

Sinclair and Coulthard (1975), in their study of the structure of classroom discourse, set up a rank scale, a hierarchy of constituents each with its own configuration of functional elements. Ruqaiya Hasan (1979) considers that this structural organization is a general feature of texts of all genres; in her studies of transactional discourse she recognizes optional and obligatory elements, variations in sequence, recursive options and the like, all of which make the text structure look rather similar to the ideational structure that is characteristic of the clause. We can sum this up by saying that, in at least some genres, and perhaps in all, a text is a configuration of functional elements, collectively representing some complex construct of experience and typically realized as discrete, bounded constituents in a partially determinate sequence.

Within the ideational component there is a category of conjunctive relations of the types of "and, or, nor, viz, yet, so then", which can be coded in a great variety of different ways. They appear in many forms within the clause and even within clause constituents; most typically, perhaps, they link clauses in a hypotactic or paratactic clause complex. But they also function as semantic links over longer passages of discourse. Martin (1992) has interpreted these relations in a generalized system network and suggested how they may be accounted for as an aspect of the ideational structure of a text.

2. Interpersonal. A clause has an interpersonal pattern of organization, including a modal structure (mood, modality and key) which expresses its character as a speech event. In the same way a text has a unified character as a rhetorical event. In a recent study, Melrose (1979) makes the suggestion that a text or portion of a text derives its character from the type of process, in the transitivity system, that is predominant in it: material including action, event, behaviour; mental, including perception, reaction, cognition; verbal; or relational, including attributive, equative, existential. This "type of process" is of course an ideational category; but a clustering of processes of the same kind expresses the rhetorical design of the text rather in the same way that a particular complex of ideational features such as "I am certain" or "I want to know" functions as the interpersonal motif of a clause. The bridging concept in this case is the *field of discourse*, which is the aspect of the context of situation of a text by which the transitivity selections in it tend to be mainly determined (Halliday 1977); the "field" is defined as the nature of the social action in which the text is playing some part, and this naturally limits the range of possible parts that are open to it to play (Appendix 4).

3. Textual. That discourse displays some kind of a wave form, with peaks of prominence at both ends, has been a commonplace of rhetorical

theory ever since it was first hypothesized that a text has a beginning, a middle and an end. (This is perhaps one of the few examples of a verifiable hypothesis in linguistics, though characteristically in order to be verified it has first to be trivialized.) The concept of the paragraph is based on the notion of culminatives, with terms such as initiating, introductory or topic sentence referring to movement downwards from a beginning, and terms such as culminating, summative or focal sentence referring to movement upwards to an end. The diminuendo–crescendo pattern we find in the clause is thus also present in the paragraph, and probably in other text units as well: a text can justifiably be thought of as a construct of waves within waves. And this nesting of wave-like structures one inside another is characteristic also of lexicogrammatical organization: among the constituents of the clause in English, endocentric word groups (verbal groups and nominal groups) display this same kind of movement from speaker prominence to listener prominence. So when a linguist says to his editor *I have been going to finish my three brilliant articles for you ever since the beginning of the year*, the verbal group *have been going to finish* goes from the speaker prominent deictic *have*, locating the process in speech time, to the listener-prominent lexical item *finish*, saying what the process actually is; and the nominal group *my three brilliant articles* likewise goes from a deictic *my*, locating the object in speaker space, to a lexical item *articles*, again giving the main piece of information. This is essentially the same complex movement as that from Theme to non-Theme and from non-New to New in the clause. So both text and clause can be seen to participate in a multilayered pattern of organization in which the movement has this same underlying periodicity repeated over structures of differing extent.

So much for what we might call the metonymic aspect of the relation of clause to text. Now we turn to the metaphorical: where the feature that we have identified in the clause is not being repeated on a larger canvas, as in the instances just considered, but rather is standing as the realization of something else that is a feature of the text.

However, not only is it realizing a text feature, but also, given the naturalness of fit that we were able to establish between the grammar and the semantics, it has a similarity, in some transformed way, to the feature which it serves to realize.

(B) 1. Ideational. Cohesion, as defined by Halliday and Hasan (1976), is the semantic resource through which textual coherence is realized. A text displays cohesion; and this cohesion is achieved by means of a variety of features of the clause, which serve to relate one clause to others that constitute its context. However, while cohesion is a necessary condition of textual coherence, it is not by itself sufficient to guarantee it; and in her subsequent studies Ruqaiya Hasan (1984) has been comparing pairs of texts, of similar nature and origin, where one is judged coherent and the other not, in order to establish what are the differences between them. She has one set of texts which are stories told by children; she has also examined texts from schizophrenic patients, including a pair of texts from one particular patient, one when undergoing treatment and the other when the same patient was judged as having been cured. In each case all the texts display typical chains of identity or similarity, ongoing representations of some participant or some other element of the semantic structure – a process, perhaps, or an attribute, or a complex concept of some kind. Now, in the texts judged to be coherent, these lexicoreferential chains were systematically interrelated: a majority of the occurrences in any one chain were related to occurrences in some other chain. They were systematically related, that is to say, in the ideational structure of the clause; for example as Agent to Process, or Attribute to Carrier, or by their both having the same role with reference to some other element, such as both being carriers of the same attribute. In the texts that were judged to be non-coherent, on the other hand, although the proportion of lexicoreferential occurrences entering into cohesive chains was no less than in the coherent texts, only a minority of these occurrences were cross-related in this way; in general, the recurring elements ran alongside each other through the text but without intermingling to any extent. The coherence of the text appears to be the product of this "interchaining". If a text is coherent there is a movement of related particles through a succession of clauses, so that not only do the individual particles persist from one clause to another, but the structural configurations, though not remaining static, also preserve a recognizable continuity. Just as individual elements form a clause not as isolated entities but as roles in a structural configuration, so chains of elements form a text not as isolated chains but as role-chains in an ongoing configurational movement (Appendix 1).

2. Interpersonal. How does one recognize the unique rhetorical flavour of a text? Partly at least from the overall pattern of interpersonal features of the individual clauses. A text has its own character as an inter-subjective event, and this **tenor of discourse** is manifested primarily through the cumulative force of the options taken up in the interpersonal systems of meaning. In Priestley's play *An Inspector Calls*, the underlying theme, or rather one of the underlying themes, is that of social responsibility: we are all members of one body. This confers obligations on all of us, each one towards others. In the course of the play these

obligations are acted out – or rather the consequences of their not being fulfilled are acted out – through the step-by-step uncovering of a chain of irresponsibility, compounded by sheer chance and observed through a confusion of prejudices and doubts. Now, the three conceptual fields of probability, opinion and obligation together comprise the semantic raw material of the complex system of modality in the grammar of English. It is not surprising therefore that the underlying semiotic of the play is worked out metaphorically, at a critical point in the action, through the highlighting of modal selections within the clause, backed up by lexical choices from the same semantic fields. The clauses in this key passage, each with its own small momentum, combine to produce a powerful semantic movement, a motif first of chance and then of duty, both hedged around by opinion, and culminating, after a narrative monologue serving as commentary, in a burst of direct assertion in which the modalities are finally swept away. As audience we respond to this movement even though the events which call it forth are in themselves trivial, no more than an argument over the identification of a photograph. Here the interpersonal features of the clause stand as a metaphor for the social semiotic of the text, as an exploration of the complex symbolic structures binding men to their fellow men (Appendix 5).

3. Textual. The last two examples suggest that we can 'read off' significant aspects of the semiotic quality of a text from looking at the transitivity and modal features that predominate in the individual clauses. When we come to consider the rhetorical organization of a text, this too can be discovered from a reading of the clause patterns, in this case those having to do with functional sentence perspective: what are the elements that function predominantly as theme, and what are the elements that function predominantly as news. In his study of the thematic organization of discourse, Fries (1981) has shown how these patterns realize the development of the paragraph. Examining a tightly constructed paragraph by Lytton Strachey, Fries found three lexicosemantic chains, one having to do with the opposition of wisdom and chance, one with the English constitution, and one with political apparatus in general; of the three, the former was overwhelmingly associated with initial position in the clause, the second with final position, while the third showed no particular pattern of distribution. Fries points out that this reflects the rhetorical interpretation of the paragraph as having the "wisdom versus chance" motif as its method of development and the English constitution as its main point. Thus the **mode of discourse** is manifested in the same cumulative manner by the ongoing selections, in each clause, from

the thematic and informational systems, those comprising the "textual" element in the meaning potential of the clause (Appendix 3).

I am not suggesting, of course, that listeners and readers process text in a conscious manner, parsing each clause as they go along. On the contrary, speaking and understanding are, as Boas and Sapir always insisted, among the most unconscious of all the processes of human culture. The conscious task is that which falls to the linguist, when he tries to find out how text is organized. Listeners and readers make predictions – they have a good idea of what to expect; if they did not make these predictions, with a greater than chance probability of being right, they would not be able to understand each other. It is the organization of a text, and in particular the relation of a text, as a semantic unit, to a clause as the primary lexicogrammatical unit through which it is realized, that makes such prediction possible. The linguistic analysis of text is a necessary step in the interpretation of how meanings are exchanged.

A clause, while it realizes directly only a very small unit of text (sometimes referred to as a "message unit"), stands also as the realization of a text as a whole, or some structurally significant portion of it, in the indirect, metaphorical sense that these examples suggest. The former is its automatic function, as determined by the system of the language. The latter is what Mukařovský (1977) recognized as "deautomatization": still, of course, part of the potential of the linguistic system but deployed in a metagrammatical way, conveying meaning by the act of systemic choice instead of (in fact always as well as) by the act of realization. A clause is a text in microcosm, a "universe of discourse" of its own in which the semiotic properties of a text reappear on a miniature scale. This is what enables the clause to function as it does. What are clauses for? – to make it possible to create text. A clause does this effectively because it has itself evolved by analogy with the text as a model, and can thus represent the meanings of a text in a rich variety of different ways.

Appendices

Appendix 1

From Hasan (1980a)

Text A

1. once upon a time there <u>was</u> a <u>little girl</u>
2. and <u>she went</u> out for a walk

3. and <u>she</u> saw a <u>lovely</u> <u>little</u> <u>teddybear</u>
4. and so <u>she</u> <u>took</u> <u>it</u> <u>home</u>
5. and when she got home she washed it
6. and when <u>she</u> <u>took</u> *<u>it</u>* <u>to</u> bed with <u>her</u> <u>she</u> <u>cuddled</u> <u>it</u>
7. and <u>she</u> <u>fell</u> *<u>straight</u>* <u>to</u> <u>sleep</u>
8. and when <u>she</u> <u>got</u> up <u>and</u> (_) <u>combed</u> <u>it</u> with a <u>little</u> wirebrush the <u>teddybear</u> <u>opened</u> *<u>his</u>* <u>eyes</u>
9. and (_) started to <u>speak</u> to <u>her</u>
10. and <u>she</u> <u>had</u> <u>the</u> <u>teddybear</u> for <u>many</u> <u>many</u> <u>weeks</u> and <u>years</u>
11. and so when <u>the</u> <u>teddybear</u> <u>got</u> <u>dirty</u> she used to <u>wash</u> <u>it</u>
12. and every time <u>she</u> <u>brushed</u> <u>it</u> <u>it</u> used to <u>say</u> some <u>new</u> words from a different country
13. and that's how <u>she</u> used to know how to <u>speak</u> <u>English</u> <u>Scottish</u> and <u>all</u> <u>the</u> <u>rest</u>

Text B

1. <u>the</u> <u>sailor</u> <u>goes</u> on the ship
2. and <u>he's</u> <u>coming</u> <u>home</u> with a <u>dog</u>
3. and <u>the</u> <u>dog</u> wants <u>the</u> <u>boy</u> and <u>the</u> <u>girl</u>
4. and <u>they</u> don't know <u>the</u> <u>bear's</u> in the <u>chair</u>
5. and <u>the</u> <u>bear's</u> coming to <u>go</u> to <u>sleep</u> in <u>it</u>
6. and <u>they</u> find <u>the</u> <u>bear</u> in the <u>chair</u>
7. <u>they</u> <u>wake</u> <u>him</u> up
8. and (-----) <u>chuck</u> <u>him</u> out the <u>room</u>
9. and (-----) take <u>it</u> to the zoo
10. <u>the</u> <u>sailor</u> takes his hat off
11. and <u>the</u> <u>dog's</u> <u>chased</u> <u>the</u> <u>bear</u> out <u>the</u> <u>room</u>
12. and <u>the</u> <u>boy</u> will sit down in <u>their</u> chair what <u>the</u> <u>bear</u> was <u>sleeping</u> in

Underlined items are those which enter into lexico-referential chains. Broken underlining indicates that one item incorporates more than one token, for example <u>they</u> referring to the girl, the boy, the sailor and the dog. Empty underlining within parenthesis (_), (-----) indicates a token or tokens presupposed by ellipsis.

The number of lexico-referential tokens in the two texts is not very different: 66 in Text A, 56 in Text B. But whereas 43 of those in Text A (65 per cent) occur in chain interaction, the comparable figure for Text B is only 20 (36 per cent). Text A thus displays considerably greater cohesive harmony.

When subjects were asked to judge the coherence of the two texts, Text A was consistently rated "more coherent" than Text B.

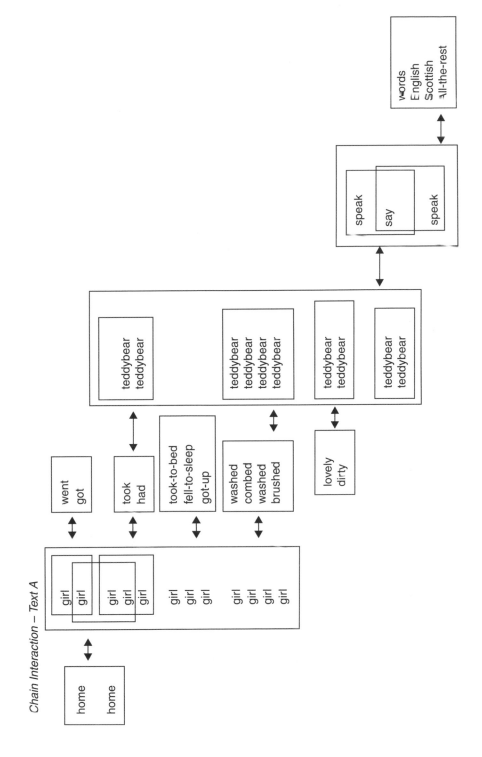

Chain Interaction – Text A

Chain Interaction – Text B

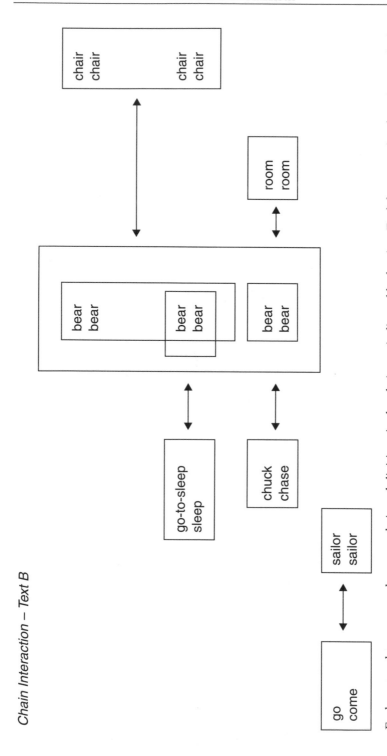

Each rectangle corresponds to one chain; subdivisions in the chain are indicated by boxing. Each box contains those items which are in a constant functional relation (shown by a double-headed arrow) to items in some box in a different chain; for example in Text A, between *girl* (4) and the box containing *washed . . . brushed* there is an actor-action relation; between the latter and *teddybear* (4), a relation of actional-goal.

Appendix 2

FROM JAMES R. MARTIN (1984)

 1. B: Lips are a must.
 2.   They're in fashion.
 3.   So . . . what are you using in your skin care?
 4. A: Oh I just – I don't know.
 5.   Something my mom gets: Ponds or something.
 6. B: Yes.
 7. A: I don't know.
 8. B: Well really uh that's not good enough really.
 9.   You want something that's going to treat the skin.
10.   You need to cleanse your skin well
11.   uh to use a good toner
12. A: Hmm.
13. B: and moisturiser is a must
14.   and of course then you can go into the make-up.
15.   But if you do all these things
16.   our skin will start to improve.
17. A: Yeah.
18. B: You're finding a few little spots under your skin, aren't you?

                    Talking Shop: scene 21 Halliday and Poole (1978).

Appendix 2 (continued)

Appendix 2 (continued)

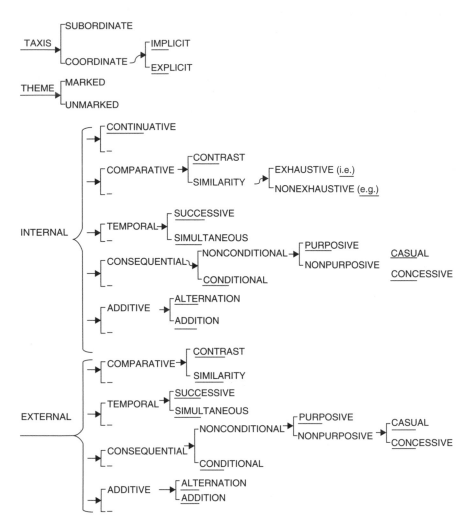

Figure 1 The system of CONJUNCTION in English

Appendix 2 (continued)

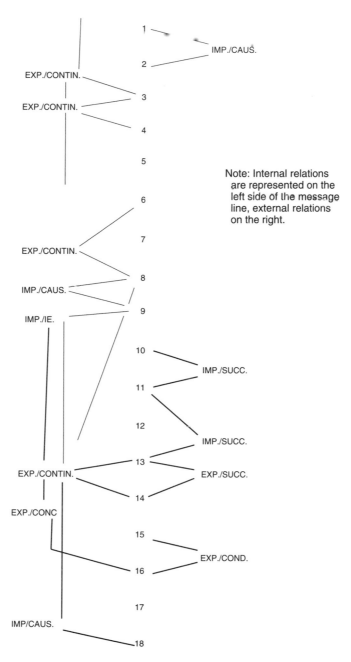

Figure 2 Conjunctive relations in *Talking Shop* (scene 21)

Appendix 3

FROM PETER FRIES (1981)

1. A. <u>The English Constitution</u> – that indescribable entity – is a living thing, growing with the growth of men, and assuming ever-varying forms in accordance with the subtle and complex laws of human character.
2. B. <u>It</u> is the child of wisdom and chance.
3.   C. <u>The wise men of 1688</u> moulded it into the shape we know.
4.   C. <u>but the chance that George I could not speak English</u> gave it one of its essential peculiarities – the system of a cabinet independent of the Crown and subordinate to the Prime Minister.
5.   C. <u>The wisdom of Lord Grey</u> saved it from petrification and set it upon the path of democracy.
6.   C. <u>Then</u> <u>chance</u> intervened once more.
7.   D. <u>A female sovereign</u> happened to marry an able and pertinacious man,
8.   D. <u>and it seemed likely</u> that an element which had been quiescent within it for years – the element of irresponsible administrative power – was about to become its predominant characteristic and change completely the direction of its growth.
9.   C. <u>But what chance gave</u> chance took away.
10.   D. <u>The Consort</u> perished in his prime,
11.   D. <u>and the English Constitution</u>, dropping the dead limb with hardly a tremor, continued its mysteric life as if he had never been.

Queen Victoria, Lytton Strachey (p. 192)

[The above] is a well constructed para graph which contains within it three lexical systems; the first concerns living, growing, changing, the second system concerns wisdom versus chance and the third system concerns concepts having to do with government. From reading the paragraph it is clear that the main point of the paragraph is that the English constitution is living, growing and changing, that the paragraph is developed via the opposition between wisdom and chance and that the lexical system having to do with government plays no particular role within the structure of the paragraph. On examining the paragraph one finds that the terms having to do with living, growing and changing typically occur within the rhemes of the component sentences of the paragraph. The terms having to do with wisdom and chance, with certain exceptions which can be explained, occur within the themes of the component sentences. The terms having to do with the form of government occur more or less equally within the themes and rhemes of the component sentences of the paragraph. Thus the consistent placement of the terms of a lexical system inside or outside the themes of the component sentences of the paragraph affect the perceived role of that lexical system within the paragraph as a whole.

[Hence] a) the lexical material placed initially within each sentence of a paragraph (i.e. the themes of each sentence of a paragraph) indicates the point of departure of the message expressed by that sentence, and b) the information contained within the themes of all the sentences of a paragraph creates the method of development of that paragraph. Thus if the themes of most of the sentences of a paragraph refer to one semantic field (say location, parts of some object, wisdom vs chance, etc.) then that semantic field will be perceived as the method of development of the paragraph. If no common semantic element runs through the themes of the sentences of a paragraph, then no simple method of development will be perceived.

Appendix 4

FROM ROBIN MELROSE (1979)

The remaining eleven sections deal with every aspect of life, regulating it at every stage and aspect, ordering everything, forcing everything into a symmetrical pattern: the cities are uniform, married life is strictly controlled, education is minutely prescribed. Philosophy is confined within rigid limits, the fine arts somewhat less so (. . .) This planned paradise is enforced by drastic penal laws. Machinery of government is paternalistic and pyramidal. It is based on division into families, tribes, cities and provinces, and, in the case of the different crafts and professions, on units of ten. To each unit of work is assigned its "master" (. . .) Each paterfamilias over fifty is a senator, each family in turn provides a tribal chief, each town in turn a city chief. Subordinate senates of cities are controlled by the Supreme Senate. At the head of the state is the General.

Totalitarianism, Leonard Schapiro (pp. 87–8)

Theme:

The remaining eleven sections; the cities; married life; education; Philosophy; This planned paradise; Machinery of government; It; To each unit of work; Each paterfamilias over fifty; each family; Subordinate senates of cities; At the head of state

Lexical Cohesion:
Group A:

> regulating ; ordering ; forcing ; uniform ; controlled ; prescribed ; confined ; planned ; enforced ; penal laws ; paternalistic and pyramidal

This is a particularly clear example of an attributive message. It begins with a summation, "every aspect of life", with the general noun "aspect" acting as Head of a nominal group. It is this summation which determines the Theme of the clauses that follow: thematic prominence is assigned precisely to aspects of life, so that there is a relationship of superordinate to hyponym between summation and Theme in the message, reinforced by Theme in the last five clauses, which is in a relationship of hyponym to "machinery of government", itself an aspect of life.

There is no explicit conjunction of interest : the chief conjunctive relationship is an implicit one, of the internal additive type. More worthy of attention is the lexical string of Group A. Just as Theme was determined by the summation, so the lexical string of Group A is determined by the non-finite clauses dependent on the clause of which the summation is an element. Together with the three verbs in these non-finite clauses, nine lexical items of the message proper constitute a string of synonyms, near-synonyms, and collocates – and of these nine, six function as Complement, and so form a kind of pattern in the Rheme. Thus it may be seen that in this attributive message the summation and the clause complex of which it is an element are both closely related to the message proper that follows: the summation is hyperonymously linked to the Theme, and the clause complex (or, more precisely, the non-finite clause) is synonymously connected – with one exception – to the Rheme. Or, to put it another way, it is most often the case that "aspects of life" are encoded in the Subject, while "regulation" is realised in the Complement.

Characteristics of message types
Table adapted from Melrose's Table 4, p. 50.

	Factual	Phenomenal	Relational
Type of Process	material (doing, happening)	mental (seeing, feeling, thinking); verbal (saying)	relational (being – attribute, identity)
Characteristic Theme	main participant	cognizant / sayer or phenomenon / discourse	synonym or hyponym of summative element

	Factual	Phenomenal	Relational
Typical Conjunction	external temporal	external or internal additive or temporal	internal additive or adversative
Summative Element	general noun, of which message is meronym	general noun, of which message is hyponym	general noun + expansion, of which message is meronym

Appendix 5

FROM M. A. K. HALLIDAY (1982)

Mrs. Birling:	I think we've just about come to an end of this wretched business.
Gerald:	I don't think so. Excuse me.
	(He goes out. They watch him go in silence. We hear the front door slam.)
Sheila:	(to Inspector) You know, you never showed him that photograph of her.
Inspector:	No. It wasn't necessary. And I thought it better not to.
Mrs. Birling:	You have a photograph of this girl?
Inspector:	Yes. I think you'd better look at it.
Mrs. Birling:	I don't see any particular reason why I should –
Inspector:	Probably not. But you'd better look at it.
Mrs. Birling:	Very well.
	(He produces the photograph and she looks hard at it.)
Inspector:	(taking back the photograph) You recognize her?
Mrs. Birling:	No. Why should I?
Inspector:	Of course she might have changed lately, but I can't believe she could have changed so much.
Mrs. Birling:	I don't understand you, Inspector.
Inspector:	You mean you don't choose to do, Mrs. Birling.
Mrs. Birling:	(angrily) I meant what I said.
Inspector:	You're not telling me the truth.
Mrs. Birling:	I beg your pardon!
Birling:	(angrily, to Inspector) Look here, I'm not going to have this, Inspector. You'll apologize at once.
Inspector:	Apologize for what – doing my duty?
Birling:	No, for being so offensive about it. I'm a public man –
Inspector:	(massively) Public men, Mr. Birling, have responsibilities as well as privileges.
Birling:	Possibly. But you weren't asked to come here to talk to me about my responsibilities.

Sheila: Let's hope not. Though I'm beginning to wonder.

Mrs. Birling: Does that mean anything, Sheila?

Sheila: It means that we've no excuse now for putting on airs and that if we've any sense we won't try. Father threw this girl out because she asked for decent wages. I went and pushed her further out, right into the street, just because I was angry and she was pretty. Gerald set her up as his mistress and then dropped her when it suited him. And now you are pretending you don't recognize her from that photograph. I admit I don't know why you should, but I know jolly well you did in fact recognize her, from the way you looked. And if you're not telling the truth, why should the Inspector apologize? And can't you see, both of you, you're making it worse? (She turns away. We hear the front door slam again.)

An Inspector Calls, J. B. Priestley (Act 2)

In the text, obligation is tied to judgements of probability: there are opinions relating to duties, and, as a minor motif, duties relating to opinions. The two themes are closely interwoven. We have already seen that this is a projection into the text of a relation that exists between them in the system. The scales of "possible–certain" and "allowed–required" both typically combine with a common semantic feature, that of "subjective", in the sense of representing the speaker's judgment; and this is symbolized by the use of modal verbs as one form of the realization of both.

The significance of the lexicogrammatical selections in the text can only be fully revealed by a consideration of their value in the semantic system. Textually, the passage under discussion centres around the scrutiny and recognition of a photograph. The words and structures which, in their automatic function as the "output" of semantic choices, carry forward the movement of the text, also become de-automatized and so take on a life of their own as engenderers of meaning.

Example of modalized clause complex

Inspector: Of course she might have changed lately, but I can't believe she could have changed so much.

Clause 1 *polarity* positive

          modality low / (indicative : probability) / (subjective : congruent)

Clause 2 *polarity* negative : transferred

          modality high /

                    (a) *can* (imperative : inclination) / (subjective : congruent)

(b) *I . . . not believe* (indicative / probability) / (subjective : explicit)

(c) *could* (indicative / probability) / (subjective : congruent)

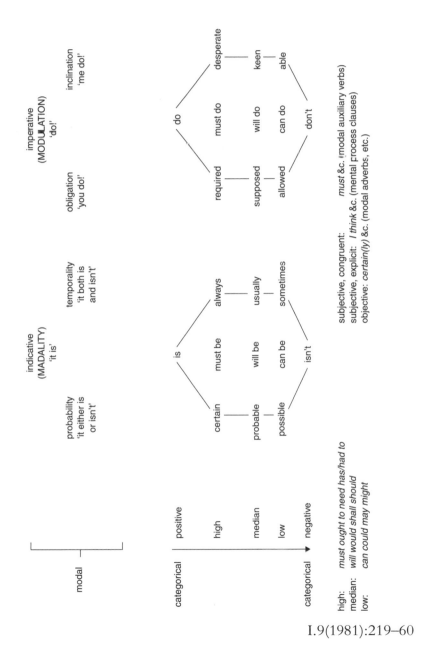

I.9(1981):219–60

Additional readings

On Grammar (Volume 1) – 8(1979):206–7; 10(1985); 12(1987):328
Linguistic Studies of Text and Discourse (Volume 2)
On Language and Linguistics (Volume 3) – 13(2001):279; 16(1992):373
The Language of Early Childhood (Volume 4) –3(1976):70; 7(1975):160, 185–96
Computational and Quantitative Studies (Volume 6) – 8(2002)
Studies in English Language (Volume 7) – 7(1985):216–31
Studies in Chinese Language (Volume 8) – 1(1959); 9(2001)

Chapter Eighteen

THEORY AND DESCRIPTION

Summary

Description is not theory, but it must be grounded in a theory of how language works at the level of grammar. The aim is to describe contextualized systematic sounds, i.e. language, on several levels, including phonic substance (realization), form (lexicogrammar), and context (semantics). The description is oriented more to the paradigmatic axis of representation, seeing language not simply as structure, but primarily as system, in which language is modeled as a meaning-making resource rather than as an inventory of items. Inherent to this paradigmatic orientation is the cline of delicacy, or 'depth in detail', at one end of which is the primary degree in the categories of structure and rank, and at the other end is some point where distinctions into secondary structures blur into homogeny. Since, even at the primary degree, the description may still be comprehensive, so any decision about the degree of delicacy to be achieved depends on the means at one's disposal.

Selected readings

On Grammar (Volume 1)

There have been in the main two approaches to description in modern linguistics: the "textual" and the non-textual or, for want of a better word, "exemplificatory". More recently a third has been added, primarily in grammar but lately also in phonology, the "generative" (strictly "transformative–generative", since generation does not presuppose transformation). Some linguists have gone so far as to suggest that transformative generation should replace other types of description[1] as a linguistic method of making statements about language.[2] Others, myself included, feel that all three approaches have a fundamental place in linguistics; that they do different things, and that the third is a valuable supplement to the first two.[3]

Description is, however, not theory. All description, whether generative or not, is related to General Linguistic theory; specifically, to that part of General Linguistic theory which accounts for how language works. The different types of description are bodies of method which derive from, and are answerable to, that theory. Each has its place in linguistics, and it is a pity to deny the value of textual description (which is appropriate, for example, in "stylistics", the linguistic study of literature) just because certain of the methods used in description are found to be inadequate.

My purpose in writing this paper is to suggest what seem to me to be the fundamental categories of that part of General Linguistic theory which is concerned with how language works at the level of grammar, with brief reference to the relations between grammar and lexis and between grammar and phonology. The theory sketched out here derives most of all from the work of J. R. Firth.[4] At the same time I do not of course imply that I think Professor Firth would necessarily have found himself in accord with all the views expressed, which in some places depart from his own; nor do I underestimate the debt to my present colleagues and the many others whose work I have, obviously, drawn on.[5]

No excuse is needed, I think, for a discussion of General Linguistic theory. While what has made linguistics fashionable has been, as with other subjects, the discovery that it has applications, these applications rest on many years of work by people who were simply seekers after knowledge. It would not help the subject if the success of these applications led us into thinking that the theoretical problems were solved and the basic issues closed.

1 STARTING-POINT

It will perhaps be helpful if the point of departure is first made clear. The following is a summary of what is taken as "given" for the purposes of this paper.

1.1 One part of General Linguistic theory is a theory of how language works. It is from this that the methods of Descriptive Linguistics are derived.

1.2 The relevant theory consists of a scheme of interrelated categories which are set up to account for the data, and a set of scales of abstraction which relate the categories to the data and to each other. The data to be accounted for are observed language events, observed as spoken or as codified in writing, any corpus of which, when used as material for linguistic description, is a "text".[6]

1.3 Description consists in relating the text to the categories of the theory. The methods by which this is done involve a number of processes of abstraction, varying in kind and variable in degree. It is the theory that determines the relation of these processes of abstraction to each other and to the theory.[7]

1.4 The theory requires that linguistic events should be accounted for at a number of different levels: this is found to be necessary because of the difference in kind of the processes of abstraction involved.[8]

1.5 The primary levels are *form*, *substance* and *context*. The substance is the material of language: *phonic* (audible noises) or *graphic* (visible marks). The form is the organization of the substance into meaningful events: *meaning* is a concept, and a technical term, of the theory (see below, 1.8). The context is the relation of the form to non-linguistic features of the situations in which language operates, and to linguistic features other than those of the item under attention: these being together "extratextual" features.

1.6 The complete framework of levels requires certain further subdivisions and additions, and is as follows:

(a) Substance may be either *phonic* or *graphic*.
(b) If substance is phonic, it is related to form by *phonology*.
(c) If substance is graphic, it is related to form by *orthography* (or *graphology*),[9] either
  (i) if the script is lexical, then directly, or
  (ii) if the script is phonological, then via phonology.
(d) Form is in fact two related levels, *grammar* and *lexis*.
(e) Context is in fact (like phonology) an *interlevel* relating form to extratextual features.

1.7 The study of phonic substance belongs to a distinct but related body of theory, that of General Phonetics. Since phonology relates form and phonic substance, it is the place where linguistics and phonetics interpenetrate. Linguistics and phonetics together make up "the linguistic sciences".[10]

1.8 Language has *formal meaning* and *contextual meaning*. Formal meaning is the "information" of information theory, though (i) it can be stated without being quantified and was in fact formulated in linguistics independently of the development of information theory as a means of quantifying it,[11] and (ii) formal meaning in lexis cannot be quantified

405

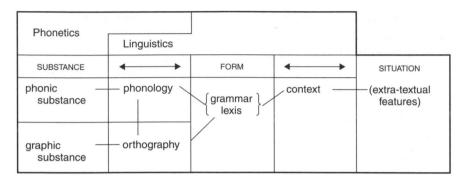

Figure 1 Levels of language

until a method is found for measuring the information of non-finite ("open") sets (see below, 2.1 and I.2(1961):60-1). The formal meaning of an item is its operation in the network of formal relations.

1.9 Contextual meaning, which is an extension of the popular – and traditional linguistic – notion of meaning, is quite distinct from formal meaning and has nothing whatever to do with 'information'.[12] The contextual meaning of an item is its relation to extratextual features; but this is not a direct relation of the item as such, but of the item in its place in linguistic form: contextual meaning is therefore logically dependent on formal meaning.[13]

1.10 It follows from 1.8 and 1.9 that, in description, formal criteria are crucial, taking precedence over contextual criteria; and that the statement of formal meaning logically precedes the statement of contextual meaning.[14]

1.11 Finally, it is necessary to distinguish not only between theory and description but also between description and presentation. Presentation, the way the linguist expounds the description, varies with purpose, and relative merit is judged by reference to the specific purpose intended. Description depends on the theory; theoretical validity is demanded, and relative merit is judged by reference to comprehensiveness and delicacy.[15]

2 GRAMMAR

2.1 Grammar is that level of linguistic form at which operate closed systems.[16,17] Since a system is by definition closed, the use of the term "closed" here is a mnemonic device; but since "system" alone will be used as the name of one of the four fundamental grammatical categories (see I.2(1961):52-5) it is useful to retain "closed system" when referring to the system as the crucial criterion for distinguishing grammar from lexis.

A closed system is a set of terms with these characteristics:

(a) The number of terms is finite: they can be listed as A B C D, and all other items E . . . are outside the system.
(b) Each term is exclusive of all the others: a given term A cannot be identical with B or C or D.
(c) If a new term is added to the system this changes the meaning of all the others.[18]

Any part of linguistic form which is not concerned with the operation of closed systems belongs to the level of lexis. The distinction between closed system patterns and open set patterns in language is in fact a cline; but the theory has to treat them as two distinct types of pattern requiring different categories. For this reason General Linguistic theory must here provide both a theory of grammar and a theory of lexis, and also a means of relating the two. A description depending on General Linguistic theory will need to separate the descriptions of the two levels both from each other and from the description of their interrelations. This paper is primarily concerned with the theory of grammar, though reference will be made to lexis at various points.

2.2 The fundamental categories for the theory of grammar are four: *unit*, *structure*, *class* and *system*. These are categories of the highest order of abstraction: they are established, and interrelated, in the theory. If one asks: "why these four, and not three, or five, or another four?", the answer must be: because language is like that – because these four, and no others, are needed to account for the data: that is, to account for all grammatical patterns that emerge by generalization from the data. As the primary categories of the theory, they make possible a coherent account of what grammar is and of its place in language, and a comprehensive description of the grammars of languages, neither of which is possible without them.

Each of the four is specifically related to, and logically derivable from, each of the others. There is no relation of precedence or logical priority among them. They are all mutually defining: as with theoretical categories in general, "definition" in the lexicographical sense is impossible, since no one category is defined until all the others are, in the totality of the theory.[19] The order chosen here for exposition is therefore simply that which seemed the easiest: namely the order in which they are listed above.

The relation of these categories to each other and to the data involve three distinct scales of abstraction, those of *rank*, *exponence* and *delicacy*;

these are considered separately (see I.2(1961):55–9) but have also to be referred to in connection with the categories. In discussing these I have used the terms "hierarchy", "taxonomy" and 'cline' as general scale–types. A hierarchy is taken to mean a system of terms related along a single dimension which must be one involving some form of logical precedence (such as inclusion).[20] A taxonomy is taken to mean a special type of hierarchy, one with two additional characteristics: (i) there is a constant relation of each term to the term immediately following it, and a constant reciprocal relation of each to that immediately preceding it; and (ii) degree is significant, so that the place in order of each one of the terms, stable as the distance in number of steps from either end, is a defining characteristic of that term.[21] A cline resembles a hierarchy in that it involves relation along a single dimension; but instead of being made up of a number of discrete terms a cline is a continuum carrying potentially infinite gradation.

2.3 In this view of linguistics description is, as already emphasized, a body of method derived from theory, and **not** a set of procedures. This has one important consequence. If description is procedural, the only way of evaluating a given description is by reference to the procedures themselves: a good description is one that has carried out the right procedures in the right order, but for any more delicate evaluation external criteria have to be invoked. Moreover, every language has to be treated as if it was unknown, otherwise procedural rules will be violated; so the linguist has to throw away half his evidence and a good few of his tools.

A theory on the other hand provides a means for evaluating descriptions without reference to the order in which the facts are accounted for. The linguist makes use of all he knows and there is no priority of dependence among the various parts of the description. The best description is then that which, comprehensiveness presupposed, is maximally grammatical: that is, makes maximum use of the theory to account for a maximum amount of the data. Simplicity has then to be invoked only when it is necessary to decide between fewer systems with more terms and more systems with fewer terms; and since both information theory and linguistic intuition favour the latter even this preference might be built in to the theory.[22]

Notes

1. It is in no way to deny the fundamental importance of Chomsky's work (1957) and elsewhere, if we suggest that the readiness of linguists who had previously

worked in the "Bloomfieldian" tradition to abandon these methods in favour of Chomsky's is in part due to their lack of theoretical foundation. The point of view adopted here is that transformation-generation is a type of description which, like other types, depends on but does not replace a theory.

2. Even Chomsky (1961) seems to imply that a textual study cannot be theoretical. But a grammar of one short text **may** be based on theory; and any theory-based grammar, transformational or not, can be stated in generative terms.

3. Those linguists who have followed up the work of Firth have always tended to give more weight to textual description than have those following Bloomfield, since for the former meaning and the statement of meaning have always been integrated in the theory. Cf. Firth (1957a): "The object of linguistic analysis as here understood is to make statements of meaning so that we may see how we use language to live" (p. 23; cf. also p. 11).

4. Professor Firth died on 4 December 1960. I had just completed this paper and was planning to show it to him on the following day. Although he had not seen it and was in no way directly responsible for any of the opinions formulated here, the influence of his teaching and of his great scholarship will, I hope, be clearly apparent. See especially Firth (1955; 1957a; 1957c, chapters 9, 10, 14–16; 1957d).

5. Of major importance to me have been discussions, both on linguistic theory as a whole and on the specific subjects mentioned, with J. C. Catford, J. O. Ellis, A. McIntosh (lexis and "delicacy" – the latter concept is of his origination), J. M. Sinclair (English grammar) and J. P. Thorne (logical structure of linguistic theory, and the work of Chomsky).

6. As used by Firth (1957c: 225). Here "text" refers to the event under description, whether it appears as corpus (textual description), example (exemplificatory) or terminal string (transformative–generative).

7. The set of these abstractions, constituting the body of descriptive method, might be regarded as a "calculus", since its function is to relate the theory to the data. It is important to distinguish between calculus (description) and theory; also between description and the set of generalizations and hypotheses by which the theory was arrived at in the first place. The latter precede the theory and are not susceptible of "rigorization"; though we may distinguish the logical stages of observation–generalization–hypothetization–theory, keeping Hjelmslev's (1953: 8) distinction between "hypothesis" and "theory"; cf. Allen (1953: 53). Here we are concerned with the stages, once the theory is formulated, of theory–description–text.

8. Since the theory is a theory of how language works, it does not matter whether the levels are considered levels of language or levels of linguistics (theory or description): it comes to the same thing. Cf. Firth (1957c): "We must expect therefore that linguistic science will also find it necessary to postulate the maintenance of linguistic patterns and systems . . . within which there is order, structure and function. Such systems are maintained in activity, and in activity they are to be studied. It is on these grounds that linguistics must be systemic" (p. 143, cf. also pp. 187, 192).

9. Cf. McIntosh (1956). Professor McIntosh followed this up subsequently in a study of the underlying theoretical problems.

10. This figure is a schematic representation of §§1.5–1.7.

11. Cf. Firth (1957c): "A nominative in a four-case system would in this sense necessarily have a different 'meaning' from a nominative in a two-case or in a fourteen-case system, for example" (p. 227). The article from which this is quoted, "General linguistics and descriptive grammar", was published in 1951; but Firth's view of the "dispersal of meaning", that (i) form is meaningful and (ii) formal meaning is distinct from contextual meaning, antedates this by some time; it is in fact already clear, though without the precise formulation of formal meaning, in "The technique of semantics" (1935), also reprinted in Firth (1957c).

12. Some of what has been written on information theory and language is vitiated by the confusion between these two levels of meaning; cf. my reviews of Whatmough (Halliday 1958) and Herdan (Halliday 1959a). It is doubtful whether, even if contextual meaning can ever be quantified, it has anything to do with "information"; the latter is a function of the operation of (a term in) a system, and a linguistic item can never be a term in a contextual system even if such a thing can be rigorously described. Cf. I.2(1961):70-2.

13. The reason why "context" is preferred to "semantics" as the name of this interlevel is that 'semantics' is too closely tied to one particular method of statement, the conceptual method; cf. Firth (1957a: 9–10, 20). The latter, by attempting to link language form to unobservables, becomes circular, since concepts are only observable as (exponents of) the forms they are set up to "explain". The linguistic statement of context attempts to relate language form to (abstractions from) other (i.e. extratextual) observables.

14. Cf. Firth (1957a): "References to non-verbal constituents of situations are admissible in corroboration of formal linguistic characteristics stated as criteria for setting up . . . word–classes" (p. 15). The approach to context from the other end, that is from non-language, has been developed in an important monograph by William E. Bull (1960), as what he (perhaps unfortunately, in view of the formal use of "system") calls "systemic linguistics". The difficulty of this method lies in deciding on what Bull calls "those features of objective reality which are pertinent to the problem" (p. 3), since this can only be known by reference to linguistic forms: cf. e.g. "it may be assumed that normal people automatically divide, on the preverbal level, all events into three categories: those anterior to PP (point present) . . ., those simultaneous with PP . . ., and those posterior to PP" (p. 17); "The languages of the dominant world cultures use vector formulas, and the discussion which follows is therefore concerned only with the structure of a hypothetical tense system based on the vector principle" (p. 20); "The system, of course, would break down if a plus form were to be used to describe a minus event or if a form indicating anticipation were used for recollection" (p. 24). This does not invalidate the approach; it does suggest that it will have to be part of a study of context which starts from form as well as from "objective

reality", as phonology works both from form and from substance; context, like phonology, is in a real sense an interlevel.

15. Theoretical validity implies making maximum use of the theory (see below, 2.3 and I.2(1961):52-3). It is not necessary to add a separate criterion of "simplicity", since this is no use unless defined; and it would then turn out to be a property of a maximally grammatical description, since complication equals a weakening of the power of the theory and hence less grammaticalness. It should perhaps also be mentioned here that the distinction between methods of description and discovery procedures is here taken for granted throughout (cf. below, 2.3). We are **not** concerned with how the linguist "finds out" how an event is to be described. This is no more capable of scientific exposition than are the steps by which the theory was arrived at in the first place − in fact less, since the latter can at least be formulated, while the former can only be summed up in the words of the song: "I did what I could".

16. Cf. Firth (1957a: 22), and above, 1.8 n. 11; Garvin (1957); see I.2(1961):53-4, n. 60; Robins (1959).

17. "Grammar" is also the name for the study of grammar; as with "level" (above, 1.4 n. 8), it is unnecessary to distinguish between "the grammar" of a language and "grammar" in theory and description − though a distinction is often made between "lexis" and "lexicology", the latter being the study of lexis. Again, **not** a set of discovery procedures, but a set of properties of what the linguist accounts for grammatically. The grammar of a language can only be "defined" as that part of the language that is accounted for by grammatical description.

18. The reference is, of course, in formal meaning: it is form that is under discussion. It may always happen that the addition of a new term changes the contextual meaning of at least one of the others, since terms that are formally mutually exclusive are likely to carry contextual distinctions; but this is not a property of a system. The "addition" of a new term is not of course considered as a process (though historical change is one type of instance of it): it may be displayed in any comparison of two related systems. For example, two possible systems of first and second person pronouns used by different speakers of Italian (quoted in oblique disjunct form; I = "interior to social group", E = "exterior ...").

1	me	me
1+	noi	moi
2I	te	te
2I+	voi	
2E	lei	voi
2E+	loro	

(The distinctions made in written Italian are ignored, since they would not affect the point.) The difference in format meaning is a function of the different number of terms: in system one *me* excludes five others, in system two only three. In contextual meaning only terms of the second group are affected.

19. Cf. Firth (1957a): "Moreover, these and other technical words are given their "meaning" by the restricted language of the theory, and by application of the theory in quoted works" (p. 2). This is true of descriptive categories too: "noun" can no more be defined in a glossary than "structure".

20. I should therefore agree with Palmer (1958) that linguistic levels do not form a hierarchy. His view is "that there are levels, but only in the widest sense, and that these are related in specific, but different, ways. The set of relationships cannot be regarded as a hierarchy, except in the loosest sense of the word". Palmer, however, appears to reintroduce procedural hierarchy when he says, "The procedure is not from phonetics via phonology to grammar, but from grammar via phonology to phonetics, though with the reminder that the phonetic statement is the basis, i.e. the ultimate justification for the analysis" (p. 240). I would rather say that there is **order** among the levels, determined by their interrelations, but (a) no hierarchy, in the **defined** sense of the word, and (b) no procedural direction. Unfortunately Palmer excludes this use of "order". "There is a statable **order** of levels ... and, therefore, a hierarchy" (pp. 231–2, in reference to Hockett).

21. Immediate Constituent analysis, for example, yields a hierarchy that is not a taxonomy: it does not fulfil criterion (ii). (It may not always fulfil (i): cf. Hockett (1957): "There must be also at least a few utterances in which the hierarchical structure is ambiguous, since otherwise the hierarchical structure would in every case be determined by form, and order, and hence not a "primitive" " (p. 391).)

22. The theory thus leads to "polysystemic"-ness in description – both syntagmatically and paradigmatically. Syntagmatic polysystemic statement follows from the linking of classes and systems to places in structure (see I.2(1961):46-55), so that the question "how can we prove that the *b* of *beak* and the *b* of *cab* are occurrences of one and the same phoneme?" (Ebeling: 1960: 17) is regarded as an unreal one; cf. Henderson (1951: 132); Carnochan (1952: 78); Robins (1953: 96); Firth (1955: 93; 1957c: 121) and Palmer (1958: 122–4). Paradigmatically, the "simplicity" referred to here follows from the requirement of making maximum use of the category of "system" by polysystemic or "multidimensional" statement in grammar; cf. Halliday (1956: 192).

I.2(1961):37–42, 72–7

* * *

7.4 Delicacy is the scale of differentiation, or depth in detail. It is a cline, whose limit at one end is the primary degree in the categories of structure and class. In the theory, the other limit is the point beyond which no further grammatical relations obtain: where there are no criteria for further secondary structures, or systems of secondary classes or formal items. In description, delicacy is a variable: one may choose to describe a language without going beyond the primary degree, still being comprehensive in rank and exponence and making use of all the categories of the theory. Each subsequent increase in delicacy delay the move to the exponents (cf. I.2(1961): 57-8) and thus increases the grammaticalness of the description. The limit of delicacy is set by the means at one's disposal.

In well-described languages, such as English, any extension in delicacy beyond what is already known requires either or both of large-scale textual studies with frequency counts and complex secondary classification based on multiple criteria, criteria which often cut across each other and may have to be variably weighted. And, as suggested above (I.2(1961): 53-4), a point will perhaps be reached where probabilities are so even as to cease to be significant[69] and classes so delicately differentiated that the description will have to decide on crucial criteria and ignore the others,[70] thus setting its own limits.

Delicacy is distinct from rank and the limit of delicacy applies at the rank of all units, for example differentiation of clause structures and of classes of the group. At one stage, therefore, it becomes a limit on the grammatical differentiation of items which then remain to be lexically differentiated: it sets an endpoint to grammar where lexis takes over. Here the scales of delicacy and exponence meet. The endpoint set to grammar on the exponence scale is where abstraction ceases: one has to move from abstract category to exponential item. That set on the delicacy scale is where differentiation ceases: the set of exponents of each class, and of each element of structure, permits no further, more delicate groupings. If the formal items are still not ranged in systems, the implication in either case is that further relations among them are lexical.

Whether or not, as discussed above (I.2(1961):53-4), grammatical delicacy can reach a point where there is a one / one category–exponent relation (where each element of structure, and each class, has only one formal item as exponent), when all formal relations, including those among what are now treated as lexical items, can be accounted for by the grammatical categories and stated grammatically – in other words, whether or not, ultimately, all linguistic form is grammar, we do not know. At present, lexical items must be treated separately, and lexical relations established in their own right. These lexical relations do not depend on grammatical categories[71] (so they are not yet "most delicate grammar") and they have their own dimensions of abstraction (so not yet "most exponential grammar"). So there must be a theory of lexis, to account for that part of linguistic form which grammar cannot handle.

Notes

69. For example, the statistical study of sequences of clause-classes, which is necessary both to the statement of sentence structures and to the description of

a unit above the sentence, would reveal the range, and cline, of the determination of probabilities by the occurrence of a member of each class. (Cf. my review of Whatmough (Halliday 1958).)

70. For example, a preliminary study of about 1000 items of the *put up* type, the purpose of which is to reveal the systems (dimensions) relevant to the identification and classification of so-called "phrasal verbs" in English, shows that fifteen different formal criteria yield fifteen different sets of classes.

71. That is, have not yet been shown to be dependent on grammatical categories, and must therefore be postulated to be independent until shown to be otherwise: on the general theoretical principle that heterogeneity is to be assumed until disproved by correlation. Recent work by McIntosh (1961) suggests that lexical relations may, in some cases, be better described by reference to grammatical restrictions of variable extent; if so, this will affect both the theory of lexis and the relations between the levels of lexis and grammar. Cf. I.2(1961):60–1.

I.2(1961):58–9, 86

* * *

12 Paradigmatic orientation and delicacy

When many years ago I first tried to describe grammar privileging the paradigmatic axis of representation (the "system" in Firth's framework of system and structure), the immediate reasons related to the theoretical and practical tasks that faced a 'grammatics' at the time (the middle 1960s): computational (machine translation), educational (first and second language teaching; language across the curriculum); sociological (language and cultural transmission, in Bernstein's theoretical framework, for example Bernstein (1971)); functional-variational (development of register theory) and textual (stylistics and analysis of spoken discourse). All these tasks had in common a strong orientation towards meaning, and demanded an approach which stretched the grammar in the direction of semantics. There were perhaps five main considerations.

i: The paradigmatic representation frees the grammar from the constraints of structure; structure, obviously, is still to be accounted for (a point sometimes overlooked when people draw networks, as Fawcett (1988) has thoughtfully pointed out), but structural considerations no longer determine the construal of the lexicogrammatical space. The place of any feature in the grammar can be determined "from the same level", as a function of its relationship to other features: its line-up in a system, and the interdependency between that system and others.

ii: Secondly, and by the same token, there is no distinction made, in a paradigmatic representation, between describing some feature and relating it to other features: describing anything consists precisely in relating it to everything else.

iii: Thirdly, the paradigmatic mode of description models language as a resource, not as an inventory; it defines the notion of "meaning potential" and provides an interpretation of "the system" in the other, Saussurean sense – but without setting up a duality between a langue and a parole.

iv: Fourthly, it motivates and makes sense of the probabilistic modelling of grammar. Probability can only be understood as the relative probabilities of the terms in a (closed) system.

v: Fifthly, representing grammar paradigmatically shapes it naturally into a lexicogrammar; the bricks-&-mortar model of a "lexicon" of words stuck together by grammatical cement can be abandoned as an outmoded relic of structuralist ways of thinking.

This last point was adumbrated many years ago under the formulation "lexis as delicate grammar" (see I.2(1961)); it has subsequently been worked out theoretically and illustrated in two important papers by Hasan (1985a; 1987). The principle is that grammar and lexis are not two distinct orders of phenomena; there is just one stratum here, that of "(lexico)grammar", and one among the various resources that the grammar has for making meaning (i.e. for "realizing" its systemic features) is by lexicalizing – choosing words. In general, the choice of words represents a delicate phase in the grammar, in the sense that it is only after attaining quite some degree of delicacy that we reach systems where the options are realized by the choice of the lexical item. The lexicogrammar is thus construed by the grammatics as a cline, from "most grammatical" to "most lexical"; but it is also a complementarity, because we can also view lexis and grammar as different perspectives on the whole. The reason people write "grammars" on the one hand and 'dictionaries' on the other is that options at the most general (least delicate) end of the cline are best illuminated by one set of techniques while options at the most delicate (least general) end are best illuminated by a different set of techniques. One can employ either set of techniques all the way across; but in each case there will be diminishing returns (increasing expenditure of energy, with decreasing gains).

To say that, as the description moves towards the lexical end, one eventually reaches systems where the options are realized by the choice of a lexical item, does not mean, on the other hand, that these are systems where there is a direct correspondence of feature to item, such that feature 1 is realized by lexical item *a*, feature 2 by lexical item *b* and so on.

What it means is that one reaches systems where the features are components of lexical items. (Thus, they are like the features of a standard componential analysis, except that they form part of the overall system network and no distinction is made between features that are "lexical" and those that are "grammatical".) Any given lexical item then appears as the conjunct realization of a set of systemic features; and "the same" lexical item may appear many times over, in different locations, much as happens in a thesaurus (where however the organization is taxonomic rather than componential).

13 A NOTE ON DELICACY

Inherent in the paradigmatic orientation is the concept of variable delicacy, in which again the grammatics mimics the grammar: delicacy in the construal of grammar (by the grammatics) is analogous to delicacy in the construal of experiential phenomena (by the grammar). Since for the most part the "lexicalized" mode of realization is associated with fairly delicate categories in the grammar, we can talk of "lexis as delicate grammar" (this refers to lexical items in the sense of "content words"; grammatical items, or "function words", like *the, of, it, not, as,* turn up in the realization of very general systemic features). But this is not the same thing as saying that when one reaches the stage of lexical realization one has arrived at the endpoint in delicacy.

What is the endpoint, on the delicacy scale? How far can the grammatics go in refining the categories of the grammar? In one sense there can be no endpoint, because every instance is categorically different from every other instance, since it has a unique instantial context of situation. We tend to become aware of this when an instance is codified in the work of a major writer and hence becomes immortalized as a "quotation". It seems trivial; but it may not be trivial in the context of intelligent computing, where the program might need to recognize that, say, *turn left!*, as instruction to the car, has a different meaning – and therefore a different description – at every instance of its use. This is the sense in which a grammar can be said to be an "infinite" (i.e. indefinitely large) system. But if we are literate, then in our commonsense engagements with language, in daily life, we behave as if there is an endpoint in delicacy: namely, that which is defined by the orthography. We assume, in other words, that if two instances look different (i.e. are represented as different forms in writing) they should be described as different types; whereas if two instances are written alike they should be described as tokens of the same type – however delicate the description, it will not tease them apart. The orthography is taken as the arbiter of paradigmatic boundaries: the way things are written determines their identity.

There is sense in this: writing represents the unconscious collective wisdom of generations of speakers/listeners. And we do allow exceptions. (a) We recognize homonymy and, more significantly, polysemy, where the delicacy of categorization does not stop at the barrier created by the writing system. (b) We accept that there are systematic distinctions which orthography simply ignores: for example, in English, all those realized by intonation and rhythm. (c) And, as already noted, it never was assumed, except perhaps among a very few linguists, that a "function word" like *of* has only one location in the terrain described by the grammatics. These exceptional cases challenge the implicit generalization that the orthographic form always defines a "type" within the wording.

A more explicit principle could be formulated: that, as far as the grammatics is concerned, the endpoint in delicacy is defined by what is systemic: the point where proportionalities no longer continue to hold. As long as we can predict that $a : a' :: b : b' :: \ldots$, we are still dealing with types, construed as distinct categories for purposes of grammatical description.

In practice, of course, we are nowhere near this endpoint in writing our systemic "grammars". (I find it disturbing when the very sketchy description of English grammar contained in Halliday (1994) is taken as some kind of endpoint. Every paragraph in it needs to be expanded into a book, or perhaps some more appropriate form of hypertext; then we will be starting to see inside the grammar – and be able to rewrite the introductory sketch!) We are only now beginning to get access to a reasonable quantity of data. This has been the major problem for linguistics: probably no other defined sphere of intellectual activity has ever been so top-heavy, so much theory built overhead with so little data to support it. The trouble was that until there were first of all tape recorders and then computers, it was impossible to assemble the data a grammarian needs. Since grammars are very big, and very complex, an effective grammatics depends on having accessible a very large corpus of diverse texts, with a solid foundation in spontaneous spoken language; together with the sophisticated software that turns it into an effective source of information.

I.15(1996):403–6

Language and Education (Volume 9)

"General linguistics" implies a general theory of language, and this in turn implies that we can identify the properties that are common to all languages and distinguish these from the features that are specific to a given language.

Many features often assumed to be universal, in the sense of 'common to all languages', are not in fact universals at all: concepts like **verb, phrase** and **syllable** are not linguistic constants and must to a certain extent be redefined for each language. The syllable in French, for example, has a very different status from the syllable in English; in some languages we do not find anything which we should want to call a "verb" because there is nothing that displays enough of the properties of what are called "verbs" in the languages to which this term was first applied. To find what is common to all languages we must invoke more abstract concepts than these. It is rather as if we said that all human beings must drink, and therefore all societies have some means of drinking; but not all societies use cups, and sometimes we are doubtful whether a particular vessel should be called a "cup" or not.

The understanding of what are the inherent properties of language as such is extremely important, since it provides a framework of categories for a powerful and accurate description of any language. We will not find a **verb** in every language, so "verb" will have no place in a general theory; but we shall find the category of which verb is a special instance, namely the category of **class**. All languages have classes, and the "class", appropriately defined, does have a place in a general theory of language. General linguistics is necessary if we seek to explain how language works. In fact all description of languages, however elementary, presupposes some theory or other; but the more adequate the theory, the simpler, more comprehensive and more exact the description will be.

Descriptive linguistics has other applications besides language teaching, although language teaching is certainly one of the most important. In all such applications the first essential is a good description of the language or languages concerned. For language teaching purposes we also need to compare languages; the methods are those of comparative descriptive linguistics, sometimes known also as "contrastive linguistics". The principal contribution of general linguistics to language teaching is thus that it makes possible the provision of adequate descriptions and comparisons of languages. A secondary but still important contribution is that it shows how a description may take different forms according to the aim that is in view.

1 THE DESCRIPTION OF A LANGUAGE

The basic principle of description is to analyse the language according to its various kinds of patterning: to break it down into what we call **levels**. Language, as said above, can be thought of as organized noise. To this we can add: 'used in situations', actual social situations. Organized noise used in social situations, or in other words 'contextualized systematic sounds'.

I shall be concerned here mainly with spoken language; not that I wish to suggest that written language is unimportant, but merely so as to avoid complicating some of the formulations. With this as a starting-point I should like to consider in outline one possible approach to the description of a language.

Language, whether spoken or written, has a substance: this is the material aspect of language The substance may be phonic or graphic, but for the moment we will consider only the phonic. The noise, then, is the substance. Language also has a form: this is the organization. In language, therefore, we recognize a level of *substance* and a level of *form*. Now the organization of language, its form, is meaningful: that is, linguistic activity participates in situations alongside man's other creative activities. Thus for a complete description of language one has to account for the form, the substance and the relationship between the form and the situation.

The study of this relationship could be called the *semantic* level; but since it involves an approach to meaning rather different from that normally implied by "semantics" we may refer to this as the *contextual* level, the "context" here being the non-linguistic environment.

There is thus a resemblance between "context" as used here and "meaning" in its non-technical sense. But what is generally understood by "meaning" is perhaps too limited to be adequate for linguistics, being confined almost entirely to referents or concepts. For the linguist any consideration and any description of language, be it formal or contextual, is concerned with meaning: this is inevitable, for language is meaningful activity. It is often said that "structural linguistics" represented an attempt to describe a language without reference to its meaning; whether or not this is so, we would rather insist that the aim of a description is to elucidate linguistic meaning at its various levels. At the same time it should be stressed that we are concerned here with linguistics and not philosophy. What "meaning" means to a philosopher may be a rather different question.

The domain of the linguistic sciences, as far as the description of language is concerned, can be illustrated as follows:

LINGUISTIC SCIENCES				
	Phonetics			
			Linguistics	
SUBSTANCE		FORM		SITUATION (environment)
phonic	phonology	{grammar/lexis}	context	extra-textual features

Language, by its nature as contextualized systematic sound, presupposes substance (phonic substance), form and situation, the last being the associated non-linguistic factors. Under "form", however, we must make a further distinction between *grammar* and *lexis* (vocabulary), a distinction likewise made necessary by the nature of language. In every language the formal patterns are of two kinds, merging into one another in the middle but distinct enough at the extremes: those of grammar and those of vocabulary (or, to use a technical term, of lexis). I shall come back later to the criteria on which the distinction between grammar and lexis depends.

The link between form and phonic substance is provided by phonology: this is the meaningful distribution of speech sounds. It is here that phonetics and linguistics overlap. Phonetics covers the study of phonic substance and also of phonology from the standpoint of phonic substance. Linguistics covers the study of form and also of phonology from the standpoint of form. Linguistics also extends to the right of the diagram so far as to take in the study, not of the non-linguistic features themselves, but of the relation between these non-linguistic features and linguistic form: that is what we are here calling the study of context.

These then are what we call the "levels of analysis" of descriptive linguistics: phonic, phonological, grammatical, lexical and contextual. For the written language, matters are a little more complicated: one cannot simply replace "phonological" and "phonic" by "graphological" and "graphic", for in most languages the orthography represents the linguistic forms not directly but via the phonology: we must therefore add the study of the relations between the two.

The levels of analysis are derived in the first place by a process of abstraction from our observations of the language material. We observe, to start with, the linguistic events we call "utterances", in which we find regular patterns of partial likeness between events. Then we generalize from these observations, grouping elements together according to the likenesses. Afterwards we make abstractions: we set up categories of language and so construct a theory, with hypotheses depending on the theory, to explain the facts observed. Finally we present our description, made in terms of the categories so established.

Observation, generalization, theory, presentation: this, one might perhaps say, is the scientific method of description. The facts of language are such that we must proceed by a set of abstractions at several levels at once, all constantly interrelated but each level having its own categories. These categories enable us to arrange systematically the mass of events constituting a language.

IX.7(1960):136–9

Additional readings

On Grammar (Volume 1) – 3(1963):98–9; 4(1966); 6(1966); 15(1996):396, 414–5
On Language and Linguistics (Volume 3) – Introduction(2003):7–15; 1(1964):37–47; 9(1992):199–212; 15(1972):327–30; Appendix(1994):433–41
The Language of Science (Volume 5) – 3(1998): 53–8
Computational and Quantitative Studies (Volume 6) – 10(1995):227–38
Studies in English Language (Volume 7) – 4(1969): 156–63
Studies in Chinese Language (Volume 8) – 6(1992)
Language and Education (Volume 9) – 7(1960):149
Language and Society (Volume 10) – 1(1964):31

Chapter Nineteen

TRINOCULAR VISION

Summary

In categorizing the grammar, the grammarian comes at the task from three perspectives, each of which corresponds to a different stratum. First, there is the stratum of semantics, or what has been referred to as the higher level. Here, the perspective is from above, and looks at what each category realizes or how it relates to meaning. Second is the stratum of lexicogrammar itself, where the perspective is from roundabout. The third perspective which looks at each category from below deals with the morphological and phonological realization of a given category. In a functional grammar, priority is given to the perspective from above, as form follows function, and the meaning of an expression will decide its phonological and morphological realization.

Selected readings

On Grammar (Volume 1)

15 TRINOCULAR VISION

The "trinocular" principle in the grammatics can be simply stated. In categorizing the grammar, the grammarian works "from above", "from roundabout" and "from below"; and these three perspectives are defined in terms of strata. Since the stratum under attention is the lexicogrammar, "from roundabout" means 'from the standpoint of the lexicogrammar itself '. "From above" means 'from the standpoint of the semantics: how the given category relates to the meaning (what it " 'realizes" ')'. "From below" means 'from the standpoint of morphology and phonology, how the given category relates to the expression (what it "is realized by")'.

What are being taken into account are the regularities (proportionalities) at each of the three strata.

Since the patterns seen from these three angles tend to conflict, the resulting description of the grammar, like the grammar's own description of experience, must be founded on compromise. This is easy to say; it is not so easy to achieve. Often one finds oneself 'hooked' on one oculation – obsessed, say, with giving the most elegant account of how some pattern is realized, and so according excessive priority to the view from below; then, on looking down on it from above, one finds one has committed oneself to a "system" that is semantically vacuous. If the view from below is consistently given priority, the resulting description will be a collapsed grammar, so "flat" that only an impoverished semantics can be raised up on it. On the other hand, if one is biased towards the view from above, the grammar will be so inflated that it is impossible to generate any output. And if one looks from both vertical angles but forgets the view from roundabout (surprisingly, perhaps, the commonest form of trap) the result will be a collection of isolated systems, having no internal impact upon each other. In this case the grammar is not so much inflated or collapsed; it is simply curdled.

Thus the categories of the grammatics, like those of the grammar, rest on considerations of underlying function, internal organization (with mutual definition) and outward appearance and recognition. But there is more than a simple analogy embodied here. I referred above to the notion of semiotic transformation: that the grammar transforms experience into meaning. The trinocular perspective is simply that: it is the process of transforming anything into meaning – of "semioticizing" it in terms of a higher order, stratified semiotic. Construing the phenomena of experience means "parsing" them into meanings, wordings and expressions (you only have to do this, of course, when form and function cease to match; this is why the task is inescapably one of achieving compromise). The entire stratal organization of language is simply the manifestation of this trinocular principle. Making this principle explicit in the grammatics is perhaps giving substance to the notion of 'language turned back upon itself'.

I.15(1996):408–9

On Language and Linguistics (Volume 3)

4 All descriptive categories are identified from three perspectives: those of (i) the higher level, (ii) the same level, (iii) the lower level. This is

sometimes referred to as (i) "from above", (ii) "from around" and (iii) "from below". For example, in English the Subject is that which

  (i) has special status in the interpersonal structure of the clause, being the element on which the argument is made to rest (by reference to which the proposition is laid open to argument);

  (ii) is mapped on to certain elements in the experiential and textual structural (e.g. Actor in active material process, Senser in one type of mental process; Theme in declarative mood, etc.);

  (iii) is the nominal group that accompanies the Finite operator and is taken up pronominally in the declarative mood tag.

This enables us to express the difference between functional and formal grammars. All grammars, of course, are concerned both with function and with form; the difference is one of orientation. In a formal grammar, perspective (iii) has priority; (i) is derived from (iii), and may not be stated at all (e.g. in some formal grammars the category corresponding to Subject in English would have no interpretation from above). In a functional grammar, such as systemic grammar, (i) has priority, and (iii) will typically be derived from it.

Since criteria from the different perspectives often conflict, there may be a substantial difference between formal and functional grammars in how the descriptive categories are aligned, and even in the categories themselves. Categories that are relatively clearly identifiable from above may be very complex to describe from below (e.g. the different types of process in English, which may simply not be recognized in a formal grammar). Again, however, it must be emphasized that the priority is not absolute: no category is fixed from one perspective alone. The description is always a compromise among all the three perspectives.

5 In a functional grammar, perspective (i) is that which **explains** (this is what is meant by saying that a functional grammar is one which offers functional explanations – a kind that is not recognized as explanations in a formal grammar). What is **to be explained** is some pattern identified from the vantage point of perspective (iii). For example: "why does a particular one of the nominal elements in an English declarative clause turn up again pronominally in the tag?" (and cf. the question "why does a particular element come first in the clause?", cited in 1 above [see III.9(1992):201] above). The explanation will be given from the vantage point of perspective (i), e.g. "this is the element which the speaker selects in order to carry the weight of the argument – the one that is held 'modally responsible' for it". In other words, a functional grammar is one which

explains the forms of the language by referring to the functions they express.

Now consider the case of **comparative** description: that is, using the categories set up for one language as tools for exploring another. Here the direction of inquiry is typically reversed. Instead of beginning with a question seeking to explain the formal pattern in (iii), we begin with what was originally the answer to such a question, namely the functional generalization under (i). So, for example, if we are using the concept of Subject to investigate the grammar of Chinese, we don't say "Is there a nominal element in the clause that accompanies the Finite operator and also turns up pronominally in the tag?" – which would not be very helpful, since we would first have to find Finite operators and mood tags in Chinese before we could ask the question! We say "Is there a nominal element that has special status in the interpersonal function of the clause, as being the one on which the argument is made to rest?" The assumption is that, if there is any such element, it will be recognizable somehow or other (that is, identifiable from perspective (iii)), although not the way it is in English.

In other words, the comparison is made from the vantage point of perspective (i). We look at the meaning of some category in the language of reference, and then ask if there is any category in the language under description that has a comparable function taken in the context of the whole. Almost all descriptive work today is in this sense comparative; and this is reasonable, since there is no point in pretending, when we come to describe a language, that no other languages have been described before, or that we cannot learn anything from those that have. Ideally – but let me say clearly that this is not what is usually done! – each language should be described twice over: first comparatively, using categories drawn from other language as guides, and then **particularly** – entirely in its own terms, as if no other language had been described before. This is the only way to ensure that it will not be misrepresented. Historically, the second one was the way the ancient Indian and Greek grammarians proceeded; first they described the forms, perspective (iii), and then they questioned why these forms arose: why is this noun in this particular case? why are there two sets of forms for certain verbs? and so on. This was the origin of syntax. The reason why syntax never evolved in China is that Chinese has no morphology; so questions of this kind were never asked.

6 We have said that comparative description begins from the vantage point of perspective (i): we look for categories which are comparable when viewed "from above". But by itself this could be misleading. We do

not, in fact, start out by trying to identify individual categories, single elements of structure, like "Subject", or single options in a system, like "passive". The basis of any comparative description is the system (a point made very many years ago by Sidney Allen; see Allen 1956).

Thus, if we are using English categories to explore Chinese, we do not ask whether there is a Subject, or whether there is a passive; we ask whether there is a comparable system, in each case. For example, the category of Subject in English realizes choice of mood; so instead of asking whether or not Chinese has a category of Subject, we first ask "Is there a system of mood? – that is, a system for exchanging information and goods-&-services, one through which speakers are enabled to argue." There is; so then we ask about its options, to see whether they can be interpreted by reference to categories of declarative, interrogative and so on. Step by step we come to the question whether there is a particular nominal element which has a special function in the clause with respect to the system of mood. There is – but not the same as in English. The Subject in English does two jobs in the mood system: it takes responsibility for the proposition, and it also plays a part in realizing the distinction between one category of mood and another. There is a nominal element in Chinese which does the first job but not the second – and since it is not required for making the distinction between declarative and interrogative, it is often "not there" where the Subject would be in English. (The temptation then is to say that something in the Chinese has been "dropped" or "omitted". But this is where the comparative approach becomes pathological. Nothing has been omitted; that is a fiction created by looking at Chinese through English eyes.) The important question then becomes, what is the difference in meaning between a clause which makes explicit this modally responsible element and one which does not. It could be a matter of ellipsis (i.e. the element is presumed from elsewhere – note that there is still a difference in meaning between putting it in and leaving it out, albeit a subtle one); or it could be realizing some other systematic semantic opposition.

III.9(1992):202–5

Additional readings

On Grammar (Volume 1) – 15(1996):398, 402
On Language and Linguistics (Volume 3) – 12(1997):254–5, 266
Computational and Quantitative Studies (Volume 6) – 10(1995):231

Chapter Twenty

VARIETIES AND VARIATION IN LANGUAGE: DIALECT, REGISTER, CODE

Summary

While individuals each possess their own idiolect, people also tend to group themselves according to their perceived sense of shared identity with a particular language and dialect. The dialect used people who regard themselves as belonging to the same speech community may vary at any or all levels from the dialects of other speakers of the same language. Typically, one dialect emerges as the standard language, serving as a lingua franca among speakers of the various dialects within the same language community. Most speakers of this standard language, however, continue to speak with the phonetics of their native dialect, i.e. accent, without loss in intelligibility.

Registers are distinguishable on the basis of a classification along the three dimensions of field of discourse, i.e. the area of operation of the language activity (e.g. shopping and games-playing as well as medicine and linguistics); tenor or style of discourse, i.e. the relations among the participants (e.g. 'casual', 'intimate', 'deferential'); and mode of discourse, i.e. the medium or mode of the language activity (e.g. spoken and written language). Codes, on the other hand, refer to sub-cultural variation in patterns or habits of speech adopted by speakers of the same language.

Selected readings

On Language and Linguistics (Volume 3)

A language is a space defined by dialectal and functional, or "registerial", variation. I think it is useful here to stress the analogy between ***dialect*** and *register*, as names for **kinds of variation**. They are both mass nouns. When we move from the category of "dialect", as mass noun, to that of "a dialect", as a count noun, we are modelling the experience whereby only certain feature combinations within this variable space are actually found to occur; they therefore stand out as rather clearly bounded patches. It is the same kind of shift we are making when we derive from the mass noun "register" the count noun "a register". What we recognize as "a register" is a clustering of features – in this case, predominantly features of the content plane, rather than features of the expression plane as with "a dialect" – that can be observed to co-occur in a regular fashion: a local resetting of the global probabilities of the system, as I expressed it earlier. Like a dialect, a register comes to exist only because the great majority of possible feature combinations never occur at all; there are huge disjunctions, empty regions in a language's variable space.

Higher stratum at which variants are unified ("higher level constant")	semantics [content plane]	social context	[no higher level constant]
Stratum ar which variation typically occurs	phonology [expression plane]	semantics	semantics
Type of variation	dialect	code	register

Figure 1 Types of variation in language

But there is also a third kind of variation within language, originally identified by Basil Bernstein (1971, 1996) and referred to by him under the name of *code*. Ruqaiya Hasan (1989) has interpreted "code", in terms of linguistic theory, as systematic semantic variation: that is, variation in the semantic features that are typically associated with a given social context. In other words, code variation (a) is **semantic** – and in this it is unlike dialect but like register; at the same time, (b) it is **variation against a higher level constant** – and in this it is unlike register but like dialect (cf. Figure 1).

III.12(1997):255–6

* * *

Hasan has interpreted Bernstein's codes, in semiotic terms, using the concept of semantic variation. This is different from functional, or register, variation in one critical respect: in semantic variation there is a higher level constant – we can talk of semantic "variants"; whereas in register variation there is not. Registers are ways of doing different things; there is no level of interpretation at which, say, technocratic discourse and casual conversation become signifiers of a common signified. With codes there is; and in this respect, codes resemble social dialects; but whereas social dialects (like dialects in general) realize their higher level constant in the semantic system (that is, within language itself), codes come together only **outside** of language, in the culture. It is only at an abstract level in the context of culture that different codes can be seen to realize a common "signified".

Following up Bernstein's work two decades later, Hasan and her colleagues analysed semantically over 20,000 messages of spontaneous conversation between mothers and their pre-school children in the home, and subjected the results to a detailed cluster analysis. The analysis showed significant differences in the patterns of meaning that were adopted, respectively, by mothers of boys and mothers of girls. Their discourse did not constitute two different language systems (two climates); they were just random fluctuations in the semiotic weather. They were different codes – that is, consistent orientations to different ways of meaning, which construed boys and girls as different social beings. And the same study – same analysis, same data, same program – showed up other differences, equally significant both ideologically and statistically, between mothers from the working class and mothers from the middle class. And the children's own part in the dialogues revealed very clearly – not by direct imitation of the mothers, which would make no sense, but by a deeper semiotic resonance in their grammar – that they were, at three and a half years old, fully paid-up members of the social bond (Hasan 1990; Hasan and Cloran 1990).

III.17(1992): 382–3

Computational and Quantitative Studies (Volume 6)

Variable: A language forms a multidimensional semiotic space, which accommodates a great deal of variation: "sub-languages" of various kinds which selectively exploit, or foreground, different regions of that space. (a) Most familiar, perhaps, is **dialectal** variation; this is typically variation in the **expression** space (the "lower" interface of the grammar, and the phonology), although dialects can also vary in content, particularly on the standard / non-standard dimension. (b) **Functional** variation, or **register**, on the other hand, is typically variation in the **content** (semantic) space; this is the variation that is associated with the different functions of a language in society – the different kinds of activities that people engage in. When new activities come into being, as often happens with changes in technology, new registers evolve along with them, opening up further regions of semantic space. (For discussion of register variation in language, see Ghadessy 1994; Matthiessen 1993b.) (3) There is also what is known as **idiolectal** variation, between one individual speaker and another. People develop different habits of meaning, individually and in small social groups.

Implications for grammatics. The variation has to be accounted for, as a normal feature of language. The variants are not different languages, or even different grammars; the differences are not categorical, but matters of relative frequency – a resetting of probabilities from global to local norms. This means that the grammatics has to accommodate probabilities.

VI.10(1995):225–6

Language and Education (Volume 9)

The distinction between dialect and register is a useful one for the English teacher: the dialect being defined 'according to the user' (the dialect you use is determined, by and large, by who you are), the register being 'according to the use' (determined by what you are using the language for). Note that "standard English" is a dialect like any other socioregional variety. The individual may speak in many dialects, in a linguistically complex community such as ours, but if so this reflects his personal history; he must certainly, however, speak (and write) in many registers, to be a citizen of the community at all. Of course, there is such a thing as 'the English language', and one should not exaggerate the differences among its varieties; nevertheless there are differences between spoken and written, formal and informal, technical and non-technical discourse, and the pupil has to understand and master them.

Some register differences are clearly motivated; they correlate with the purpose for which the language is being used, or with the medium, or with the relations among the participants. When the teacher talks of 'effective English' he can explain why certain patterns are used in certain types of situation, and show that effectiveness is to be assessed in relation to given aims and environments. It is not enough to postulate an idealized English that is 'effective', or 'logical' or 'clear' or simply 'good'. The replacing of the monolithic concept of 'good English', a mythical register assumed to be superior for all purposes and in all contexts, by the notion of an English rendered effective precisely by its ability to assume various styles in response to different needs, has been one of the major sources of advance in English teaching theory and practice. Among the most far-reaching of its consequences has been the readiness to take spoken language seriously, to recognize "oracy", in Wilkinson's terms, as an aim parallel in importance to the aim of literacy.

At the same time other differences between register seem entirely unmotivated: they belong to the region of linguistic table-manners, being conventional markers of acceptable behaviour and nothing more. Here the teacher must be able to stand back (whether or not he takes the children with him) and recognize these linguistic conventions for what they are. Since it is one of the school's tasks to socialize its pupils, no doubt it is as reasonable for the teacher to teach the proprieties of language as those of any other form of social behaviour; he should, however, be aware of the distinction (even if it is fuzzy at the edges, as with any other form of social activity) between the dietetics of language and its table-manners. This is the linguistic basis of the distinction between productive and prescriptive teaching as used above.

The teacher, in fact, needs to be objective in all his social attitudes, and it is because the social attitudes of English people towards their language and its varieties are so marked and vehement that the particular sub-branch of linguistics that deals with the study of such attitudes is relatively of such great importance. The training of teachers in this country seems not yet to make adequate provision for developing objective attitudes towards society; much more progress has been made in inculcating objective attitudes towards the individual. It is assumed that the teacher needs to know some psychology, but not yet that he should be trained in sociology or social anthropology. In fact these three subjects – sociology, psychology and linguistics – are the disciplines that are most crucial to the understanding of one's fellow men; every teacher has to be able to step outside the mythology of his own culture, and the teacher of English as a native language is operating in what is perhaps the most myth-prone area of all.

IX.1(1967):29–31

* * *

To say that linguistic and cultural diversity is a positive feature of the community implies more than merely recognizing that it exists, more even than recognizing it and taking pride in it. It implies that this diversity has significance for the culture, that it is a significant aspect of people's lives.

The fact that there are different modes of meaning in the community has now become part of the total environment within which meanings are exchanged. In this situation it is no longer possible to treat monolingual societies as the norm and to regard all others as special cases, as if they were somehow deviations from the norm.

To express this in the terms of linguistics, we invoke the concept of language variation. As linguists see it (although they have taken a long time to reach this point), language is a variable system; there is linguistic variation both in the life of the community and in the life of the individual. A totally homogeneous society, in which everyone speaks the same way as everyone else all the time, is as much a fiction as a totally heterogeneous society in which no two individuals speak alike. Constructs like these are idealizations; they are the opposite poles that it is useful to keep in mind because we know that reality lies somewhere in between.

In real life, it typically happens that an individual does not speak the same way as all other individuals. More than that, he does not always speak the same way as himself. He switches; and the switching takes two forms. He may switch among different languages, and he may switch among different registers. Let us look at each of these in turn.

1 The language a person uses depends on who he is: his geographical and social origins. Everyone is born into some micro-community, whose language he learns. Typically, the micro-community is a family, and the child learns the language that is the language of the family and of his parents, although even in the family there will often be two or more languages spoken. When he starts to meet members of other linguistic micro-communities, one party has to switch to the language of the other; or else both parties switch to some agreed third language that is known to both and accepted by them as appropriate for this purpose.

2 The register a person is using depends on what he is doing at the time: the particular social situation in which he finds himself, and the part that language is playing in that situation. This may be the informal, nontechnical register of everyday conversation, spontaneous, lively and fluent; or any one of a variety of more formal or more technical registers, spoken or written, and ranging (as far as the part played by language is concerned) from situations of a more active kind, various forms of collaborative work and play in which the language used is confined to brief exchanges of instructions and most of the activity is non-verbal, to contexts such as meetings and public lectures, where talk is almost the only thing that matters.

It is possible to translate between different languages. People generally assume that different languages consist of the same meanings, but with different means of expression. In real life we know that it is not quite as simple as this; we search for equivalences and often cannot find them. By and large, however, the assumption is valid. It is not normally possible, on the other hand, to translate between different registers, since registers consist of different meanings. Technical English cannot be translated into English gossip; the two are not different modes of expression but different modes of meaning. There are perhaps occasional instances where translation between registers is possible, when a special ritual style that has come to be associated with a particular purpose is replaced by a more informal popular style. Recently the leading motor car insurers in Australia brought out a new insurance policy which they called a "Plain English Policy"; this was a "translation" of a more formal document the public had found difficult to understand. But even this was objected to by a legal expert, who claimed that the meaning was no longer the same as in the original.

It is clearly possible to go through life using only one language; but it is scarcely possible to go through life using only one register. Typically all adults are multilingual in the 'register' sense: they use language in a variety of different ways, for a variety of different purposes, and hence they are constantly changing their speech styles. This ability to control different registers is a natural human ability; it is built up in adolescence, and school plays a significant part in it. It also seems to be a natural human ability to control different languages, given the right conditions for doing so. Not all adults, obviously, are multilingual in this other sense, of controlling different languages. But if we extend the notion of variation in language to include variation in dialect, we shall find that very many more adults are multilingual in this sense: they may not switch among different languages, but they do switch among different dialects of the same language. Some linguists have suggested terms that might be used to cover both, meaning 'language or dialect of a language'. The British linguist Trevor Hill used the term *tongue*; the American C.-J. Bailey talks of *lects*, and refers to multilingualism as *polylectalism*.

In principle, choice of language (tongue) and choice of register are independent of each other; they are determined by different sets of conditions. In practice, however, the two tend to be closely bound together. In most societies where more than one language or dialect is used, there is some kind of a 'division of labour' among them; certain kinds of activity, such as commerce or schooling, are carried out in one 'tongue', and others, such as informal conversation in the home or playground, in another, or in various others. In this way a particular register comes to imply a particular language or dialect; and this leads to the emergence of

433

standard languages (which are really standard dialects) and national languages – varieties that are specially associated with those areas of activity that are supra-local in character. The influence of the register is so strong that even people from the same locality will often switch from the local to the standard variety when the register is one that by implication transcends local differences.

This interplay of language varieties, the tendency for a given register to determine a given dialect or language, reflects something that is a fundamental aspect of life in complex societies: namely the variable scope of social interactions. The exchange of meanings between two or more people at any one moment may involve the home, the neighbourhood, the locality, the region, the nation or the world. All these represent, in an idealized sense, different speech communities, each with its own language or dialect; and since there are infinitely many homes in any one region or nation, most people are faced with the need to vary their dialect or language if they want to move very far along the scale. There are no doubt some who use the same dialect of the same language in all the social contexts in which they find themselves: the 'standard English' of an upper-middle-class speaker from London or Los Angeles may vary relatively little whether he is at home with his children or at an international conference of heads of state. But such people are in a minority, and in most parts of the world, including all of Southeast Asia, there is considerable linguistic variation not only between different levels of social context but also within one level. In a typical multilingual society, the national language may differ from all the languages of home, neighbourhood or locality; and at any of these levels there may be more than one language in use, not only more than one home language but often more than one national language as well. At the upper end of the scale, in regional, national and international contexts, there is scope for language policy and planning; whereas at the lower end, whatever developments take place usually take place naturally.

In using these terms "local", "regional", "national", and so on, we are setting up a conceptual framework, one that will help in interpreting the variable scope of sociolinguistic interactions. Such a framework is of course an idealization; the actual situations of language use are by no means neatly separable into such clear-cut categories. It should be made clear, moreover, that using language in a 'national' context does not necessarily mean communicating with people from outside one's locality or region; nor does an 'international' context necessarily imply a situation of talking to foreigners. These labels may simply indicate the subject matter of the discourse; as Blom and Gumperz discovered in Norway, even a group of villagers meeting in their own locality would tend to switch to the standard language when talking about national affairs. The labels are useful for indicating the extent of the communication network that is presupposed or implied by a particular instance of linguistic interaction. To say that a particular language is a "regional language" or a "national language" does not by itself tell us in what actual encounters any actual speaker will be using it. What it does tell us is the status that is accorded to that language in the community, the symbolic value that is placed on it by the members, and the meaning they attach to its use; and from this we can make intelligent guesses about the contexts in which it will typically be heard.

This scale of language status, from the home upwards, can also be interpreted as a developmental one, relating to how children learn language; it represents the widening linguistic horizons in the natural development of a child. A child begins by building up the linguistic patterns of the home, and he learns these almost entirely from his own family. Next come those of the neighbourhood, which are learnt mainly from his playfellows, the peer group. At this point society intervenes, and we put the child in school; he now starts to learn language patterns from his teachers. The school is a new environment for him, and may impose considerable discontinuity, both linguistic and cultural; for this reason it is all the more important to stress the essential continuity of the phases of language development through which he is passing as he grows up. Although a child coming into school may suddenly find himself coping with one or even more new languages, the linguistic experiences he is going through, and through which it is to be hoped the teacher is helping to guide him, are closely related to experiences he has been undergoing in one form or other since he was born; the more he is able to build on what he knows, the less formidable will be the task of assimilating what he does not know.

IX.11(1979):240–3

Language and Society (Volume 10)

Fundamentally, educational failure is a social problem, not a linguistic one; but it has a linguistic aspect, which we can begin to understand if we consider the cultural environment in the second of the two senses mentioned above. It is not the linguistic environment in the sense of which language or dialect the child learns to speak that matters, so much as the cultural or subcultural environment as this is embodied in and transmitted through the language. In other words, the 'language difference' may be significant, but if so it is a difference of function rather than of form.

It is this fundamental insight which lies behind Professor Bernstein's theoretical and empirical work in the field of language and society; together with a further insight, namely that what determines the actual cultural-linguistic configuration is, essentially, the social structure, the system of social relations, in the family and other key social groups, which is characteristic of the particular subculture. Bernstein (*Class, Codes and Control*, Vol. 1., p. 122) writes: "A number of fashions of speaking, frames of consistency, are possible in any given language and . . . these fashions of speaking, linguistic forms or codes, are themselves a function of the form social relations take. According to this view, the form of the social relation or, more generally, the social structure generates distinct linguistic forms or codes and *these codes essentially transmit the culture and so constrain behaviour*" (his italics). Since, in the words of the American sociologist and linguist William Stewart, "so much of human behaviour is socially conditioned rather than genetically determined", it is not difficult to suppose an intimate connection between language on the one hand and modes of thought and behaviour on the other.[3]

Bernstein has investigated **how** this connection is made, and suggests that it is through linguistic codes, or fashions of speaking, which arise as a consequence of the social structure and the types of social relation associated with it. As Mary Douglas put it, "The control [of thought] is not in the speech forms but in the set human relations which generate thought and speech" (1972, p. 312).

What are these linguistic codes, or fashions of speaking? They relate, essentially, to the functional account of language. It is not the words and the sentence structures – still less the pronunciation or "accent" – which make the difference between one type of code and another; it is the relative emphasis placed on the different functions of language, or, to put it more accurately, the kinds of meaning that are typically associated with them. The "fashions of speaking" are sociosemantic in nature; they are patterns of meaning that emerge, more or less strongly, in particular contexts, especially those relating to the socialization of the child in the family. Hence although each child's language-learning environment is unique, he also shares certain common features with other children of a similar social background; not merely in the superficial sense that the material environments may well be alike – in fact they may not – but in the deeper sense that the forms of social relation and the role systems surrounding him have their effect on the kind of choices in meaning which will be highlighted and given prominence in different types of situation. Peter Doughty comments "the terms *elaborated* and *restricted* refer to characteristic ways of using language to interact with other human beings; they do not suggest that there are two kinds of 'meaning potential' (*Exploring Language*, pp. 104–5).

This dependence on social structure is not merely unavoidable, it is essential to the child's development; he can develop only as **social** man, and therefore his experience must be shaped in ways which make him a member of society and his particular section of it. It becomes restrictive only where the social structure orients the child's thinking **away from** the modes of experience that the school requires. To quote Bernstein again, "the different focusing of experience . . . creates a major problem of educability only where the school produces discontinuity between its symbolic orders and those of the child" (1971, pp. 183–4). In other words, the processes of becoming educated require that the child's meaning potential should have developed along certain lines in certain types of context, especially in relation to the exploration of the environment and of his own part in it. To what extent this requirement is inherent in the very concept of education, and to what extent it is merely a feature of education as it is at present organized in Britain and other highly urbanized societies, we do not know; but as things are, certain ways of organizing experience through language, and of participating and interacting with people and things, are necessary to success in school. The child who is not predisposed to this type of verbal exploration in this type of experiential and interpersonal context "is not at home in the educational world", as Bernstein puts it. Whether a child is so predisposed or not turns out not to be any innate property of the child as an individual, an inherent limitation on his mental powers, as used to be generally thought; it is merely the result of a mismatch between his own symbolic orders of meaning and those of the school, a mismatch that results from the different patterns of socialization that characterize different sections of society, or subcultures, and which are in turn a function of the underlying social relations in the family and elsewhere. Mary Douglas says of Bernstein that he asks "what structuring in society itself calls for its own appropriate structures of speech" (1972, p. 5); and she goes on to add "A common speech form transmits much more than words; it transmits a hidden baggage of shared assumptions", a "collective consciousness that constitutes the social bond".

It is all too easy to be aware of subcultural differences in speech forms, because we are all sensitive to differences of dialect and accent. Unfortunately this is precisely where we go wrong, because differences of dialect and accent are in themselves irrelevant; in Bernstein's words, "There is nothing, but nothing, in the dialect as such, which prevents a child from internalizing and learning to use universalistic meanings", and dialect is a problem only if it is **made** a problem artificially by the prejudice and ignorance of others. It is much harder to become aware of the **significant** differences, which are masked by dialectal variation (and by no means always correspond to dialect distinctions), and which do not appear in any obvious form, as differences in vocabulary or grammatical structure. We are still far from being able to give a comprehensive or systematic account of the linguistic realizations of Bernstein's codes or of the ways in which language operates in the transmission of culture. But the perspective is that of language and social man, and the functional investigation of language and language development provides the basis for understanding.

In essence, what seems to happen is this. The child first constructs a language in the form of a range of meanings that relate directly to certain of his basic needs. As time goes on, the meanings become more complex, and he replaces this by a symbolic system – a semantic system with structural realizations – that is based on the language he hears around him; this is what we call his "mother tongue". Since this is learnt, and has in fact evolved, in the service of the same basic functions, it is, essentially, a functional system; but its functionality is now built in at a very abstract level. This is what was referred to at the beginning of this section, when we said that the adult linguistic system has, in effect, the four generalized functional components, or **metafunctions**, experiential, logical, interpersonal and textual. These form the basis for the organization of meaning when the child moves from his original protolanguage into language proper.

But he does not abandon the original concrete functional elements of the system as he invented it. These still define the purpose for which language is used; and out of them evolve the social contexts and situation types that make up the patterns of use of language in daily life – including those contexts that Bernstein has shown to be critical in the socialization process. Herein lies the basis of the significant subcultural variation that we have been looking at. In **which** particular contexts of use will the child bring to bear **which** portions of the functional resources of the system? Seen from a linguistic point of view, the different "codes", as Bernstein calls them, are different strategies of language use. All human beings put language to certain types of use, and all of them learn a linguistic system which has evolved in that context; but what aspects of the system are typically deployed and emphasized in one type of use or another is to a significant extent determined by the culture – by the systems of social relations in which the child grows up, including the roles he himself learns to recognize and to adopt. All children have access to the meaning potential of the system; but they may differ, because social groups differ, in their interpretation of what the situation demands.

Note

3. This view is associated first and foremost with the work of the great American linguist Benjamin Lee Whorf, who wrote "An accepted pattern of using words is often prior to certain lines of thinking and modes of behaviour". Whorf emphasized that it is not so much in "special uses of language" (technical terms, political discourse etc.) as "in its constant ways of arranging data and its most ordinary everyday analysis of phenomena that we need to recognize the influence [language] has on other activities, cultural and personal" (*Language, Thought and Reality*, pp. 134–5). Bernstein points out that, in Whorf's thinking, "the link between language, culture and habitual thought is *not* mediated through the social structure", whereas his own theory "places the emphasis on changes in the social structure as major factors in shaping or changing a given culture through their effect on the consequences of fashions of speaking. It shares with Whorf the controlling influence on experience ascribed to "frames of consistency" involved in fashions of speaking. It differs from Whorf by asserting that, in the context of a common language in the sense of a general code, there will arise distinct linguistic forms, fashions of speaking, which induce in their speakers *different* ways of relating to objects and persons."

X.3(1974):85–8, 129–30

★ ★ ★

6. REGISTER

This last point is a reflection of the contexts of situation in which language is used, and the ways in which one type of situation may differ from another. Types of linguistic situation differ from one another, broadly speaking, in three respects: first, as regards what is actually taking place; secondly, as regards what part the language is playing; and thirdly, as regards who is taking part. These three variables, taken together, determine the range within which meanings are selected and the forms which are used for their expression. In other words, they determine the "register".

The notion of register is at once very simple and very powerful.[5] It refers to the fact that the language we speak or write varies according to the type of situation. This in itself is no more than stating the obvious.

What the theory of register does is to attempt to uncover the general principles which govern this variation, so that we can begin to understand **what** situational factors determine **what** linguistic features. It is a fundamental property of all languages that they display variation according to use; but surprisingly little is yet known about the nature of the variation involved, largely because of the difficulty of identifying the controlling factors.

An excellent example of register variation (and of how to investigate and describe it) is provided by Jean Ure in a paper entitled 'Lexical density and register differentiation' (1971). Here Jean Ure shows that, at least in English, the lexical density of text, which means the proportion of lexical items (content words) to words as a whole, is a function first of the medium (that is whether it is spoken or written – written language has a higher lexical density than speech) and, within that, of the social function (pragmatic language, or 'language in action', has the lowest lexical density of all). This is probably true of all languages; but whether it is or not, it is a basic fact about English and a very good illustration of the relation between the actual and the potential that we referred to at the beginning of this section. We could say, following Dell Hymes, that it is part of the speaker's "communicative competence" that he knows how to distribute lexical items in a text according to different kinds of language use; but there is really no need to introduce here the artificial concept of 'competence', or 'what the speaker knows', which merely adds an extra level of psychological interpretation to what can be explained more simply in direct sociolinguistic or functional terms.

It is easy to be misled here by posing the question the wrong way, as a number of writers on the subject of register have done. They have asked, in effect, 'what features of language are determined by register?' and then come up with instances of near-synonymy where one word differs from another in level of formality, rhetoric or technicality, like *chips* and *French fried potatoes*, or *deciduous dentition* and *milk teeth*. But these are commonplaces which lie at the fringe of register variation, and which in themselves would hardly need any linguistic or other kind of 'theory' to explain them. Asked in this way, the question can lead only to trivial answers; but it is the wrong question to ask. **All** language functions in contexts of situation, and is relatable to those contexts. The question is not what peculiarities of vocabulary, or grammar or pronunciation, can be directly accounted for by reference to the situation. It is **which** kinds of situational factor determine which kinds of selection in the linguistic system. The notion of register is thus a form of prediction: given that we know the situation, the social context of language use, we can predict a great deal about the language that will occur, with reasonable probability of being right. The important theoretical question then is: what do we need to know about the social context in order to make such predictions?

Let us make this more concrete. If I am talking about gardening, I may be more likely to use words that are the names of plants and other words referring to processes of cultivation; and this is one aspect of the relation of language to situation – the subject matter of gardening is part of the social context. But, in fact, the probability of such terms occurring in the discourse is also dependent on what I and my interlocutor are doing at the time. If we are actually engaged in gardening while we are talking, there may be very few words of this kind. Jean Ure quotes an amusing example from some Russian research on register: "The recording was of people frying potatoes, and frying potatoes was what they were talking about; but since, it seems, neither frying nor potatoes were represented lexically in the text, the recording was a mystification to all who had not been in the kitchen at the time." The image of language as merely the direct reflection of subject matter is simplistic and unsound, as Malinowski pointed out exactly 50 years ago; there is much more to it than that, and this is what the notion of register is all about.

What we need to know about a context of situation in order to predict the linguistic features that are likely to be associated with it has been summarized under three headings: we need to know the *field of discourse*, the *mode of discourse* and the *tenor of discourse*.[6] We shall say a little more about these in Section 7 (X.3(1974):97); here it will be helpful to quote John Pearce's summary, from Doughty, Pearce and Thornton 1972:

Field refers to the institutional setting in which a piece of language occurs, and embraces not only the subject-matter in hand but the whole activity of the speaker or participant in a setting [we might add: 'and of the other participants'] . . .

Mode refers to the channel of communication adopted: not only the choice between spoken and written medium, but much more detailed choices [we might add: 'and other choices relating to the role of language in the situation'] . . .

Tenor or Style refers to the relationship between participants . . . not merely variation in formality . . . but . . . such questions as the permanence or otherwise of the relationship and the degree of emotional charge in it.

These are the general concepts needed for describing what is linguistically significant in the context of situation. They include the subject matter, as an aspect of the 'field of discourse' – of the whole setting of relevant actions and events within which the language is functioning; for this is where subject matter belongs. We do not, in fact, first decide what we want to say, independently of the setting, and then dress it up in a garb that is appropriate to it in the context, as many writers on language and speech events seem to assume. The 'content' is part of the total planning that takes place. There is no clear line between the 'what' and the 'how'; all language is language-in-use, in a context of situation, and all of it relates to the situation, in the abstract sense in which we are using the term here.

We should here make a passing reference to dialects, which are part of the picture of language and social man, although not primarily relevant in the educational context except as the focus of linguistic attitudes. Our language is also determined by who we are; that is the basis of dialect, and in principle a dialect is with us all our lives – it is not subject to choice. In practice, however, this is less and less true, and the phenomenon of "dialect switching" is widespread. Many speakers learn two or more dialects, either in succession, dropping the first when they learn the second, or in coordination, switching between them according to the context of situation. Hence the dialect comes to be an aspect of the register. If for example the standard dialect is used in formal contexts and the neighbourhood one in informal contexts, then one part of the contextual determination of linguistic features is the determination of choice of dialect. When dialects come to have different meanings for us, the choice of dialect becomes a choice of meaning, or a choice between different areas of our meaning potential.

Like the language of the child, the language of the adult is a set of socially contextualized resources of behaviour, a 'meaning potential' that is related to situations of use. Being 'appropriate to the situation' is not some optional extra in language; it is an essential element in the ability to mean. Of course, we are all aware of occasions when we feel about something said or written that it might have been expressed in a way that was more appropriate to the task in hand; we want to 'keep the meaning but change the wording'. But these are the special cases, in which we are reacting to purely conventional features of register variation. In the last resort, it is impossible to draw a line between 'what he said' and 'how he said it', since this is based on a conception of language as existing in isolation from any context. The distinction between one register and another is a distinction of **what** is said as much as of **how** it is said, without any enforced separation between the two. If a seven-year-old insists on using slang when you think he should be using more formal language, this is a dispute about registers; but if he insists on talking about his football hero when you want him to talk about a picture he has been painting, then this is equally a dispute over registers, and one which is probably much more interesting and farreaching for both teacher and pupil concerned.

Thus our functional picture of the adult linguistic system is of a culturally specific and situationally sensitive range of meaning potential. Language is the ability to 'mean' in the situation types, or social contexts, that are generated by the culture. When we talk about "uses of language", we are concerned with the meaning potential that is associated with particular situation types; and we are likely to be especially interested in those which are of some social and cultural significance, in the light of a sociological theory of language such as Bernstein's. This last point is perhaps worth stressing. The way that we have envisaged the study of language and social man, through the concept of 'meaning potential', might be referred to as a kind of 'sociosemantics', in the sense that it is the study of meaning in a social or sociological framework. But there is a difference between 'social' and 'sociological' here. If we describe the context of situation in terms of *ad hoc* observations about the settings in which language is used, this could be said to be a 'social' account of language but hardly a 'sociological' one, since the concepts we are drawing on are not referred to in any kind of general social theory. Such an account can be very illuminating, as demonstrated in a brilliant paper, published some 20 years ago, by T. F. Mitchell (1957), called 'The language of buying and selling in Cyrenaica' – though since the language studied was Cyrenaican Arabic and the paper was published in a learned journal in Morocco, it is not widely known. But for research of this kind to be relevant to a teacher who is professionally concerned with his pupils' success in language, it has to relate to social contexts that are themselves of significance, in the sort of way that Bernstein's "critical contexts" are significant for the socialization of the child. The criteria would then be sociological rather than simply social – based on some theory of social structure and social change. In this respect, the earlier terms like Firth's "sociological linguistics", or "sociology of language" as used by Bernstein, are perhaps more pointed than the currently fashionable label "sociolinguistics".

Notes

5. Useful discussions of the concept of register, in the present context, will be found in Hasan (1973) and in Ure and Ellis (1972).

6. See Halliday, McIntosh and Strevens (1964), where the term "style of discourse" was used instead of "tenor". Here we shall prefer the term "tenor" introduced by Spencer and Gregory, in Enkvist, Spencer and Gregory (1964). A number of other, more or less related, schemata have been proposed; see especially Jeffrey Ellis (1965, 1966).

X.3(1974):93–7, 130

★ ★ ★

Theoretically a social dialect is like a regional dialect, in that it can be **treated as** invariant in the life history of the speaker. This in fact used to be regarded as the norm. In practice, however, it is misleading; as Labov remarks in this connection (1970; in 1971: 170): "As far as we can see, there are no single-style speakers". Labov refers to "style shift" rather than "code shift", understanding by this a shift in respect of certain specified variables that is governed by one particular situational restraint, namely the level of formality. The variables he finds are grammatical and phonological ones, such as the presence or absence of *be* in copular constructions, e.g. *he (is) wild*; negative concord, as displayed in the music-hall Cockney sentence *I don't suppose you don't know nobody what don't want to buy no dog*, or its absence; θ vs. $t\theta$ vs. t in initial position, e.g. in *think*; plus or minus post-vocalic *r*, etc. Labov's work has shown that one cannot define a social dialect, at least in an urban context, except by having recourse to variable rules as well as categorical rules: in other words, variation must be seen as inherent in the system. Labov's own earlier definition of an urban speech community, as a group of speakers sharing the same linguistic attitudes, which he arrived at after finding that speech attitudes were more consistent than speech habits, could therefore, in the light of his own studies of variation, be revised to read "a group of speakers showing the same patterns of variation" – which means, in turn, reinstating its original definition as a group of speakers who share the same social dialect, since social dialect is now defined so as to include such variation (see Wolfram 1971).

However, as Labov remarks, although "there are a great many styles and stylistic dimensions, . . . *all such styles can be ranged along a single dimension, measured by the amount of attention paid to speech*" (1970; in 1971: 170, Labov's italics). Hence, for example, the five stylistic levels that are postulated in order to show up variation in post-vocalic *r*: casual speech, careful speech, reading, word lists and minimal pairs. In other words the **type** of linguistic variation that is associated with these contexts, through the "amount of attention paid to speech", is itself largely homogeneous; it can be represented in the form of points along a scale of deviation from an implied norm, the norm in this case being a prestige or "standard" form. The speaker is not switching between alternative forms that are equally deviant and thus neutral with regard to prestige norms (contrasting in this respect with rural speakers in dialect boundary areas). He is switching between variants that are valuecharged: they have differential values in the social system. This by no means necessarily implies that the so-called "prestige" forms are most highly valued for all groups in all contexts (Labov, 1970; in 1971: 204), but simply that the effect of such variation on linguistic change cannot be studied in isolation from the social system which determines the sets of values underlying the variation.

X.4(1975):138–9

★ ★ ★

2.3 REGISTER

The term **register** was first used in this sense, that of text variety, by Reid (1956); the concept was taken up and developed by Jean Ure (Ure and Ellis 1972), and interpreted within Hill's (1958) "institutional linguistic" framework by Halliday, McIntosh and Strevens (1964). The register is the semantic variety of which a text may be regarded as an instance.

Like other related concepts, such as "speech variant" and "(sociolinguistic) code" (Ferguson 1971, Chapters 1 and 2; Gumperz 1971, Part I), register was originally conceived of in lexicogrammatical terms. Halliday *et al.* drew a primary distinction between two types of language variety: dialect, which they defined as variety according to the user, and register, which they defined as variety according to the use. The dialect is what a person speaks, determined by who he is; the register is what a person is speaking, determined by what he is doing at the time. This general distinction can be accepted, but, instead of characterizing a register largely by its lexicogrammatical properties, we shall suggest, as with text, a more abstract definition in semantic terms.

A register can be defined as the configuration of semantic resources that the member of a culture typically associates with a situation type. It is the meaning potential that is accessible in a given social context. Both the situation and the register associated with it can be described to varying degrees of specificity; but the existence of registers is a fact of everyday experience – speakers have no difficulty in recognizing the semantic options and combinations of options that are 'at risk' under particular environmental conditions. Since these options are realized in the form of grammar and vocabulary, the register is recognizable as a particular selection of words and structures. But it is defined in terms of meanings; it is not an aggregate of conventional forms of expression superposed on some underlying content by 'social factors' of one kind or another. It is the selection of meanings that constitutes the variety to which a text belongs.

2.4 CODE

Code is used here in Bernstein's sense; it is the principle of semiotic organization governing the choice of meanings by a speaker and their interpretation by a hearer. The code controls the semantic styles of the culture.

Codes are not varieties of language, as dialects and registers are. The codes are so to speak 'above' the linguistic system; they are types of social semiotic, or symbolic orders of meaning generated by the social system (see Hasan 1973). The code is actualized in language through the register, since it determines the semantic orientation of speakers in particular social contexts; Bernstein's own use of "variant" (as in "elaborated variant") refers to those characteristics of a register which derive from the form of the code. When the semantic systems of the language are activated by the situational determinants of text – the field, tenor and mode – this process is regulated by the codes.

Hence the codes transmit, or control the transmission of, the underlying patterns of a culture or sub-culture, acting through the socializing agencies of family, peer group and school. As a child comes to attend to and interpret meanings, in the context of situation and in the context of culture, at the same time he takes over the code. The culture is transmitted to him with the code acting as a filter, defining and making accessible the semiotic principles of his own sub-culture, so that as he learns the culture he also learns the grid, or sub-cultural angle on the social system. The child's linguistic experience reveals the culture to him through the code, and so transmits the code as part of the culture.

X.5(1975):181–3

★ ★ ★

1. Language as institution

1.1 DIALECT

Classical dialectology, as developed in Europe, rests on certain implicit assumptions about speakers and speech communities. A speech community is assumed to be a social unit whose members (i) communicate with each other, (ii) speak in a consistent way and (iii) all speak alike. This is obviously, again, an idealized picture; but in the type of settled rural community for which dialect studies were first developed, it is near enough reality to serve as a theoretical norm.

Dialectal variation, in such a model, is essentially variation between speech communities. We may recognize some variation also within the community – squire and parson, or landlord and priest, probably speak differently from other people – but this is at the most a minor theme; and we do not envisage variation as something that arises **within** the speech of an individual speaker.

When dialectology moved into an urban setting, with Labov's monumental New York city studies, variation took on a new meaning. Labov showed that, within a typical North American urban community, the speech varies (i) **between** the members according to social class (low to high), and (ii) **within** each member according to "style scale" (amount of monitoring or attention paid to one's own speech, casual to formal). The effect of each of these factors is quantitative (hence probabilistic in origin), but the picture is clear: when single dialect variables are isolated for intensive investigation, some of them turn out to be socially stratified. The forms of the variable ('variants') are **ranked** in an order such that the 'high' variant is associated with higher social status **or** a more formal context of speech, and the 'low' with lower social status **or** a more casual context of speech.

1.2 SOCIAL DIALECT

As long as dialect variation is geographically determined, it can be explained away: one group stays on this side of the mountain, the other group moves to the other side of the mountain, and they no longer talk to each other. But there are no mountains dividing social classes; the members of different social classes do talk to each other, at least transactionally. What is the explanation of this socially determined variation? How do "social dialects" arise?

One of the most significant of Labov's finding was the remarkable uniformity shown by people of all social groups in their attutudes towards variation in the speech of others. This uniformity of attitude means that the members are highly sensitive to the social meaning of dialectal variation, a form of sensitivity that is apparently achieved during the crucial years of adolescence, in the age range of about 13–18.

We acquire this sensitivity as a part of growing up in society, because dialect variation is functional with respect to the social structure. And this is why it does not disappear. It was confidently predicted in the period after World War II that, with the steadily increasing dominance of the mass media, dialects would disappear and we should soon all be speaking alike. Sure enough, the **regionally**-based dialects of rural areas **are** disappearing, as least in industrial societies. But with the urban dialects the opposite has happened: diversity is increasing. We can explain this by showing that the diversity is socially functional. It expresses the structure of society.

It would be a mistake to think of social structure simply in terms of some particular index of social class. The essential characteristic of social structure as we know it is that it is hierarchical; and linguistic variation is what expresses its hierarchical character, whether in terms of age, generation, sex, provenance or any other of its manifestations, including caste and class.

Let us postulate a perfectly homogeneous society, one without any of these forms of social hierarchy. The members of such a society would presumably speak a perfectly homogeneous language, one without any dialectal variation. Now consider the hypothetical antithesis of this: a society split into two conflicting groups, a society and an anti-society. Here we shall expect to find some form of matching linguistic order: two mutually opposed linguistic varieties, a language and an anti-language. These are, once again, idealized constructs; but phenomena approximating to them have arisen at various times and places. For example, the social conditions of sixteenth-century England generated an anti-society of 'vagabonds', who lived by extorting wealth from the established society; and this society had its anti-language, fragments of which are reported in contemporary documents. The anti-language is a language of social conflict – of passive resistance or active opposition; but at the same time, like any other language, it is a means of expressing and maintaining the social structure – in this case, the structure of the anti-society.

Most of the time what we find in real life are dialect hierarchies, patterns of dialectal variation in which a "standard" (representing the power base of society) is opposed by non-standard varieties (which the members refer to as "dialects"). The non-standard dialects may become languages of opposition and protest; periods of explicit class conflict tend to be characterized by the development of such protest languages, sometimes in the form of 'ghetto languages', which are coming closer to the anti-language end of the scale. Here dialect becomes a means of expression of class consciousness and political awareness. We can recognize a category of 'oppressed languages', languages of groups that are subjected to social or political oppression. It is characteristic of oppressed languages that their speakers tend to excel at verbal contest and verbal display. Meaning is often the most effective form of social action that is available to them.

1.3 Register

Dialects, in the usual sense of that term, are different ways of saying the same thing. In other words, the dialects of a language differ from each other phonologically and lexicogrammatically, but not, in principle, semantically.

In this respect, dialectal variation contrasts with variation of another kind, that of **register**. Registers are ways of saying different things.

Registers differ semantically. They also differ lexicogrammatically, because that is how meanings are **expressed**; but lexicogrammatical differences among registers are, by and large, the automatic consequence of semantic differences. In principle, registers are configurations of meanings that are typically exchanged – that are 'at risk', so to speak – under given conditions of use.

A dialect is 'what you speak' (habitually); this is determined by 'who you are', your regional and/or social place of origin and/or adoption. A register is 'what you are speaking' (at the given time), determined by 'what you are doing', the nature of the ongoing social activity. Whereas dialect variation reflects the social order in the special sense of *the hierarchy of social structure*, register variation also reflects the social order but in the special sense of *the diversity of social processes*. We are not doing the same things all the time; so we speak now in one register, now in another. But the total **range** of the social processes in which any member will typically engage is a function of the structure of society. We each have our own repertory of social actions, reflecting our place at the intersection of a whole complex of social hierarchies. There is a division of labour.

Since the division of labour is **social**, the two kinds of language variety, register and dialect, are closely interconnected. The structure of society determines who, in terms of the various social hierarchies of class, generation, age, sex, provenance and so on, will have access to which aspects of the social process – and hence, to which registers. (In most societies today there is considerable scope for individual discretion, though this has not always been the case.) This means, in turn, that a particular register tends to have a particular dialect associated with it: the registers of bureaucracy, for example, demand the "standard" (national) dialect, whereas fishing and farming demand rural (local) varieties. Hence the dialect comes to symbolize the register; when we hear a local dialect, we unconsciously switch off a large part of our register range.

In this way, in a typical hierarchical social structure, dialect becomes the means by which a member gains, or is denied, access to certain registers.

So if we say that linguistic structure "reflects" social structure, we are really assigning to language a role that is too passive. (I am formulating it in this way in order to keep the parallel between the two expressions "linguistic structure" and "social structure". In fact, what is meant is the linguistic *system*; elsewhere I have not used "structure" in this general sense of the organization of language, but have reserved it for the specialized sense of constituent structure.) Rather we should say that linguistic structure is the *realization of* social structure, actively symbolizing it in a process of mutual creativity. Because it stands as a metaphor for society, language has the property of not only transmitting the social order but also maintaining and potentially modifying it. (This is undoubtedly the explanation of the violent attitudes that under certain social conditions come to be held by one group towards the speech of others. A different set of **vowels** is perceived as the symbol of a different set of **values**, and hence takes on the character of a threat.) Variation in language is the symbolic expression of variation in society: it is created by society, and helps to create society in its turn. Of the two kinds of variation in language, that of dialect expresses the diversity of social structure, that of register expresses the diversity of social process. The interaction of dialect and register in language expresses the interaction of structure and process in society.

X.9(1978):252–5

Additional readings

Linguistic Studies of Text and Discourse (Volume 2) – 1(1964):17; 2(1977):58; 6(1990):168–70; 8(1994):231–4

On Language and Linguistics (Volume 3) – 12(1997):268; 13(2001):283; 16(1992):360, 362–3; 18(1995):416–7

The Language of Early Childhood (Volume 4) –13(1975):287

Computational and Quantitative Studies (Volume 6) – 4(1991):66; 5(1992):84; 8(2002):160; 11(1995): 248, 263–4

Studies in English Language (Volume 7) – 7(1985):214–6

Language and Education (Volume 9) – 14(1986):296–300

Language and Society (Volume 10) – 1(1964); 3(1974):103–7, 115–6; 4(1975): 140–2, 147; 5(1975):174–5, 196–7; 6(1975):205–9; 8(1994):235, 242–3; 9(1978):259–61

BIBLIOGRAPHY

Allen, W. S. (1953) 'Relationship in comparative linguistics', *Transactions of the Philological Society*.

Allen, W. S. (1956) 'Structure and system in the Abaza verbal complex', *Transactions of the Philological Society*.

Bateman, J. and Matthiessen, C. M. I. M. (1991) *Systemic Linguistics and Text Generation: Experiences from Japanese and English,* London and New York: Frances Pinter.

Bateson, G. (1936) *Naven.* Stanford: Stanford University Press (2nd edn 1958).

Bateson, M. C. (1975) 'Mother-infant exchange: the epigenesist of conversational interaction', in D. Aaronson and R. W. Rieber (eds), *Developmental Psycholinguistics and Communication Disorders.* New York (Annals of the New York Academy of Sciences 163).

Bazell, C. E. (1953) *Linguistic Form.* Istanbul: Istanbul University Press.

Benson, J. D. and Greaves, W. S. (eds) (1985) *Systemic Perspectives on Discourse.* Vol. 1. Norwood NJ: Ablex.

Benson, J. D. and Greaves, W. S. (eds) (1988) *Systemic Functional Approaches to Discourse.* Norwood, NJ: Ablex.

Berger, P. L. and Luckmann, T. (1966) *The Social Construction of Reality: A Treatise in the Sociology of Knowledge.* London: Allen Lane (Penguin Press).

Bernstein, B. (1970) 'A critique of the concept "compensatory education"', in S. Williams (ed.), *Language and Poverty: Perspectives on a Theme.* Madison: University of Wisconsin Press.

Bernstein, B. (1971) *Class, Codes and Control, Vol. 1: Theoretical Studies Towards a Sociology of Language.* London: Routledge and Kegan Paul (Primary Socialization, Language and Education).

Bernstein, B. (1973) *Class, Codes and Control, Volume 2: Applied Studies Towards a Sociology of Language,* London: Routledge and Kegan Paul (Primary Socialization, Language and Education).

Bernstein, B. (1990) *The Structuring of Pedagogic Discourse.* Vol. 4, *Class, Codes and Control.* London: Routledge & Kegan Paul.

Bernstein, B. (1996) 'Codes and research', in *Pedagogy, Symbolic Control and Identity: Theory, Research, Critique*. London: Taylor and Francis.

Birch, D. and O'Toole, M. (eds) (1988) *Functions of Style*. London: Pinter.

Bohm, D. (1980) *Wholeness and the Implicate Order*. London: Routledge & Kegan Paul (Art Paperbacks, 1983).

Briggs, J. P. and Peat, F. D. (1985) *Looking Glass Universe: The Emerging Science of Wholeness*. Glasgow: Simon & Schuster.

Bruner, J. (1975) 'The ontogenesis of speech acts', *Journal of Child Language* 2.

Bűhler, K. (1934) *Sprachtheorie: Die Darstellungfunktion der Sprache*. Jena: G. Fischer.

Bull, W. E. (1960) *Time, Tense and the Verb*. Berkeley: University of California Press (University of California Publications in Linguistics 19).

Bullowa, M. (ed.) (1979) *Before Speech: The Beginning of Interpersonal Communication*. Cambridge: Cambridge University Press.

Butt, D. G. (1984) 'The Relationship between Theme and Lexicogrammar in the Poetry of Wallace Stevens.' Unpublished PhD dissertation, Macquarie University.

Butt, D. G. (1988) 'Ideational meaning and the existential fabric of a poem', in R. P. Fawcett and D. J. Young (eds), *New Developments in Systemic Linguistics. Vol. 2, Theory and Application*. London and New York: Pinter.

Butt, D. G. (1989) 'The object of language', in R. Hasan and J. R. Martin (eds), 1989.

Carnochan, J. (1952) 'Glottalization in Hausa', *Transactions of the Philological Society*.

Carroll, J. B. (ed.) (1956) *Language, Thought and Reality: Selected Writings of Benjamin Lee Whorf*. Cambridge, MA: MIT Press.

Chomsky, N. (1957) *Syntactic Structures*. The Hague: Mouton (Janua Linguarum 4).

Chomsky, N. (1961) 'Generative grammar', *Word* 17.

Cloran, C. (1989) 'Learning through language: the social construction of gender', in R. Hasan and J. R. Martin (eds), 1989.

Colby, B. N. (1973) 'A partial grammar of Eskimo folktales', *American Anthropologist* 75.

Colby, B. N. and Colby, L. M. (1980) *The Daykeeper: The Life and Discourse of an Ixil Diviner*. Cambridge, MA.: Harvard University Press.

Dahl, Ö. (1985) *Tense and Aspect Systems*. Oxford and New York: Basil Blackwell.

Daneš, F. (1960) 'Sentence intonation from a functional point of view', *Word* 16, 34–54.

Daneš, F. (1964) 'A three-level approach to syntax', *Travaux Linguistiques de Prague* 1, 225–240, 1964.

Davey, A. (1978) *Discourse Production: A Computer Model of Some Aspects of a Speaker*. Edinburgh: Edinburgh University Press.

Davidse, K. (1991) 'Categories of Experiential Grammar.' Unpublished PhD dissertation, Catholic University of Leuven.

Davidse, K. (1992) 'Transitivity/ergativity: the Janus-headed grammar of actions and events', in M. Davies and L. Ravelli (eds), 1992.

Davidse, K. (1996) 'Ditransitivity and possession', in R. Hasan *et al.* (eds), 1996.

Davies, M. and Ravelli, L. (eds) (1992) *Advances in Systemic Linguistics: Recent Theory and Practice*. London and New York: Pinter.

Delavenay, E. (1960) *Introduction to Machine Translation*. London. Thames & Hudson.

Delbridge, A. (1970) 'Intonation and ambiguity', *Kivung* 3.2.

Dore, J. (1974) 'A pragmatic approach to early language development', *Journal of Psycholinguistic Research*, 4.

Dore, J. (1976) 'Conditions on the acquisition of speech acts', in I. Markov (ed.), *The Social Context of Language*. New York: Wiley.

Doughty, P., Pearce, J. and Thornton, G. (1971) *Language in Use*. London: Arnold (Schools Council Programme in Linguistics and English Teaching).

Doughty, P., Pearce, J. and Thornton, G. (1972) *Exploring Language*, London: Edward Arnold.

Douglas, M. (1971) 'Do dogs lunch? A cross-cultural approach to body symbolism', *Journal of Psychosomatic Research* 15.

Douglas, M. (1972) 'Speech, class and Basil Bernstein', *The Listener* no. 2241, London: BBC (9 March).

Dunbar, R. (1992) Summary in 'Secret life of the brain', *New Scientist* 1850 (Supplement 4).

Ebeling, C. L. (1960) *Linguistic Units*. The Hague: Mouton (Janua Linguarum 12).

Edelman, G. (1992) *Bright Air, Brilliant Fire: on the Matter of the Mind*. New York: Basic Books; London: Allen Lane.

Eiler, M. A. (1979) *'Meaning and choice in writing about literature: a study of cohesion in the expository texts of ninth graders.'* Unpublished PhD dissertation, Illinois Institute of Technology.

Ellis, J. M. (1993) *Language, Thought and Logic*. Evanston IL: Northwestern University Press.

Ellis, J. O. (1965) 'Linguistic sociology and institutional linguistics', *Linguistics* 19.

Ellis, J. O. (1966) 'On contextual meaning', in C. E. Bazell *et al.* (eds), *In Memory of J. R. Firth*. London: Longmans.

Elmenoufy, A. M. E. S. (1969) 'A study of the role of intonation in the grammar of English', 2 vols, PhD thesis, University of London.

Enkvist, Nils Erik; Spencer, John and Gregory, Michael (1964) *Linguistics and Style,* London: Oxford University Press (*Language and Language Learning* 6).

Fawcett, R. P. (1981) 'Generating a sentence in systemic functional grammar' in Halliday and Martin (eds).

Fawcett, R. P. (1983) 'Language as a semiological system: a reinterpretation of Saussure', in J. Morreall (ed.), *The Ninth LACUS Forum*. Columbia, South Carolina: Hornbeam Press.

Fawcett, R. P. (1988) 'What makes a "good" system network good?', in J. D. Benson and W. S. Greaves (eds), *Systemic Functional Approaches to Discourse*. Norwood, N.J.: Ablex.

Fawcett, R. P. (1992) 'The COMMUNAL project: how to get from semantics to syntax', *Proceedings of COLING 92, Fourteenth International Conference on Computational Linguistics, Nantes.*

Fawcett, R. P. (1994) 'Some recent developments in Systemic Functional Grammar'. Paper presented to Linguistics Association of Great Britain, April 1994.

Fawcett, R. P. and Tucker, G. H. (1990) 'Demonstration of GENESYS: a very large semantically based systemic functional grammar', *Proceedings of the Thirteenth International Conference on Computational Linguistics, Helsinki,* Vol. 1.

Fawcett, R. P., Tucker, G. H. and Lin, Y. Q. (1993) 'How a systemic functional grammar works: the role of realisation', in H. Horacek and M. Zock (eds), *New Concepts in Natural Language Generation.* London: Pinter.

Ferguson, Charles A. (1971) *Language Structure and Language Use: Essays Selected and Introduced by Anwar S. Dil,* Stanford, California: Stanford University Press.

Firth, J. R. (1955) 'Structural linguistics', *Transactions of the Philological Society.* Reprinted in F. R. Palmer (ed.), *Selected Papers of J. R. Firth 1952–1959.* London: Longman.

Firth, J. R. (1957a) 'A synopsis of linguistic theory', in J. R. Firth *et al.* (eds), *Studies in Linguistic Analysis.* Oxford: Blackwell (Special Volume of the Philological Society). Reprinted in F. R. Palmer (ed.) (1968), *Selected Papers of J. R. Firth 1952–1959.* London: Longman.

Firth, J. R. (1957b) 'Ethnographic analysis and language, with reference to Malinowski's views', in Raymond Firth (ed.), *Man and Culture: An Evaluation of the Work of Bronislaw Malinowski,* London: Routledge and Kegan Paul.

Firth, J. R. (1957c) *Papers in Linguistics 1934–1951,* London: Oxford University Press.

Firth, J. R. (1957d) 'Applications of general linguistics', *Transactions of the Philological Society.* Reprinted in F. R. Palmer (ed.) (1968), *Selected Papers of J. R. Firth 1952–1959.* London: Longman.

Firth, J. R. (1968) 'Linguistic Analysis as a Study of Meaning', in Palmer, F. R. (ed.) *Selected Papers of J. R. Firth 1952–59,* London: Longman.

Fishman, Joshua A. (ed.) 1971 *Advances in the Sociology of Language, Vol. 1.* The Hague: Mouton.

Five to Nine: Aspects of Function and Structure in the Spoken Language of Elementary School Children (1972) Toronto: English Department, York University, and Board of Education for the Borough of North York.

France, M. N. (1975) 'The Generation of the Self: A Study of the Construction of Categories in Infancy'. University of Essex PhD thesis.

Fries, P. H. (1981) 'On the status of theme in English: arguments from discourse', *Forum Linguisticum* 6.1. Reprinted in J. S. Petőfi and E. Soőzer (eds), *Micro and Macro Connexity of Texts.* Hamburg: Buske.

Fries, P. H. (1995) 'Patterns of information in initial position in English', in P. H. Fries and M. Gregory (eds), *Discourse in Society: Systemic Functional Perspective.* Norwood, N.J.: Ablex.

Garvin, P. (1957) *Report of the Seventh Annual Round Table Meeting on Linguistics and Language Study.* Washington, D.C.: Georgetown University Press (Languages and Linguistics 9).

Ghadessy, M. (1994) *Register Analysis: Theory and Practice.* London: Pinter.

Giglioli, Pier Paolo, (ed,) (1972) *Language and Social Context*, Harmondsworth: Penguin Books (Penguin Modern Sociology Readings).

Gregory, M. J. (1967) 'Aspects of varieties differentiation', *Journal of Linguistics* 3. 2.

Gregory, M. J. (1985) 'Linguistics and theatre – Hamlet's voice: aspects of text formation and cohesion in a soliloquy', *Forum Linguisticum* 7.

Gumperz, J. J. and Hymes, D. H. (eds) (1972) *Directions in Sociolinguistics.* New York: Holt, Rinehart & Winstion.

Gumperz, John J. (1971) *Language in Social Groups: Essays Selected and Introduced by Anwar S. Dil,* Stanford, California: Stanford University Press.

Guy, G. R. and Vonwiller, J. (1984) 'The meaning of an intonation in Australian English', *Australian Journal of Linguistics* 4.1.

Haas, W. (1957) 'Zero in linguistic description', in J. R. Firth *et al., Studies in Linguistic Analysis.* Oxford: Blackwell (Special Volume of the Philological Society).

Hagège, C. (1997) 'Language as a faculty, languages as "contingent" manifestations and humans as function builders', in A.-M. Simon-Vandenbergen, K. Davidse and D. Noel (eds), *Reconnecting Language.* Amsterdam/Philadelphia: Benjamins.

Hagège, C. (2000) *Halte à la mort des langues.* Paris: Odile Jacob.

Halliday, M. A. K. (1956) 'Grammatical categories in modern Chinese'. *Transactions of the Philological Society.* 177-224. In Collected Works, Vol. 8.

Halliday, M. A. K. (1958) Review of Whatmough: *Language: A Modern Synthesis, Archivum Linguisticum* 10. 2.

Halliday, M. A. K. (1959a) Review of Herdan: *Language as Choice and Chance, Archivum Linguisticum* 11. 2.

Halliday, M. A. K. (1959b) *The Language of the Chinese: 'Secret History of the Mongols'.* Oxford: Blackwell (Philological Society Publications 17).

Halliday, M. A. K. (1961) 'Categories of the theory of grammar', *Word* 17.3: 242–92.

Halliday, M. A. K. (1967) *Intonation and Grammar in British English.* The Hague: Mouton (Janua Linguarum Series Practica 48).

Halliday, M. A. K. (1967/68) 'Notes on transitivity and theme in English, Parts 1-3', *Journal of Linguistics* 3.1, 3.2, 4.2.

Halliday, M. A. K. (1969) 'Relevant models of language', *The State of Language (Educational Review* 22.1: 26-37).

Halliday, M. A. K. (1971) 'Language in a social perspective', *The Context of Language (Educational Review,* University of Birmingham 23.3) Reprinted in M. A. K. Halliday, *Explorations in the Functions of Language.* London: Edward Arnold (Explorations in Language Study), 1973.

Halliday, M. A. K. (1973) *Explorations in the Functions of Language.* London: Edward Arnold (Explorations in Language Study Series).

Halliday, M. A. K. (1974) *Language and Social Man*, London: Longman (Schools Council Programme in Linguistics and English Teaching. Papers Series II, Vol. 3), in *Collected Works*, Vol. 10.

Halliday, M. A. K. (1975a) 'Language as social semiotic: towards a general sociolinguistic theory' in A. Makkai and V. B. Makkai (eds), *The First LACUS Forum 1974*. Columbia, SC: Hornheam Press. Abridged version reprinted in Halliday 1978.

Halliday, M. A. K. (1975b) *Learning How to Mean: Explorations in the Development of Language*. London: Edward Arnold.

Halliday, M. A. K. (1977) 'Text as semantic choice in social contexts', in A. van Dijk and J. Petőfi (eds), *Grammars and Descriptions*. Berlin: de Gruyter.

Halliday, M. A. K. (1978a) 'Meaning and the construction of reality in early childhood', in H. L. Pick, Jr and E. Saltzman (eds), *Modes of Receiving and Processing of Information*. Hillsdale, NJ: Lawrence Erlbaum Associates.

Halliday, M. A. K. (1978b) *Language as Social Semiotic: The Social Interpretation of Language and Meaning*. London: Edward Arnold.

Halliday, M. A. K. (1979a) 'Modes of meaning and modes of expresson: types of grammatical structure, and their determination by different semantic functions', in D. J. Allerton, E. Carney and D. Holdcroft (eds), *Function and Context in Linguistic Analysis: Essays Offered to William Haas*. Cambridge: Cambridge University Press.

Halliday, M. A. K. (1979b) 'One child's protolanguage', in M. Bullowa (ed.), 1979.

Halliday, M. A. K. (1982) 'The de-automatization of grammar: from Priestley's *An Inspector Calls*', in J. Anderson (ed.), *Language Form and Linguistic Variation: Papers Dedicated to Angus McIntosh*. Amsterdam: J. Benjamins (Current Issues in Linguistic Theory 15).

Halliday, M. A. K. (1984) 'Listening to Nigel: Conversations of a Very Small Child'. Unpublished manuscript, University of Sydney, Linguistics Department, Sydney, Australia. (The data is on an accompany CD to *Collected Works Vol. 4*).

Halliday, M. A. K. (1985/1994) *An Introduction to Functional Grammar*. London: Edward Arnold [2nd edn 1994].

Halliday, M. A. K. (1987) 'Spoken and written modes of meaning', in R. Horowitz and S. J. Samuels (eds), *Comprehending Oral and Written Language*. New York: Academic Press. In Collected Works, Vol. 1, chap. 12, 2002.

Halliday, M. A. K. (1991a) 'Towards probabilistic interpretations', in E. Ventola (ed.), *Functional and Systemic Linguistics: Approaches and Uses*. Berlin: Mouton de Gruyter.

Halliday, M. A. K. (1991b) 'Corpus studies and probabilistic grammar', in K. Aijmer and B. Altenberg (eds), *English Corpus Linguistics: Studies in Honour of Jan Svartvik*. London: Longman.

Halliday, M. A. K. (1992) 'How do you mean?' in M. Davies and L. Ravelli (eds), 1992.

Halliday, M. A. K. (1993a) 'Towards a language-based theory of learning', *Linguistics and Education* 5.2.

Halliday, M. A. K. (ed.) (1993b) *Language as Cultural Dynamic (Cultural Dynamics 6, 1-2)*, 1-10.

Halliday, M. A. K. (1994) *Introduction to Functional Grammar*, 2nd rev. edn. London: Edward Arnold.

Halliday, M. A. K. (1995) 'Computing meanings: some reflections on past experience and present prospects'. Paper presented to the second conference of the Pacific Association of Computational Linguistics (PACLING II), University of Queensland, Brisbane.

Halliday, M. A. K. and Hasan, R. (1976) *Cohesion in English*. London: Longman.

Halliday, M. A. K. and Hasan, R. (eds) (1980) *Text and Context: Aspects of Language in a Social-Semiotic Perspective*. Tokyo: Sophia University Graduate School of Linguistics (Sophia Linguistica 6).

Halliday, M. A. K. and Hasan, R. (1985) *Language, context and text: a social semiotic perspective*. Geelong, Victoria: Deakin University Press.

Halliday, M. A. K. and James, Z. L. (1993) 'A quantitative study of polarity and primary tense in the English finite clause', in J. M. Sinclair, M. Hoey and G. Fox (eds), *Techniques of Description: Spoken and Written Discourse (A Festschrift for Malcolm Coulthard)*. London and New York: Routledge.

Halliday, M. A. K. and Martin, J. R. (eds) (1981) *Readings in Systemic Linguistics*, London: Batsford.

Halliday, M. A. K. and Martin, J. R. (1993) *Writing Science: Literacy and Discursive Power.* London: Falmer Press.

Halliday, M. A. K. and Matthiessen, C. M. I. M. (1999) *Construing Experience through Meaning: a language-based approach to cognition*. London and New York: Cassell (Open Linguistics Series).

Halliday, M. A. K. and Matthiessen, C. M. I. M. (2000) *Systemic Linguistics: a First Step into the Theory*. Macquarie University. National Centre for English Language Teaching and Research.

Halliday, M. A. K. and Poole M. (1978) *Notes on Talking Shop: Demands on Language for Use with the Film Australia Production*. Lindfield: Australian Film Commission.

Halliday, M. A. K., Gibbons, J. and Nicholas, H. (eds) (1990) *Learning, Keeping and Using Language*. Selected Papers from the 8th World Congress of Applied Linguistics, Sydney, 16-21 August 1987. Amsterdam/Philadelphia: Benjamins.

Halliday, M. A. K., McIntosh, A. and Strevens, P. (1964) *The Linguistic Sciences and Language Teaching*. London: Longmans (Longmans' Linguistics Library).

Hammond, Jennifer (1990) 'Oral and written language in the educational context', in Halliday, Gibbons and Nicholas (eds).

Harris, Z. S. (1951) *Methods in Structural Linguistics*. Chicago: University of Chicago Press.

Harris, Z. S. (1952) 'Discourse analysis', *Language* 28.1,4.

Hasan, R. (1971) 'Syntax and semantics', in Morton, J. (ed.) *Biological and Social Factors in Psycholinguistics*, London: Logos Press.

Hasan, R. (1973) 'Code, register and social dialect', in Bernstein (ed.) (1973).

Hasan, R. (1979) 'On the notion of text', in J. Petőfi (ed.), *Text Versus Sentence: Basic Questions of Text Linguistics*. Hamburg: Helmut Buske Verlag.

Hasan, R. (1980a) 'The texture of a text', in M. A. K. Halliday and R. Hasan (eds), 1980.

Hasan, R. (1980b) 'What's going on: a dynamic view of context', in J. E. Copeland and P. W. Davis (eds), *The Seventh LACUS forum*. Columbia, SC: Hornbeam Press. 106-121.

Hasan, R. (1983) 'Coherence and cohesive harmony', in J. Flood (ed.), *Understanding Reading Comprehension*. Newark, DE.: International Reading Association.

Hasan, R. (1984a) 'The structure of the nursery tale: an essay in text typology', in L. Coveri (ed.), *Linguistica Testuale: Proceedings of the 15th Internatonal Congress of the Italian Linguistics Society*. Rome: Bulzoni.

Hasan, R. (1984b) 'Ways of saying: ways of meaning', in R. P. Fawcett, M. A. K. Halliday, S. M. Lamb and A. Makkai (eds), *Language as Social Semiotic*. Vol. 1, *The Semiotics of Culture and Language*. London and Dover: Pinter (Open Linguistics Series).

Hasan, R. (1984c) 'Coherence and cohesive harmony', in J. Flood (ed.), *Understanding Reading Comprehension*. Newark, DE.: International Reading Association.

Hasan, R. (1985a) 'Lending and borrowing: from grammar to lexis', in J. E. Clark (ed.), *The Cultivated Australian: Festschrift for Arthur Delbridge*. Hamburg: Helmut (Buske Beiträge zur Phonetik und Linguistik 48).

Hasan, R. (1985b) 'The texture of a text', in M. A. K. Halliday and R. Hasan, *Language, Context and Text*. Geelong, Vic.: Deakin University Press. (Reprinted London: Oxford University Press, 1989.)

Hasan, R. (ed.) (1985c) *Discourse on Discourse*, Canberra: Applied Linguistics Association of Australia (Occasional Paper 7).

Hasan, R. (1986) 'The ontogenesis of ideology: an interpretation of mother-child talk', in T. Threadgold *et al.* (eds), *Semiotics, Ideology, Language*. Sydney: Sydney Association for Studies in Society and Culture (Sydney Studies in Society and Culture, vol. 3).

Hasan, R. (1987) 'The grammarian's dream: lexis as most delicate grammar', in M. A. K. Halliday and R. P. Fawcett (eds), *Theory and Description*. Vol. 1, *New Developments in Systemic Linguistics*. London: Pinter.

Hasan, R. (1989) 'Semantic variation and sociolinguistics', *Australian Journal of Linguistics* 9.2.

Hasan, R. (1992) 'Rationality in everyday talk: from process to system', in J. Svartvik (ed.), *Directions in Corpus Linguistics: Proceedings of Nobel Symposium 82, Stockholm, 4–8 August 1991*. Berlin: de Gruyter.

Hasan, R. (1996) *Ways of Saying: Way of Meaning. Selected Papers of Ruqaiya Hasan*, ed. C. Cloran, D. Butt and G. Williams. London: Cassell.

Hasan, R. and Cloran, C. (1990) 'Semantic variation: A sociolinguistic interpretation of everyday talk between mothers and children', in M. A. K. Halliday, J. Gibbons and H. Nicholas (eds).

Hasan, R. and Fries, P. H. (eds) (1995) *On Subject and Theme: a discourse functional perspective.* Amsterdam and Philadelphia, PA: John Benjamins.

Hasan, R. and Martin, J. R. (eds) (1989) *Language Development: Learning Language, Learning Culture. (Meaning and Choice in Language,* vol. 1.) Norwood, NJ: Ablex.

Henderson, E. (1951) 'The phonology of loanwords in some southeast Asian languages', *Transactions of the Philological Society.*

Henrici, A. (1966/1981) 'Some notes on the systemic generation of a paradigm of the English clause', in M. A. K. Halliday and J. R. Martin (eds).

Hill, A. A. (1958) *Introduction to Linguistic Structures.* New York: Harcourt, Brace & World.

Hill, Trevor (1958) 'Institutional linguistics', *Orbis* 7.

Hjelmslev, L. (1953) *Prolegomena to a Theory of Language,* trans. by F. J. Whitfield. Bloomington: Indiana University Press (Danish original *Omkring Sprogteoriens Grundlaeggelse.* Copenhagen: Munksgaard).

Hockett, C. F. (1955) *Manual of Phonology.* Baltimore: Waverly Press (Memoirs of the International Journal of Anthropological Linguistics 2, Indiana University Publications of Anthropology and Linguistics).

Hockett, C. F. (1957) 'Two models of grammatical description', in M. Joos (ed.), *Readings in Linguistics.* Washington: American Council of Learned Societies.

Hockett, C. F. (1958) *Course in Modern Linguistics.* New York: Macmillian.

Hockett, C. F. (1961) 'Linguistic elements and their relations', *Language* 37.

Huddleston, R. D. (1965) 'Rank and depth', *Language* 41, 574–86. (Reprinted in Halliday and Martin (eds), 1981.)

Huddleston, R. D., Hudson, R. A., Winter, E. O. and Henrici, A. (1970) *Sentence and Clause in Scientific English.* London: Communication Research Centre, University College London [for Office of Scientific and Technical Information].

Hudson, R. A. (1967) 'Constituency in a systemic description of the English clause', *Lingua* 18.

Hudson, R. A. (1971) *English Complex Sentences: An Introduction to Systemic Grammar* (Linguistic Series 4). Amsterdam: North Holland.

Hymes, D. H. (1971) 'Competence and performance in linguistic theory', in R. Huxley and E. Ingram (eds), *Language Acquisition: Models and Methods.* London: Academic Press.

Joos, Martin (1967) *The Five Clocks,* New York: Harcourt, Brace and World.

Junker, K. S. (1979) 'Communication starts with selective attention', in M. Bullowa (ed.), 1979.

Katz, J. J. and Fodor, J. A. (1963) 'The structure of a semantic theory', *Language* 39.

Labov, William (1970) 'The study of language in its social context', *Studium Generale* 23. Reprinted in Fishman (ed.) 1971 and in Giglioli (ed.) 1972.

Labov, William (1971) 'The notion of "system" in creole languages', in Hymes (ed.) 1971.

Lamb, S. M. (1964) 'On alternation, transformation, realization and stratification', in C. I. J. M. Stuart (ed.), *Report of the Fifteenth Annual (First International) Round Table Meeting on Linguistics and Language Study.* Washington, DC: Georgetown University Press (Monograph Series on Languages and Linguistics 17).

Lamb, S. M. (1971) 'Linguistic and cognitive networks', in Paul Garvin (ed.) *Cognition: A Multiple View*, New York: Spartan Books.

Lamb, S. M. (1974) Discussion, in H. Parret, *Discussing Language*, The Hague: Mouton.

Lamb, S. M. (1999) *Pathways of the Brain: The Neurocognitive Basis of Language.* Amsterdam and Philadelphia: Benjamins.

Langendoen, T. D. (1968) *The London School of Linguistics: A Study of the Linguistic Theories of B. Malinowski and J. R. Firth.* Cambridge, MA: MIT Press (Research Monograph 46).

Lees, W. R. (1963) *The Grammar of English Nominalizations.* The Hague: Mouton.

Lemke, J. L. (1984) *Semiotics and Education.* Toronto: Victoria University. (Toronto Semiotic Circle Monographs, Working Papers and Prepublications, no. 2.)

Lemke, J. L. (1990) *Talking Science: Language, Learning, and Values.* Norwood, NJ: Ablex.

Lemke, J. L. (1993) 'Discourse, dynamics, and social change', *Cultural dynamics* 6.1-2 (*Language as Cultural Dynamic*).

Léon, J. (2000) 'Traduction automatique et formalization du langage: les tentatives du Cambridge Language Research Unit (1955-1960)', in P. Desmet, L. Jooken, P. Schmitter and P. Swiggers (eds), *The History of Linguistics and Grammatical Praxis.* Louvain/Paris: Petters. 369-94.

Lewis, M. M. (1936) *Infant Speech: A Study of the Beginning of Language.* London: Routledge and Kegan Paul. (International Library of Psychology, Philosophy and Scientific Method) (2nd edn, enlarged, 1951).

Lewis, M. M. (1951) *Infant Speech: A Study of the Beginnings of Language.* 2nd edn, enlarged. London: Routledge & Kegan Paul.

Mackay, D., Thompson, B., and Schaub, P. (1970) *Breakthrough to Literacy*, London: Longman (see especially Teacher's Manual).

Malinowski, B. (1923) 'The problem of meaning in primitive languages', Supplement I to C. K. Ogden and I. A. Richards, *The Meaning of Meaning*, London: Kegan Paul.

Malinowski, B. (1935) *The Language of Magic and Garden.* Vol. 2, *Coral Gardens and their Magic.* New York: American Book Co. Reprinted as *The Language of Magic and Gardening.* Bloomington: Indiana University Press (Indiana University Studies in the History and Theory of Linguistics).

Mann, W. C. (1985) 'An Introduction to the Nigel text generation grammar', in J. D. Benson and W. S. Greaves (eds). 84-95.

Martin, J. R. (1980) 'How many speech acts?', *University of East Anglia Papers in Linguistics* 14–15.

Martin, J. R. (1983) 'Conjunction: the logic of English text', in J. S. Petőfi and E. Sőzer (eds), *Micro and Macro Connexity of Texts*. Hamburg: Buske.

Martin, J. R. (1984) 'Lexical cohesion, field and genre: parcelling experience and discourse goals', in J. E. Copeland (ed.), *Text Semantics and Discourse Semantics: Proceedings of the Second Rice Symposium in Linguistics and Semiotics*. Houston. Rice University.

Martin, J. R. (1986) 'Intervening in the process of writing development', in C. Painter and J. R. Martin (eds), *Writing to Mean: Teaching Genres Across the Curriculum*. Applied Linguistics Association of Australia, Occasional Paper 9.

Martin, J. R. (1990) 'Literacy in science: learning to handle text as technology', in F. Christie (ed.), *Literacy for a Changing World*. Hawthorn: Australian Council for Educational Research.

Martin, J. R. (1992) *English Text: System and Structure*. Amsterdam: Benjamins.

Martin, J. R. and Matthiessen, C. M. I. M. (1991) 'Systemic typology and topol ogy' in F. Christie (ed.), *Literacy in Social Processes*. Drawin, N.T. (Australia): Northern Territory University, Centre for Studies of Language in Education.

Martin, J. R. and Rothery, J. (1980-1) *Writing Project: Report 1980, 1981*. Sydney: Linguistics Department, University of Sydney.

Matthiessen, C. M. I. M. (1983) 'Choosing primary tense in English'. *Studies in Language*. 7.3. 369–430.

Matthiessen, C. M. I. M. (1985) 'The systemic framework in text generation', in J. D. Benson and W. S. Greaves (eds). 96–118.

Matthiessen, C. M. I. M. (1991) 'Language on language: the grammar of semiosis', *Social Semiotics* 1.2.

Matthiessen, C. M. I. M. (1992) 'Interpreting the textual metafunctions', in M. Davies and L. Ravelli (eds), *Advances in Systemic Linguistics: recent theory and practice*. London and New York: Pinter.

Matthiessen, C. M. I. M. (1993a) 'The object of study in cognitive science in relation to its construal and enactment in language'. *Cultural Dynamics*. 6. 1-2.

Matthiessen, C. M. I. M. (1993b) 'Register in the round: diversity in a unified theory of register analysis', in M. Ghadessy (ed.), *Register Analysis: Theory into Practice*. London and New York: Frances Pinter.

Matthiessen, C. M. I. M. (1995) *Lexicogrammatical Cartography: English Systems*. Tokyo and Taipei: International Language Sciences Publishers.

Matthiessen, C. M. I. M. (1996) 'Systemic perspectives on tense in English', in M. Berry, C. S. Butler and R. P. Fawcett (eds), *Grammatical Structure: a Systemic Perspective,* Norwood NJ: Ablex [Meaning and Choice in Language, Vol. 2].

Matthiessen, C. M. I. M. (1998) 'Construing processes of consciousness: from the commonsense model to the uncommonsense model of cognitive science', in J. R. Martin and R. Veel (eds), *Reading Science: Critical and Functional Perspectives on Discourse of Science*. London: Routledge.

Matthiessen, C. M. I. M. (n.d.) 'Fuzziness construed in language: a linguistic perspective'. [mimeo]

Matthiessen, C. and Bateman J. (1992) *Systemic Linguistics and Text Generation: Experiences from Japanese and English,* London: Pinter.

McIntosh, A. (1956) 'The analysis of written Middle English', *Transactions of the Philological Society.*

McIntosh, A. (1961) 'Patterns and ranges', *Language* 37.3.

Melrose, R. (1979) '*General word and particular text: a study of cohesion in academic writing*'. Unpublished PhD dissertation, University of Sydney.

Mitchell, T. F. (1957) 'The language of buying and selling in Cyrenaica: a situational statement', *Hesperis* 26. Reprinted in T. F. Mitchell, *Principles of Firthian Linguistics.* London: Longman.

Mukařovský, J. (1977) *The Word and Verbal Art: Essays,* trans. by J. Burbank and P. Steiner. New Haven, CT.: Yale University Press.

Nelson, K. and Levy, E. (1987) 'Development of referential cohesion in a child's monologues', in R. Steele and T. Threadgold (eds), *Language Topics,* vol. 1, Philadelphia: John Benjamins.

Nesbitt, C. and Plum, G. (1988) 'Probabilities in a systemic grammar: the clause complex in English', in R. P. Fawcett and D. J. Young (eds), *New Developments in Systemic Linguistics, 2: Theory and Application.* London and New York: Pinter. 6-38.

Newton, I. (Sir) (1952) *Opticks, or a Treatise of the Reflections, Refractions, Inflections and Colours of Light.* New York: Dover Publications (based on the fourth edition, London 1730; originally published 1704).

O'Connor, J. D. and Arnold, G. F. (1961) *Intonation of Colloquial English,* London: Longmans.

Ogden, C. K. and Richard, I. A. (1923) *The Meaning of Meaning.* London: Kegan Paul (International Library of Psychology. Philosophy and Scientific Method).

Oldenburg, J. (1986) 'The transitional stage of a second child – 18 months to 2 years', *Australian Review of Applied Linguistics* 9.

Oldenburg-Torr, J. (1987) *From Child Tongue to Mother Tongue: A Case Study of Language Development in the First Two and a Half Years.* University of Nottingham: Department of English Studies (Monographs in Systemic Linguistics 9).

Oldenburg-Torr, J. (1990) 'Learning the language and learning through language in early childhood', in M. A. K. Halliday, J. Gibbons and H. Nicholas (eds), *Learning, Keeping and Using Language: Selected Papers from the 8th World Congress of Applied Linguistics, Sydney, 16–21 August 1987.* Amsterdam: John Benjamins, pp. 27-38.

O'Toole, M. (1989) 'Semiotic systems in painting and poetry', in M. Falchikov, C. Poke and R. Russell (eds), *A Festschrift for Dennis Ward.* Nottingham: Astra Press.

O'Toole, M. (1994) *The Language of Displayed Art.* London: Leicester University Press (Pinter).

O'Toole, M. (1995) 'A systemic-functional semiotics of art', in P. H. Fries and M. J. Gregory (eds), *Discourse in Society. Vol. 3, Meaning and Choice in Language*. Norwood, NJ: Ablex.

Painter, C. (1984) *Into the Mother Tongue: A Case Study in Early Language Development*. London: Frances Pinter.

Painter, C. (1989) 'Learning language: a functional view of language development', in R. Hasan and J. R. Martin (eds), 1989.

Palmer, F. R. (1958a) 'Linguistic hierarcy', *Lingua* 7.

Palmer, F. R. (1958b) 'Comparative statement and Ethiopian semitic', *Transactions of the Philological Society*.

Petőfi, J. S. and Sözer, E. (eds) (1983) *Micro and Macro Connexity of Texts*. Hamburg: Helmut Buske.

Phillips, J. (1986) 'The development of modality and hypothetical meaning: Nigel 1;7½-2;7½', *Working Papers in Linguistics*, 3, Linguistics Department, University of Sydney.

Pike, K. L. (1959) 'Language as particle, wave and field', *Texas Quarterly* 2.

Plum, G. and Cowling, A. (1987) 'Social constraints on grammatical variables: tense choice in English', in R. Steele and T. Threadgold (eds), Vol. 2. 281-305.

Postal, P. M. (1964) *Constituent Structure: A Study of Contemporary Models of Syntatic Description*. Bloomington, IN: Indiana University Publications in Anthropology. Folklore and Linguistics, Publication 30.

Prigogine, I. and Stengers, I. (1982) *Order Out of Chaos: Man's New Dialogue with Nature*. London: Heinemann (Fontana Paperbacks, 1985).

Qiu, S. J. (1985) 'Transition period in Chinese language development', *Australian Review of Applied Linguistics* 8.

Reichenbach, H. (1947) *Elements of Symbolic Logic*. New York: Macmillan.

Reid, T. B. W. (1956) 'Linguistics, structuralism, philology', *Archivum Linguisticum* 8.

Robins, R. H. (1953) 'Formal divisions in Sundanese', *Transactions of the Philological Society*.

Robins, R. H. (1957a) 'Vowel nasality in Sundanese', in J. R. Firth *et al.* (eds), *Studies in Linguistic Analysis*. Oxford: Blackwell (Special Volume of the Philological Society).

Robins, R. H. (1957b) 'Aspects of Prosodic Analysis'. Vol. 1, *Proceedings of the University of Durham Philosophical Society* 1. Durham: Durham University Philosophical Society (series B).

Robins, R. H. (1959) 'Status of grammar', *Lingua*.

Robins, R. H. (1963) 'General linguistics in Great Britain 1930-1960', in Christine Mohrmann *et al.* (eds), *Trends in Modern Linguistics*, Utrecht: Spectrum.

Sankoff, Gillian (1974) 'A quantitative paradigm for the study of communicative competence', in Richard Bauman and Joel Sherzer (eds) *Explorations in the Ethnography of Speaking*, Cambridge: Cambridge University Press.

Schegloff, E. A. (1968) 'Sequencing in conversational openings', *American Anthropologist* 70. Reprinted in J. J. Gumperz and D. Hymes (eds), 1972.

Schubiger, M. (1958) *English Intonation: Its Form and Function*. Tübingen: Niemeyer.

Shannon, C. E. and Weaver, W. (1963[1949]) *The Mathematical Theory of Communication*. Urbana: University of Illinois Press.

Sinclair, J. M., Daley, R. and Jones, S. (1970) *English Lexical Studies, Report No. 5060*. Office of Scientific and Technical Information, London.

Sinclair, J. McH. (1972) *A Course in Spoken English: Grammar*. London: Oxford University Press.

Sinclair, J. McH. and Coulthard, R. M. (1975) *Towards an Analysis of Discourse: The English Used by Teachers and Pupils*. London: Oxford University Press.

Sinclair, J. McH., Forsyth, I. J., Coulthard, R. M. and Ashby, M. (1972) *The English Used by Teachers and Pupils*. University of Birmingham, Department of English.

Spencer, J. and Gregory, M. (1964) 'An approach to the study of style', in J. Spencer (ed.), *Linguistics and Style*. London: Oxford University Press.

Steiner, E. (1988) 'The interaction of language and music as semiotic systems: the example of a folk ballad', in J. D. Benson, M. J. Cummings and W. S. Greaves (eds), 1988.

Stubbs, M. (1996) *Text and Corpus Analysis: Computer-Assisted Studies of Language and Culture*. Oxford: Blackwell.

Sugeno, M. (1993) 'Intelligent fuzzy computing'. Paper presented at PacLing [Pacific Conference on Computational Linguistics].

Sugeno, M. (1995) 'Intelligent fuzzy computing'. Paper presented to the second conference of the Pacific Association of Computational Linguistics (PACLING II), University of Queensland, Brisbane.

Svartvik, J. (1966) *On Voice in the English Verb* (Janua Linguarum Series Practica, 63). The Hague: Mouton.

Svartvik, J. (1992) *Directions in Corpus Linguistics: Proceedings of Nobel Symposium 82, Stockholm, 4–8 August 1991*. Berlin: Mouton de Gruyter.

Svartvik, J. and Quirk, R. (eds) (1980) *A Corpus of English Conversation*. Lund: C. W. K. Gleerup (Lund Studies in English 56).

Taylor, C.V. (1979) *English for Migrant Education Curriculum*. Canberra: Education Development and Research Committee (Report 18).

Thibault, P. J. (1991a) *Social Semiotics as Praxis: Text, Social Meaning Making and Nabokov's 'Ada'*. Minneapolis: University of Minnesota Press.

Threadgold, T. (1988) 'Stories of race and gender: an unbounded discourse', in D. Birch and M. O'Toole (eds), 1988.

Trevarthen, C. (1974a) 'Conversation with a two-month-old', *New Scientist*, 62 (2 May).

Trevarthen, C. (1974b) 'The psychobiology of speech development', in E. H. Lenneberg (ed.), *Language and Brain: Developmental Aspects* (Neuroscience Research Program Bulletin 12).

Trevarthen, C. (1979) 'Communication and cooperation in early infancy: a description of primary intersubjectivity', in M. Bullowa (ed.), 1979.

Turner, G. J. (1973) 'Social class and children's language of control at age five and age seven', in B. Bernstein (ed.).

Ure, J. (1971) 'Lexical density and register differentiation', in G. E. Perren and J. L. M. Trim (eds), *Applications of Linguistics: Selected Papers of the Second International Congress of Applied Linguistics.* Cambridge: Cambridge University Press.

Ure, J. and Ellis, J. (1972) 'Register in descriptive linguistics and linguistic sociology', in O. U. Villegas (ed.), *Las concepciones y problemas actuales de las sociolinguistica.* Mexico City: University of Mexico Press.

Ure, J. N. and Ellis, J. O. (1979) 'Register in descriptive linguistics and linguistic sociology', in O. U. Villegas (ed.), *Issues in Sociolinguistics.* The Hague: Mouton.

Van Leeuwen, T. (1988) 'Music and ideology: towards a sociosemantics of mass media music', *Working Papers 2.* Sydney: Sydney Association for Studies in Society and Culture.

Watts, A. F. (1944) *The Language and Mental Development of Children.* London: Heath.

Wells, R. S. (1960) 'Nominal and verbal style', in T. A. Sebeok (ed.), *Style in Language.* New York: MIT Technology Press and Wiley.

Whorf, B. L. (1956a) 'A linguistic consideration of thinking in primitive communities', in J. B. Carroll (ed.), 1956.

Whorf, B. L. (1956b) *Language, Thought and Reality: Selected Essays, edited by John B. Carroll,* Cambridge: MA and New York: MIT Press and Wiley.

Wignell, P., Martin, J. R. and Eggins, S. (1987) 'The discourse of geography: ordering and explaining the experiential world', in J. R. Martin, P. Wignell and S. Eggins (eds), *Writing Project Report 1987.* Sydney: University of Sydney Linguistics Department.

Winograd, T. (1972) *Understanding Natural Language.* Edinburgh: Edinburgh University Press.

Winter, E. (1977) 'A clause–relational approach to English texts: a study of some predictive lexical items in written discourse', *Instructional Science 6.*

Wolfram, W. (1971) 'Social dialects from a linguistic perspective', in *Sociolinguistics: a crossdisciplinary perspective,* Washington, DC: Center for Applied Linguistics.

Yngve, V. H. (1960) 'A model and an hypothesis for language structure', *Proceedings of the American Philosophical Society 104.5.*

Zadeh, L. (1995) 'Fuzzy logic and its applications'. Paper presented at FUZZ-IEEE/IFES '95.

Zipf, G. K. (1935) *The Psychobiology of Language.* Boston: Houghton Mifflin.

INDEX